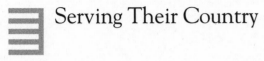Serving Their Country

Serving Their Country

American Indian Politics
and Patriotism in the
Twentieth Century

PAUL C. ROSIER

Harvard University Press
Cambridge, Massachusetts
London, England

For my wife, Debra,
and my boys, Maxwell and Casey

First Harvard University Press paperback edition, 2012

Library of Congress Cataloging-in-Publication Data
Rosier, Paul C.
  Serving their country : American Indian politics and patriotism in the twentieth century / Paul C. Rosier.
    p. cm.
  Includes bibliographical references and index.
  ISBN 978-0-674-03610-9 (cloth: alk. paper)
  ISBN 978-0-674-06623-6 (pbk.)
  1. Indians of North America—Politics and government—20th century. 2. Indians of North America—Government relations—1869–1934. 3. Indians of North America—Government relations—1934– 4. Patriotism—United States—History—20th century. 5. Democracy—United States—History—20th century. 6. Citizenship—United States—History—20th century. 7. United States—Territorial expansion. 8. Imperialism—History. 9. United States—Race relations—Political aspects. I. Title.
  E98.T77R67 2009
  323.1197—dc22   2009019968

Contents

Abbreviations

AAIA   Association on American Indian Affairs
AICC   American Indian Chicago Conference
AIF   American Indian Federation
AIM   American Indian Movement
BIA   Bureau of Indian Affairs

ICC   Indian Claims Commission
IRA   Indian Reorganization Act
NCAI   National Congress of American Indians
NIYC   National Indian Youth Council
SAI   Society of American Indians
SAIA   Survival of American Indians Association

VRP   Voluntary Relocation Program

Prologue: An Empire for Liberty

I am proud to be an American citizen, and have four years in the United States Navy to prove it. I am just as proud to be a Seneca Indian. And I do not see any reason why I cannot be both.

—George Heron, president of the Seneca Nation, to the U.S. Congress, 1960

In October 1972 a controversy began brewing on the White Mountain Apache reservation in Arizona when the Apache Tribal Council moved to change the name of Achesnay Memorial Hall, which honored the last Apache "chief" of the nineteenth century, to Ralph Aday Memorial Hall, which would have honored a young Apache soldier killed in World War II. Apache officials thought the change befitted "the memory of Apaches who had lost their lives while serving their country." According to the reservation newspaper, the *Fort Apache Scout*, a "considerable" number of Apache, including Geronimo's great-grandson, condemned the proposed name change, in part because Achesnay was "a legend." The council's apparently minor decision to rename a communal building mushroomed into a far-reaching debate about whose version of the Apache past would prevail. On the surface it appears that many Apache were defending a figure who defined nineteenth-century Apache nationalism rather than one who represented the modern United States. But Achesnay was noted largely for his service to the United States in the 1886 capture of Geronimo, a symbol of final resistance to American imperial expansion in the West. This controversy nicely illustrates the complex and layered ways in which American Indians, especially during wartime, wrestled with their history and their identity as both American and Indian. Unfolding as the Vietnam War reached its conclusion, the controversy also points to the ways in which American Indians tried to balance their loyalty to the American state and to their Indian nation as the Cold War intersected with a burgeoning decolonization movement. These intersections of patriotism, nationalism, and international affairs animate this book.[1]

The activist and historian Vine Deloria Jr. (Standing Rock Sioux), Native America's most influential intellectual of the post–World War II period, believed that America's international failure in Vietnam reflected its domestic failure to honor its Indian treaties and to place its relations with American Indians "in a world historical perspective." Deloria's comments reflect both the international context within which I examine modern Native American political history and the internationalist perspective that activists such as Deloria used in Native Americans' own campaign of decolonization. Historians of Native America have neglected this connection between national and international issues, preferring to analyze Native politics and life in discrete chronological units such as nineteenth-century wars, World War II, the termination era, and the era of Red Power. Historians of the United States also have failed to situate Native American issues in an international context. Arthur N. Gilbert has observed that "domestic historians pushed Indians into footnotes and appendices secure in the knowledge that they would be treated better by those who study foreign policy. Diplomatic historians could ignore Indians by claiming that they were essentially an internal problem. The former insisted that Indians are nations, the latter that they were a domestic issue." American Indians (or Native Americans; I use both terms interchangeably) thus became a liminal subject, marginalized in American historiography as they were in American society. But, as Gilbert contended, it is precisely "because Indian affairs are in the grey area between domestic and foreign that there are so many significant issues *of a diplomatic nature* to examine."[2]

Indeed, because American Indians figure in significant ways in constructing the discourse and dimensions of the American empire, *Serving Their Country* is a work of American history, though it examines American Indians' place in and perspectives on that imperial history. In doing so, the book helps to correct a central fallacy of American history. Writing in 1927, the journalist Walter Lippman noted: "The rest of the world will continue to think of [America] as an empire. Foreigners pay little attention to what we say. They observe what we do. We on the other hand think of what we feel. And the result is that we go on creating what mankind calls an empire while we continue to believe quite sincerely that it is not an empire because it does not feel to us the way we imagine an empire ought to feel." Echoing Lippman years later, Paul Carter contended in his 1989 intellectual history of the United States that Americans "still like to think of themselves as non-imperial . . . In extenuation, paleface Americans contended that they had previously expanded only into land that was empty—well, almost empty; and only the kind of expansion that jumped off the home continent, they argued, could properly be put down as imperialism." This book takes as a basic premise that the United States has practiced imperialism since its founding, that America as a particular geography was constructed by force rather than conceived by ideological notions such as manifest destiny, and that its imperial expansion in what became the American West shaped U.S. soldiers' and officials' subsequent engagement with new peoples on new global frontiers—"Indian country" migrating westward to the Philippines and beyond.[3]

Americans developed and maintained this *feeling* that they did not play the empire game at home through foundational ideologies linking race and space. "In the beginning," the British political theorist John Locke wrote, "all the World was America." Locke's conception of American Indian land as unimproved premodern space added an important link to the chain of American social thought which denied Indians the quality of the civilized and then the modern. Lockean views, in combination with the theology of expropriation espoused by William Bradford and other religious leaders, underwrote colonial Americans' justification for the taking of Indian lands as a natural process. Emmerich de Vattel's influential work *The Law of Nations* (1758) complicated this argument. Echoing Locke, he contended: "If each nation had, from the beginning, resolved to appropriate to itself a vast country, that the people might live only by hunting, fishing, and wild fruits, our globe would not be sufficient to maintain a tenth part of its present inhabitants. We do not, therefore, deviate from the views of nature, in confining the Indians within narrower limits." The containment of American Indians "within narrower limits" became the operating principle of American expansion well into the twentieth century. But Vattel added an important caveat that treated American Indians as enjoying a Lockean sovereignty, noting that colonial Americans "pur-

chased of the Indians the land of which they intended to take possession."[4]

Early federal Indian policy expressed the contradictory frames of nature
and nations. General Henry Knox argued in 1789 that "Indians possess
the right of the soil. It cannot be taken from them unless by their free consent, or by the right of conquest in case of a just war." Knox's ideas, supported by George Washington, legitimized the *inter*national nature of In-
dian-American relations, which became embedded in a suite of treaties.
At the same time, federal officials, including Knox and Washington, believed that Native Americans had to sell much of their territory to meet
the material demands of manifest destiny. Early-nineteenth-century Indian policy promoted the notion of national "expansion with honor." In
short, expansion was inevitable. Whether it proceeded in a moral fashion,
without taint to the nation's Christian conscience, depended on whether
American Indians embraced the bundle of cultural attributes known as
"civilization." The 1793 Trade and Intercourse Act embodied these two
prescriptions, bringing to life the first incarnation of the federal "Civilization Program" that funded educational, vocational, and religious instruction among Native Americans. But the success of expansion with honor
would also come down to how Americans measured that civilization in an
increasingly polarized racial context. It remained to be seen whether President Thomas Jefferson's proclaimed "empire for liberty" would extend liberty to the empire's indigenous peoples.[5]

Native Americans' post-Revolutionary perspective was one of a sustained crisis of sovereignty stemming from a tidal wave of white settlers,
many of them willing to take land or resources at gunpoint, and a federal
government willing to ride that wave westward in the name of empire.
These factors led tens of thousands of Native Americans to remove themselves beyond the Mississippi River well before the federal government did
it for them in the 1830s. And it led those who remained in the South to
embrace evangelically the belief that adopting the federal government's
Civilization Program would prevent their dispossession and forced integration into the American body politic. To codify their political sovereignty, the Cherokee adopted a constitution in 1827 along the lines of the
United States Constitution. It created a legislature and judiciary and established rules prohibiting the sale of land to non-Cherokee. The constitution and the publication of the bilingual newspaper *Cherokee Phoenix* a

year later strengthened Cherokee nationalism. By 1828 the Cherokee, as well as other Indian nations of the Southeast, had, to varying degrees, become a "mirror of the American Nation," to use historian Mary Young's trenchant phrase. But they also remained Indian in name and in appearance. With slave-based agribusiness increasingly profitable, Georgians intent on gaining the rich cotton lands and gold of the Cherokee Nation began waging what they considered a just war to get them. The federal policy of containment soon became one of termination of American Indian sovereignty.[6]

The U.S. Congress's passage of the Removal Act in 1830 exposed the agonistic tension between the Law of Nature and the Laws of Nations. In his address outlining the impetus for the federal policy of removing Indians from their lands, President Andrew Jackson contrasted "a country covered with forests and ranged by a few thousand savages to our extensive Republic, studded with cities, towns, and prosperous farms." Jackson framed the relocation of Native Americans as a natural process. "Our children by thousands yearly leave the land of their birth to seek new homes in distant regions . . . [They] remove hundreds and almost thousands of miles at their own expense, purchase the lands they occupy, and support themselves at their new homes from the moment of their arrival." Jackson wanted to have it both ways: to maintain that Indians were different from whites and thus removable by coercive state power, and that they should be like whites and accept that removal in the spirit of the great tradition of American westward movement. To assert this Law of Nature, Jackson first had to contend with the Law of Nations. In *Cherokee Nation v. Georgia* (1831), the U.S. Supreme Court ruled that Indian nations were "domestic dependent nations," denying them the full sovereignty of a "foreign nation." But the following year the Court ruled in *Worcester v. Georgia* that Georgia officials had no right to apply state laws in Indian country because Indians retained sovereign powers guaranteed by federal treaties. Using Vattel's book *The Law of Nations* to frame its decision, the Court argued that the U.S. Constitution

adopted and sanctioned the previous treaties with the Indian nations, and consequently admits their rank among those powers who are capable of making treaties. The words "treaty" and "nation" are words of our own language, selected in our diplomatic and legislative proceedings, by ourselves, having each a definite and well understood meaning. We have applied them to Indians, as we have applied them to the other nations of the earth.

But America, Jackson contended, was not Europe. He nullified the Court's decision in the spirit of manifest destiny, the Law of Nature trumping the Law of Nations. And thus Native Americans by the tens of thousands left their ancestral homelands on trails of tears, terror, and terminated treaties, a process that would be repeated in the American West throughout the nineteenth century and into the twentieth.[7]

The colonial theorist Homi Bhabha has argued that nations depend on "a strange forgetting of the history of the nation's past: the violence involved in establishing the nation's writ. It is this forgetting . . . that constitutes the *beginning* of the nation's narrative." The violence and the complex constitutional, economic, and social dimensions of the removal period became forgotten, synthesized in the simple but potent phrase "manifest destiny," which enunciated the American nation's narrative of the victory of a civilized people obeying the Law of Nature in their just war against a savage people. Simultaneously, Native Americans embraced a different manifest destiny, creating a parallel narrative of decolonization to restore the Law of Nations, a narrative that reminded America of the legal and ethical commitments embedded in international treaties it signed with Indian nations from the late eighteenth century to the end of the nineteenth century, a diplomatic process and product codified by the supreme law of the land.[8]

Native Americans constructed this narrative in an international context, both by never forgetting their rights guaranteed by those international treaties and by connecting their experiences of subjugation with those of foreign peoples. Citizens of the Choctaw Nation and Cherokee Nation, now relocated to Indian Territory (present-day Oklahoma), sent contributions to aid the Irish people after reading of the 1847 famine, which created a similar forced migration of thousands. "Although we may never receive any pecuniary benefit or aid in return," stated a Cherokee newspaper, "we will be richly repaid by the consciousness of having done a good act, by the moral effect it will produce abroad." Beyond Christian benevolence, framed by memories of their own privations, such activism reflected the international perspective of the Cherokee and Choctaw, their sense of belonging to a league of nations and of the imperative to construct a humane world beyond their borders. The following year, citizens of the Seneca Nation, facing unrelenting pressure from New Yorkers for their land, cast their eyes abroad as they devised their constitution, finding inspiration in "the political agitations abroad . . . imitating the movements of France and all Europe and seeking a larger liberty" and more independence. The Palestinian scholar Edward Said defined an intellectual as someone who works to "universalize the crisis, to give greater human scope to what a particular race or nation suffered, to associate that experience with the sufferings of others." Throughout the nineteenth and twentieth centuries, Native American intellectuals drew on their international experiences, at home and abroad, in negotiating for a larger liberty in and more independence from the American empire.[9]

The internationalism of these intellectuals developed more fully during World War I, World War II, and the international Cold War, in large measure because Native Americans as well as African Americans gained broader contact with other colonized or marginalized peoples while serving in the U.S. armed forces. Subsumed into the American empire even as they were shunted to its racialized fringes, Native Americans used their international perspectives to shape the moral center of America as it expanded its material borders in the twentieth century. The history of empire "must be told from the border, which is the new center," to borrow historian Modris Eksteins's phrase. In illuminating the complex ways in which Native Americans have conceived of democracy, citizenship, and patriotism in modern America, this book addresses critical questions about national identity in the twentieth century by exploring Native Americans' engagement with what Swedish sociologist Gunnar Myrdal called the "American dilemma," the contradictions of a creed which posited civic inclusion and social equality in theory while simultaneously codifying racial boundaries to contain the mobility of minority groups in practice. Gary Gerstle examined this tension between civic nationalism and racial nationalism in his influential work *American Crucible: Race and Nation in the Twentieth Century*, but he neglected the experiences of Native Americans.[10]

This tension between racial nationalism and civic nationalism and American Indians' use of patriotic rhetoric to mediate it emerged most clearly during the Cold War. But since much recent scholarship on the intersection of race and the Cold War has ignored Native Americans, the story of Indian-white relations remains segregated from the narratives of twentieth-century American history and international history. Exploring the involvement of Native Americans with the local, national, and international politics of the Cold War era, I trace the evolution of Native Americans' contemporary identities in the crucible of the Cold War, from the end of World War II to the end of the Vietnam War. When American Indians faced new threats of wholesale removal by the federal government during the so-called termination era (broadly, 1948–1970), activists reimagined their struggle for sovereignty through an internationalist perspective shaped by the material dimensions of Cold War nation-building programs and the moral dimensions of Third World decolonization. The heart of this book considers where the Cold War took place for Native Americans, how they conceived of its relevance to their lives, through what institutions they mediated its pressures, and how it shaped their national and ethnic identities and thus their vision of American citizenship and patriotism. In addition, I trace connections between U.S domestic Indian policy and U.S. Cold War foreign policy and examine how the struggles of Native Americans to preserve their ancestral lands helped to shape Americans' conceptions of the Cold War at home and abroad, in particular American citizens' awareness of their new global role in constructing an empire for liberty abroad and American politicians' engagement with Third World peoples intent on securing their independence from imperial rule.[11]

There is more continuity than change in these Cold War stories, as the epilogue to this book makes clear. It was during the 1830s, the original era of termination, that white Americans first "reified 'the Indian' into an object of contemplation that both reflected and provided imaginative space for reflection on the meaning of national identity." George Cheever, a student activist from the Andover Seminary, protested that Andrew Jackson's removal policy "has disgraced us as a people, has wounded our national honor, and exposed us to the merited reproach of all civilized communities in the world." During the Cold War, American citizens used similar language in attacking politicians' efforts to abrogate Native treaty rights, arguing that termination policies weakened America's international goodwill and gave Soviet communists grist for their active propaganda mill. More important, American Indians' resistance to federal termination policies engendered political rhetoric that mirrored that of Americans' resistance to Soviet communism, creating the grounds for what journalists and Native activists deemed a domestic "cold war" with American politicians hostile to treaty rights and thus the Law of Nations. But the fullest expression of an ideological conflict over a way of life American politicians and boosters deemed foreign and thus a threat to the construction of empire began during the removal era of the 1830s. As that empire expanded, American Indians' efforts to contain Americanism and to protect the particular political and cultural geography of "Indian country" gave shape first to a series of hot wars in the American West and then to a simmering cold war, by which I mean, broadly speaking, a sustained and ritualized practice of ideological conflict. American Indians' experiences reveal the continuities between American imperial and Cold War histories and the blurring of lines demarcating domestic from international contexts. "Indian country" became both a particular place, an ancestral homeland with its own history, and a protean space invested with symbolism by Americans, East Germans, Russians, Cubans, Pakistanis, and other citizens of an interconnected world.[12]

American Indians' brand of patriotism mediated this cultural cold war. Scholars of American patriotism have investigated Americans' and immigrants' various reasons for serving flag, country, empire. But they have included American Indians only by using them as a trope against which Americans forged their national identity or by exploring how Native Americans were force-fed patriotic rhetoric as part of the imperial project of the late nineteenth and early twentieth centuries, particularly in Indian boarding schools. Scholars have failed to consider how American Indians negotiated that patriotic rhetoric, imagined an American nationalism that drew upon rather than destroyed their values, and developed an ideology of hybrid patriotism—both Indian and American—to define the heart of "America." That is, the social interactions between Natives and Americans worked in dialogical rather than dictatorial ways, Indians trying to reform America as a pluralist society even as non-Indians coercively pushed for a homogeneous society. This hybrid American patriotism was promoted in large measure by American Indian veterans of the armed forces, who served in international conflicts ranging from the U.S.-Philippines War as the nineteenth century ended to post-9/11 military operations as the twenty-first century began. Army Reserve Sergeant Leonard Gouge

(Muscogee Creek) captured the ways in which Native Americanism and Americanism acted symbiotically when he wrote shortly after the 9/11 attacks, "By supporting the American way of life, I am preserving the Indian way of life."[13]

Native Americans demonstrated this hybrid patriotism in multiple ways. For example, in Montana in the 1960s a misnamed Northern Cheyenne journalist called Hollowbreast swelled with pride in reporting that Memorial Day "was again well-received with a traditional celebration with Indian dances, parade, giveaway, feats, and a rodeo in Lame Deer" as Northern Cheyenne celebrated both the heroics of Cheyenne veterans who fought in America's wars of the twentieth century and the heroics of Cheyenne chiefs and warriors who resisted America's war on Indians in the nineteenth century. Hollowbreast later covered Fourth of July festivities by noting: "Independence Day is here and once more comes the time to celebrate the 4th as seen fit, be it a rodeo or Indian dance, elsewhere throngs head for the National Parks, recreational areas, etc. The 4th of July as interpreted in the Cheyenne lingo is mid-summer festival." Native Americans adapted "American" holidays to their particular public history culture, as did most ethnic Americans who helped maintain freedom at home by serving in the U.S. military abroad. For Native Americans, though, their service was part of a more complex narrative of loyalties. To act patriotically meant both to celebrate the continuities of tribal patriotism and its protection of ancestral homelands and to foster change in America by holding it to the standards that generate patriotism in the first place, to reify the tropes of freedom and democracy that animated the American narrative at home and abroad. Ronnie Lupe, the chairman of the White Mountain Apache government, provided a particularly evocative expression of this Native patriotism in responding to non-Indians who frequently ask "why Indians serve the United States with such distinction and honor? They consider it a vast contradiction that we zealously help defend a country that first attempted to exterminate us and now does everything possible to impede our progress." Lupe, a Korean War veteran, was writing during the Gulf War of 1991–92, in which Native American soldiers served to protect the independence of the Kuwaiti people. He explained: "Our loyalty to the United States goes beyond our need to defend our home and reservation lands . . . Only a few in this country really understand that the indigenous people are a national treasure. Our values have the potential of creating the social, environmental and spiritual healing that could make this country truly great."[14]

Lupe's message echoed three generations of Native politicians, intellectuals, and activists who promoted the idea that if the United States did not recognize its obligations to and the value of its indigenous people, then it would never succeed in fulfilling the moral and material obligations of its "empire for liberty" abroad. Serving the United States and their Indian nations with distinction and honor, American Indians defended their right to be both American and Indian, representing that right as the promise of American life while the United States engaged the world in the twentieth century.

1   Westward the Course of Empire

> When visiting the Sioux, I was led to the wigwam of the chief. It was just like the others in external appearances, and even within the difference was trifling between it and those of the poorest of his braves. The contrast between the palace of the millionaire and the cottage of the laborer with us to-day measures the change which has come with civilization.
>
> —Andrew Carnegie, "Wealth," 1889

On March 4, 1905, the Apache leader Geronimo rode among five Native Americans dressed in traditional Indian garb in the inaugural parade marking Theodore Roosevelt's new term as president. A contingent of Native Americans from the Carlisle Indian School, dressed in the school's military-style uniforms, followed at a distance, representing the space and time that "the Indian" had traveled from the old days, the distance between the "savage" and the "civilized." Geronimo, who as one of the last American Indian leaders to resist the U.S. Army served as a symbol of final resistance to American imperialism in the West, rode between trolley tracks, literally contained within the iron rails of industrial development that helped shape his defeat.

Roosevelt had played a bit part in the drama of Native Americans' military defeat, both promoting the subjugation of Indian "savages" and chronicling their conquest in his multivolume account *The Winning of the West*. Roosevelt was the object of the parade and the hero of the narrative it told. "I wanted to give the people a good show," he told critics of Geronimo's inclusion. As historian Angie Debo claims: "Geronimo stole the show. Only the president attracted more attention." The ceremony marked the start of Roosevelt's presidency but linked it to the narrative of the nation's ascendancy as an imperial power through the conquest of the Geronimos of the American West. The "good show" Roosevelt wanted to

1.1 "Indian chiefs," headed by Geronimo, on parade during President Theodore Roosevelt's inauguration, March 4, 1905, Washington, D.C. The party included Quanah Parker (Comanche), Little Plume (Blackfeet), Buckskin Charley (Ute), Hollow Horn Bear (Brule Sioux), and American Horse (Oglala Sioux). Behind them march members of the Carlisle Indian School band and over three hundred Carlisle Indian School cadets. Courtesy of Library of Congress LC-USZ62-56009.

stage resembled the Roman Triumph, the ritual parading of the conquered barbarian through the imperial capital, which displayed the victor and the vanquished, the ruler and the subject.[1]

Geronimo had his motives for joining the show, of course. He had furthered his commodification in the early twentieth century as a touchstone of the nineteenth by selling his autograph and photograph at various public events including the Pan-American Exposition at Buffalo in 1901 and the St. Louis World's Fair in 1904. But he hoped that his participation in the parade would lead Apaches back to their ancestral homeland. In a post-inaugural meeting Geronimo pleaded with Roosevelt for such an out-

come, but Roosevelt could not abide the Apache's "return to your country" on the grounds that it would provoke a new war in Arizona. The
American Century would brook no such war. Geronimo remained a prisoner of war, an exile from his "country."[2]

Echoing Thomas Jefferson and two subsequent generations of white reformers, Roosevelt supported Indians' "ultimate absorption into the body
of our people." Like most white Americans of his generation, Roosevelt
subscribed to the notion that Indians were "savages" and had no legitimate claim to their land. In *The Winning of the West* he had written that
"the most ultimately righteous of all wars is a war with savages." Roosevelt's
statement demonstrates continuity with General Henry Knox's 1789 declaration that Indians' land "cannot be taken from them unless by their free
consent, or by the right of conquest in case of a just war." From the beginning, chroniclers of Americans' movement west described it as a "just war"
or "righteous war," as a divinely inspired expansion or a natural evolution,
not as imperialism; it was, according to an early-nineteenth-century text-
book, a movement based on "growth, not acquisition; by internal development, not by external accession." Such views animated new periods of
manifest destiny in the 1830s, 1850s, and 1890s. As Roosevelt put it, "The
simple truth is there is nothing even remotely resembling imperialism in
the development of the policy of expansion which has been part of the
history of America since the day she became a nation."[3]

Obstructing the powerful combination of Christianity and capitalism,
the twin engines of American imperialism, had grave consequences for
Native Americans in the nineteenth century and beyond. With visions of
righteousness and riches driving them to new frontiers, white Americans
waged a military, cultural, and legal "just war" against Native Americans,
a war of imperialism that took place on battlefields and on reservations, in
the Congress and in the courts, and in the public discourse that linked industrialization and civilization as the American empire made its way ever
westward to the Pacific and beyond.

Across the Continent

The federal government's forced march of Native Americans from their
ancestral homelands in the Southeast and in the Ohio River valley to
their trails of tears and terror during the so-called removal era of the 1830s

proceeded in the West, supported by the same racialist ideology that denied Indians the capacity to rise above their "natural" and "savage" state but advanced by new bureaucratic mechanisms of dispossession. Although the first formal use of the term "reservation" appears in the 1825 Treaty of Prairie du Chien, Commissioner of Indian Affairs Luke Lea articulated the idea of a reservation "system" in 1850, shortly after the gold rush generated enthusiasm among millions of Americans and Europeans for traversing Native Americans' mother earth on their way to finding the mother lode. Addressing what he called "our northern colony of Indians," Lea maintained that the government should "concentrate them within proper limits." Concentration, he contended, would lead to Native Americans' domestication and "ultimate incorporation into the great body of our citizen population." Concentration, domestication, and incorporation became the operating principles of federal Indian policy well into the twentieth century.[4]

Although an original justification for concentrating Indians was to protect them from the millions of white emigrants traveling west through Indian country, the major impetus stemmed from the need to maintain the division between "savage" space and "civilized" space and thus prevent Indians from inhibiting national progress from sea to shining sea, especially as the idea of manifest destiny took hold in the American imagination. "What shall we do with the Indians," asked Alfred Riggs in *The Nation* in 1867, to ensure that they did not obstruct the railroads, "the highways to the Pacific." Two choices existed for Native Americans in post–Civil War America, according to Riggs: they could be "exterminated" or incorporated as partners in "law and habits of industry."[5]

Phase One: Concentration

In the vanguard of a clash between cultural economies of the American West, citizens of the so-called Five Civilized Tribes in Indian Territory wrestled with these figurative and literal boundaries separating Indian and white life. Facing enormous pressure first from railroads and then from mining corporations for access to their lands, pro-corporation and anti-corporation factions formed among the Cherokee, Creek, and other Indian nations trying to retain their political and economic sovereignty. Native American leaders resisted efforts by the railroads to traverse their

lands, fearing that their projects would bring with them the vices of railway workers and require Indian land, timber, and water resources for track
construction and eventually town sites. A Cheyenne delegate told an audience at the Cooper Institute in New York in 1871: "Before they ever
ploughed or planted an acre of corn for us they commenced to build railroads through our country. What use have we for railroads in our country?
What have we to transport from other nations? Nothing." Such Native
leaders asked why their nations could not prosper within the American
nation as *imperium in imperio*. Other Cherokee and Creek citizens, however, rejected the feasibility or desirability of an autarkic future, supporting industrial development to facilitate economic growth, but on their
terms. Pragmatic as ever, the Cherokee worked in Indian Territory as they
had in the Southeast before removal to develop a capitalism that fit their
social ecology rather than that of corporate monopolies. Cherokee chief
William Ross addressed the need to adapt to changing conditions, adopting the discourse of progress in the process: "When the most restless and
enterprising and greedy population on the face of the earth is mantling
and flowing all around us . . . there is not time for the children of the country to grow up in idleness and ignorance."[6]

In 1870 Cherokee and Creek diplomats asked the federal government
to help them build their own railroads; Cherokee politicians claimed such
a project would further the goal of "Christian civilization" but by Cherokee means. Commissioner of Indian Affairs Ely S. Parker (Seneca) denied
their requests on the grounds that such actions would perpetuate "semi-
civilized customs and forms of society," a clear expression of the inability
of government officials, even one of Indian ancestry, to abide "in-between"
or hybrid methods of market integration. The case embodies the "Great
Divide" separating people of the West from the racial "other," separating
the modern and the un-modern; the biological and cultural interaction
between these two groups paradoxically led to a proliferation of "hybrids"
such as the Cherokee, who were rendered invisible and thus illegitimate.
The "tribe," with its supposedly ingrained communal character, could not
function as a corporation because American policymakers saw the corporation as functioning *as* an individual *for* the individual. The incorporation of Indians would occur along lines of resources—human and natural—not corporate ownership. In supporting an open door policy in Indian
Territory, one U.S. senator argued that it would extend to Indians "that

civilization of the highest character of which a railway is a symbol." With-out a railroad, Indians could not be civilized. Without civilization, they could not have their own railroad. The Cherokee and other Native people were caught in a liminal space, "declared both inside and outside the American polity: subject to its jurisdiction, but without rights of citizenship."[7]

Railway companies, the Atlantic and Pacific Railroad (A&P) in particular, produced sophisticated public relations campaigns calling for the formation of a territorial government in Indian country to break Indian sovereignty and facilitate growth, complaining, as A&P officials did, of the hardships imposed by the recalcitrant and "degraded, shabby, do nothing set" of Indians. This campaign accelerated after Congress ended the policy of treaty making in 1871, which delegitimized the sovereignty of Indian space. Writing in his 1871 tract *Atlantic and Pacific Railroad and the Indian Territory*, A&P attorney C. J. Hillyer described the effect of this "radical change" in U.S.-Indian relations as "the end of Indian nationality." Hillyer concluded, "There is no sacredness in a treaty stipulation made years ago with an Indian tribe as to require or permit it to obstruct the national growth." Americans' manifest duties and rights would preserve national growth, regardless of its bloody consequences. Asserting a material rather than a moral calculus, Hillyer wrote, "Whether one Indian or five thousand be killed in the operation, the result must be obtained." To sell his genocidal story, Hillyer had to present Indian space as savage and static. Native inhabitants of Indian Territory, he asserted, "have insisted the country remain a wilderness because they prefer to live in a wilderness." As late as 1882 railroad companies distributed Hillyer's seventy-three-page lawyerly rant against "Indian nationality" to Congress to legitimize their "rights of way" through Native American space.[8]

Hillyer and other promoters drew upon the diverse set of historical assumptions that marked Indian-white relations and the attendant boundaries between legitimate and illegitimate uses of space and forms of social and political organization. In the 1870s this river of social thought received the new ideological current of social Darwinism, which gave the "Law of Nature" a new power. The head of the House Committee on Indian Affairs put it bluntly in 1872: "The laws of trade are more powerful than those of Congress—the thing is inevitable." The Laws of Trade, the inevitability of market capitalism, trumped the Laws of Nations. In this context it was the white Americans who were restricted in their use of

1.2 "Across the Continent: Westward the Course of Empire Takes Its Way"
(Currier and Ives, 1868) delineates "savage" Indian space from "civilized" white
space, depicted as the product of improving the land and creating outposts of
Christian life by means of the railroad, the central nervous system of the body
politic. Currier and Ives took the subtitle from Anglican bishop George Berkeley's 1726 poem "On the Prospect of Planting Arts and Learning in America,"
which celebrated America as the end point of civilization's progress. Courtesy of
Library of Congress LC-DIG-ppmsca-03213.

space. "We will not be penned up; we will not be hindered," trumpeted a
senator from Texas. Governments were to prosecute violators of the natural law, not of the Law of Nations, especially since promoters rejected Indian nations' sovereignty. A battle over cultural conceptions of space had
always defined Indian-white relations, but the grounds of division could
change rapidly, drawing on new ideas to strengthen the case for expropriation and thus maintaining the fiction of American "internal development"
rather than "external accession." In the 1870s the motto of American promoters of progress remained one of "confining the Indians within narrower limits," which meant that as long as Indians were defined as Indians,
seen as racial and savage "others," and thus as "un-American," their space
would continue to narrow.[9]

Native Americans' efforts to dissolve the imposed intellectual boundary between civilization and savagery and thus preserve their terrestrial
boundaries became even more difficult after 1871 with the emergence of
the idea that "communistic" behavior threatened social order. The events
of the 1871 Paris Commune reshaped whites' perceptions of Native American space at a critical point in Indian-white relations. Lasting between
March 28 (formally declared) and May 28, 1871, the short-lived Commune arose when a working-class French militia staged a revolution after
the Franco-Prussian War ended the previous January. The French government abandoned Paris for Versailles, leaving the city controlled by the
Central Committee of the National Guard, which proclaimed a communal form of governance in the tradition of rural France and adopted a red
flag to replace the French national banner. Though animated by a mixture
of ideas, the Commune became identified by its opponents as an expression of dangerous "communism." They called the Communards "Red Indians" and "blood-thirsty Indian squaws," likening them to "fierce Apaches"
or a Comanche horde. The use of the Indian as archetypal savage to paint
as dangerous those social groups on the margins of political power found
its way east across the Atlantic before 1871. The British critic Samuel
Smiles had argued earlier that the "poorer classes . . . resemble the savage
tribes, who know no better, and do no worse. Like the North American
Indians, they debase themselves by the vices which accompany civilization, but make no use whatever of its benefits and advantages." The conflation of Paris "Reds" and American Indian "Reds" created a new discourse marking Indians' broader threat to industrial civilization, at home
and abroad.[10]

In a post–Civil War United States undergoing civic reconstruction and
fantastic economic growth, Americans were sensitive to disruptions of the
social order. The Paris Commune gave opponents of Indian sovereignty
tangible proof of the ways in which "communist" ideas could threaten a
nation recovering from war. The use of the Red Indian trope became functional for politicians in the East and boosters in the West, adding a new
ideological justification for expropriating Indian land and for concentrating Indians beyond the boundaries of an expanding industrial civilization.
The internationalization of Indian-white frontier conflict, especially in
the Southwest, painted Indian resistance not as a defense of an ancestral
homeland but as a savage attack on the sacred institutions of American

life. Less than a month after the Paris Commune met its violent end, the
New York World termed Indian resistance in Texas "the Red Spectre."
Boosters in Nebraska, New Mexico, and Colorado conflated "savage" Indians and French "Communists" to further their land-grab schemes. The
Commune crisis thus helped to sharpen class and racial divisions along a
straight line between savagery and civilization with no middle ground allowed. The first "Red scare" in the United States extended to burgeoning
urban spaces in which immigrant workers or poor Americans could be
linked to the savagery of the American frontier. The rhetoric of concentration in rural and urban America was the rhetoric of containment. The
containment of the poor in city slums marked these as urban reservations
for workers who failed to adapt to the norms of civilization.[11]

After the 1871 Paris Commune and Congress's decision that same year
to abandon treaty making, the attitudes of federal officials invested in resolving the "Indian problem" hardened. Appointed commissioner of the
Bureau of Indian Affairs (BIA) that year, Francis A. Walker posed two related questions: "What shall be done with the Indian as an obstacle to
national progress?" and "What shall be done with him when, and so far as,
he ceases to oppose or obstruct the extension of railways and settlements?"
Walker's views on how work discipline could reform the uneducated Indian drew upon laissez-faire economics, early ideas of scientific management, and the New England Whig culture in which he was raised. The son
of a railroad executive and manufacturer, Walker supported the reservation system as a means to concentrate American Indians away from rail
lines and settlements, thus protecting them from "obstruction or molestation" by the Indians. He envisioned the reservation system employing a
"rigid reformatory discipline" to instill "a severe course of industrial instruction and exercise under restraint." In this rural version of the asylum
or factory that began dotting the American landscape before the Civil
War, reservations were not "reserved" to American Indians for their use
but rather constructed as an industrial space engineered for maximum efficiency along the lines of factory discipline. Reservation agents would employ surveillance and control, prohibiting Indians from crossing the legal
and moral boundary between Indian space and white space, in part to promote "compulsion to labor." Once reformed, Walker believed, Indians
would not "go to the dogs" but would "find a place for themselves in the
social and industrial order." The reservation became part of an evolving

"disciplinary society"; within the new rationalized boundary lines defining Native America, "disciplinary power became an 'integrated' system, linked from the inside to the economy and to the aims of the mechanism in which it was practiced." In the spirit of postwar industrialization, Walker promoted the idea, never implemented, of concentrating all American Indians on one or two big reservations, thus attempting to operate the reform agenda on the principle of economies of scale.[12]

Custer's defeat in the Dakotas in July 1876 and the Great Railroad Strike of 1877 reinforced views that reservation Indians had to be disciplined and violators who crossed reservation boundaries punished. Both the Red Indians of the rural West and the Red workers of industrial America became symbols of resistance to the progress of the railroad system and other elements of industrial growth. The battle for American industrial civilization, then, took place on two fronts. Writing after the Sioux and Cheyenne wiped out Custer's army in July 1876, *New York Tribune* columnist James Gordon Bennett called the Sioux "communistic" and compared them to the Molly Maguires and other "dangerous classes." When the Great Railroad Strike exploded in 1877, the strikers were seen as impediments to growth, in particular to the movement of trains, the literal and figurative engine of industrial expansion. As the *Tribune* put it in late July 1877, "Every striker made war upon all civilized society when he countenanced the stopping of trains." At the time of the strike, the Nez Perce were waging their final act of resistance to the BIA's concentration policy. Linking contexts, federal troops pursued the "murderous reds" of Chief Joseph's Nez Perce while suppressing union officials such as "Chief Arthur" who were leading a tribe of "fighting strikers" in their resistance to an industrial order not of their making.[13]

Phase Two: Domestication

U.S. Army officers constructed strategies for containing Native Americans within a global frame of empire building. General William T. Sherman, who played a prominent role in subjugating Indians in the American West, had studied "how a small force of British troops, aided by the native troops, govern two hundred millions of people" in India; Sherman also made reference to the English-Afghan War in a visit to the White House in 1878. General George Crook noted in 1885 that "things that may ap-

1.3 "The First Chapter of America" appeared in the November 1877 issue of *Scribner's Monthly*. Published as Indian wars continued in parts of the American West and during the year of the Great Railroad Strike, the image posits Indians' continued threat to American civilization as it began its second century. The threat necessitated a new program to subdue Indians in order to prevent a domestic version of the Sepoy Rebellion, which reshaped social relations in British India in 1857 and beyond.

pear trivial at Washington, are frequently all important in the management of . . . dangerous Indians. The Sepoy Rebellion [of 1857] was supposed to have been caused by greased cartridges." Gilded Age reformers' efforts to ameliorate the "savagery" of workers and Indians and thus remake America's ethnic and racial social space, urban and rural, also had much in common with the various British and European "civilizing missions" then under way in Africa and Asia. The American civilizing mission, reborn in the late 1870s under the guidance of Secretary of the Interior Carl Schurz, whose immigration from Germany and success in America colored his perspectives on Indian policy, sought to implement the program of "domestication," the second stage of Luke Lea's vision of concentration, domestication, and incorporation. Journeying to the ethnic islands called "reservations," reformers went to work domesticating the wildness out of Indians through education, religion, and industry.[14]

Federal Indian policy resulted from collaboration between congressmen, private reformers, and federal officials such as Schurz. The so-called Civilization Program was inspired by the "Friends of the Indian," East Coast–based white Anglo-Saxon Protestants in government and in private organizations such as the Indian Rights Association, the Board of Indian Commissioners, and the Women's National Indian Association. In 1883 the Quaker Albert Smiley hosted a series of meetings at his resort home on Lake Mohonk in upstate New York that became known as the Lake Mohonk Conferences of Friends of the Indians. Reformers from this Mohonk Tribe sought to protect Native Americans as people but not as "Indians," believing that they were headed for extinction unless they adapted to the modern conditions of industrial America by adopting Christianity, the English language, American citizenship, and individual land tenure. As historian Francis Paul Prucha put it, "The otherness was to be destroyed and a homogenous mass was to be formed, of which the Indian would be an indistinguishable part." In pushing the contradictory goals of individualization and Americanization, reformers sought to "Americanize" the Indian as they would any Irish, German, or Italian immigrant.[15]

Even though treaties "reserved" to Native Americans a fixed territory demarcating their reduced homelands, white Americans identified reservations as first a confining space to prevent Indians' "obstruction or molestation" of American industrial civilization and then as a training ground for Indians' incorporation into that civilization. The reservation, a physical space marking the boundaries of indigenous Americans' newly circumscribed world as defined by the legal and national instrument of the treaty, became immediately, for white Americans, foreign cultural space. As one commissioner of Indian affairs framed it, the overarching goal was to "make the Indians feel at home in America." Thus Indians could go "home" only by leaving the reservation, their self-described "homeland." Such a view found popular expression, as in a reader's response to a *New*

York Tribune editorial supportive of Indian rights: "What right have [Indians] to be in the country, anyhow?" And it found political expression in the form of Henry L. Dawes, a senator from Massachusetts and a prominent member of the Mohonk Tribe, who complained that Americans had "struggled with [the "Indian problem"] for two hundred and fifty years" without making any progress. Indians remained "a savage people speaking a strange jargon we did not understand"—foreigners squatting on undeveloped American land.[16]

Reformers promoted above all the elimination of the reservation system and all the "savage" and "strange" traditions it protected. Schurz, writing in an 1881 issue of the prominent journal *North American Review*, contended in social Darwinist terms that "a stubborn maintenance of the system of large Indian reservations must eventually result in the destruction of the red men, however faithfully the Government may endeavor to protect their rights. It is only a question of time." Once again the Law of Nature qua commerce trumped the Law of Nations. Charles C. Painter, representing the Indian Rights Association, saw the reservation boundary as a buckskin curtain, "a wall which fences out law, civil institutions, and social order, and admits only despotism, greed, and lawlessness. It says to all the institutions, methods, and appliances of civilized life, 'Thus far shalt thou come and no further' . . . So long as we were weak we bargained for a small reservation for ourselves; when we grew stronger we gradually forced them [the Indians] on to smaller and smaller reservations, which of our generosity." And soon the reservation was to be no more. As Merrill Gates summarized it simply, the goal was to "put the reservation in the past tense." Gates, who served as president of Rutgers College and Amherst College in addition to presiding over the Mohonk Conference, sanctioned destroying the "two peculiarities" of Indian life that impeded progress: the reservation and the tribe. Promoting plans to force Indians to adopt the nuclear family, what he called "God's unit of society," Gates argued that the key to the Indian problem was destroying loyalty to notions of tribe and chief, which prevented Indian men from attaining their "highest manhood" and thus denied them "the highest right of man . . . the right to be a man." To grow up, to gain full manhood, would come in conjunction with citizenship, both available only through ownership of private property. Individualization of property and economic production would lead to full manhood, as each Indian American could then take responsibility for his land and his nuclear family.[17]

Like Schurz and Gates, Senator Dawes had an evangelical belief that eliminating tribal economic production and communal distribution would push Indians toward what he called "citizenship and manhood." Citizenship would engender consumption, which was tied to notions of manhood. Dawes claimed that the "last and the best agency of civilization is to teach a grown up Indian to *keep*." He and other reformers embraced the principle of individual "selfishness." Superintendent of Indian Schools John Oberly put it best in claiming that reform would succeed when Native Americans say "'I' instead of 'We,' and 'This is Mine,' instead of 'This is ours.'" Echoing Dawes and Oberly, Gates argued that "to bring him out of savagery into citizenship we must make the Indian more intelligently selfish before we can make him unselfishly unintelligent. We need to *awaken in him wants*," which would manufacture "an Indian wearing trousers with a pocket in them, and with a *pocket that aches to be filled with dollars*." To paraphrase Montaigne, what was the point of the civilization program if Indians didn't wear breeches with pockets? [18]

Not only were Native Americans pushed toward consuming the gifts of industrial civilization, but also they became commodified in the narratives of Gilded Age capitalism, their reclamation from savagery documented in the discursive spaces of imperial advertising. Just as the British marketed the notion of a benevolent empire through commodity advertising, so too did American companies tap into the unfolding drama of a great reclamation project remaking the social geography of the American West.

Ivory soap campaigns, for example, integrated the civilizing mission under way in Indian country in narrative accounts of the transformative effects of soap on the great unwashed of the American West. Appearing in magazines such as *Harper's Young People: An Illustrated Weekly* beginning in 1884, the advertisements told a story of a people "reclaimed" by contact with Ivory soap, which would "change their nature day by day and wash their darkest blots away." In the second frame the "reclaimed" Indian wears Uncle Sam's breeches, coat, and hat while carting the soap in fetish form as a ticket to the civilization of the white world. The name of the soap, Ivory, its whiteness, and its slogan, "99 44/100 percent Pure," testified to its scientifically proven qualities and thus the soap represented both means and end, both material and metaphor. The transformation, or reclamation, of the Indians is also structural; pictured as a group of males in the first frame, they appear as members of "God's unit of society" in the second, exemplifying the Indian male's rise to "full manhood" by way of

A NEW DEPARTURE.

Said Uncle Sam : "I will be wise,
And thus the Indian civilize:
Instead of guns that kill a mile,
Tobacco, lead, and liquor vile,
Instead of serving out a meal,
Or sending Agents out to steal,
I'll give, domestic arts to teach,
A cake of Ivory Soap to each.
Before it flies the guilty stain,

The grease and dirt no more remain :
'Twill change their nature day by day,
And wash their darkest blots away.
They'll turn their bows to fishing-rods,
And bury hatchets under sods,
In wisdom and in worth increase,
And ever smoke the pipe of peace;
For ignorance can never cope
With such a foe as Ivory Soap."

1.4 Ivory Soap advertisement, 1880s. The cleanliness motif, featuring soap as a fetish and as a ticket for indigenous peoples to gain entrance to civilized society, recurs in various British and American publications and promotions of empire in the late 1800s. Courtesy of Baker Library Historical Collection, Harvard Business School.

RECLAIMED.

WE once were factions, fierce and wild,
To peaceful arts unreconciled;
Our blankets smeared with grease and stains
From buffalo meat and settlers' veins.
Through summer's dust and heat content,
From moon to moon unwashed we went;
But IVORY SOAP came like a ray
Of light across our darkened way.

And now we're civil, kind and good,
And keep the laws as people should.
We wear our linen, lawn and lace,
As well as folks with paler face.
And now I take, where'er we go,
This cake of IVORY SOAP to show
What civilized my squaw and me
And made us clean and fair to see.

1.5 Ivory Soap advertisement, 1880s. The Indians "reclaimed" by cleanliness, with the man now dressed like Uncle Sam, mimic the family structure of Christian America but remain defined by their racialized features. Courtesy of Baker Library Historical Collection, Harvard Business School.

consumer practices. Yet as in the case of the British Monkey Brand "soap monkey," whose body was washed but whose head remained "dark" and thus ignorant, these soap Indians retain the racialized features common to nineteenth-century representations of the "barbaric" Irish Americans and African Americans. Even though Ivory Soap fell "like a ray of light across [Indians'] darkened way," their way remained blocked, the result of the (scientifically proven) racial infirmities of their darkness. Achieving pure (or "99 44/100 percent Pure") whiteness would be impossible. Indians would remain closer to the "mottled-red" soap product that Procter and Gamble originally proposed.[19]

But there remained a major complication. "The Indian will never be reclaimed," former commissioner of the Bureau of Indian Affairs George E. Ellis explained in his 1881 book *The Red Man and the White Man in North America*, "till he ceases to be a communist." The centerpiece of the government's reform became the allotment of the Indian land base in severalty to destroy Indians' communal land tenure, a campaign that found legislative expression in the General Allotment Act of 1887, which some reformers called the "Indian Emancipation Act." Allotment had been a legacy of the Indian removals in the Southeast, but the instability of Indian land tenure due to sustained settler pressure and endemic racism never necessitated a formal government program. Sponsored by Senator Dawes, the General Allotment Act (which became known as the Dawes Act) set into motion federal machinery to divide American Indian reservations into 160-acre parcels of land for distribution to tribal members. The new federal real estate service charged with allotting millions of acres of Indian land sold the "surplus land" to white settlers; the proceeds funded the government's Civilization Program. The act stipulated that the federal government had to hold the allotments "in trust" for a twenty-five-year period to prevent their sale or lease to non-Indians, thus giving Indian farmers sufficient opportunity to learn the tools of the trade and adjust to a new system of individual land tenure. In 1891, however, Congress weakened the trust provisions, bowing to relentless pressure from white land speculators and settlers. And in the 1906 Burke Act it liberalized the rules even further by permitting the outright sale of land.[20]

The allotment policy, the centerpiece of the Civilization Program, proved to be a failure and a fraud. Predicting such an outcome, some members of Congress, populist reformers, and of course Native Americans themselves argued against the mandated division of Indian lands along the linear and cultural lines of the yeoman homestead model. In 1880, as allotment bills began winding their way through the legislative pipeline, members of the House Committee on Indian Affairs issued a minority report that challenged the civilizing elements of the law. "The main purpose of this bill," the report charged, "is not to help the Indian, or solve the Indian problem, so much as it is to provide a method for getting at the valuable Indian lands and opening them up to white settlement." Defending Native political economy, the committee argued, "Whatever civilization has been reached by the Indian tribes has been attained under the tribal system," citing the work of the Cherokee, Choctaw, Sioux, and Chippewa, all of whom were "working out their own deliverance, which will come in their own good time if we but leave them alone and perform our part of the many contracts we have made with them. But that we have never yet done, and it seems from this bill we will never yet do. We want their lands, and we are bound to have them." It is important to note that these congressional critics of forced allotment argued that if the U.S. government honored the "many contracts" or treaties signed with Indian nations, then allotment would be unnecessary. In the Senate, Henry Teller of Colorado argued that no blanket legislation would work because "Indians differ as much one from another as the civilized and enlightened nations of the earth differ from the uncivilized and unenlightened nations of the earth." Teller also contended that not only were most American Indians not ready for land in severalty but also any such program should require Indians' "unanimous consent," given that "many contracts" or treaties required such consent. He suggested that congressional supporters title the 1880 legislation "a bill to despoil the Indians of their lands and to make them vagabonds on the face of the earth." But these were voices crying in the legislative wilderness. Even Senator Teller himself, an ardent assimilationist, soon jumped on the Dawes bandwagon.[21]

Lake Mohonk reformers had resurrected for the model of the "reclaimed Indian" the archetypal yeoman farmer of Jeffersonian and Jacksonian tradition, who at the time of the allotment debate was waging a populist revolt against the forces of agricultural and industrial capitalism in the West and in the South. In 1885, as the allotment policy picked up supporters in Congress, the National Indian Defense Association (NIDA) formed to protest mandatory land allotment. A strange admixture of populists, Native Americans, and assimilationists such as former Kansas Territory governor James Denver and former Indian affairs commissioner Francis A. Walker, the NIDA membership was nearly half American Indian, unlike that of other Indian reform groups of the time. NIDA founder Thomas Bland, a Quaker and former Union Army surgeon, printed Native Americans' protests against allotment legislation in *The Council Fire*, its publication on Indian affairs until 1889. Bland's efforts to gain the perspective of Sioux leaders such as Red Cloud, a member of NIDA, engendered great resistance by Sioux reservation agents, BIA officials, and Senator Dawes himself. Forced to leave the Great Sioux Reservation under threat of violence, Bland questioned the freedom of Indians on reservations in an 1884 *Council Fire* essay in which he attacked the BIA's control of reservations as "un-American." NIDA echoed Senator Teller in arguing that Indians should, if they desired, retain their communal lands and integrate into the American economy on their own terms, a call that mirrored the angst of white farmers in the emerging populist belts of rural America who were also undergoing wrenching economic transformations. Laissez-faire capitalism threatened the integrity of many rural communities, such as the Indiana community in which Bland grew up, which drew strength from traditional notions of communal assistance. Unifying Populists in the South, Midwest, and far West was the alarming privatization of common spaces and communal resources through new enclosure and stock laws and the power of railroad monopolies to fix prices. In the context of allotment, Bland asserted that the government could be a moral agent by protecting Native Americans' assets and property rights, contesting the argument that the Law of Trade trumped the Law of Nations, that the material right of property was stronger than the moral right of the treaty. "Let no knee be bowed in submission to the great corporations, whose motto is that 'might makes right,'" Bland told NIDA supporters. NIDA board member and U.S. Senate chaplain Bryon Sunderland attacked Congress for submitting to the interests of "railroad men" and condemned the Indian Rights Association for its support of allotment, opining that it should change its name to the "Land Shark's Rights Association." Bland, Sunderland, and others invoked royalist and class language but also biblical language in painting mandated allotment as an attack on the spirit of brotherhood and community. Contesting the chief argument that allotment would extend to Native Americans the glories of American civilization and

Christianity, Sunderland harrumphed: "Such civilization! Such Christianity! . . . We have already had enough of it to cover the history of the Nation with disgrace . . . [N]o Eastern idolatry was ever more merciless in its bloody rites than our modern Mammon worship."[22]

Other critics of agricultural and industrial capitalism, linking rural and urban contexts, valorized Indian communal traditions and incorporated them into *their* vision of American industrial civilization. Karl Marx and Friedrich Engels were both influenced by Lewis Henry Morgan's analysis of Iroquois political and social traditions in his 1877 book *Ancient Society*. In 1884 Engels published *The Origin of the Family, Private Property, and the State: In Light of the Researches of Lewis H. Morgan*, which he wrote with the aid of Marx's notes on Morgan's book. Both Marx and Engels held up the Iroquois Confederacy, by way of Morgan's assessments, as a model for communal economic production, an alternative to industrial capitalism and the class stratification it produced. In the preamble to its constitution, the Knights of Labor union connected the expropriation of the rights of industrial labor to that of Native Americans' rights, insisting that if the United States drove "the native from the land of his father" in "the name of civilization, then in that name their possessions should be common property." The Knights condemned the taking of Indian lands, which were "originally common property," by "physical power, by robbery or fraud." To cite a third example, Chicago labor organizer Albert Parsons contended in his November 1884 essay "The Indians," published in the anarchist journal *The Alarm*, that "the Indian has been 'civilized' out of existence and exterminated from the continent by the demon of 'private property' . . . Driven from the soil, disinherited, robbed and murdered by the piracy of capitalism, this once noble but now degraded, debauched and almost extinct race have become the 'national wards' of their profit-mongering civilizers." Native Americans no doubt would have resented such a characterization of their "race," as it employed language similar to that of the Lake Mohonk reformers, who were then designing programs to eliminate Indianness. But the tribe of Knights and the tribe of Indians, both under siege by the forces of industrial capitalism, shared common ideological ground and similar pressures.[23]

Jack London, William Haywood, and Hamlin Garland, among others, also championed the retention of American Indians' rights in their critiques of American capitalism. Garland, who toured parts of Native America in the late 1890s, depicted a bleak future for American Indians under the new allotment policy, arguing that Lake Mohonk reformers "have an ideal to which they wish the Indian to conform. This is the poor farmer." Thus a new generation of Indians would become "supine and stupid toilers." Garland appealed to President Theodore Roosevelt in 1902 to stop allotment: "To make solitary homesteaders of them [the Indians] is to destroy them. Their land should be allotted in such ways that they can live as the French peasants do, in villages, and farm their outlying lands. Others of them, like the Navajo, are natural herders and should be allowed to continue as such. They must have time of adjustment." But time was shrinking as fast as space. The West was won. Roosevelt was fighting new battles in 1902 as the American frontier expanded across the Pacific Ocean.[24]

Workers' and anarchists' use of American Indian images, heroes, and traditions went both ways, reinforcing for some commentators the linkage between urban and rural centers of protest against the prevailing social order, opinions which found expression in the popular press in 1886, a year before Congress passed the Allotment Act. Historian Franklin Rosemont notes that "for most of 1886, Apaches and anarchists were almost equivalent bugaboos in American newspapers and pictorial weeklies. Many an editor and not a few cartoonists and wits alluded to outbreaks of 'savagery' in Arizona and Chicago." Before and after the passage of the Allotment Act, both Native Americans and discontented laborers were attacked for failing to respect the laws of private property; both were described as people who "when banded together lose their individualism and become a conglomerate mass of undesirable citizens," as one anti-labor pamphlet described workers who impeded industrial civilization. Workers, likened to wolves as Indians once were, had to be managed accordingly. A Colorado weekly expectorated that radical workers should be treated "like the Indian . . . hunted down and exterminated." Wobblies were later described as "roaming about in bands making trouble . . . infest[ing] great regions of the West," the industrial Apaches of the early twentieth century.[25]

It is difficult to assess the ways in which this public discourse affected American reformers, both public and private, as they implemented their domestication agenda. The elimination of communal traditions clearly animated their agenda as a whole. How they defined these traditions in ideological terms varied, but they certainly engaged the rhetorical significance of "communism." Some reformers employed small "c" communism to describe communal traditions, while others used capital "C" Communism, implying linkages with European communism or socialism. The aforementioned 1880 House of Representatives report critical of allotment made a distinction between tribal communism and European communism: "From the time of the discovery of America, and for centuries probably before that, the North American Indian has been a communist. Not in the offensive sense of modern communism, but in the sense of holding property in common." The cultural trope of tribal "savage" rather than the political trope of foreign "communist" drove American conquest and control and then federal policy reforms. But in the end both "modern communism" and indigenous communism were antithetical to the American way. And when the conflation of the two came into sharper focus ideologically in the 1870s and beyond, especially after 1886, both variants were presented as foreign ideologies and thus un-American and dangerous to the social order. In the words of that House of Representatives report, "the idea of the separate possession of property by individuals is as foreign to the Indian mind as communism is to us." Western newspaper editorials employed anticommunist rhetoric to paint Indians as un-American, adding to the traditional weapons used in ongoing expropriation campaigns. For example, Colorado booster William Vickers, fusing antagonisms against Indians' royalist and communist traditions, contended in his 1880 coverage of the "Ute War" that "the Utes are actual, practical Communists, and the Government should be ashamed to foster and encourage them in their idleness and wanton waste of property . . . The Government might, with almost, if not quite equal propriety, plant a colony of Communists upon the public domain, maintaining them in idleness at public expense, as to leave the Colorado Utes in possession of their present heritage and present privileges." Vickers called Utes "the original 'tramps' of the country," equating them with jobless whites of the industrial age.[26]

Public discourse simply reinforced the ways in which Native American communal traditions existed in stark contrast to "American" traditions of both the new modern consumer and the old yeoman farmer. Those white Americans pushing allotment, then, did not need the foreign communist analogy to compel Congress to reform Indian society. The analogy supported their views while helping to frame the Indian as "foreigner" for those lawmakers less familiar with or committed to the Mohonk agenda.

Captain Henry Pratt of the Carlisle Indian School could speak for multiple constituencies when in December 1886 he congratulated Senator
Dawes on the pending passage of his "[allotment] law looking to the di-
vorcement of the Indian from the worse than slavery of his old Communistic systems."[27]

But the employment of such anticommunist rhetoric proved functional,
given what was at stake in passing the Allotment Act: the rejection of
treaties still on the books, an ethical hangover from the era of General
Knox and of the Supreme Court's challenge to Indian removal in the
1830s. When Congress abandoned treaty making in 1871, it had stipulated that nothing contained in the act "shall be construed to invalidate
or impair the obligation of any treaty heretofore lawfully made and ratified
with any such Indian nation or tribe." The problem of treaties and thus
their standing as "international law," as one reformer described the
politico-legal context, resurrected the agonistic tension between the Law
of Nations and the Law of Nature.[28]

Philip C. Garrett, a lawyer and member of the Indian Rights Association executive committee, complained that in trying to make new policy
"we are stopped again by the existence of hundreds of *alleged* treaties,
which imply the perpetual existence of the tribes, or contain some obligation unfulfilled." Garrett and other members of the Mohonk Tribe wrestled with how to discharge those obligations semantically and prevent the
treaties from serving as a barrier to the implementation of legislation without Indians' consent, which treaties required. Several reformers explicitly
attacked the notion of "domestic dependent nations," or *imperium in imperio,* still on the Supreme Court books. William Strong, a former associate
justice of the U.S. Supreme Court who attended various Lake Mohonk
conferences, contended in 1885, "We began by making treaties with these
Indian tribes; we treated them as independent tribes. It was a little absurd;
it was within our borders, a little *imperium in imperio.* But we did not recognize them as independent." Expediency led to the signing of treaties.
Expediency, sold as social crisis, now led to their rejection as legal documents, freeing the federal government to treat individual Indians as independent of tribal political authority. Echoing Strong, Garrett concluded,
"The great mistake has been one which it is now too late to avoid, that of
dealing with these numerous races of savages within our borders as nations, as if there could be nations within nations without some organic
provision of constitutional law." Hundreds of federal treaties served as a

legal and moral barrier to the physical incorporation of Indian America, maintaining the intellectual and international Great Divide between the United States and Indian nations. In his effort to resolve the Indian problem, Garrett provided a solution that nicely frames terminationists' thinking: "How can this anomaly be remedied, at least, but by painfully cutting the Gordian knot, and declaring that this National recognition was a mistake, and henceforth the United States will only deal with the individual Indian." Garrett presented "as food for thought" a few ideas on how reformers could rethink the treaty in ahistorical terms and find just cause for cutting the legal Gordian knot of treaties that, he believed, choked expansion and development: "(1) Are all of these so-called treaties really treaties? (2) What would be the legal and moral relations of the two high contracting parties were it conceivable that it was subsequently discovered that one of them was not a nation? (3) If the termination of the treaty by the United States is undeniably against her own interests, and in the interest of the Indian tribe, does that alter the moral question involved[?]" Garrett sought to manipulate a past that had refused to obey the Laws of Nature.[29]

Garrett and other reformers and federal officials were not the first imperialists to wrestle with such questions. They may have drawn on the lessons provided by their British counterparts, who first negotiated the 1840 Treaty of Waitangi with the Maori of New Zealand and then used disingenuous means to deny the Maori those treaty rights. The minister of justice of the New Zealand parliament had justified the intent of the treaty as "the detribalization of the Maoris—to destroy if it were possible, the principle of communism . . . and to amalgamate the Maori race into our social and political system." When the Maori exercised their treaty right not to sell land to settlers, thus complicating that agenda of amalgamation, a British colonial judge pulled a legal rabbit out of his wig in declaring the Treaty of Waitangi "a simple nullity." American officials would do the same when faced with Garrett's central question: "Are all of these so-called treaties really treaties?"[30]

Phase Three: Incorporation

Final resistance to the legality of the allotment program and thus the formal "cutting" of America's Gordian knot, to use Garrett's metaphor, ended in January 1903 with the Supreme Court decision *Lone Wolf v. Hitchcock.*

While white Americans conveniently ignored treaties as legitimate instruments of international relations, Native Americans did not. Lone Wolf, a leader of the Kiowa nation (Indian Territory) forced to adopt the allotment policy, sued Secretary of the Interior Ethan Allen Hitchcock, arguing that the policy violated the 1867 Treaty of Medicine Lodge Creek, which had granted the Kiowa the right to reject tribal land sales with a three-fourths majority vote. Tribal opponents of allotment, as well as white supporters benefiting from favorable reservation leasing arrangements, believed that sacred American legal principles concerning contracts made inviolable the contract of the treaty. But the Supreme Court ruled against Lone Wolf and elucidated the principle of plenary power that invested Congress with the right to abrogate treaties, ending judicial review of congressional expropriation of Indian land and rejecting the notion of domestic dependent nations explicated by the Court in 1832. White reformers had thus waged a successful "just war" in Congress and in the Court to redefine the nature of international agreements made between the United States and the nations of Native America.[31]

On the heels of Lone Wolf, the Bureau of Indian Affairs established competency commissions which fanned out through Indian America to mark particular Native Americans as "competent" to sell their land. Once labeled competent, Native Americans were left vulnerable to the forces of land acquisition common to the American West. Facilitated by corrupt federal agents, another round of epic fraud resulted, which historian Philip Deloria calls "without doubt one of the vilest episodes in the long history of American colonialism." These competency commissions expanded greatly under the direction of Commissioner of Indian Affairs Cato Sells, who in 1914 summarized a century of government policy by declaring: "I hold it to be an economic and social crime, in this age and under modern conditions, to permit thousands of acres of fertile land belonging to the Indians and capable of great industrial development to lie in unproductive idleness." Twentieth-century boosters of industrial expansion depicted Indians as criminals breaking the natural law of human progress for maintaining their reservations as wasted space, sustaining views articulated in the early years of the American republic, enunciated across the spaces of the American West, and finally established in the modern conditions of industrial America.[32]

The 1887 General Allotment Act, supported by Lone Wolf v. Hitchcock and other decisions and implemented in various guises, such as Sells's criminalization of small-scale Indian farmers, had passed despite its central contradictory dynamic: the use of socialistic means to further an "American" end of capitalism and the abandonment of the structural elements of international law. Thus federal officials forced upon American Indians a program "unimaginable in U.S. society—the wholesale redistribution of property," according to the historian Alexandra Harmon. Dispossession was the result. Native Americans' collective land base dropped from 138 million acres in 1887 to 52 million acres in 1934, when Congress abandoned the allotment policy. By that time nearly two-thirds of the Indian population either had lost their land or were living on land incapable of providing subsistence.[33]

Some Native Americans, especially those in Indian Territory, had harnessed the capitalist energy flowing around them, in so doing contesting the label of "communism" to preserve their political sovereignty and cultural space. For example, Cherokee politicians complained to Congress in 1880: "The statements made to you that we, or any of the Indians, are communists . . . are entirely erroneous. No people are more jealous of the personal right to property than Indians . . . [Our] farms and lots are practically just as much the property of the individuals as yours are." Indian citizens of the Five Civilized Tribes, employing the spirit of acquisitiveness or "selfishness" that Senator Dawes claimed was at the bottom of civilization, amassed large estates, which reformers and politicians attacked as evidence of Indians' royalist traditions rather than as an exemplification of trends regnant in Gilded Age America; Commissioner of Indian Affairs J. D. C. Atkins for one called such American Indian estates "baronial" in 1886. But American Indian governments remained committed to ameliorating class conflict by restraining economic practices that emphasized individual interests over tribal, mediating an agonistic tension between the individual ideal and the communal ideal.[34]

In September 1904 the German scholar Max Weber traveled to Indian Territory and Oklahoma Territory, two politically distinct regions on the verge of unification through statehood. Weber witnessed there the end of Native Americans' assiduous efforts to steer the engine of progress along tracks of their making, a subsidiary ethnic trunk line that nonetheless intersected with the main line of Americanness. He interviewed the various actors in the sordid drama of evolving Oklahoma statehood, from the Creeks and Cherokees to the selfish land sharks who were fine-tuning their schemes to defraud them. At the time of his visit Weber was known as a specialist in agrarian economics, but he was soon to publish his most famous work, *The Protestant Ethic and the Spirit of Capitalism*. Like many Europeans, Germans in particular, Weber was fascinated by the changing sociological conditions of Indian life. His interest grew in part from his father, Max Weber Sr., whose travels in America in 1883 included a trip from Minneapolis to Seattle on the Northern Pacific railroad in the company of Secretary of the Interior Schurz. Weber subsequently followed frontier developments, reading American histories provided by family friends. After attending a conference in St. Louis in September 1904, Weber elected to spend several days touring Oklahoma Territory and Indian Territory, the latter about to be incorporated into the former, politically, economically, and culturally, despite the best efforts of the Cherokee politician Robert Owen, who would soon serve in the U.S. Senate as a progressive Democrat. In a letter of September 28, 1904, Weber told his mother that until the critical mass of settlers generated sufficient pressure to restructure Indian life, "the entire old Indian Territory belonged to the Indians, who were dealt with like a foreign power." But after "private ownership [was] forced upon the Indians," the result was the rapid transfer of Indian land to white ownership, the dissolving of boundaries of foreign and American soil, and the end of "agricultural communism." Weber noted the "vehement objection" of Creek full-bloods to the abolition of "communal land" ("Land-Communismus," in Weber's German). He saw this transition to American capitalism in ethnic terms: the full-bloods "are surely doomed to decline, but among the others one sees intelligent faces. Their clothes are almost invariably European." Like many Americans, and many Germans, Weber employed the vanishing Indian trope common to that era, but he also added his voice to the chorus of American critics of industrial expansion who depicted the Indian as victim of hegemonic capitalism, a populist metaphor for the end of rural communities' independence. Muskogee, the capital of Indian Territory, was no longer "Indian," he lamented. "In a year this place will look like Oklahoma, that is, like any other American city. With almost lightning speed everything that stands in the way of capitalistic culture is being crushed."[35]

The Next Chapter

In *Lone Wolf v. Hitchcock* we see the legal incorporation of Native America, in Oklahoma the final act of its territorial incorporation. Geronimo's participation in Roosevelt's March 1905 inaugural parade symbolized the ways in which Native Americans became incorporated into American history. The story of the winning of the West, expressed in the parade's narrative account of the narrowing of the Great Divide between the "savage" and the "civilized," closed the first chapter of U.S. imperial expansion. By 1905 its new chapter and the American Century were well under way in the Philippines, an extension of America's conquest of Indian country, a new righteous war with "savages." Emilio Aguinaldo, the leader of the Filipinos' resistance, became "Tecumseh, Sitting Bull, Old Cochise, or some other celebrated Indian warrior," as Senator William Stewart framed it in 1899. Veterans of American Indian wars carried out most of the military operations in the Philippines. Nearly 90 percent of the U.S. officer corps had experience fighting Indians, including General "Hell Roaring" Jacob Smith, a veteran of the 1890 Wounded Knee Sioux massacre, who advocated turning the Philippines into a "howling wilderness" by establishing concentration camps and massacring Filipino youth. Militia men, many of them the sons of veterans of Indian wars, echoed the genocidal rhetoric of their generals. One Kansas soldier boldly told a reporter that the Philippines "won't be pacified until the niggers [meaning the Filipinos] are killed off like the Indians." Another soldier claimed that "the only good Filipino is a dead one," repeating the popular American refrain that echoed from sea to shining sea: "The only good Indian is a dead Indian." President Roosevelt supported this hard line in the Philippines, vowing not to "repeat the folly of which our people were sometimes guilty . . . when they petted hostile Indians." The Filipinos, for their part, also looked to the bloody history of Indian-white relations in framing their resistance to U.S. imperialism. A representative of the Aguinaldo government warned General Marcus Miller in January 1899 that Filipinos would not surrender but "withdraw to the mountains and repeat the North American Indian warfare."[36]

General Henry Lawton, who had helped capture Geronimo, also served in the Philippines, leading one newspaper to describe his unit's actions as pursuing "the rebel Filipinos just as they relentlessly pursued the Modocs and Apaches in the triumph of civilization." American newspapers expressed ambivalence about this "triumph of civilization," however. A number of anti-imperialist newspapers employed "the Indian" as a warning against taking on a new civilizing mission. For some Americans, the Wounded Knee massacre lay like a shadow across the country's new phase of imperial expansion, even as soldiers responsible for it re-created its grue-some outcome thousands of miles away. In one notable example, the *Chicago Record* editorialized on the Philippines occupation by claiming that "in dealing with the Indian question the United States government has not been brilliantly successful, unless ability to exterminate be accounted success." The *New York Herald* was more sanguine in its assessment of U.S. prospects in the Philippines, opining that "the United States is not entirely inexperienced in the handling of native tribes, and it is to be hoped that the lessons which we have learned in dealing with the North American Indians may bear fruit in deciding as to what is best for our oceanic possessions."[37]

In this second great debate on U.S. imperialism, the leaders of the Mohonk Tribe also weighed in on the Philippines question by offering a justification modeled after the cultural conquest of Native American space. Senator Dawes supported the war in the Philippines and the subjugation of its "alien" race, maintaining that America's experience with Indians should serve as "an object lesson worthy of careful and candid study." Championing support for the overseas concentration, domestication, and incorporation of the Filipinos, the Lake Mohonk Conference resolved that federal Indian policies should "govern [U.S.] dealings with other dependent peoples." In 1904 the group codified this notion by changing its name to the Lake Mohonk Conference of the Indian and Other Dependent Peoples.[38]

The Filipino-American War thus functioned as a foreign extension of the domestic military and cultural "just war" waged against American Indians. It is important to note the ways in which the Philippines context interacted with the ongoing legal "just war" conducted against Native American sovereignty. The 1903 *Lone Wolf v. Hitchcock* decision operated in a dual international context. In deciding *Lone Wolf* the Supreme Court supported the right of Congress to abrogate treaties between Indian nations and the American nation "when circumstances arise which will not only justify the government in disregarding the stipulations of the treaty, but may demand, in the interest of the country and the Indians themselves, that it should do so." By 1903 those circumstances included a war in the Philippines that conflated Filipinos with American Indians. The United States denied sovereignty to the Filipinos on the basis of policies denying it to Indians. Perhaps thinking of Geronimo, Theodore Roosevelt claimed in his influential essay "The Strenuous Life" that adopting anti-imperialists' doctrines "would make it incumbent upon us to leave the Apaches of Arizona to work out their own salvation, and to decline to interfere in a single Indian reservation." Acting "in the interest of the country," an interest that now extended all the way to the new frontier of the Philippines, the Supreme Court codified the right of the Congress to deny sovereignty to "the Indian and Other Dependent Peoples" at the same time.[39]

Folded into international history by events in the Philippines that were shaped by imperial ideologies of racial conquest, stripped of sovereignty by the law of the land in the *Lone Wolf* decision, and finally rendered stateless by Oklahoma statehood, Native Americans collectively found themselves entering the twentieth century in a liminal political, cultural, and social position. And yet in the narrative of Roosevelt's inauguration and the new chapter of American history he helped to launch abroad lay the groundwork for Indian peoples' survival as American Indians. The Carlisle students marching in the inaugural parade of 1905 represented the "modern" Indian who had crossed the intellectual and physical boundaries dividing Indian and white America. These graduates, and others of the federal Indian boarding school system, a central component of the government's domestication agenda, would lead Native Americans' assiduous efforts over the course of the twentieth century to restore the legal strands of the Gordian knot of international relations between the United States and Indian nations and thus reassert the moral prerogatives of the Law of Nations. These graduates would employ the ideological themes of America's engagement with international events to reimagine themselves as both Indian and American. Incorporated into the expanding American empire, these "new Indians" would serve that empire both as patriotic soldiers and as patriotic intellectuals, participating not only in furthering its material dimensions but also in shaping its moral dimensions "in the interest of the country" by fighting for self-determination for "the Indian and Other Dependent Peoples."

2   The Defense of the Reservation

In some curious way, it is the Indians still who are American.

—D. H. Lawrence, *New York Times Magazine*, December 24, 1922

Richard Henry Pratt, a veteran of the Civil War and of Indian wars in the American West, was the most outspoken critic of what he called the "un-American" system of reservations, which he believed perpetuated a "Communistic" Indian life. Pratt contended that African Americans and immigrants had shown "progress" because of their proximity to and participation in institutions of American life, while Indians remained "prisoners on reservations." Pratt failed to note the limitations of that progress because of racial and ethnic prejudice in American industrial society, but he fixed the roots of the "Indian problem" in "the indurated system of segregating and reservating the Indians and denying them all chances to see and thus to learn and to prove their qualities through competition"; containing Indians on reservations and "away from and outside [white] civilization" destroyed reformers' goal of "promoting their Americanization." Pratt assiduously promoted his "Americanization" agenda through off-reservation schools, establishing the Carlisle Indian School in Pennsylvania as the foundation of the federal boarding school system, an important element of the government's domestication program. Carlisle's slogan became: "To civilize the Indian, get him into civilization. To keep him civilized, let him stay." Like other Gilded Age reformers, Pratt saw such "civilization" leading to citizenship and thence to "manhood" and full incorporation into American society. Carlisle and other boarding schools thus became sites for transforming "savage" Indians into the "civilized" specimens of modernity who followed proudly in Geronimo's wake during Theodore Roosevelt's 1905 inaugural parade.[1]

To promote "Americanization," in April 1911 members of this Carlisle generation organized the Society of American Indians (SAI), the pan-Indian equivalent of the National Association for the Advancement of Colored People (NAACP), which had formed two years earlier. Prominent SAI members had been students at Pratt's Carlisle Indian School, had taught at the school, or embodied its philosophical principles. In July 1911 SAI co-founder Charles Eastman (Santee Sioux), a Dartmouth College–trained doctor, traveled to London to represent "the North American Indian" at the First Universal Races Congress, a four-day gathering of over one thousand representatives of fifty-three nationalities. In his July 28 address Eastman championed what he called Pratt's "unanswerable logic: 'To civilize the Indian, get him into civilization!'" He told his audience that American Indians had struggled with "civilization," in particular with the attenuation of communal practices of sharing eroded by capitalism. But when they were forced onto reservations and into a "miserable prison existence . . . the manhood of the Indian suffered its final eclipse . . . We may say now without much fear of contradiction that the reservation policy was a mistake." Like Eastman, Carlos Montezuma (Apache), who had lectured at the Mohonk Conference and served as a physician at the Carlisle School, denounced reservations as "demoralized prisons." Writing in 1916, another founding SAI member, Arthur C. Parker, an anthropologist of Seneca heritage, noted that on reservations "Indians were communists and frequently work cooperatively." Equating reservation life with "segregation," Parker insisted that *the evils of the reservation system have continued to corrupt the Indian and render a just understanding of citizenship, taxation and social service, things difficult to inculcate or to achieve.*[2]

The host of the first SAI meeting, the white sociologist Fayette McKenzie, had proposed that the SAI become a "Mohonk by Indians." This new generation of Indian intellectuals employed the Mohonkian discourse of civilization that shaped the ideological battle over the contested cultural space of the reservation. To complete the process of incorporation begun in the 1850s, Eastman, Montezuma, Parker, and other SAI leaders lobbied for the abolition of the reservation system and of the Bureau of Indian Affairs that managed it as well as for granting citizenship to all Indians. Yet their agenda and their identities would develop what Eastman called a "confusing and contradictory" character that Mohonk reformers and Pratt would have found anachronistic, the result in part of their ambivalence toward American "civilization." As Eastman put it in his memoirs, documenting America's poverty and violence, "I had not seen half the savagery of civilization."[3]

SAI intellectuals defended Indianness in ethnic terms, especially during World War I and beyond. For them the Indian was a "vanishing race" in purely full-blood biological terms, but not in intellectual, social, or cultural terms. Montezuma promoted moving the 1917 SAI annual conference from an academic venue to one closer to the people the SAI was purportedly serving. "This is an Indian country: let the Indians attend and let the Indians rule," he argued. "Heretofore the sentiment of the Indians has been lacking." In the end, despite his anti-reservation rhetoric, Montezuma returned to "Indian country" and his Apache roots by choosing to die in a hut on the reservation where he was born. Parker championed the biological and philosophical hybrid "new Indian," a "well-bred Indian, who is familiar with modern culture." Eastman, too, talked about creating a "new Indian." Inspired by his international experiences, the rhetoric of World War I, and his witness to the poverty of industrial America, Eastman later professed the agonistic dynamics of his hybridity: "I am an Indian; and while I have learned much from civilization . . . I have never lost my Indian sense of right and justice. I am for development and progress along social and spiritual lines, rather than those of commerce, nationalism, or material efficiency. Nevertheless, so long as I live, I am an American." Eastman's "American," however, was a new American as much as he was a new Indian.[4]

In articulating *their* version of "Americanization," SAI intellectuals promoted a hybrid patriotism: supporting America and fighting in its name meant fighting in the name of cultural tolerance; Indianness and Americanness in combination would strengthen America. In the address opening the SAI's October 1919 conference in Minneapolis, Eastman argued: "We are part of this great American Nation, and must be some good to the country . . . We Indians started the whole basis of Americanism. We Indians laid the foundation of freedom and equality and democracy long before any white people came here." In asserting the spiritual values of Indians against the values of white civilization, which were based on "dollar,

dollar, dollar," Eastman claimed that "the Indian will save this country." Progressive Era Indian intellectuals selected "the best attributes of the tribes but would no longer be bound by tribal parochialism. The new Indian would also adopt the best qualities of the larger society; his Indianness and Americanness would complement and refresh each other. The American nationality always in the process of being created would be strengthened and broadened by its Indian infusion."[5]

It remained to be seen what kind of citizenship the SAI envisioned: Wilsonian global citizenship, "99 44/100 Pure" citizens, or "mottled-red" citizens, hybrid citizens who celebrated elements of Americanness in Indian ways. And it remained to be seen whether such a conception could appeal to Native Americans beyond the membership of the SAI, which remained an off-reservation voice for a well-traveled and well-educated group; only college graduates could serve as editors of its quarterly journal, *American Indian Magazine*. The slogan of the journal—"For the Honor of the Race and the Good of the Country"—framed the dual identity of these Native Americans and the dynamic of hybrid patriotism that emerged from their memories of the domestic conflict of Indian wars and their engagement with the international conflict of World War I. In trying to reconcile the debilitating tensions between American civic nationalism and American racial nationalism that bubbled to the surface during wartime, Native Americans thus added their voices to larger debates about the character of American modernity, the role of imperialism in shaping that modernity, and its implications for America's leadership in the world.[6]

Participating in—and Resisting—the War

Federal Indian boarding schools, Captain Pratt's Carlisle Indian School in particular, emphasized disciplinary rigor based on military models of instruction. When it came time for the United States to send men to the savage battlefields of World War I, the armed forces recruited in these schools because of this military-oriented curriculum but also because of their assiduous efforts to "inculcate patriotism." Dovetailing with public school programs, an 1889 BIA directive had instructed school superintendents to require Indian students to sing patriotic songs, fly the American flag, and celebrate important patriotic holidays, including the date marking the passage of the Dawes Act to "impress upon Indian youth the en-

larged scope and opportunity given them by this [act] and the new obligations which it imposes." The "new obligations" of Native Americans
included defending the American nation into which they had been forcibly incorporated.[7]

American Indians had participated in American military campaigns
during the Revolutionary War and beyond, fighting in the War of 1812,
the Civil War, and with units of the army in the West waging their "just
war" against other American Indians. In all cases they did so as auxiliary
units, fighting alongside rather than within regular units because of their
noncitizen status and whites' racist perceptions that they were not disciplined or trustworthy enough for regular army service. Debates on integrating Native Americans into the army as individual soldiers rather than
as segregated units intensified as the boarding school system expanded
but especially after 1914, when the debate took place in an international
context. The chief of staff of the U.S. Army, General Hugh L. Scott, a
supporter of Indian assimilation programs, contended that "the idea that
an American can not make a good soldier of an Indian is preposterous.
The people of Egypt were made into good soldiers by the English." A key
supporter of Indian-only regiments, Joseph Kossuth Dixon, made note of
the U.S. allies' deployment of Sikh, Gurkha, and African troops, especially the use of Senegalese troops by the French. Supporters also pointed
to Canada's experience of integrating Canadian Indians into army service,
where they performed heroically. U.S. officials, then, grappled with the
same questions as their imperial peers and conflated American Indians
with other colonized peoples who served as soldiers of empire.[8]

Debates over including Indian soldiers in the regular army fractured
along lines of preserving Native culture or furthering assimilation. Dixon
argued that the employment of Indian-only regiments might preserve the
"Vanishing Race," the title of his 1913 book; serving in segregated units
would allow Indians to maintain their warrior traditions, among other
"noble" aspects of Indian life. Key opponents of segregated units included
Henry Pratt, who told Secretary of War Newton Baker that "it would be
far better for [Indians] to be recognized as individual men than as masses,"
highlighting his objection to anything resembling anachronistic tribal activities. Commissioner of Indian Affairs Cato Sells, a devout assimilationist, echoed Pratt in contending that "the military segregation of the Indian
is altogether objectionable. It does not afford the associational contact he

needs and is unfavorable to his preparation for citizenship." Native Americans divided on the question. On the one hand, the Society of American Indians objected to the segregation of units because it implied that Indians were unfit for regular service and thus impeded their access to American institutional life. On the other hand, Cherokee and Lumbee Indians of North Carolina objected to serving with white troops, as did many of the Iroquois who volunteered. Baker's objections, reinforced by Sells's and Pratt's views, won out: the U.S. Army did not establish segregated units for Native Americans, though it maintained the practice of segregating African Americans from the regular army until 1948.[9]

Although many Native Americans were noncitizens and thus not required to adhere to regulations imposed by selective service legislation, 17,313 Native Americans registered for the draft; another 6,509 were inducted. Nearly all eligible students in the off-reservation boarding school system served in the war; roughly 90 percent of them volunteered, a rate of participation and voluntarism far greater than the 20–40 percent for the reservation communities. The Carlisle Indian School itself contributed 205 soldiers. The range of participation between different native communities was great, ranging from roughly 1 percent of Navajo to 30–60 percent among Oklahoma Indian communities, reflecting various degrees of acculturation in Indian country. The casualty rate for Native American soldiers was much higher than for other ethnic groups, in part because army commanders used Indians in the most dangerous positions such as scouts, arguing that it was in their "nature" to perform such tasks. In the end, Native American soldiers earned the most prestigious awards of the war, including the French Croix de Guerre. In addition, Choctaw and Cherokee soldiers provided unbreakable telephone communication codes, prefiguring the use of Comanche and Navajo "code talkers" during World War II.[10]

Motivations for volunteering for army service varied greatly. Some Native Americans fought overseas to gain citizenship, others for reasons of adventure, economics, patriotism, or tribal traditions that celebrated the warrior ethos. White Americans and Europeans were not alone in believing that war regenerated the national spirit. Some Native American soldiers echoed the Wilsonian rationale for U.S. participation in the war. Loney Sawell, for example, explained that he joined the army to help "make the world safe for democracy." Native Americans would fight for

2.1 Corporal George Miner (Winnebago) from Wisconsin, sent overseas to make the world safe for democracy and self-determination, stands guard in Niederahren, Germany, January 1919. Courtesy of National Archives and Records Administration.

freedom and democracy precisely because they knew what it meant *not* to have them. Chauncey Yellow Robe, an 1895 graduate of Carlisle and a disciplinarian in the federal boarding school system, delineated American Indians' "patriotic motives" at the SAI's 1918 annual convention. He asserted that Native Americans, in contrast to the "Un-American" German immigrants, were examples of the "true patriot," the "native of America" who had always fought in the name of the Declaration of Independence. Yet even as he told his fellow SAI members, "We must Americanize," Yellow Robe declared, "We, the American Indians, are not all dead, and we will fight on and die fighting for this freedom." Americanization for many Native Americans reflected this hybrid patriotism, the belief that fighting in the name of an America that would respect their Indianness served to reify the founding ideals of the American Revolution for which Americans, Indian and non-Indian, were fighting overseas.[11]

Although most draft-age Native Americans registered for the draft or volunteered for service, it is important to note that some objected to army service and thus resisted conscription. Not surprisingly, given the history of Indian-white relations, not all Native Americans jumped at the chance to die overseas for freedoms they believed were denied them at home. Resistance took multiple forms and derived from various influences, including Native Americans' correct assessment that the government had no right to induct noncitizens. Another major factor was increased pressure on Native Americans' land base, the product of both wartime demand for agricultural and industrial production and of government policies that expanded the allotment policy to increase that production. In April 1917 Commissioner Sells unveiled his so-called Liberal Policy, which liberalized rules in the granting of allotments to "competent" Indians, identified as such by roving bands of white commissioners eager to expand the number of Indians eligible to sell their land during the boom years of the war. Repeating a familiar BIA mantra, Sells argued that the Liberal Policy "means the ultimate absorption of the Indian race into the body politic of the Nation. It means, in short, the beginning of the end of the Indian problem." What it really meant, however, was the exacerbation of the Indian problem of losing land to white speculators and settlers at below-market rates because of BIA corruption or indifference. The effects of the policy, as well as wartime pressures to conform to the state, and the inability of many Indians to vote in state or federal elections, led to draft resistance among Native Americans from New York to New Mexico who linked the federal government's efforts to integrate them into the war machine to the integration of their land into the American economy. Both processes diminished their sovereignty.[12]

Open resistance to conscription developed in isolated Pueblo, Hopi, and Navajo communities, in parts of Oklahoma, and among the Iroquois nations of New York. The Seneca, despite the patriotic exhortations of prominent Seneca citizen Arthur C. Parker, resisted induction, in part because of renewed allotment pressure that accelerated after speculators discovered oil and gas reserves on the reservation in the 1890s. Dividing communal property threatened the unity of the Seneca and thus their sovereignty. Asserting tribal autonomy, two other Iroquois nations, the Oneida and the Onondaga, declared war on Germany on their own terms. On the White Earth Reservation in Minnesota, journalist Gustave Beaulieu championed an antiwar stance in his newspaper the *Tomahawk*, publishing stories about local antiwar demonstrations and printing editorials under headings such as "Is This a Free Country?" that criticized federal officials for conscripting Indians to fight a war that benefited American capitalists. The White Earth Chippewa faced enormous pressure to allot communal lands prior to and during the war, engendering great bitterness toward federal officials and white speculators. Here, as in New York, the resistance to induction of Native Americans did not stem solely from their distrust of coercive initiatives that denied them basic rights but was tied to ongoing allotment campaigns that undermined their sense of stability and place. The *Tomahawk* lost this critical edge in August 1917 when Gustave died and his brother Clement, a Christian minister, replaced him as editor and used the newspaper in support of what he called a "righteous war."[13]

American Indians in Oklahoma also sharply divided during the war, producing some of its most vocal proponents and some of its most vociferous opponents. Some Oklahoma Indians joined the Green Corn Rebellion, a group of agrarian socialists who echoed the populist critiques of agricultural capitalism, embracing a version of Gustave Beaulieu's argument that entering World War I served the interests of Wall Street rather than Main Street, especially the Main Streets of American Indian reservations. Ellen Perryman (Muscogee Creek) championed draft resistance, asserting: "Indians are not going to the slaughter fields of France. To Hell with the Government and the Allies . . . They are nothing but a bunch of Grafters and Sons of Bitches." Perryman's animus stemmed from her belief that "there was a movement on among the white people to drive the Indians from their native lands." Perryman's efforts to dissuade American Indians from registering led to charges that she had violated the Espionage Act, but she was not imprisoned. In the end, the federal government arrested draft resisters but elected not to jail them, in part because of the international implications of creating American Indian prisoners of war at home.[14]

The U.S. Committee on Public Information (CPI), formed to sell the war to the American public, advertised American Indians' high participation rate, declaring in one campaign that "the spirit and blood of the race seems to have risen in one hot compound of militant Americanism." Federal officials viewed Native Americans' army service as validation of their efforts, historical and contemporary, to assimilate Indians. But incorporating noncitizens into an institution such as the army generated international exposure of "the Indian problem," including the increasingly visible effects of the Liberal Policy. While they used Native American patriotism to sell the war, federal officials also sought to prevent a different view of Native American life from finding an overseas audience, for the first time demonstrating sensitivity to the ways in which issues of race played out internationally. To combat negative portrayals of American freedom and democracy, for which Native Americans were dying, the CPI formed a censorship team with U.S. Customs. A film titled *Ermine of the Yellowstone*, released during the war, alarmed censors of the Division of Foreign Picture Service because it featured a romance between a white woman and "a half breed Indian" as well as battles between Indians and American soldiers. "The question," the censor asked, "is whether this picture could be used as evidence that the U.S. treated a race inferior in numbers and a prior occupant of American soil in a manner which would stir up antagonistic feeling." A fellow censor elaborated: "It could be said that we are preaching liberty to all the world, when we are depriving Indians, an inferior race, not only of liberty, but of their property and exploiting them . . . Hence Germans could say their doctrine of biology, 'survival of the fittest,' is even true of us."[15]

Such concerns would find fuller expression during the propaganda battles of World War II and the Cold War. Their expression during World War I marked the difficulty of reconciling the realities of Native Ameri-

can life with the outbreak of patriotism that war engendered and the expectations of progress that patriotism created. As the war ended, questions
about fair treatment of ethnic and racial minorities took center stage,
pushed forward by Native Americans intent on marshaling the moral and
the material components of postwar nation building to restore Native
Americans' rights and sovereignty.

Citizens of the World

Native Americans situated their service and patriotism in an international
context before the war ended. The *New York Evening Herald* claimed that
Native Americans fought for America because it was their nature to fight;
they did not understand "the international aspects" of the war, including
the purpose of defending the "self-determination of small nations." But
Native Americans in fact understood very clearly "the international aspects" of the war precisely because of their troubled history of international relations with the United States. "Loving liberty as he does, he will
fight for it. Knowing the tragedy of 'broken treaties,' he will fight that
there not be more treaties broken," Arthur C. Parker wrote in a 1917 issue
of the *Carlisle Arrow and Red Man*. "Challenged, the Indian has responded
and shown himself a citizen of the world and an exponent of an ethical
civilization wherein human liberty is assured." In a different forum Parker
called the American Indian "a world patriot." *American Indian Magazine*
published a series of editorials during the war that highlighted Native
American intellectuals' and activists' analysis of the war's implications.
For example, in the spring 1917 issue the editors noted:

> Indians are viewing the world war with a deep interest and seeking to
> understand the principles that lie at the bottom of it. Somehow they
> seem to believe that the civilization of which the European has
> boasted is after all a defective thing . . . Some of the Indians see that
> the outcome of this appalling catastrophe will be a better understand-
> ing among men and nations and a more just recognition of the rights
> of the smaller divisions of mankind.

Facing east to view the slaughter of the West's enlightened ideals, Native
Americans explicitly and publicly erased the intellectual boundary be-

tween Indians' "savagery" and whites' "civilization" that underwrote the
U.S. government's racist policies. And they offered an important vision of
America as a champion of decolonization, as a model "ethical civilization"
in an unsettled world of savagery in which the traumas of war afflicting
"modern" nation-states stemmed from the related processes of industrialization and imperialism that shaped their development. These American
Indian intellectuals thus served as the conscience of a nation trying to resolve the tensions between its modern and its imperial identity as it sought
to promote the promise of American life abroad.[16]

The events of World War I and the rhetoric of freedom and democracy
which framed them advanced an internationalism among Native Americans which fostered the belief that waging war abroad in the name of
democracy would improve democracy at home, thus creating the moral
foundation for a "just war" for Native American rights. Demonstrating intellectuals' "interaction between universality and the local," the Lakota
activist Gertrude Bonnin (Zitkala-Sa) declared in the summer of 1918:
"Truth and justice are inseparable component parts of American ideals. As
America has declared democracy abroad, so must we consistently practice
it at home." The conflation of international and local contexts created a
new discourse among Native Americans that linked their prewar experiences to the moral and material dimensions of postwar Native nationalism. Serving the interests of the United States as soldiers and as champions of its democratic ideals, Native Americans embraced the obligations
of this relationship while demanding obligations in return, a mutually reinforcing set of commitments that animated their hybrid patriotism after
the war.[17]

Native Americans' views of international events and world citizenship
found fuller expression when activists appropriated Wilsonian language to
demand their rights in a post–World War I world. Charles Eastman asked
the question at the heart of internationalized Indian-white relations in
"The Indian's Plea for Freedom," published in the winter 1919 issue of
American Indian Magazine: "How can our nation pose as the champion of
the 'little peoples' until it has been fair to its own?" Echoing Eastman,
Bonnin proclaimed in the same issue: that "The eyes of the world are upon
the Peace Conference sitting at Paris . . . Little peoples are to be granted
the right of self-determination! Small nations and remnants of nations are
to sit beside their great allies at the Peace Table; and their just claims are

2.2 "Can This Be the Light of the East?" This political cartoon appeared in the Society of American Indians publication *Quarterly Journal* (ca. 1916). The American Indian, for so long represented as a savage in the West, shifts his gaze to the east to situate savagery in the heart of Europe while standing tall and dignified above the imperialistic fray.

to be duly incorporated in the terms of a righteous peace." For Bonnin, the "small nations and remnants of nations" included Indian nations seeking resolution of their "just claims" related to the trauma of the "just war" waged against them in the nineteenth century. "The Red man asks for a very simple thing,—citizenship in the land that was once his own,—America . . . What shall world democracy mean to his race?"[18]

To address Bonnin's question, Native American leaders reached beyond the pages of a magazine geared toward educated and off-reservation Indians. Crow politician Robert Yellowtail, a graduate of the Sherman Institute boarding school in California, declared to the Senate Committee on Indian Affairs in September 1919 that his Crow reservation was "a separate, semi-sovereign nation in itself," making this claim because Woodrow Wilson had "assured . . . the people of the whole world, that the right of self-determination shall not be denied to any people." At the end of his speech he reminded the Senate committee members of the sacrifices Native Americans had made during the war and demanded citizenship in return, which would mean "nothing else than freedom; freedom in the broadest and most comprehensive sense of the word." Citizenship, for Yellowtail, meant something broader than Bonnin's conception of it: the freedom to maintain "separate, semi-sovereign" cultural and political space, a hybrid citizenship that drew from the mutually supporting set of obligations of nineteenth-century treaties that protected Indian nationalism and of twentieth-century world citizenship that demanded service to an American state that helped make the world safe for democracy for all peoples. The contrast between Bonnin's and Yellowtail's notions of citizenship reflected the tension between two conceptions of national integration, between off-reservation intellectuals who promoted political amalgamation and on-reservation politicians who were intent on rebuilding what they considered their national political economy.[19]

Laura M. C. Kellogg (née Cornelius), a founding member of the SAI, also argued for fair treatment of American Indians within an international context. Publishing her views in her 1920 book *Our Democracy and the American Indian*, Kellogg (Iroquois) claimed that the democratic ideals of Indian America were embedded in the constitution of white America. Addressing her first chapter "To the American People," she argued that "the idea of the League of Nations and Democracy . . . came from an American Indian," citing the experience of the Iroquois Confederacy, which was founded on "the message of peace and love" and of "govern-ment, order, progress." "And so I love my country," she wrote, speaking of both Iroquois country and an America that she believed reflected its dem-ocratic genius. Now that the United States was poised to play a larger role in the world, she paused to reflect on its implications for local Native de-mocracies: "But what shall I say to you now, Americans of my America . . . Have not 98 per cent of your treaties with the Indian been 'scraps of pa-per'? Are you going to be guilty of these things while you preach from the housetops the self-determination of peoples and the democratization of the whole world?"[20]

In addition to asserting this moral dimension of postwar self-determination, Native Americans demanded their share of its material di-mensions, linking the two in a context of national obligation and honor. In the opening speech of the SAI's 1919 annual convention, Charles East-man noted that "millions [of dollars] are sent back over the seas, to the Belgians, the Armenians, the Poles, and to this and that." He insisted that "the United States owes us something." Thomas Sloan (Omaha) spoke at the same convention, emphasizing too the obligation of the United States to honor its commitments: "This nation has given to the needy of Europe many billions of dollars. The Indians have contributed to this their share or more. It would take but a few millions of dollars to pay the claims of the Indian tribes against the government. Obligations that should be paid . . . Let us apply the justice we are carrying to the weak nations abroad to the weak nations at home." Having met their "obligations" to fight for the United States, Native Americans now wanted the United States to meet its obligations, both historical and contemporary. Mabel Powers, a non-Native woman adopted by the Seneca, echoed Eastman's and Sloan's calls for domestic justice. Supporting Native Americans' right to maintain "an independent government," she contended in the summer 1919 issue of *American Indian Magazine*: "The autonomy of little peoples is not a prob-lem and experiment confined to the world across the big sea water, nor south of the Rio Grande. It lies at the very door of New York . . . If billions of dollars and millions of lives can be spent to secure the rights of little peoples across the sea, is it not consistent to give to a little people at home an equal chance?" Powers appealed to the American people to give Indi-ans a "square deal." That deal included an adjudication of land claims in-volving stolen territory such as the Black Hills of Sioux country and the reassertion of treaty rights neglected by U.S. courts, the product of the slow unraveling of the strands of America's Gordian knot of treaties. Such claims were, Gertrude Bonnin argued in the spring of 1919, "the progeny of broken treaties."[21]

What the United States owed Indians was therefore not "charity" but the promises of its many treaties, the lingua franca of international relations. In linking citizenship to treaty rights and constitutional rights, Eastman resuscitated the discourse of the Law of Nations, arguing that American officials had an obligation to uphold "the highest contract in the world, the civilized world. An agreement between nations." Illustrating this new discourse of treaty rights, the editors of *American Indian Magazine* saw fit to reprint in the winter 1919 issue a passionate speech made by Senator Theodore Frelinghuysen in 1830 at the height of the Indian removal crisis, in which he rejected the removal of southeastern Indians because of the "inviolate character of a treaty." Bonnin, Eastman, Kellogg, and other Native American intellectuals sharpened their identity as American Indians and their ideas of Indianness and Americanism in the crucible of a global conflict. The war impelled them to view their own freedoms and access to democracy within a new context of political self-determination whose terms were defined by both nineteenth-century treaty provisions and a twentieth-century conception of a new postcolonial order enunciated by Woodrow Wilson and other internationalists.[22]

The Contours of Termination

For white Americans, postwar debates on Native Americans also centered, as they had during the Gilded Age, on questions of citizenship and the elimination of both reservations and the Indian traditions that they sustained. Native Americans' service in World War I and the second Red scare, which resulted from the Russian Revolution of 1917, generated a new round of opposition to the reservation. Shortly after the war, Representative Melville C. Kelly of Pennsylvania attacked the reservation as "a prison pen where human beings are doomed to live amid sad memories of their ancestors and among the ghosts of the dead." Kelly promoted a terminationist agenda of closing the BIA and giving citizenship to all Native Americans, claiming that American Indians had returned home from the war to face the "Hohenzollern rule of the Indian Bureau . . . They helped free the world from armed brutality," he reminded his colleagues. "We should now free them from autocratic bureaucracy." Kelly's sentiments, issued as coercive Americanization campaigns spread throughout the country, both reflected politicians' traditional animus toward reservations and responded to new conceptions of Native American patriotism engendered by Natives' heroic army service. Kelly and other like-minded policymakers interpreted this national service as evidence that all Native Americans considered the reservation anachronistic space. His views were echoed by members of the Indian Rights Association, one of the "friends of the Indians" groups that sprang up during the 1880s. At its January 1918 convention, officers of the association resolved that "when the Great Effort is to make the world safe for Democracy, we must not forget that Democracy at home ought to be safe for the Indian." The group's antidemocratic plan to institute democracy for American Indians involved "the complete absorption of the Indian into our body politic," "greater responsibility . . . placed upon Indians in the management of their own affairs," and "the *termination* of communal relations."[23]

The terminationist views of white policymakers such as Kelly and groups such as the Indian Rights Association resembled, and may very well have duplicated, those of SAI intellectuals who had publicly employed the trope of reservation as prison in championing both full citizenship for American Indians and the end of the reservation system. Carlos Montezuma had opposed the drafting of noncitizen Indians, but he supported American involvement in the war in part because it would further the rights of American Indians at home. Writing in the May 1918 issue of the journal *Wassaja* he asserted: "When the world is fighting for freedom, equal rights, and humanity, it is a poor policy to wait until after the war to ask for freedom, equal rights, and justice . . . We must then strike while the iron is hot to have the [BIA] abolished" and to extend citizenship to all Native Americans. These two goals animated the work of the SAI during and after the war, expressed in Montezuma's essays in *Wassaja*, the *American Indian Magazine*, and elsewhere, which carried titles such as "Break the Shackles Now—Make Us Free," "Abolish the Indian Bureau," and "Let My People Go." "Abolish the Indian Bureau" became the mantra of the SAI, a terminationist agenda that both echoed the ideas of Gilded Age reformers and the World War I campaigns of the Indian Rights Association and prefigured the Cold War–era termination movement that would spark a crisis in Indian country during the 1940s and 1950s.[24]

Native American leaders promoted Indian patriotism and attacked the paternalistic BIA in an international framework, contrasting their democratic aspirations with the autocratic programs of the Germans, the Russians, and, after 1917, the Bolsheviks. As Arthur C. Parker argued, "We are making war against autocracy in order, as we have stated our aims, 'to make the world safe for democracy.'" Laura Kellogg complained that the bureau had aggregated power to "such an extreme that Russia ten years before the war, when at the height of her despotic power, was not more depleting than the Indian Bureau. Where Russia had one Czar, this Bureau had a hundred and fifty," referring to reservation superintendents who had instituted a "reign of terror." Kellogg called on a new generation of postwar and postcolonial Indians, "the sons of men who bled for Liberty," to stand up to "the insolent arrogance and arbitrary dictation of political bosses" that she compared to "the wanton outrages of Bolshevism." Putting it simply, Gertrude Bonnin called BIA paternalism and the denial of Indian citizenship "un-American."[25]

Fluid linguistic and physical boundaries shaped the rhetorical battles over "the reservation" and the attendant debates over incorporation of Indians within America as "citizens." Native American intellectuals condemned the reservation system in part because of the BIA's autocratic management of it, but they also saw "the Indian" imprisoned by nineteenth-century traditions in a twentieth-century world and therefore incapable of becoming a "new Indian"; white American and (some) Native American reformers depicted American Indians as trapped in a physical space that perpetuated a cultural process, neither of which these reformers considered modern and thus worth protecting. Parker had argued that "the only just and logical way to understand the Indian and judge his capacity is to watch the Indian who is *away* from the reservation." But many Native Americans in the early twentieth century, including others of the first generation of boarding school graduates, had no interest in leaving the reservation, for various cultural and social reasons including endemic racism in American society. Reservations provided a crucial breathing space at a critical time for Native communities to reconstitute themselves culturally and to reimagine themselves politically. The reservation, for most Native Americans, was not a prison but a homeland.[26]

By the early 1920s, then, Native Americans envisioned the reservation in three principal ways: as a prison, as a homeland, and, in the middle ground between them, as a refuge for those "new Indians" like Montezuma,

Bonnin, and Eastman who still walked in two worlds. The SAI editorialized that "the red man and the white man must learn and develop together, and living in one country, both serve its common need." Self-
determination thus took two forms: individual or self-sovereignty and
tribal sovereignty, which maintained the porous boundary between two
"countries" that permitted crossing in times of crisis such as war and sustained the resultant hybrid patriotism. American citizenship for many Native Americans, including SAI intellectuals critical of the reservation as
an anachronism, would remain a matter of dual identity in the twentieth
century.[27]

Citizenship Arrives

American Indians' heroic service during World War I and the arguments
of politicians such as Kelly and SAI intellectuals such as Montezuma led
to the passage on November 6, 1919, of a bill granting citizenship to World
War I veterans, but only to those who asked for it. Few did, as most of the
army volunteers already had citizenship, granted by allotment or competency commissions. The campaign to apply citizenship to all Native
Americans thus lasted until 1924, when the Indian Citizenship Bill
granted citizenship to all Native Americans, whether they wanted it or
not. Supported by a mixture of Indian and non-Indian groups, including
the Society of American Indians and the American Legion, the bill represented the culmination of efforts of Lake Mohonk reformers and the generation of Indian activists their program spawned. Yet the bill left unresolved as many questions as it answered. The legislation allowed each state
to determine suffrage requirements, thus setting the stage for a round of
state-level battles over voting rights that would extend into the 1950s.
Fundamentally, citizenship by itself provided little protection against the
endemic theft of Indian land and resources. Reporting on the passage of
the bill, the New York Times opined that "not even the new legal status af-
fords [Native Americans] practical protection from the jealousy and ignorance of white men determined to 'civilize' them by gradual elimination."[28]

Most residents of Indian country paid little attention to the passage of
the act. They remained vigilant against the pressures described by the
Times and committed to the retention of traditional religious rituals and

social organization even as many Native Americans became more integrated into regional and national commodity markets. But the Citizenship
Act emboldened some Native leaders to delineate the boundary between
nations even as the act linked Native and American across that boundary.
Robert Hamilton, the Carlisle-educated leader of the Blackfeet Nation in
northwestern Montana, contended that as a result of the Citizenship Act,
"the Indian is equal before the law . . . The Indian is no longer to be dominated . . . and I say the sooner the Indians assert themselves the better off
they will be."[29]

In 1924 reformers' nineteenth-century goal of incorporating Indians'
lands and bodies into the American nation faced resistance from reservation leaders such as Hamilton and Yellowtail who expressed the twentieth-
century idea of cultural pluralism and a new conception of incorporation
that strengthened rather than erased the boundaries marking Native
Americans' physical and political space. SAI cofounder Laura Kellogg was
the first to articulate this new conception of incorporation. Like Eastman
and Parker, she envisioned a hybrid American Indian who would work "to
combine [Indians' and non-Indians'] higher values, and then to weave
them into the hardest-headed kind of BUSINESS." Yet she had declared at
the 1911 SAI conference, "I am not a new Indian, I am the old Indian
adjusted to new conditions." By this she meant that her home remained
the nineteenth-century legal construction of the "reservation," a physical
space whose boundaries were defined by international treaty; but managing that "old" home would need to be done with twentieth-century tools,
under the "new conditions" of modern industrial America. Rejecting the
"Carlisle point of view" of breaking up the Indian reservation, she argued
that keeping the reservation "intact gives a chance for the better day to
arrive, while the dismemberment of the Indian domain puts the Indian
out into the labor world of the white man, landless." She opposed what
"Montezuma and his Carlisle followers want—doing away with the Bureau without any substitution whatever, leaving the helpless Indian open
to the exploitation of every grafter in the land." To save Indian assets Kellogg promoted economic organization of "industrial committees" to support self-governing political communities, positing a different version of
the "incorporation" of the American Indian: "Incorporation presupposes a
state of self-government in which to succeed." Her hybrid program embraced the organizational efficiency and power of American corporations,

which had "brought a new era of development into the world," with the communal traditions of American Indians. Asserting the social values of nineteenth-century Indian "communism," set off against the dictatorial elements of twentieth-century Soviet communism, Kellogg wrestled with the question of how to equalize shares and burdens in the new tribal corporations. "The failure to do this is one of the great draw-backs to Indian Communism or any other Communism which has not been modernized."[30]

Her vision of a workable modern communism presented a syncretic Indian community that drew on the economic impetus of American corporations, the moral philosophy of the Hopi, and the political culture of the Iroquois Confederacy. It was a diverse admixture of ideas that would find few takers in the increasingly homogeneous and laissez-faire environment of 1920s America. But it offered a provocative vision that found expression in the Indian New Deal of the 1930s, which marked a new trajectory for Indian-white relations and created a new set of rhetorical weapons in the battle over the contested space of the reservation.

A New Vision of Incorporation

In the early 1920s new efforts to dispossess Native Americans and new studies that documented their poor material conditions generated vocal protests from Indians and supportive white writers. These protests shaped the ongoing debate over the value of the reservation and reflected emerging notions of cultural pluralism that defended Indian identity on Indians' terms and served as bulwarks against a coercive Americanization campaign fueled by the reactionary rhetoric of postwar Red scare America.

The tipping point came in the campaign to defeat the Bursum Bill during the early 1920s. The bill, supported by the unfailingly corrupt Secretary of the Interior Albert Fall, proposed to end Pueblo Indians' control of their land base in New Mexico by supporting local whites' bogus claims of title ownership. As D. H. Lawrence put it, "The Bursum bill plays the Wild West scalping trick a little too brazenly." Horrified by the savagery of World War I and inspired by Pueblo spiritual life as its countervailing force, forty-eight white artists and writers who frequented the cultural colony of Taos, New Mexico—including Lawrence, Carl Sandburg, Zane Grey, and William Allen White—issued a statement that called on the

American people to protest the bill "as a test of national honor." The fight over the Bursum Bill unified the Pueblo through the All-Pueblo Council, which had not met for over two centuries. The Pueblo jointly appealed to the American conscience in a statement signed by 121 delegates representing twenty Pueblo communities. Titled "An Appeal by the Pueblo Indians of New Mexico to the People of the United States," the Pueblo statement declared: "This bill will destroy our common life and will rob us of everything we hold dear—our lands, our customs, our traditions. Are the American people willing to see this happen?" They framed their argument in the language of hybrid patriotism, contending that the Pueblo people had "kept our old customs and lived in harmony with each other and with our fellow Americans."[31]

What followed was a national controversy, driven by such appeals, by a Pueblo delegation's visit to the New York Stock Exchange, and by protests made by famous and not-so-famous Americans (and the infamous D. H. Lawrence), all of which newspapers and journals covered extensively. The *New York Times* ran numerous articles on the crisis; the great Progressive intellectual Herbert Croly published an appeal in *The Nation*. The Pueblo crisis did in fact become a "test of national honor" as well as a litmus test of America's embrace of Wilsonian notions of self-determination for all nations. A *New York Times* editorial conflated international and domestic self-determination in calling on the federal government to "secure for the little minorities whom [the Pueblo] represent the justice we are so eager to assure to ancient minorities in other parts of the world . . . Do we not on our side need some historical wampum to remind us of our obligations to these minorities whom we found on this continent?" Some *Times* readers expressed their protests in international terms. Millicent Smyth of New York City contended that "law-abiding" American Indians had been "pushed aside on to lands where no white man could exist . . . If the Turks were to confine the Armenians to such a territory a cry would go up to Heaven from the whole United States." Smyth likely overstated Americans' interest in the status of Armenians, but she did point to the fact that Americans responded with concern to international crises while failing to see domestic crises such as the Pueblo's as a similar national problem of colonialism. Also drawing on international events, Secretary Fall went on the offensive to defend the Bursum Bill by painting opponents, especially the General Federation of Women's Clubs, as un-American. "Such propaganda, if allowed to go unchecked," he complained, "will eventually break down this democratic Government by substituting for it a government by propaganda. The present Soviet conditions in Russia would be preferable to such an outcome." Other critics attacked related campaigns to preserve Native cultural and religious practices, especially tribal dances, by claiming that they were "financed by Soviet money from Moscow." But the extensive publicity generated by pro-Pueblo forces ensured that the Bursum Bill would end up in the congressional dustbin of bad ideas.[32]

The campaigns to defend the Pueblo helped lead to a federal investigation of Indian affairs that culminated in the release in 1928 of a massive report called *The Problem of Indian Administration* (known as the Meriam Report), which precipitated a series of reforms in federal Indian policy that reinforced government "obligations to these minorities." A team of investigators, which included a Native American anthropologist from Yale University, chronicled in numbing detail the poverty of Indian country and the extent to which federal polices, especially allotment, had produced it. The report called for the reform of American Indian economies, recommending that "an experiment be tried . . . with the modern business device of the corporation. The corporation would own the property, keep it intact, and conserve and operate it as a great national asset." Government officials would serve as corporation managers until Indian leaders demonstrated their understanding of modern business methods. Investigators concluded that "thorough mature consideration should be given to the possibilities of using the corporate form of organization for tribal property that consists of great natural resources which cannot be economically administered or developed in small allotments." The Meriam Report laid out a Laura Kellogg–like "vision" for the advancement of American Indians through the incorporation of their assets on Indian terms rather than through the incorporation of those assets into white society. The report was fundamentally assimilationist at heart, however, and thus sustained the terminationist agenda of the Civilization Program designed by Thomas Jefferson in the early 1800s, expanded in the 1880s by Lake Mohonk reformers, and promoted anew after World War I by the Indian Rights Association and other groups. Secretary of the Interior Ray Lyman Wilbur defined the BIA's main objective in 1930 as "the gradual break-up of the old reservation system."[33]

Animated by his work to reduce urban poverty through the Progressive

Era settlement house movement during the 1910s, John Collier helped spearhead the protection of Pueblo land rights as the executive director of the American Indian Defense Association during the 1920s. In the 1930s he broke with assimiliationist federal policy in championing a new agenda as commissioner of Indian affairs under President Franklin Roosevelt. He promoted the Indian New Deal, a series of initiatives related to the federal New Deal to ameliorate Native American poverty and strengthen tribal self-government by not only rejecting the policy and philosophy of allotment but also providing federal funds for land repurchase programs. The Indian Reorganization Act (IRA) of 1934, the cornerstone of the Indian New Deal, presented a different process of "incorporation," one that strengthened rather than broke up "the old reservation system" by giving Native communities new sovereign powers over reservation boundaries and resources through regulations established by tribal corporations and codified in constitutions and charters of incorporation. To Collier, reservations were not prisons that degraded Indian life; it was the "school prisons" of the boarding school system that were intent on the annihilation of Native Americans' communal traditions and pride in Indianness.[34]

During the 1930s Collier sought to use his BIA administration to protect Native Americans from the twin scourges of colonial racism and corporate "looting." In writings from the 1920s he had connected Americans' treatment of their Indian minority with Europeans' treatment of their colonial subjects, placing the process of imperial capitalism firmly in the American interior. In his 1923 essay "The American Congo," Collier wrote of the American "equivalent of the Belgian and the French Congo. The denial of land rights of the Congo—it is here. The decimation of victims—it is here . . . And finally, the discouragement of public sympathy for the victims by propaganda directed against the victims, familiar from the Congo—it, too, is here." As a result, he argued in 1929, the Bureau of Indian Affairs had become "the nexus of a conspiracy of robbery under quasi-legal forms—a conspiracy in which numerous great corporations and local voting constituencies are receptive or active partners." In likening America to Europe, Collier attacked Americans' cherished cultural notions of exceptionalism and cherished historical perceptions that national growth was the process of internal rather than imperial expansion. He thus gave voice to Native Americans' demands for decolonization that would find fuller expression in the 1950s and beyond. Fundamentally, Collier sought to reverse federal policy that rejected the legitimacy of what he called "the personality of the other."[35]

Native Americans' first exposure to the Collier vision of cultural pluralism was his January 20, 1934, circular letter titled "Indian Self-government," which he sent to all Native communities to introduce the philosophy of the Indian New Deal. The twelve-page letter focused on the "evils of allotment" and promoted Native administration of reservation resources to improve "the community life and political responsibility of the Indian," which previous federal policy had "largely destroyed." Indian self-government and the concomitant expansion of economic opportunity would be the twin engines of Native American progress in the 1930s and beyond; tribal governments should be "organized and chartered as municipal corporations" and "entrusted with powers and responsibilities . . . exercised by a village or county government." Like former Secretary of the Interior Wilbur, Collier laid out a blueprint for the gradual termination of federal supervision of Indian affairs, recommending that state governments assume the responsibilities of Indian education and health and ultimately that a reconstituted Native American community should be given "complete supervision over its internal affairs." In Collier's view, however, Native Americans' consent was essential for self-determination, the vernacular cousin of termination, and the reservation system would be expanded rather than destroyed.[36]

The Indian Reorganization Act

Collier's vision found legislative expression in the Wheeler-Howard Bill, sponsored by Burton Wheeler and Edgar Howard of Nebraska, chairmen of the Senate and House Committees on Indian Affairs, respectively. The debate on the bill began in the House on February 22, 1934, and in the Senate five days later. Collier announced during the first House hearing that he would take his reform program to the people it would affect by organizing a series of Indian conferences, the first time the BIA gave Native Americans an opportunity to consider important legislation before it was imposed on their reservations.[37]

Tribal representatives of nearly sixty thousand Plains Indians gathered in Rapid City, South Dakota, on March 2, 1934, to hear Collier himself delineate the important facets of his program promoting Indian self-determination; the four-day Great Plains Congress was the first of nine conferences that Collier and his associates held to address Native Americans' questions about the Indian New Deal. In his general remarks to start the conference, Collier proclaimed to great applause that "it was the duty of the Indians themselves to determine what their own life shall be." He argued that the basis of the modern world was organization, which took its form in corporations, associations, cooperatives, and municipal governments. As Collier explained, what was "almost the heart" of the plan was the organization of Native Americans "for local self-government and for doing business in the modern, organized way." In the United States, Collier told the crowd of Native leaders and entrepreneurs, "you can't govern yourselves, you can't do business, you can't protect yourself, unless you organize." The American Indian, he said, was an example of Roosevelt's "forgotten man," who had been "carrying a privileged class" and "big business" on his back. Sounding like a cross between Henry Luce and Dwight Macdonald, Collier returned to the philosophical "heart of the plan": the need for Indian America to create countervailing organizations to those of white America. His plan offered a different form of incorporation, one designed to alter significantly the nineteenth-century version of an imperial incorporation that had furthered the social and territorial integration of Indian country and the "annihilation" of Indian cultural traditions. For Collier, the Indian New Deal was as much about class as it was about race.[38]

The heterogeneity of Native America ensured diverse reactions to Collier's idea of self-determination, which ranged from enthusiastic support to condemnation on the grounds that the forces of assimilation were too strong to resist or that it was a form of "communism" or "socialism." For example, Joe Irving, chairman of the Crow Creek delegation, argued that "the whole idea as to the self-government . . . is Socialism." If the legislation passed, Irving claimed, "we could not exercise our own rights and we might just as well live in Russia." Collier countered such arguments by maintaining that "white people all over the United States own land in partnerships and companies and corporations. It is not communism to allow Indians to do the same if they want to." Collier ended the conference by encouraging Native leaders to "assert their rights" in protecting their land and resources from the predations of white neighbors, warning them not to listen to "local interests" who would call the bill "communism."[39]

Similar sociological and ideological divisions emerged at other BIA conferences held during the spring of 1934 in the Southwest, in Oklahoma, in Oregon and California, and in the Great Lakes region. As at the Great Plains Congress, some Indian participants at these meetings claimed that Collier's bill represented communism or socialism; at the California conference, for example, a Mrs. Costa condemned elements of the bill as un-American: "I am one hundred percent American. I tell you this bill preaches communism and socialism." Other participants stated that the bill allowed them to hold on to their land and gave them, as San Carlos Apache John Rice put it, "a voice in all things pertaining to my reservation." A number of Native Americans saw Collier as the first sympathetic federal official, a hybrid uniting white and Indian sensibilities. Joseph Hayes (Chippewa) called him a "white man with a red man's heart"; a Stockbridge minister asserted, "My heart tells me John Collier is an Indian."[40]

The conferences and the debates over the Wheeler-Howard Bill more generally exposed the great diversity of Native Americans, many of whom had rejected traditional tribal life and the rituals that sustained it for a more secular or Christian worldview that emphasized the primacy of the nuclear family and individual property holdings. At the heart of the debates was the role of the reservation in ordering social life and the legitimacy of maintaining traditional boundaries between Indian and non-Indian space through the modern mechanisms of political economy.

The debates over the Wheeler-Howard Bill also exposed fault lines in the 1934 U.S. Congress, whose members faced the prospect of altering the trajectory of imperial policies of assimilation put into motion by their nineteenth-century political ancestors. Many members of Congress, in particular those representing western states still experiencing great demographic expansion, had little interest in altering the status quo and encouraging Indian nationalism. But after a series of contentious debates, and in the reformist milieu of depression America, Congress adopted the bill on June 16, 1934; a supportive President Roosevelt signed it two days later. The final version—which became known as the Indian Reorganization Act—differed dramatically from the original. Senator Wheeler wielded his power to prevent the codification of Collier's vision of cultural pluralism and Indian self-determination. Wheeler and his supporters reduced the forty-eight-page program to five pages, deleting Collier's language of self-determination and weakening his vision of Indian home rule. Yet the bill did, as Collier intended, legislate a formal end to the allotment policy, extend the trust period of existing allotments, and return reservation surplus lands to Native control. The bill also facilitated the creation of economic and political organizations by allowing each Native community that voluntarily adopted the IRA to develop a constitution and by-laws through which a central government could manage the domestic affairs of its members. Such a government could employ a tribal attorney, manage tribal assets and land sales, and negotiate with federal, state, and county governments. In addition, along the lines proposed by Laura Kellogg, each nation could secure from the secretary of the interior a charter of incorporation to increase the power of the Native government to manage its economic assets. To assist in the creation of Indian enterprises, Congress allotted $10 million for a revolving credit fund, twice the amount Collier had requested. In sum, the IRA improved Collier's original bill in the area of economic development but weakened or eliminated important provisions for cultural development and self-government.[41]

The bill was imperfect, the result of a struggle between two competing visions of Indian America: one sought to protect Native Americans' right to construct their own version of the American community; the other fought to sustain their forced integration into mainstream American society. Congress, torn between two powerful impulses, humanitarian and historical, compromised. It wanted to assist America's Native population in making economic progress and thus ameliorate a poverty generated largely by previous federal policies. But it did not want to retie the American Gordian knot and provide a mechanism for Indian communities to reenvision themselves as domestic dependent nations, as *imperium in imperio*, and thus undo the assimilationist work of the Tribe of Mohonk of the late 1800s.

The IRA incorporated Native Americans within a framework of American democratic practices and market economics, which for many represented more continuity than change. More important, the IRA reset a foundation for many American Indians' conceptions of nationhood, allowing them to establish formal rules for defining boundaries—demographic, geographical, political, and economic. The result was a more carefully delineated and circumscribed Native America. Fundamentally, it legitimized the boundaries of the reservation system and provided a constitutional mechanism to expand and maintain those boundaries, thus creating literal and figurative roadblocks to white Americans' goal of Indians' "ultimate incorporation into the great body of our citizen population," as Commissioner of Indian Affairs Luke Lea described his "final solution" to the "Indian problem" in 1851. Within two years of the birth of the IRA in June 1934, 181 Native communities had adopted it in special elections, while 77 communities had rejected it. Thus not all Native Americans accepted the law, which was unique in the history of federal Indian policy for not being mandatory. But even the communities that rejected the IRA benefited from the democratic conversations it generated, which centered on the meaning of Indian identity and the ways to protect it. More important than the BIA conferences and the legislation was the idea, as Collier put it, that "Indians shall take the responsibility, here and now, of thinking out their own problems and arriving at their own conclusions, and determining their own future." Self-determination through self-government represented the Native means to the desired end of federal control of Indian life, an indigenous form of decolonization driven by Native consent rather than the coercion of mandated termination. Native American politicians' legal and intellectual incorporation of reservation space, whether through the IRA or not, became an important weapon in the larger struggle to protect Indianness on Indians' terms.[42]

The debates over the IRA and the critiques of it also made the Indian New Deal mainstream, assimilating Native American leaders and citizens into a broader political context that legitimized state protection of the rights of newly defined American constituencies: the elderly, dependent children, and workers. Native Americans were no different. They became citizens in the 1930s rather than in the 1920s, as did millions of other Americans who came to see citizenship as a reciprocal relationship, the result of programs that made tangible the federal government's commitment to this increasingly broad set of constituencies. And yet, because of the unique relationship they had with ancestral land, Native Americans understood that American citizenship in whatever form would not guarantee protection from the "the wolves," as Blackfeet Nation politician Oscar Boy described white ranchers and developers who circled reservations in search of new victims, or from the many politicians who continued to view reservations as foreign spaces in need of termination.[43]

3　World War II Battlegrounds

Yes, I really have seen the world but right now I am wishing I was back to good ole Santa Fe.

—Private Tony Aguilar (Pueblo), writing from Iran, 1943

Private Keats Begay left his home in 1942 to serve America and his Navajo Nation. Sent to fight in the Philippines, Begay, along with several other Native Americans, was taken prisoner by the Japanese that same year. A survivor of the infamous Bataan Death March, he spent three years in a Japanese prison camp in Manchuria before Russian soldiers liberated him and his campmates in 1945. He first rehabilitated in Kunming, China, "recovered a bit" in Calcutta, then spent a week in a Cairo hospital. From there he traveled to Casablanca, then to the Azores and to Bermuda, before landing in a Staten Island hospital for a two week stay. Leaving the Walter Reed hospital in Washington, D.C., after a month of additional rest, he made a pit stop in Chicago before finally returning to New Mexico. He had traveled the globe, departing to the west and returning from the east. He had seen the world, with all of its brutality and heroism, and no doubt was happy to get home to "good ole" New Mexico. Begay's was an extraordinary journey that culminated in a Squaw Dance healing ceremony led by the Navajo medicine man Totsoni Tsosie, one of several kinds of ceremonies conducted for veterans suffering from what doctors now call posttraumatic stress syndrome.[1]

Although Begay's set of destinations was more extensive than most Native American soldiers', he had in common with many of them the experience of coming into contact with diverse peoples of color and their diverse customs. For example, Sergeant Julian Smith (Sioux), serving with the Persian Gulf Command in Iran, noted that "the people in that [Kurdish] village were like my own people back on the Fort Peck Reservation [Montana]. They had the same ailments, suspicions, simplicity and poverty. Seems all poor people talk the same language." Such contact for Native Americans strengthened their Indian identity and led many of them to adopt the language of internationalism. Native Americans serving abroad became aware, as Marc Gallicchio wrote about African American internationalists, "that color (or race) determined world politics." The Sioux scholar Ella Deloria, who had conducted ethnographic research with Franz Boas, wrote in her 1944 book *Speaking of Indians* that the war "wrought an overnight change in outlook, horizon, and even habits of the Indian people—a change that might not have come about for many years yet." This change, according to Deloria, was expressed by soldiers fighting abroad and by prayers for their return at home. Deloria noted the Dakota Sioux's publication of *Victory News*, edited by a Dakota graduate of Carleton College and sponsored by the Victory Club on the Rosebud Reservation in South Dakota. The monthly journal sent "cheer and home news to the boys all over the world. Think of it, a little Indian paper with a mailing list that covers the globe!" *Victory News* in turn published the letters of Sioux sent from "all over the world."[2]

Native Americans' experiences in World War II showed great continuity with those of World War I. American Indians employed similar arguments in fighting on behalf of the U.S. government, engaged in similar debates on the use of segregated troops, and practiced similar acts of resistance to draft registration. World War II, however, brought dramatic changes to Native Americans' ideas about their literal and figurative place in American society and in the world. In particular, as the stories just described reveal, Native soldiers' participation in the war involved more contact with colonial "others" than during World War I. Native veterans' conflation of their people's struggles against colonialism at home and foreign peoples' struggles against colonialism abroad fostered Indian nationalism on a broader level than after World War I, in part because debates about the Indian Reorganization Act had strengthened the physical and cultural boundaries between white America and Native America even as Native Americans remained willing to cross those boundaries during times of war in order to protect them. Connecting the local to the global through

the language of internationalism, Native Americans developed a sharpened sense of themselves as Native and as American, largely because they
perceived themselves fighting for two linked geographical spaces—their
ancestral homelands and the United States of America—both facing a
crisis of national security. World War II created a centrifugal effect on Native American space, drawing tens of thousands of Native Americans away
from reservations to serve in industry and the armed forces. This dynamic
inspired a new generation of white Americans to see this migration as evidence that Native Americans wanted to leave those reservations perma-
nently and thus justified their efforts to terminate Native sovereignty, recently fortified by IRA programs. The war and the terminationist agenda
that emerged during it also had a centripetal effect by strengthening
American Indian nationalism, which found expression in a new pan-tribal
group, the National Congress of American Indians. Unlike the Society of
American Indians active in the 1910s and the American Indian Federation that emerged during the late 1930s, the NCAI promoted the protection of reservation space rather than its elimination. The advent of World
War II, then, both diverted attention from and heightened an ongoing
ideological battle over Native American self-determination.

As Native Americans crossed physical and intellectual boundaries during World War II, they along with white Americans imagined the significance of these crossings in an international context. Commissioner of Indian Affairs John Collier in particular used his experiences with American
Indians to promote an international role for the Bureau of Indian Affairs
as U.S. interests expanded overseas during the war. His campaign in turn
helped shape the ideas of a new generation of Native activists who reimagined Indian nations as among the other colonized peoples of the world,
thus broadening the Native American context to one of international human rights.

American Nazis and American Indians

The contentious fight over the BIA's retribalization agenda of the 1930s
mirrored tensions within the larger American political narrative of the
interaction of state power and individual rights which emerged during the
New Deal. Native Americans' views on the Indian Reorganization Act
articulated during the BIA's regional conferences found national expres-

sion as the debate over the legislation intensified within an international frame. Flora Warren Seymour, a white lawyer and author, waged one of the most public campaigns against the IRA. Characterizing Indian policy as a new direction for the country, she attacked the law as "the most extreme gesture yet made by the administration in this country toward a Communistic experiment." Employing the same anticommunist rhetoric, a group of Native Americans formed the American Indian Federation (AIF) on June 8, 1934, to protest Collier's agenda. After the passage of the IRA on June 16, the federation campaigned for its repeal, the withdrawal of federal services from Indian reservations, and the abolition of the Bureau of Indian Affairs, what collectively became the kernel of the congressional termination agenda of the late 1940s and early 1950s.[3]

The AIF offered these views to Congress, fueling a congressional campaign to repeal the IRA and "emancipate" the Indian from tribal life and federal supervision. AIF president Joseph Bruner, from the Muskogee Creek community of Oklahoma, told the House Committee on Indian Affairs in a 1935 hearing that "the fundamental ideas of the commissioner's plan or program are Communistic." The AIF distributed to members of Congress pamphlets arguing that point, including one titled "Collierism and Communism in North Carolina." The following year AIF leaders conflated Collierism and communism in testifying to the Senate Committee on Indian Affairs that the Indian New Deal program promoted "atheism, communism and un-Americanism in the administration of Indian Affairs."[4]

AIF secretary Alice Lee Jemison (Seneca) became one of the most vocal opponents of Collier and President Roosevelt, attacking them and the IRA at AIF meetings, in congressional testimony, and through her own pamphlet *The First American*. She claimed that Native Americans were controlled by a group of federal officials "who have well-known regard for radical activities and association with, or admiration for, atheists, anarchists, communists and other 'fifth columnists,'" including in that group Secretary of the Interior Harold Ickes, Collier, and Dr. Willard Beatty, the director of Indian Education programs. Under the IRA, "Indians are being regimented into little reservation Soviets, patterned after the Russian 'colhozes' and 'sovhozes' . . . Briefly summarized, under the Roosevelt administration, the Indian wards of a Christian nation have been made the guinea pigs in a communist experiment, financed with public funds and tribal money." Jemison also spoke at meetings organized by Nazi sympathizers such as William Dudley Pelley, whose attacks on Roosevelt and the New Deal condemned the IRA as Roosevelt's effort to "instill communism among Indian tribes," especially the Cherokee of North Carolina, so that Native Americans would be "natural allies of the Red in case of a revolutionary showdown." As one historian put it, "such an accusation, of course, was as absurd as linking the Kremlin with the Cincinnati Reds baseball team." But these accusations point to the ways in which the trope of the communist Indian remained functional for both white American and Native American critics of Indian New Deal programs as well as for Nazi agents looking to gain traction in parts of ethnic America traditionally neglected by government agencies.[5]

Pelley's pamphlet warning against tribal communism, titled *Indians Aren't Red*, became functional for Nazi propagandists, who received it from German American Bundists and reissued it as part of their broader propaganda campaign. Jemison formed alliances with Pelley's anti-Semitic Silver Shirts of America Christian Patriots and with several German Bund organizations, which also appropriated the aggrieved Indian as a vehicle to promote Nazism. In August 1936 Jemison spoke at the Silver Shirts' pro-Nazi American National Conference; then in late 1936 representatives of various Nazi groups attended the AIF conference. The following March, Pelley's organ, *The New Liberation*, formalized the Silver Shirt Legion's support of the AIF and its anti-IRA agenda by publishing an article titled "Silver Shirts Propose Justice to the American Indian" and promising funding for AIF programs. By mid-1937 the network of support between the AIF and pro-Nazi groups extended from North Carolina to California, with groups trading mailing lists and articles linking federal Indian policy to communism and Judaism. Jemison in particular became a darling of various groups. The fascist group Militant Christian Patriots paid her for her articles railing against Indian policy reforms, and the Los Angeles German American Bund distributed her AIF articles.[6]

On Jemison's subversive trail, U.S. Naval Intelligence discovered that the car she used in her speaking tour of the Great Plains was paid for from German American Bund funds and channeled through James True, whose group, James True Associates, promoted Nazi views. True, giving Jemison the code name "Pocahontas," paid her money that came from Henry Allen, who organized pro-Nazi activities on the Mexican border. Allen in turn influenced Fritz Kuhn, the president of the German American Bund, which claimed 25,000 members. Kuhn incorporated Jemison's condemnation of the IRA and Collier in his speeches and writings and called for Native Americans to join the Nazi Party for protection against federal domination. For example, in his 1939 article "Our Indian Wards and Their Guardian," Kuhn ranted that "Indian wards of a Christian Nation are being forced into a program of anti-Christian Communism." Portraying Indians as Christians and as passive wards, as well as contemporary Pocahontases loyal to the racialist cause of imperial interlopers, Kuhn, like other American fascists, objectified American Indians for a political agenda not of their making and thus made little progress in establishing common ground in Indian country.[7]

Nazi propagandists, who granted American Indians "Aryan" racial characteristics to secure their allegiance, stressed that Germany would protect Native Americans from communist programs perpetrated by Roosevelt. In addition to facilitating Bundist activities in the United States, Nazi officials sent spies pretending to be interested in Native cultures to gauge Native Americans' interest in supporting Nazi policies, document Native Americans' conditions, and, given their use in World War I, learn Indian languages in anticipation of their potential use in a new war. A German linguistic anthropologist consulted with the Comanche of Oklahoma as early as 1932. In 1939 the FBI arrested and deported a group of German "students" who tried to establish contact with Comanches. Another Nazi agent, Dr. Colin Ross, initially benefiting from Collier's imprimatur, toured Native American communities for research on a book and a film on America. In his book *Unser Amerika* (Our America), Ross claimed that Native Americans "would look forward to [Nazi] intervention." Such remarks and State Department investigations ended his career as a German agent and filmmaker in the United States and helped expose the Nazis' broader campaign in America to generate support for their agenda.[8]

Collier was forced to wage a costly defense against the AIF's campaign because of its impact on congressional opponents of IRA-based Indian sovereignty. By the late 1930s some members of Congress had embraced the notion that the IRA was communistic, adding their voices to those critical of the national New Deal on the same grounds. Collier's counterattack against the AIF for its links to pro-Nazi groups such as the German American Bund and the Silver Shirts prevented Congress from repealing or even altering the IRA. Collier benefited from Alice Jemison's testimony to Representative Martin Dies's Committee on un-American activities in 1939 in which she admitted her financial links to pro-Nazi groups, in particular acknowledging that the Bund had paid her to incite resistance to the draft among Plains Indians; she also claimed that Hitler had promoted her articles in German magazines. Such confessions undermined the legitimacy of the AIF, which Jemison left later that year. The organization backed off from its Nazi connections to maintain its viability, turning to local Indian issues instead. And by this time the actions of the Nazis had made fascism more dangerous than communism for most Americans. Public protests against the IRA and Collier went silent when the guns of September 1939 boomed.[9]

In the end, the American Indian Federation of the 1930s, like the Society for American Indians of the 1910s, became a fringe group that garnered little support from Native Americans beyond a few small constituencies. At its height the AIF had just over a thousand members, but its meetings were sparsely attended by Native Americans, and it received much of its funding from non-Indian groups. Its significance stems from its ability to resuscitate the trope of the "Red Indian" to further its cause, tapping into a long-standing tradition of defining Indians by a radical otherness that attracted elements in the federal government hostile to the Roosevelt New Deal in general and Indian New Deal programs promoting Indian sovereignty in particular.

The Nazi Threat and the Hemispheric "Indian"

Nazi propaganda efforts in the United States in part reflected Germans' long-standing fascination with American Indians, popularized by the late-nineteenth-century fiction of Karl May, one of Hitler's favorite authors, who helped to shape his racialist views. May's work, featuring a Teutonic Tonto figure, condemned white Americans for their "destruction and degeneration of the Indian nation." Germans' affinity for Native Americans also stemmed from an appreciation of their historic fighting ability and structured warrior societies. The U.S. military magazine *PIC* commented on "the mysteries of Nazi propaganda," remarking specifically that "Goebbels has kept up a continuous radio barrage, calling on the American Indians to turn against the white men who have despoiled them of their lands and property." *PIC* cited German World War I records which contained a 1918 report on the American Indian as combatant: "The most dangerous of all American soldiers is the Indian . . . He is an army within himself. He is the one American soldier Germany must fear." The Nazi campaign to create alliances with Native Americans thus combined appreciation of traditional American Indian culture with an awareness of Indians' fighting skills in a modern context, despite the fact that minority groups such as American Indians were likely disgusted by Nazi racial theories and the genocidal policies they spawned. When a Nazi propaganda broadcast asked "How could the American Indians think of bearing arms for their exploiters?" it both reflected ingrained attitudes about Indians' experiences and asserted the functionality of using those experiences to develop allies abroad. Spanish fascists also employed these experiences in their attacks on the United States. *El Alcázar*, a Madrid newspaper, published an article titled "Yankees and Yankeeland" which claimed that white Americans "shoot [Indians] in the street, if they do not hang them with the popular legal formula of the lynching law."[10]

Painting American society as racist, capricious, and dangerous, such fascist propaganda found audiences in the United States, in Europe, and, via Nazi shortwave transmissions, in Central and South America. In evaluating the success of German broadcasting in the United States and Latin America, one American analyst called it in 1938 the "biggest and most powerful propaganda machinery in the world . . . the most frightening institution for the spread of political doctrine." After the war began in September 1939, the Roosevelt administration became convinced that Nazi activity in Latin America would destabilize the region, mainly because of its large population of German emigrants. Influenced by British propaganda designed to secure U.S. intervention in the war, sensationalist newspaper accounts of evil Nazis on America's southern doorstep, and resurgent notions of the Monroe Doctrine, the Roosevelt administration paid great attention to the possible Nazi threat. Colombia's ambassador to the United States reported to his superiors that the U.S. government routinely "exaggerate[d] the dangers of Nazi penetration" in Latin America. During the war the administration arranged the deportation of 4,058 Germans (along with 2,264 Japanese and 228 Italians) from Latin American countries to internment camps in the United States. The deportations resulted from economic rather than military insecurities, however. Many

U.S. companies enjoyed monopolistic positions within Latin American economies, and business leaders and government officials viewed economic competition from Latin American Germans as a threat to American prosperity and national security during the recovery from the depression. In addition, U.S. officials lacked confidence in the ability of Latin American regimes to inhibit Nazi Party growth, a legacy of the paternalism that had shaped U.S.–Latin American affairs since the nineteenth century. U.S. intervention hastened the end of Roosevelt's Good Neighbor Policy, especially with Argentina, Brazil, and Chile, which resisted American attempts to get their German citizens deported. In the end, the Nazi threat in Latin America was overblown; only eight of the Germans deported were accused of espionage. Yet fears of the "Nazi menace" resonated with many U.S. officials concerned with hemispheric destabilization, including Secretary of the Interior Harold Ickes and Commissioner of Indian Affairs John Collier, who increasingly framed Native American issues as international issues.[11]

To a limited extent during World War I, federal officials paid attention to the ways in which racial issues complicated the nation's role in waging war and in championing peace. World War II, according to the journalist Carey McWilliams, represented "a clash between the idea of racial superiority (central to the Nazi doctrine) and the idea of racial equality (central to the concept of democracy)." Accordingly, it became imperative for U.S. officials to ameliorate the racial conflicts that proved useful for German, Spanish, and Japanese propagandists, who seized on the mistreatment of African Americans and Native Americans as evidence that the United States had no claim to the moral high ground. In addition to asserting racial solidarity with American Indians by classifying them as "Aryan," Nazi propagandists used white Americans' treatment of Native Americans in their campaigns to secure support in Latin America. Given the size of Latin America's Indian population and its grievances against non-Indians, the importance of the region's material resources—especially Bolivian tin, Mexican oil, and Brazilian rubber—and the extent to which Indians were needed to secure these resources, U.S. officials did not take this propaganda lightly and thus worked to further inter-American collaboration on Indian affairs. Nazi propaganda served two main purposes, according to McWilliams: "It is skillfully utilized to smear the government of the United States and to counteract the indignation which Hitler's treatment of the

Jewish minority in the Reich has aroused. Even more important, however, is the manner in which this propaganda is aimed at the Indian element of the republics of Central and South America." For example, in one Latin American broadcast Nazis claimed that the Battle of Wounded Knee, which took place in 1890, had instead happened recently, creating a timeless narrative of an ongoing massacre of "the Indian" that could transcend the national boundaries of the Americas.[12]

Nazi propaganda, including its Wounded Knee narrative, may have drawn on the very words of John Collier, who met the criticism of AIF members and their congressional supporters with a public relations campaign that stressed Native Americans' wider significance in the world. In a speech titled "America's Handling of Its Indigenous Minority," distributed nationwide on the radio by the National Broadcasting Company in December 1939, Collier began with a visceral account of a survivor of the 1890 Wounded Knee massacre, which Collier called "a comparatively recent event in the history of the American Indian problem." The survivor had described American soldiers ignoring "the flag of truce" while "butchering" young Indian boys and killing "women as they were fleeing with their babes on their back." Although the United States had made great progress since the "violence" of 1890, Collier argued, "through our breaking of hundreds of solemn treaties with the tribes, [government officials] destroyed in many Indian minds their faith in us and their faith in their own future." On such words could a Nazi propaganda campaign be built. Yet Collier connected the Nazi threat with Indian affairs in the conclusion to the speech, where he championed Indian New Deal policies as a payment of "our nation's debt" to Native Americans and thus "the way the democracy of the United States is solving the minority problem of its first Americans." He also asked his radio listeners to "let me carry your thought beyond our own national borders" and consider the larger implications of the nation's treatment of Native Americans. Meeting "our own Indian minority problem has a deep significance," he claimed, to the "30,000,000 other Indians, and to all the countries where they are located. Here we enter within the battleground and effort-ground of our Western Hemisphere destiny. It is upon this scale of two continents . . . that world-history will view our own record with our Indian minority."[13]

Collier's efforts to promote and protect his Indian New Deal increasingly depended on his ability to link the comparatively small Native

American population of four hundred thousand to the 30 million Indians of Latin America and the growing importance of both in a world context. He began publicizing this linkage as early as September 1934 during an Indian Day celebration in Iroquois country. Addressing "The International Significance of the New Indian Policy of Our Own Government," Collier maintained that the U.S. attempt to "apply science, morality and common sense to Indian affairs, is being watched by many neighboring countries" and will thus generate "reactions throughout the two continents." As the war wore on, he promoted this view in the mainstream press. For example, in a 1942 *Atlantic Monthly* article Collier acknowledged that "by themselves the mere numbers tell little enough." But, he wrote, "important and significant is the fact that remote and desert places of the Western world contain the great strategic materials . . . and in these places, with a few exceptions, the Indian population is most dense." The Indian, in North America and in South America, in the Great Plains, and in the Andes, "emerges as the shadowy portent which may mark our days for all time to come." Collier thus connected the moral concerns of the "Indian minority problem" to strategic material concerns, which included hemispheric economic development. Both pragmatic and evangelical in his effort to provide a "New Deal" for all Indians in the Americas, he explained to Robert G. Caldwell, chairman of the State Department's Cultural Relations Program, that beyond the political and cultural benefits of inter-American exchanges on Indian problems, they were of

> extreme importance to the economic stability of the entire Western Hemisphere. In addition to the untapped productive energy and material resources of these thirty million Indians, we have a great potential undeveloped market which, by educating the Indians to desire an improvement in their standard of living and by increasing their purchasing power, would relieve greatly the economic strain caused by the loss of European markets.[14]

Collier's belief in the hemispheric "Indian" and the integration of the Indian into an evolving regional economy led him to collaborate with Latin American social scientists and politicians, including Mexico's part-Indian president Lázaro Cárdenas, who grew up in the state of Mochoacan, which had a large impoverished Indian population. Collier was among a number of academics and activists who crossed borders in the 1920s and 1930s to address the common cause of indigenous groups. He worked closely in particular with the Mexican anthropologist and educator Moisés Sáenz, who, having studied the 1928 Meriam Report and its attacks on allotment, discussed solutions to Indian land loss when Collier visited Mexico in 1930 and 1931. Collier in turn invited Sáenz to the United States in 1934 as the former began his campaign to codify land restoration schemes in the Indian Reorganization Act. Cárdenas's measures to bolster Indian *ejidos* (common lands) by redistributing hacienda lands and providing government credit to Indian farmers—which mirrored Collier's Indian New Deal programs—reflected this collaboration and common cause of U.S. and Mexican reformers.[15]

This collaboration led Collier and Sáenz to organize the First Inter-American Conference on Indian Life, held in Pátzcuaro, Mexico, in April 1940. Sponsored by Cárdenas and supported by U.S. officials, the conference brought together representatives of nineteen American governments to discuss a variety of topics, including Collier's Indian New Deal programs, which were familiar to many participants. Collier claimed, perhaps referring to incidents such as Wounded Knee, that "for many years, the record of the United States in its handling of its Indian minority served only to create fear among the countries south of the Rio Grande with large Indian groups." The success of his Indian New Deal agenda served as an adjunct to President Roosevelt's Good Neighbor policy, as the agenda "constituted," according to Collier, "a vast reassurance to our neighboring countries. It has provided one of the needed foundations for hemisphere co-operation." Employing Collier's language of the Indian New Deal, conference delegates unanimously supported "Indian local self-government." The presence of representatives of nine Native American communities—including the Papago, the Jicarilla and San Carlos Apache, the Hopi, and three Pueblo groups—reinforced Collier's message of promoting Indian sovereignty. Seventeen years after they had sent delegates east to Washington to protest the Bursum Bill, the Pueblo communities sent ambassadors from New Mexico south to Mexico to strengthen pan-Indianism across international borders. According to Carey McWilliams, the Pueblo "were the best representatives that this country could have selected as its ambassadors of good will. They took a leading part in the deliberations of the conference and made a deep impression on the other delegates."[16]

U.S. involvement in the 1940 Pátzcuaro conference reflected the internationalist thinking of Collier and of the Pueblo as well as officials' fears of Nazi influence in Latin America. Shaped by U.S. concerns about Nazi infiltration, and echoing the pronouncements of Collier, with whom he had a close working relationship, Secretary of the Interior Harold Ickes noted in his official 1941 report that there were "only 400,000 Indians in this country . . . but in all the Americas there are 30 million full-blood Indians." Ickes, too, stated the significance of those demographics in material as well as moral terms, again echoing Collier's contention that those millions of Indians "represent a latent purchasing power which, if developed, might well help to stabilize [the] western economy." Drawing on Collier's belief in the Indian New Deal as a model for colonial governments to rehabilitate their own indigenous populations, Ickes suggested that "administrators and students of Indians in Latin-American countries, many of them faced with problems similar to those our Government has struggled with through several generations, should study and, perhaps, profit from the trial-and-error policies of Indian administration in the United States." With funding from the Office of the Coordinator of Inter-American Affairs, run by Nelson Rockefeller, the Interior Department sponsored surveys of Latin American Indian programs by the Bureau of Indian Affairs and visits of representatives of countries interested in studying the work of the BIA. On one such occasion an Australian anthropologist named Donald Thomson, visiting the United States on a Rockefeller Fellowship, toured Indian reservations and met with Collier to discuss the Indian Reorganization Act, writing in a letter home that Americans' "social and mental attitudes" toward Native peoples had much to offer Australians; as a consequence Thomson promoted the IRA as a platform for Australian Aborigine rights. The Interior Department also set up the Division of Inter-American Cooperation to act as a clearinghouse for information about and collaboration on Indian problems with other American governments, including those of Costa Rica, Cuba, Ecuador, El Salvador, Honduras, Mexico, Nicaragua, Panama, and Peru. And it facilitated the distribution of Office of War Information reports of Native Americans' wartime patriotism and heroism to South American countries. In addition, both the Interior Department and the State Department supported U.S. participation in the Inter-American Indian Institute (Instituto Indigenista Interamericano) to sustain the "hemisphere co-operation" that started at the

April 1940 Pátzcuaro conference. As the chairman of the institute's governing board, Collier disseminated through it several of his internationalist speeches translated into Spanish, especially on Indian Day, "the hemispheric day of the Red Indian."[17]

In the end, however, the efforts of Collier and Ickes to export the Indian New Deal met with opposition from within the U.S. government and from Latin American governments less interested in Indian sovereignty than Collier, Ickes, and Sáenz. Collier's evangelism clouded his recognition of divisions within Indian Latin America, where, as in the United States, there was no such thing as "the Indian." The decision of the House Subcommittee on Interior Appropriations to cut funding for cross-border collaboration in 1944, which represented congressional opposition to the internationalization of Collierism, was just one manifestation of a renewed effort to roll back Collier's programs and replace them with a traditional detribalization agenda, a portent of the congressional termination campaign to come in the 1950s. In addition, with their eyes on the prize of the resources of the Latin American interior, which resembled the American West of the nineteenth century, U.S. officials prosecuting World War II worked to undermine programs strengthening Indian control of land. Collier's appeals to the State Department for continued funding of his internationalist programs fell on deaf ears. By 1944 the State Department had other matters to contend with, in particular the challenge of defining the postwar order in Europe. The pressures of the Cold War that emerged would temper the politics of subsequent pan-Indian congresses, leading to even less input by Indians to devising a solution to their problems. Indeed, by the time the Second Inter-American Indian Congress took place in 1949, a new group of administrators had replaced Collier, Sáenz, and Cárdenas. Collier himself was denied travel funding by the State Department. He would write in his memoirs, published in 1963, that after "sixteen cold war years" his efforts to incorporate Latin American Indian societies along the lines of his IRA program had failed to reach their potential.[18]

Defending Mother Earth

Striving to expand his ideas of Indian reorganization abroad during World War II, Collier worked hard to sustain his protection of that agenda at home. He fought to improve collaboration in the Western Hemisphere, but he also set his sights across the oceans. Proclaiming that Native Americans' participation in the war "has significance far beyond the boundaries of the United States" and that "our Indians are an important symbol to colonial peoples all over the world," Collier contended that "native" peoples in Egypt, India, Iran, and China, in addition to South America, "feel strong cultural bonds with our Indians." Richard Neuberger, a journalist for the *Portland Oregonian*, provided one example of these "strong cultural bonds," noting that "millions in India . . . conducted special prayers in behalf of their oppressed brethren in far-off America" after reading about poverty among the Navajo.[19]

In his 1942 essay "The Indian in a Wartime Nation," Collier posed a question that white Americans had asked during World War I: "How could [Native Americans] be expected to understand the clash of ideologies which has precipitated the world crisis?" Listing all the various ways in which Native American men and women were contributing to the war effort, Collier answered:

> The Indians seem to have an amazingly clear understanding of the major issues involved . . . It is a life-and-death struggle for the survival of those things for which they have been unceasingly waging an uphill fight for many generations. This has been a fight to retain their cultural independence, the right to their native religions, and the right to local democracy. It has been a struggle against the totalitarian concept of a superrace dominating, absorbing, and reducing to serfdom the small minority group of a different culture.

Having spent over a century trying to prevent white Americans from dominating and assimilating their different cultures, Collier concluded, Native Americans connected "the struggle of democracies the world over with their own struggle of the last century. It may be that they see in a victory of the democracies a guarantee that they too shall be permitted to live their own lives."[20]

Collier's internationalist framing of Native American participation in the war inspired Neuberger to document the ways in which Native Americans connected their struggles to other colonial peoples' struggles against oppression. In a November 1942 article titled "The American Indian Enlists: He Feels His Kinship to the Chinese, the East Indians, the Arabs and the Filipinos, and to Colonial Peoples All Over the World," he echoed Collier's contention that Native Americans understood the international significance of the war. The Native Americans he interviewed, Neuberger wrote, "believe it will lead to more opportunity and less inequalities for the people of China, India, South America and the island nations, and that in any such readjustment the American Indian will benefit, too." A member of the Celilo tribe of Oregon told him that the U.S. government "defends our rights. We know that under Nazism we should have no rights at all." Refuting Nazi claims that Indians had close biological ties with Nazis, he stated, "We are not Aryans." Representatives of Iroquois nations proclaimed, with Vice President Henry Wallace in attendance: "We represent the oldest, though smallest, democracy in the world today . . . It is the unanimous sentiment among the Indian people that the atrocities of the Axis nations are violently repulsive to all sense of righteousness of our people." Echoing the Iroquois, members of the Cheyenne tribe called the Axis powers an "unholy triangle whose purpose is to conquer and enslave the bodies, minds and souls of all free peoples." Orval Ricketts, editor of the *Times Hustler* of Farmington, New Mexico, observed that the Navajo showed an understanding of the war that stemmed from their own colonial history, citing the example of three Navajos who decided to contribute money to a Red Cross campaign to benefit Finland because the money, they said, would help "the little nation that was fighting a big nation." Native Americans viewed the expanding war through the lens of a colonial past imposed by Americans and a vision of a colonial future imposed by the Nazis. As Collier put it in a speech to the Rotary Club of New York, Native Americans "remember what Fascism was like when they experienced it. They do not intend to experience it again."[21]

Animated by their colonial history, Native Americans feared the prospects of a Nazi takeover of their society and responded to the exigencies of that threat by closing ranks. Amid reports of a stranger prowling the Navajo reservation, presumed to be an agent of the "so-called fifth column," telling Navajo that they would be "better off under another government," Navajo Council chairman J. C. Morgan warned Navajo citizens to be alert for "strange people" who "may be spies" taking pictures or offering bribes for information. The Navajo Council was responding to the "crisis now facing the world" because "there exists no purer concentration of Americanism than among the First Americans." Referring to reports of Nazi agents probing the reservation for converts, the council adopted a resolution stating, "It has become common practice to attempt national destruction through the sowing of seeds of treachery among minority groups such as ours." The council resolved that "any un-American movement among our people will be resented and dealt with severely." As during World War I, the Navajo pledged their loyalty "to the system which recognizes minority rights." Navajo citizen Roger Davis approved of the resolution but added one important caveat: "Due to the fact that we stand ready to defend our country at this time, let no one say the land we occupy is not ours . . . We are still not free from the captivity we have been under." In waging a war against the Nazis on behalf of the "great country" of the United States, the Navajo would continue to defend Navajo territory from ongoing American colonial subjugation in part by continuing to define Americanism in terms of Native American patriotism.[22]

As with members of other American ethnic groups, Native Americans served in the war not only because of patriotism but also because of martial traditions embedded in family or tribal community histories, for economic opportunity, and, of course, because they were drafted. In serving the United States, Indian soldiers developed bonds with non-Indian soldiers. Yet even as they found common cause in fighting for the common ground of the same nation, Native soldiers articulated reasons specific to their experience as Native Americans, in particular, the added dimension of fighting for an ancestral homeland, for a specific piece of ground that sustained a nation within a nation. One Navajo, Cozy Stanley Brown, explained, "My main reason for going to war was to protect my land and my people because the elderly people said that the earth was our mother." Another Navajo draftee acknowledged: "I don't know anything about the white man's way. I never went outside the reservation." Explaining why he fought, he wrote, "To protect my country, my people, my head men, the chiefs of my people." The Navajo eventually provided over a thousand soldiers, including the famed code talkers. Albert Smith, who joined a code talker unit, noted, "This conflict involved Mother Earth being dominated by foreign countries," and it was the Indian's "responsibility to defend her." Serving the United States enabled Native Americans to protect their "people" and their "country," which included sacred lands that nurtured their spirituality and sustained their Indianness. Assuming a respon-

sibility to defend both the United States of America and Native America
in a time of great crisis, they would travel "outside the reservation" by
the tens of thousands, crossing a boundary between Native America and
America at large, and between America and the world, in the name of
preserving that boundary.[23]

Highlighting the centrality of Indians' "homeland" in shaping their
outlook on world affairs, Secretary of the Interior Harold Ickes documented Native Americans' contributions to national defense in his 1941
annual report. "If the Indian's love of his homeland once proved an obstacle to the white man," he wrote, "today it is making an unique contribution, as it did in the last World War, to the total national defense effort."
Native Americans enlisted by the thousands even before the attack on
Pearl Harbor. By July 1941 "almost 1 out of every 10 Indians of military
age was in the armed forces." As during World War I, Native Americans of
all ages and conditions volunteered for army service. All told, roughly
25,000 Native Americans, including 800 women, served in the armed
forces. Many others were turned down because of illiteracy or poor health.
A Leech Lake Ojibwe from Minnesota protested his rejection from the
army because of his lack of teeth, saying of his potential enemies, "I don't
want to bite 'em, I want to shoot 'em." Kirtus Tecumseh, a descendant of
the great Chief Tecumseh of the early 1800s, tried to enlist in the U.S.
Navy but was rejected because of disabilities suffered from serving on a
submarine during World War I. Because of the success of code talkers during the First World War, the U.S. Army recruited Oneida, Chippewa, Sac,
and Fox, Comanche, Cherokee, Choctaw, and Navajo for similar service
during World War II. The Navajo, by dint of the large number of soldiers
who enlisted or were drafted, and because of their subsequent exploits in
the Pacific, especially at Iwo Jima, have received most of the attention
from historians and the public. But other groups, notably the Sioux and
Comanche, provided critical intelligence in the European theater, either
by speaking in their native languages or using a code based on those languages.[24]

Native Americans also worked on the home front in various ways, pre-
cipitating movement off reservations to urban factories, rural farm operations, and new military installations to a much greater extent than during
World War I. Defense companies recruited and trained Native American
men and women from boarding schools for welding and machine shop

jobs; thousands more worked in West Coast defense plants and found employment at new ordnance depots established around the country. And as during World War I, Native Americans also contributed to the war effort by purchasing U.S. war bonds at a rate equal to that of any other American ethnic group. A group of Navajo women bought $75 worth of bonds earned from selling scrap metal. The Quapaw donated $1 million to the government and accepted the bonds only after federal officials insisted. Jemez Pueblo dancers toured to raise money for war bonds. The Blackfeet, among others, grew "victory gardens" to contribute to the nation's collective food supply.[25]

American Indian women participated during World War II to a much greater extent than during World War I. Cecilia DeFoe (Ojibwe) noted the salience of Native Americans' fighting in the war: "Not too long ago [Americans] were killing us and we're going over there [Europe] to take their part." Another Ojibwe, Marge Pascale, joined the Women's Auxiliary Air Corps (WAAC) in 1943 to escape the grinding poverty of her reservation, explaining, "One thing about the service, you get two pair of shoes and you get a bed and you get to eat." Native American women, many of them from the federal boarding school system, also enlisted in women's auxiliaries such as the WAAC. Their schools proudly noted graduates' contributions. The *Indian Leader*, published by the Haskell Institute of Kansas, editorialized, "Haskell takes great pride in these patriotic young women who once attended school here." Margie Williams, a Lakota Sioux graduate of Haskell, wrote in the 1943 commencement issue: "It is with much pride that the Indian woman dons the uniform of her country to aid in settling the turmoil. As in battles before, the Redman is proving to his white brother that he can make an outstanding contribution, both on the home front and behind the firing lines. With the same pride and devotion, the Indian woman is proving herself to be one of Uncle Sam's priceless daughters." That home front service included, for Chippewa women, forming a domestic defense brigade. Said one Chippewa woman, "We have rifles, we have ammunition and we know how to shoot."[26]

The service of Native American women and men, promoted in various BIA and Interior Department publications, received widespread attention in Congress and in the press. The BIA's public relations efforts reflected Collier's genuine pride in Native Americans but also his need to insulate his Indian New Deal program from attacks by championing the patriotism

3.1 Three Native American Marine Corps reservists, Camp Lejeune, North Carolina, October 1943. Native American women demonstrated their patriotism in multiple ways during World War II. From left to right: Minnie Spotted Wolf (Blackfeet), Celia Mix (Potawatomi), and Violet Eastman (Chippewa). Courtesy of National Archives and Records Administration.

of American Indians and their refusal to ingest "the propaganda of foreign countries hostile to the American way of life." Senator D. Worth Clark of Idaho remarked that Native Americans' wartime activities were "an inspiration to patriotic Americans everywhere." Congressman John M. Coffee noted that "after the injustices the Indian has suffered, he is still ready for an all-out defense of democracy, because only democracy can better his lot . . . America's Indians are fighting for America because America has made a conscientious effort to right old wrongs and improve the lot of our Indians." Newspapers trumpeted Native Americans' contributions to audiences eager to reimagine Indians' nineteenth-century martial activities in a modern American context. The *Saturday Evening Post* opined in 1942 that the United States "would not need the Selective Service if all volunteered like Indians." One newspaper, not quite embracing the social integration of Native Americans on equal terms, extolled their patriotism by contrasting the "Red Indians" of America with the Red "anarchists, saboteurs, ingrates, traitors and teachers of treason . . . European red has deteriorated and American red has advanced." Collier himself expressed his belief that Native Americans were uniquely equipped to understand what the people of Europe were facing: "Who should know all of this . . . better than the Red Indians?"[27]

As during World War I, federal officials debated whether Native Americans should fight for their country in segregated units or within the armed services at large. The BIA initially supported all-Indian units, arguing that these would make "the best possible use of Indian special skills." Interestingly, some BIA officials also believed that the units would reflect the IRA's goal of affirming sovereignty and thus would "appeal to the Indian himself" by offering the benefit "of having his identity specifically and specially recognized." In addition, the BIA promoted the possible use of bilingual speakers to transmit codes over the telephone lines. Finally, the BIA supported the idea because the "Indian of today is the product of an adjustment of tradition and modernism—an adjustment of means of which has managed to retain much of the old native pattern and still has assimilated those portions of the white civilization which particularly suit his needs and arouse his interest." Repeating the popular notion that Indians retained race-specific fighting abilities, the BIA offered that the "modern Indian" still retained some his "warlike prowess" learned through "combat with nature and with equally crafty tribal enemies." Some Native Ameri-

3.2 The first Navajo U.S. Marine Corps code talker recruits were sworn in at Fort Wingate, New Mexico, 1942. The code talkers' military exploits remained classified until 1968, but many Navajo understood their significance as an act of patriotism that justified increased self-determination. Courtesy of National Archives and Records Administration.

cans rejected this view of innate differences, offering their services in integrated units. J. C. Morgan of the Navajo Tribal Council appealed to Collier to create a unit of "Navajo trainees as an indigenous regiment" on the reservation until they were acclimated to "the white man's way of military life." Morgan's efforts stemmed in part from the fact that few of the roughly four thousand Navajo who planned to volunteer or to register for the draft spoke English. He sought a slow integration of Navajo into regular units, though he noted in October 1940 the value of using the Navajo language "in secret code practice." Individual soldiers also appealed to the BIA to establish separate units. Private William T. Snake (Ponca) eagerly offered his services to the United States in a January 1942 letter to Collier: "I am only trying some way to help *defend* OUR COUNTRY and by organizing a PONCA INDIAN SIGNAL CORP, and using the Indian Dialect, I think it will help a little, in *defending* OUR COUNTRY." But, as during World War I, army officials rejected the idea of creating another segregated unit based on race; two were enough. "Utter confusion" would reign if the service fractured beyond black and white divisions, Assistant Chief of Staff General William E. Shedd argued in the spring of 1941. In the end Collier came to oppose the creation of segregated units, unwilling to contest War Department policy but also intent on demonstrating that his BIA agenda did not in fact promote segregation as his critics claimed. As a result, Collier strove to resolve cases of resistance to either selective service registration or induction.[28]

Protecting Native Sovereignty

With some exceptions, American Indian nations cooperated fully with Selective Service officials and with local draft boards. In North Carolina all eligible males of the Eastern Band of Cherokee registered for the draft. But many did so with considerable anger because the state of North Carolina denied them the right to vote. After two Cherokee veterans of World War I were turned away by voter registration officials in the fall of 1940, the Cherokee Tribal Council complained that the inability of the Cherokee to vote affected their status before local draft boards. The council believed that those draft boards, composed of whites only, had carte blanche to fill draft quotas with Cherokees rather than whites. Employing the foundational language of American freedom, the council resolved that "any organization or group that would deprive a people of as sacred a right as the right of suffrage would not hesitate to deprive them of other constitutional rights including the three inalienable rights—life, liberty and the pursuit of happiness, if the opportunity to do so presents itself." The council resolution took pains to emphasize the willingness of the Cherokee to honor their service obligations, noting that "there is not a more patriotic people to be found anywhere in this country of ours than the Cherokee of North Carolina." After World War II ended, Cherokee veterans marshaled this patriotic rhetoric to claim the franchise, part of a larger national struggle among Native American and African American veterans to secure the rights for which they had fought in the war.[29]

Organized resistance to draft registration did develop among Hopi (Arizona), Ute (Colorado), Seminole (Florida), Iroquois (New York), Yakima (Washington), and Papago (Arizona). Collier delineated to Selective Service officials the reasons why "misguided Indians" might resist induction while clarifying that some "draft recalcitrants" did not oppose army service so much as conscription. "Underlying the whole matter," he told one official, "is, of course, the understandable Indian psychology of distrust of a Government which has not always treated the Indian with justice and sympathy." But Collier would brook no opposition from Native Americans to registration, believing that they had an obligation to defend their country in the name of democracy, and in the name of protecting his Indian New Deal programs. Collier maintained that the 1924 Citizenship Act made all Native Americans citizens of the United States, and moreover that the Selective Service registration applied to citizens and noncitizens alike. He took pains to educate Selective Service officials, who in many cases were unfamiliar with the laws affecting Native Americans. He explained to one official: "Were we dealing with slackers, or professional trouble-makers, I should . . . urge punitive measures, but the Indians on these reservations are not slackers. They are not radicals or agitators." Only through registration could one contest service on the grounds of conscientious objection, which Collier found legitimate, especially among the Hopi. In some cases of resistance, Native Americans sought to contribute to the war effort in different ways. A Zuni "rain priest" was granted a deferral classification and thus treated like "ministers of other religions." The Zuni had contended that his services were "needed to bring rain not only for the semi-arid western New Mexico reservation but for the whole world." Other Natives protested conscription rather than army service itself. In an October 8, 1940, resolution three "Chiefs of the St. Regis Mohawk Nation" argued that to maintain "allegiance to our own country (Six Nations Confederacy) . . . [w]e do not desire and object to being conscripted. We desire that our men enlist of their own accord."[30]

The Six Nations of the Iroquois Confederacy in particular refused to accept U.S. sovereignty and pursued legal avenues to protect their treaty rights more aggressively than other Indian nations, the result of 150 years of living among a sea of white Americans hostile to Native American exceptionalism as well as of memories of World War I–era draft resistance. The Iroquois fought a legal battle at home before allowing their sons to fight and die overseas. Arguing that her son, Warren Green, was not a U.S. citizen, Green's mother, acting on behalf of Iroquois leaders, sought Green's release from military duty through a writ of habeas corpus from a district court. Denied, Green appealed to the U.S. Second Circuit Court of Appeals, which ruled against him in November 1941 on the grounds that the Citizenship Act of 1924, which the Nationality Act of 1940 had reinforced, trumped Iroquois treaty claims. The three-member court's decision was unanimous but ambivalent. Judge Thomas Swan lamented, "The white men have treated Indians shabbily for so long that I would like to give them a break on compulsory military service, but I don't see how we can work it out in any lawyer-like way." Judge Jerome Frank offered a similar sentiment, noting that the three judges had "taxed [their] ingenuity in vain to find any interpretation which would result in a decision in [Green's] favor."[31]

The compelling aspect of the case, beyond the judges' reluctance to affirm the decision, was that Warren Green agreed to serve as the "legal guinea pig," as the *New York Herald Tribune* called him, for the Iroquois Confederacy's fight against conscription as a test of its sovereign rights, much as Rosa Parks would intentionally generate publicity for African American civil rights by refusing to move to the back of the bus a decade later. As John Collier noted in opposing the legal efforts of the Iroquois, Green himself did not object to military service but simply represented the attempt of the Iroquois to retain their "status as 'imperium in imperio,'" as a nation within a nation. Iroquois leaders had always framed their struggle to retain sovereignty in internationalist terms. This case was no different. In a letter to the American Civil Liberties Union appealing for its assistance, a young Iroquois named Ernest Benedict explained his people's resistance:

Many wonder why we hold to our reservation so tenaciously. They advise us to stop our weak struggling and give in to the State and National governments and lose our racial identity in competition with the outside world. We answer that one cannot do that so easily. Why does not the United States join itself with the Soviet Republic whose numbers and territory are greater than its own? Because Americans feel that their social system is so much superior to that of Russia. Similarly, we Six Nations Indians feel we have potentially a superior social system to that of the United States. If ownly [sic] we were left alone, we could redevelop our society to part of its original form which was old in democracy when Europe knew only monarchs.

For the Iroquois, resisting U.S. hegemony was akin to Americans resisting Soviet communism's infiltration of their institutions. The Iroquois case provides an early example of the ways in which Native Americans' struggles against government coercion modeled the cultural dynamics of the international Cold War that developed after World War II.[32]

The *Ex parte Green* decision, which was upheld when the U.S. Supreme Court declined to hear the case, closed off all Native Americans' legal options for resisting compulsory military service. But it failed to quench the thirst of the Iroquois for cultural and political independence from U.S. authority, for reaffirming their "status as 'imperium in imperio.'" Appearing before the three judges of the Court of Appeals, Six Nations' representatives, dressed in traditional ceremonial garb, protested that after stripping Indians of their land and mineral wealth in Colorado, Pennsylvania, the Black Hills, and elsewhere, "practically all of the beautiful country that once was ours," the United States now looked to "break once again our treaty and take from us our last possession, our freedom." The United States found more "beautiful country" to take during the war and after it. As a result, the Iroquois, and other Native Americans, would wage new legal battles in the years to come for their land and their freedoms, animated by the same national service many of them were forced to provide in the name of fighting for freedom abroad.[33]

The Erosion of Native Land

During the war, Native American men and women gave their lives and their labor for the United States and for their own nations. They also gave their land, in many cases without their consent. According to the secretary of the interior's 1942 *Annual Report*, "blocks of Indian land also have been requisitioned for military use, and the removal of Indian families, which resulted in some instances, constituted a direct war service for the [BIA]." The use of the word "removal" highlights the visceral nature of the military's action. The War Department's efforts to use Native land sustained the ongoing cultural clash over land use and the value of "the reservation." To military officials, reservation land was perfect for gunnery practice; sparsely populated and lacking infrastructure, it could be bombed with little risk to people or property. But to Native Americans the land remained part of their cultural and spiritual landscape, the sacred acreage that remained after nineteenth-century treaties and policies had circum-scribed and commodified their tribal homelands. To give up more land, and to be "removed" from it, despite the promise that the situation was temporary, did not appeal to Native Americans, who saw the requisitions as extending military subjugation and government appropriation of their land.[34]

Southwestern Indian communities, while generally supportive of the U.S. war effort, remained opposed to militarism and fought against the use of their land for violent purposes in accord with philosophical objections to war itself; Laguna Pueblo elders protested to Collier that they would not cede their land for use as a bombing site, as did Papago leaders. The Sioux, who lost the most land in the nineteenth century, also lost the most during World War II. In early 1942 the army appropriated nearly 400,000 acres of land on the Pine Ridge Reservation in South Dakota for an aerial gunnery range. One Sioux reported, the local BIA official "said that we would be shot if we didn't leave." Sioux families lost 300,000 acres of pasture or farmland, for which most of them received the paltry sum of seventy-five cents per acre. They were forced to leave behind their homes, land allotments, and unharvested crops and had to sell livestock at a loss. Iron Hail (Dewey Beard) was one of those Sioux who lost his land. A vet-eran of the 1876 Battle of Little Bighorn, he lost his parents, three siblings, his wife, and his infant son in the 1890 Wounded Knee massacre. Adopt-ing the name of Admiral George Dewey of Spanish-American War fame, he then carved out a living as a rancher on what was left of his Sioux homeland. Having lost so much in the nineteenth century, he lost more in the twentieth, the two centuries combined on his own long trail of tears. It was indeed a cruel fate for Beard and for a people willing to assist the war effort in other ways. After the Sioux won a court of claims award of $5 million for nineteenth-century treaty violations, Sioux leaders told Presi-dent Franklin Roosevelt: "When our country is at war, we feel payment of these claims should be deferred. If it will help the country, a few more years of waiting will be patiently accepted." Such loyalty went unre-warded.[35]

Wartime land losses for Native Americans amounted to roughly 1 mil-lion acres, reversing Indian New Deal policies designed to stabilize and expand their land base. World War II neutralized or reversed a number of national New Deal programs, and the Indian New Deal was no exception.

The federal government also appropriated Native American land for housing Japanese American citizens removed from their homes on the West Coast and sent on their own trails of tears and trauma. The War Relocation Authority, headed by future commissioner of Indian affairs Dillon Myer, established two of the ten "relocation centers" on Native American reservations: the Poston center on the Colorado River Reservation and the camp at Gila River Reservation, both in Arizona. John Collier promoted the plan, in part because he thought Native Americans would later benefit from the physical infrastructure built to house Japanese prisoners. But he also saw it as an opportunity to apply the lessons the BIA had learned in working with American Indians, claiming that interning Japanese Americans on Native American lands would "demonstrate for the whole country the efficiency . . . of the [Indian] cooperative way of living." Proving Native Americans useful in this context would provide yet another source of validation of his Indian New Deal agenda.[36]

Fred Daiker, a member of Collier's Indian New Deal brain trust, thought Collier's program would demonstrate for the country a different process, arguing that "there is still enough sentiment left for the Indian so that the public may criticize using Indian reservations for these aliens and causing the Indians to be associated with these people. The *logical question* will be why place them among the Indians after all the wrong that has been done to these people? It will be construed as just another instance of forcing something on the Indian because he can do nothing about it." Indeed, in looking past Native Americans' interests to advance his Indian New Deal agenda, Collier betrayed the ideals of that agenda by pushing the internment program without the consent of the Pima of the Gila River Reservation and of the Mohave and Chemehuevi Indians of the Colorado River Reservation. During the 1930s both Native groups had embraced the Indian Reorganization Act, which emphasized consent-based decision making. During the 1940s they witnessed its limitations as their protests went unheeded. And by the end of 1942 roughly 25,000 Japanese Americans were housed on Native American lands in buildings that would be destroyed after the war rather than transferred to Native ownership as Collier had hoped. He would not be the first reformer to misjudge war as a means of shaping American social relations to a progressive end.[37]

The real and rhetorical juxtaposition of American Indians and Japanese Americans, another ethnic population removed from homes and businesses to what were commonly called concentration camps, raised important questions about the status of American Indians' sovereign space. Looking through the fences of these camps and seeing another ethnic group stripped of its rights on the basis of a different appearance and set of cultural traditions must have made many American Indians uncomfortable, as it did Indian New Deal figures like Daiker, in part because, as Daiker argued, the Japanese presence reflected Indians' continuing struggle against colonial pressures to maintain the hard-fought boundaries they were willing to cross for the purpose of defending their right to be American *and* Indian. The "logical question" for BIA officials, social scientists, and Native Americans themselves was whether or not such conflicts heralded a new direction for Indian-white relations as World War II approached its end.

American Indians "Away from Home"

Well before the war ended, Collier promoted the narrative of Indian self-determination as a model for a stable postwar world. Writing in 1942, Collier argued:

> Indians face a problem which is in essence a problem of the whole world and one which must be solved if we are to achieve any ordered stability in the international and internal relations of states. It is the problem of reconciling the rights of small groups of people to cultural independence with the necessity for larger economic units demanded by modern methods of production and distribution. This is the problem of small states and small cultural groups everywhere. If here in the United States with our Indian groups we can show the solution to this problem we shall have made a material contribution to the maintenance of world peace.

In June 1944 he restated this message, highlighting the success of his Indian New Deal program, which had worked to integrate American Indians into market capitalism while preserving their cultural values. For example, he preached the salience of self-determination in a speech to the Rotary Club of New York, telling the audience that "what the Indians have shown, the peoples of China, India, and Indonesia, and the peoples of Africa, and the huge Indian masses of the Latin American countries, just as certainly will show, if the future world-order be such as to throw responsibility upon these peoples, to give them liberty, and to supply them a minimum of intellectual purpose." Other white commentators and a new generation of Native American intellectuals and activists presented the narrative of a free Native America as a model for solving the problems of global racism and imperialism. Carey McWilliams publicized Native Americans' struggles in his 1943 book *Brothers under the Skin*. Influenced by Indian New Deal thinkers, McWilliams shed light on "the skeletons in the closet so far as American democracy is concerned," the "long-standing neglect of colored minorities, particularly the Indian and the Negro." In his chapter titled "The Non-Vanishing Indian," McWilliams extolled the virtues of Indian New Deal initiatives and the philosophy of racial tolerance and cultural pluralism that underlay them. Responding to calls to "assimilate the Indian," McWilliams asked: "But just what is meant by assimilation? In the political sense, assimilation might imply merely the full and equal exercise of political rights and privileges. In this sense, the Indians have been largely assimilated. But assimilation does not necessarily imply cultural uniformity; nor does it imply that, for certain purposes, ethnic groups cannot be regarded as separate or distinct entities." McWilliams defended Indian New Deal programs by arguing that they were not "atavistic" but focused on "providing for a gradual and orderly adjustment of Indian culture to the demands of a modern industrialized society," and in a way that guaranteed Native Americans' religious and cultural freedoms and protected them from the vagaries and violence of American racism. McWilliams cited the argument of BIA official John Embree that assimilation would not work without addressing the institutionalized racism of "modern industrialized society." As Embree put it, "The great American middle classes are so full of color prejudice that Indians, no matter how fully they adopt white ways, will not for many years be accepted into the white world."[38]

Like Collier, McWilliams believed that America's approach to resolving the universal problem of racism had implications for a stable postwar order. He closed his chapter on American Indians by writing, "If a solution of this problem can be effected in the United States, then there is at least reason to believe that a similar solution might be made of similar world problems." McWilliams framed this racial dynamic by maintaining,

"When we say that imperialism must be banished from the postwar world, we forget that it must also be eliminated at home." The Swedish sociologist Gunnar Myrdal captured this dynamic in his influential 1944 book *An American Dilemma: The Negro Problem and Modern Democracy*. The American dilemma, according to Myrdal, was the country's inability to resolve the disjunction between the ideological declarations of equality embedded in the founding texts of the late eighteenth century and the endemic racism that continued to permeate American society in the mid-twentieth century.[39]

During the war, Native Americans' internationalist perspectives further developed from their wrestling with their own version of the American dilemma. Native soldiers' hybrid patriotism was manifested in their writings from abroad, in particular in a series of letters sent by Navajo and Pueblo soldiers to Margretta Steward Dietrich of the New Mexico Association on Indian Affairs, a group which sent Christmas care packages and the newsletter *Indian Club News* to Native soldiers from New Mexico. The letters capture the soldiers' pride in fighting for the United States, their homesickness, and their perspective on other peoples affected by colonialism. And they express a renewed belief in being "Indian" and the related importance of their ancestral homeland. Writing from Africa in July 1943, Private First Class Justino Herrera (Cochiti Pueblo) told Dietrich that he was trying "to help win this war and restore our Freedom, rights to do as we've done in the past at our beloved homes in our great country (America)." After visiting Bombay and Australia, Private Tony Aguilar (Santo Domingo Pueblo) reported from Iran that "the people here are similar to our own Pueblos, especially Taos and Isleta Pueblos. It really is very interesting taking from a view point of anthropologists or ethnologists." In his January 1943 letter Private First Class Joseph Roybal noted that he was happy to do his duty by fighting in the army but that as soon as the war ended, he would return immediately to San Ildefonso Pueblo in New Mexico. Like Aguilar, he would bring with him a new perspective gained from contact with Alaskan natives, from whom he "learned that the U.S. Gov't did away with their ceremonials . . . In my opinion I think it's a pity that fate had stepped in and this should come their way. These living here are like any tax paying citizens." Hearing of the decline of Alaskan ceremonials, he was "thankful that I came from the adobe land where I hope that in the years to come no ill-thinking white man will attempt to change our way of living or even our ceremonials in the Southwest, the land I wouldn't trade for any part of the world. Since the other boys feel the same way I say this because now I know the significance of the Pueblo land."[40]

In this passionate letter Roybal connected the prerogatives of American citizenship, the impact of lost cultural traditions, and the significance of land in maintaining those traditions. For Roybal, Aguilar, and other Pueblo soldiers, the threat to their people's land base and thus the maintenance of their ceremonies was very real in 1943. A number of Pueblo responded viscerally to news that Congress was considering legislation, H.R. 323, that would authorize construction of dams on the Rio Grande in New Mexico, threatening the homes and lands of numerous Pueblo communities in New Mexico. Private Octavio Suina (Cochiti Pueblo) told Dietrich in his poignant April 1943 letter that hearing of the legislation "is hurting us boys who are in the Army fighting for you and our homes. I want you to write to Washington to the Congressman that I don't want any dams or any damage to be done to our homes & Pueblos while we are absent. After the war we want to go home & want to find our homes the way we left them. We don't want nothing but our dear homes." Suina and other soldiers felt betrayed that Congress would act in this way while they fought overseas—"while we are away from home," as Suina put it. Private Lewis Naranjo (Santa Clara Pueblo) protested that such an action "would be a poor reward for our present services in the war. We thought this a free country for everybody . . . I don't think it is a free country after all." Echoing Roybal's concern about Alaskan natives losing their ceremonies, Naranjo objected to Dietrich that the "white man" would "attempt to change our way of living or our Ceremonies. We enlist in the army cause we thought we could live peacefully after we win victory. As the old Indian saying 'Our land our religion all bound together.'" Other soldiers made reference to the Pueblo ceremonies that were threatened by the loss of land. Writing from "somewhere" in the South Pacific, a Private Pino (San Ildefonso) told Dietrich that he had heard of the legislation from friends, who asked him to write his congressmen to protest H.R. 323. He did so, having "realized my Indian people needed my help to protect and save the people their pueblos and their tribal ceremonies furthermore I have the same rights to protest what I believe is wrong." Private Aguilar had also noted, "I hope I've helped out what little I've done writing Congressmen about that Bill—H.R. 323."[41]

The battle over H.R. 323 represented in many ways a repeat of the Bursum Bill crisis of the early 1920s, a renewed effort by white Americans to gain access to Pueblo resources. As the Bursum Bill did in the 1920s, this new campaign galvanized supporters of American Indians' rights. To protect Pueblo lands, the New Mexico Association on Indian Affairs, the Indian Committee of the General Federation of Women's Clubs, and the Indian Rights Association, in addition to Pueblo representatives, protested the proposed legislation during congressional hearings held in May 1943. The Association on American Indian Affairs (AAIA), based in New York City but led by anthropologists specializing in Southwest Indian cultures, also worked on behalf of the Pueblo. Oliver LaFarge, an AAIA founder serving in the army, wrote in the inaugural issue of the association's magazine, *The American Indian*, that "the will to blitz [American Indians'] homes while they are gone makes me feel savage . . . I do not want them [the Pueblo] or any other Indians . . . to come home with a chestful of medals and a sleeveful of stripes to find their Reservation wrecked." LaFarge noted that American Indians who were sent "incredibly far away" from their homes "hope the American people will repay their loyalty, but experience keeps them from being quite sure."[42]

LaFarge and his AAIA colleagues saw H.R. 323 as a symbol of a growing congressional campaign to terminate federal funding for Indian affairs, a portent of Indian peoples' being "shoved back into the old mire of debt and helplessness, the hospitals gone and the schools closed, as has been recommended." At the time Pueblos and their supporters were campaigning to kill or modify H.R. 323, the Senate Indian Affairs committee issued a report titled "Survey of Conditions . . . in Justification of Appropriations for 1944, and the Liquidation of the Indian Bureau." Known as Senate Partial Report 310, the "Survey of Conditions" was the first of many reports and policies that both resuscitated the spirit of reservation termination that stretched back to nineteenth-century policies of incorporation and reflected growing congressional opposition to Collier's IRA policies, which had helped to blunt that incorporation. The editors of *The American Indian* called the Senate report a "tyrannical proposal" put forward by "pressure groups that would destroy our American Indian minority in a truly dictatorial manner." The AAIA expanded its fund raising using this theme of an emerging crisis of un-Americanism. In a brochure published in late 1944 the AAIA argued that Native Americans "gallantly PROTECT

US on all fronts." Now it was time for American citizens to repay that debt in protecting America's "first minority group." The brochure reminded potential supporters that the "pitfall to progress in 1944 is the fact that world chaos tends to make us forget the rampant exploitation and abuse in our own backyard, and those Americans deeply concerned with India—should protect their own Indians!" Making this linkage between the conflicts abroad and in Indian country, John Collier asserted that "the final battleground is at home." Indeed, even as Pueblo and Navajo soldiers wrote their congressmen or congresswomen from distant battlegrounds to protest H.R. 323, they did so stripped of their fundamental democratic right to vote in the state of New Mexico.[43]

As World War II began, Nazi agents prowled American Indian reservations in search of converts. As the war ended, Indians saw a different kind of "dictatorial" agent prowling their reservations and eyeing their natural resources. American Indians' and Indian rights supporters' allusions to the dictatorship of Germany would become more frequent after World War II, with communists replacing fascists as the model for repressive U.S. legislators and bureaucrats. The pressures of World War II therefore revealed the contours of an evolving struggle between Native Americans and the U.S. government, a conflict with ideological roots in the late nineteenth century which emerged again during the mid-twentieth century to resemble the contours of the coming international Cold War.

The crisis of H.R. 323 politicized a new generation of Native American activists, who framed their struggle in the language of hybrid patriotism. Lewis Naranjo (Pueblo) put it most clearly in stating: "We are doing our best to win the war to be free from danger as much as the white man. We are fighting with Uncle Sam's army to defend the right of our people to live our own life in our own way." The Pueblo joined the Navajo, Sioux, Iroquois, Pima, and other Native groups that, during the war, had identified "danger" to their way of life and their sacred places lurking at home as well as abroad.[44]

This "danger," manifesting itself in the form of H.R. 323, Partial Report 310, and terminationist statements from white American reformers and politicians, helped lead to the formation of the National Congress of American Indians in 1944. The idea for a new pan-Indian group arose from Indian New Deal conferences and programs that brought Native

Americans together to affirm the value of Indianness and further the goals
of Native self-determination. Inspired by these conversations, by the in-
ternationalist rhetoric of World War II, and by their experiences at inter-
American conferences organized by John Collier, including a 1939 Canadian conference on North American Indians held in Toronto and the
1940 Pátzcuaro conference in Mexico, Native employees of the Bureau of
Indian Affairs began meeting to address the lack of a national American
Indian organization. Founding members of the NCAI included D'Arcy
McNickle, of Cree and French heritage, and an enrolled member of the
Flathead tribe; Archie Phinney (Nez Perce), whose experiences included
serving as a superintendent of the Northern Idaho Indian Agency and as
an instructor at the Leningrad Academy of Sciences in the Soviet Union;
and Charles Heacock (Lakota Sioux), who began working for the BIA in
1935.

NCAI founders took note of the failings of previous pan-tribal organizations, the Society of American Indians in particular; the American Indian
Federation, with its divisive and strident rhetoric, had never found wide
appeal in Native America. The SAI, which held its last convention in
1923, had failed to create a conversation between reservation and nonres-
ervation Indians, alienating a significant constituency of American Indians committed to maintaining their ancestral homelands. At the same
time, as Phinney put it, the NCAI would appeal to Native Americans
"who think beyond their reservation borders." NCAI founders also resolved to prohibit non-Indians from serving in the organization, after con-
sulting with Arthur C. Parker, an influential SAI founder; some Native
Americans had criticized the SAI and the AIF for allowing non-Indians to
set their respective agendas. And after initially considering linking the
NCAI to a branch of the BIA or to the Inter-American Indian Institute,
which emerged from the Pátzcuaro conference, the founders decided to
preserve the organization's independence to ensure Indian leadership and
to preclude charges of its serving BIA interests. Non-Indian BIA employees, including Collier, and members of the Association on American Indian Affairs, supported the NCAI's efforts to remain independent even as
they offered advice and funding to help the organization get off the ground.
The ambitious aim of the NCAI founders, then, was to develop an inclu-
sive all-Indian organization that would work to protect Indianness on and
off the reservation.[45]

3.3 Native Americans staged the inaugural meeting of the National Congress of American Indians in Denver in November 1944. This group of NCAI members graduated from the Carlisle Indian School, representing a paradox of the Indian boarding school system: rather than facilitating assimilation, it furthered pan-tribal political activism. Courtesy of National Archives and Records Administration, Pacific Alaska Region (Seattle).

Months before allied countries met in San Francisco to form the United Nations organization, representatives of united Indian nations met in Denver in November 1944 to discuss American Indians' postwar future. The preamble to the NCAI constitution stated the organization's mission: "to enlighten the public toward a better understanding of the Indian race; to preserve cultural values; to seek an equitable adjustment to tribal affairs; to secure and to preserve rights under Indian treaties with the United States; and to otherwise promote the common welfare of the American Indians." The convention delegates also emphasized concrete goals of securing voting rights for Native Americans in Arizona and New Mexico and promoting the establishment of a claims commission to provide compensation for treaty violations. In short, the NCAI pledged to mediate both the American dilemma and the worsening cold war between Indian nations and the U.S. government by retying the strands of the Gordian knot of nineteenth-century treaties.[46]

The sociological and ideological divisions in Native America, however, made the NCAI a tenuous alliance; it represented a constellation of Native politicians whose ideas were shaped by an integrationist (or terminationist) discourse which asserted the primacy of assimilation and an internationalist discourse which championed self-determination for colonial peoples. Ruth Muskrat Bronson (Cherokee), another NCAI cofounder, embodied the divided mind of the NCAI. Bronson reflected the biological and intellectual hybridity of most twentieth-century Native activists, including Charles Eastman, Arthur C. Parker, Laura Kellogg, and fellow NCAI founders, many of them educated in federal boarding schools and employed in those schools or federal bureaucracies such as the Bureau of Indian Affairs; Bronson was a graduate of Mount Holyoke College and a former teacher at the multitribal Haskell Institute in Kansas. After the first NCAI convention she posed several questions in a series of essays intended to explain American Indian life to young Methodists, fellow members of her church. In "What Does the Future Hold?" Bronson contended that Native Americans had been politicized by domestic and overseas experiences during the war and were now inclined to "participate in government of the people, by the people, for the people. Everywhere Indians are given opportunity to think through their own problems and act for themselves, there is a new spirit of courage, a dynamic new hopefulness." Native soldiers would return with "a new perspective" from seeing "how people all over the world do things . . . Many will come home demanding full status in American life. They have fought for America. Now they will want to be truly a part of America." As after World War I, it remained to be seen to what extent and in what ways Indians would now become "a part of America": Would it be complete incorporation by leaving the reservation, or acculturation to the practices of market capitalism on the reservation, embrace of the Christian values that shaped Bronson's perspectives, or traditional ceremonies tied to sacred homelands? Would Native Americans become "new Indians" in the Parker and Bronson mold or "old Indians adjusted to new conditions," as Kellogg had framed it in her systematic defense of the reservation in 1920?[47]

Even as she promoted an integrationist point of view, Bronson championed an internationalist one. In another section of the essay, subtitled "The Indian's Message for America," Bronson asserted the "significance" of America's "smallest racial minority" to race relations within the United States and with other countries. "If, when her [America's] time comes to help determine the destinies of other conquered people across the reaches of the world, the United States can be willing to apply the lessons she has learned from her handling of the one race she has conquered and kept within her boundaries, then the Indian may be an instrument in saving world civilization from total destruction." One of the lessons, Bronson concluded, at a time when terminationist sentiments were beginning to spill into public discourse, was that "even well-intentioned people have no right to settle the destinies of other people without their consent or cooperation." America would indeed assume a responsibility for determining the "destinies of other conquered peoples" around the world as World War II ended and the Cold War began. When it did, the future of America and of Native America would be linked. "All event is world event now," Collier had written in *The American Indian*.[48]

Native Americans, then, continued to believe in the significance of their past, both as history lesson for the future of America and as part of an ongoing decolonization narrative of restoring their treaty rights to protect their sacred ancestral homelands, newly imagined during a war fought on and for homelands all over the world. During the Cold War, Native American activists such as Bronson would offer important history lessons on the need to secure the "consent and cooperation" of minority peoples to help resolve the tension between American exceptionalism and the American dilemma that deepened after World War II and thus advance the promise of American life for which tens of thousands of Native Americans had fought, well beyond the borders of their "dear homes."

4 The Cold War on the Indian Frontier

So the question of what we do about our Indians, important as it used to be for the sake of justice, is enhanced in importance now because it is part of the fight which we and other democracies must wage, day in and day out, in perfecting our governmental household so that it will not be vulnerable to attack by the Communists.

—Eleanor Roosevelt, "To Arms, Indians! The Congressmen Are Coming!" October 5, 1949

In *The Air-Conditioned Nightmare*, published in 1945, the writer Henry Miller chronicled his travels through America during the war years, including urban "hell-holes" such as Pittsburgh and Manhattan. Pittsburgh, where he began his tour, was "the crucible where all values are reduced to slag." Miller imagined himself surveying the industrial nightmare of Pittsburgh's steel mills with an American Indian by his side: "I can almost hear him thinking, 'So it was for this that you deprived us of our birthright.'" Calling the reservation of the North Carolina Cherokee "a virtual paradise," he claimed that "the contrast between [the Indian] world and ours is almost unbelievable." Miller ended his 1947 book *Remember to Remember*, the sequel to *The Air-Conditioned Nightmare*, with a broad condemnation of American industrial progress: "To what end, to what end? Ask the Indian who sits and watches, who waits and prays for our destruction." It was an ironic statement, coming soon after the end of a war in which Native Americans gave their labor, their land, and their lives to defeat the forces of fascism and to earn access to the benefits of industrial life that many white Americans took for granted: electricity, running water, health care, education, and jobs. Miller, employing the trope of the ecological Indian to good effect, nevertheless missed several elements central to American Indian life in the twentieth century: the measured acculturation of Native Americans, their patriotism, and their belief that Indian values could help fashion a just international order.[1]

Yet at the root of Miller's critique, which used Native Americans as a foil for the nation's spiritual bankruptcy, was his salient notion that "the Indian" maintained a relationship with the land that encompassed more than the commodities it produced, in part because Native Americans felt rooted in a particular place, static as it was, according to Miller. For white Americans, however, "endless was the trek and endless the search. As in a mirage the bright nuggets of gold lay always beyond them." The American frontier beckoned yet again, Americans' restless capitalist energy fueling their search for more gold nuggets, in this case overseas in war-shattered Europe and Asia. Indeed the pressures and logic of the postwar period and of the Cold War pushed Americans west again as well as east, bringing with them Native Americans who both participated abroad as soldiers spreading democracy and freedom as part of the nation's newly defined mission and criticized federal officials at home for not recognizing their sacrifices made in the name of that mission.[2]

Native Americans' patriotic service continued into the Korean War and beyond, animating the efforts of Native politicians to gain access to the material and moral dimensions of nation building that underwrote Cold War struggles. After World War II, as they did after World War I, Native American leaders expected the United States to honor its commitment to its own people as it sought to extend freedoms and foreign aid to more distant peoples of the world. Native Americans prayed not for America's destruction but for its development of *their* ancestral homelands, marrying a material goal of progress, outlined in international Cold War aid programs such as the Marshall Plan, to the moral obligations of domestic treaties which promised them that progress. Native Americans' experiences negotiating Cold War pressures highlight links between U.S. domestic and international policies, open a window into the consciousness of American citizens wrestling with the implications of their country's new power, and reveal new intersections between the international Cold War and the domestic cold war.

The Contested Space of the Indian Reservation

Henry Miller had written in *Remember to Remember:* "Don't let any one think, especially South of the Mason-Dixon line, that the Four Freedoms means freedom for blacks and whites to intermarry! That belongs to the fifth or sixth freedom, and will probably demand another war." During the Cold War, African Americans continued to fight their war of the color line. Faced with another round of forced land allotment and relocation, Native Americans waged their own battles of the color line to maintain the cultural and political boundaries of the reservation. The rhetoric of World War II and of the Cold War complicated these battles over reservation space, the roots of which stretched to the late 1880s and the first great showdown over the reservation, deemed a "prison" by many reformers and politicians. World War II, as we have seen, produced a new description of the reservation: concentration camp. Miller employed this conception of Indian space in *The Air-Conditioned Nightmare*, presenting a narrative in which

> our forefathers came along and, seeking refuge from their oppressors, began by poisoning the Indians with alcohol and venereal disease, by raping their women and murdering their children. The wisdom of life which the Indians possessed they scorned and denigrated. When they had finally completed their work of conquest and extermination they herded the miserable remnants of a great race into concentration camps and proceeded to break what spirit was left in them.[3]

It is difficult to pinpoint the first use of the term "concentration camp" to describe a reservation, but it predated 1942, when U.S. officials, including President Franklin D. Roosevelt, called Japanese American detention centers "concentration camps." And it was used before knowledge of the Nazis' genocidal programs gave the term its most horrific connotation. An American politician compared a reservation to a concentration camp as early as March 1940, during a congressional hearing on a bill recommending "relief of needy Indians," when Representative John Schaefer of Wisconsin asked Blackfeet Nation politician Levi Burd whether the U.S. record on Indian affairs "more than parallels the atrocities and so-called concentration camps abroad." The historical record, Schaefer said, was that "the white man took the Indians' land, debauched their women, killed many of them, and herded the survivors in concentration camps which we now call Indian Reservations." Burd rejected the analogy because it painted Blackfeet as passive victims confined against their will, instead sounding a theme that emerged clearly in the postwar period: "If there are any people that are neglected, it is the Indians." To cite another example, in 1944 a congressional committee seeking to repeal the Indian Reorganization Act explained that the committee's goal was to "rehabilitate the Indians so they may be assimilated into the American way of life and not be in the reservation like a concentration camp; for, after all, a reservation is only a step or two from a concentration camp." The statement represented the reemergence of congressional critiques of the IRA, which served as the foundation of the termination movement of the late 1940s and 1950s. After World War II, during an era of Cold War conformity, critics of federal Indian policy used the term "concentration camp" or "socialistic environment" more openly to describe the reservation as either an oppressive or a subversive space from which Indians wanted to be freed and "assimilated into the American way of life."[4]

Even as Native Americans acted patriotically and heroically to defend both the United States and their hybrid conception of the American way of life, white commentators began calling for an end to federal Indian programs and to the reservation system. As after World War I, non-Indians viewed Native Americans' contributions during the war as testimony to their interest in leaving the reservation and joining the American "mainstream." Oswald Villard, a journalist who had turned against the New Deal, promoted this position in a 1944 *Christian Century* article, writing that Native Americans "no more wish to stay at home and be confined within the reservations than did the children of the early communist settlement." Villard saw one future: eventually "the Indians themselves will tire of being considered circus exhibits, human museum pieces seeking to keep alive vestiges of a life that was picturesque." The following year *Reader's Digest* published O. K. Armstrong's influential article "Set the American Indians Free!" Armstrong, a *Reader's Digest* editor and Missouri state legislator, echoed Villard in championing the liquidation of the Bureau of Indian Affairs, contending that the Indian New Deal forced "a collectivist system upon the Indians, with bigger doses of paternalism and regimentation," while reinforcing a policy of "racial segregation." Some Native Americans joined this attack on BIA paternalism. One Winnebago veteran told Armstrong, "When we Indian servicemen get back [from the war], we're going to see that our people are set free to live and act like American citizens." Perhaps he had read Villard's piece, as he noted to Armstrong, "We're tired of being treated like museum pieces."[5]

Villard's and Armstrong's attacks on the Indian New Deal were part of an increasingly public anti–New Deal movement intent on cutting the federal government's newly expanded bureaucracy, eliminating or restricting new welfare programs, and facilitating Americanization of the nation's diverse ethnic population. The termination agenda, promoted by private reformers such as Villard and Armstrong and crafted by federal officials and politicians, fused the nineteenth-century language of the allotment era with the new language of World War II and of the emerging Cold War: anticommunism, individualism, Americanism, emancipation, and liberation. The reservation became a touchstone of conflict between opposing conceptions of social space in Cold War America, embodying "the conflicts . . . which foster the explosion of abstract space and the production of a space that is *other*." In the discourse of the 1940s and 1950s, "reservation" became a code word for confining space, othered or racialized space, socialistic space, and even emasculated space. Despite the patriotism of Native Americans who had served the United States to defend both American and Indian homelands, the reservation remained, for these politicians and critics, *Indian* and therefore *un-American* space. Thus began a new stage in a long-running battle to deconstruct reservations as sites of ethnic difference and to complete the process of cutting America's legal Gordian knot of treaties.[6]

BIA officials negotiated the emerging ideology of termination that threatened the ideals of the Indian New Deal—cultural pluralism, Indian self-determination, and reservation development—with new leadership. John Collier had resigned in March 1945, exhausted from his World War II battles with an increasingly stingy and hostile Congress. The headquarters of the BIA had been relocated from Washington to Chicago during the war years and its funding cut, both moves halting the programmatic and ideational momentum of the Indian New Deal. Collier would maintain his focus on inter-American affairs even as he continued to monitor the terminationist legislation that threatened his administration's legacy. William Brophy assumed control of the BIA, with Collier's imprimatur. During the Indian New Deal years Brophy served as an attorney for the Pueblo, then during World War II he headed the Puerto Rican branch of the Interior Department's Division of Islands and Possessions. Although many Native American groups had promoted Native candidates for the commissioner position, Brophy quickly won support in many parts of Native America by touring numerous reservations, meeting with Native leaders, and studying conditions there.[7]

Brophy recognized both the dangers of the growing termination movement at home and its implications for the United States abroad. In a statement sent to the Association on American Indian Affairs in late 1945, Brophy outlined his program as the new commissioner of Indian affairs. Identifying the normalization of terminationist thinking, he attacked Armstrong's "Set the Indians Free," published earlier that year. "I believe everybody nailed the speciousness of the argument there set forth," wrote Brophy. "What [Armstrong] was promoting was a plea for a grab of Indian property." Native Americans and their non-Indian supporters presented this "argument" as the core of the termination agenda. The BIA, Brophy told the AAIA, had to fight to contain that agenda: "There must be mutual agreement, as I see it, between the parties, or there must be on the part of the United States so impeccable a record of right doing with respect to the Indian people that we can stand before the world and say that we have done our share, and more, and we can now wash our hands in public." Other BIA staffers also envisioned the expanded role the United States would play after the war and the important role of the BIA in ensuring that the U.S. image remained a clean one. John Evans, general superintendent of the United Pueblo Agency, told Brophy in April 1946:

> The world is confronted with the terrible urgency of bringing into full play every element of basic goodness and social awareness which humanity possesses if it is to keep pace with its own self-imposed but as yet, alas, unaccepted responsibilities. Our own nation, with its enormous responsibilities in the world scene becoming daily more clearly defined, if not yet clearly recognized, needs desperately to evaluate its potentialities in this field. Racing against time, these elements must be put to their fullest use in our own and in the world's best interests. The alternative may well be catastrophic.

Evans cited the Pueblo people's embodiment of that "basic goodness," calling the Pueblo "real American citizens."[8]

Brophy and Evans articulated three major themes of the postwar period in Indian-white relations: first, that white Americans intended to renew their assault on Native Americans' land base and, therefore, on Native

Americans' treaty rights, an assault begun anew during World War II; second, that such action would have consequences internationally as the United States assumed "enormous responsibilities in the world scene"; and third, that Native Americans could contribute to Americans' assumption of those responsibilities and help further the country's newfound mission abroad by holding U.S. leaders to the obligations owed to the nation's oldest minority and thus ensuring America's "record of right doing," as Brophy had put it. Three developments involving Native American treaty rights and civil rights soon put these themes into motion. The first was specific to Indian-white relations: the continuing legal crisis of land claims arising from the Gordian knot of national treaties signed in the nineteenth century. The second development was related to a new moral discourse of civil rights that emphasized the nation's obligation to improve its treatment of African Americans and Native Americans. Both domestic contexts intersected with the emerging international tensions that shaped the Cold War and found clear expression in a third development, a dramatic crisis in the Navajo Nation that captured the attention of all Americans, including Native Americans, and other peoples of the world trying to navigate the rocky contours of the postwar world.

Claiming Justice and Reputation

For decades American Indians as well as non-Indians had been calling for the creation of a formal government mechanism to resolve the hundreds of land claims that never made their way through the regular U.S. Court of Claims because of an 1863 statute barring Native Americans from filing such actions. As the number of treaty violations piled up in the late nineteenth century and beyond, Indian rights groups began to push for the creation of a separate Indian claims commission. The Society of American Indians had called for such a vehicle to adjudicate treaty violations. Collier's original IRA plan had proposed an Indian claims commission, but Congress rejected it. And at its founding convention in 1944, the National Congress of American Indians made the establishment of an independent Indian court of claims a priority. In the spring of 1945 a part-Choctaw congressman from Oklahoma, William Stigler, introduced a bill drafted by the NCAI calling for the creation of a commission to resolve outstanding American Indian claims. After debate in the House of Repre-

4.1 In Joe Rosenthal's iconic photo of the second flag raising on Iwo Jima on February 23, 1945, Ira Hayes is reaching for but not quite touching the flag, his position an unintended symbol of his inability to secure the rights represented by the flag. He could not vote when he returned to New Mexico. But his presence in the photo came to symbolize the success of ethnic integration. Courtesy of National Archives and Records Administration.

sentatives the bill, H.R. 4497, made its way through the Senate and then to the desk of President Harry S. Truman, who signed it in August 1946, bringing to life the Indian Claims Commission (ICC).[9]

American politicians had three principal motivations for supporting the ICC. The spirit of the bill had been endorsed in both the Democratic and Republican platforms since 1940. And in the wake of Native Americans' outstanding military service, personified in 1945 in the raising of the flag on Iwo Jima by Ira Hayes (Pima), an image publicized in subsequent tours of the flag raisers and emblazoned on War Bond posters, the bill earned bipartisan support in both houses of the 1946 Congress. The first reason for supporting the bill, therefore, was to grant Native Americans the same right as other Americans to have their day in court, which they had earned through this national service. Numerous Indian and non-Indian groups sent telegrams in favor of the bill. The Seminole of Oklahoma, for example, urged, "Indians feel justly entitled to this consideration and have won it by our war record if on no other ground." The second reason, representing the continuing battle over Indian reservations, reflected how this dynamic of equality animated the interest of congressional terminationists in resolving all treaty claims as part of a larger program to fulfill the nineteenth-century mission of ethnic and territorial incorporation of the American Indian. In defending termination, Senator Arthur Watkins, a Utah Republican, claimed that Congress had "deviated from its accustomed policy" of assimilation by passing the Indian Reorganization Act in 1934 but that it now "sought to return to the historic principles of much earlier decades," meaning the nineteenth-century "Civilization Program" that promoted allotment, Christianity, citizenship, and the attendant end of the reservation system, the original termination program. The third reason U.S. officials supported the ICC stemmed from America's new postwar role as global power. In his August 1946 letter to Truman supporting the ICC, Secretary of the Interior Julius Krug noted the "international repercussions," explaining to Truman: "The bill before you will be widely viewed as a touchstone of the sincerity of our national professions of fair and honorable dealings toward little nations. In abolishing a racial discrimination affecting resort to the courts, we will strengthen our moral position in the eyes of many other minority peoples." Krug warned Truman's budget director that it would be an "international and national disgrace" if Truman failed to sign the legislation. Commissioner of Indian Affairs William Brophy later made a similar point, applauding Truman for signing a bill that served as "a fine example of our will to do justice to all" and "re-emphasizes a fundamental premise which distinguishes our Government from the totalitarians. Permitting, as it does, independent judicial proceedings against the Sovereign, it protects the citizen against any inadvertent act of injustice by the Government."[10]

Truman considered the ICC bill in this domestic and international frame. Prodded by his secretary of the interior to use it to make a statement to the world, encouraged by bipartisan congressional support and by public support which included that of Native Americans, and assured by his budget director that it would not create a financial "Frankenstein,"

Truman signed the bill (Public Law 726) on August 13, 1946. In his statement announcing what he called a "final settlement" of Indian claims,
Truman addressed "men and women, here and abroad," who might have
misread the U.S. government's "fair and honorable dealings" and "respect
for all Indian property rights." In discussing what he called "the largest
real estate transaction in history," he acknowledged that the United States
had "made some mistakes and occasionally failed to live up to the precise
terms of our treaties and agreements with some 200 tribes." But, he said,
the signing of the bill marked "the beginning of a new era for our Indian
citizens. They have valiantly served in every battle front. They have
proved by their loyalty the wisdom of a national policy built upon fair
dealings and respect for the rights of little peoples." Native Americans
could now "share fully in the march of [America's] progress."[11]

The passage of the ICC had three broad effects. First, it emboldened
terminationists who believed that they were championing the second
"emancipation" of the American Indian, the first having come during the
allotment era, when reformers freed the American Indian from "the slavery of his old Communistic systems," to quote the Carlisle School's Henry
Pratt. Congressman Stigler, the ICC bill's cosponsor, told a friend that the
ICC "will go a long way in emancipating the American Indian and permitting him to take his place with the white brethren." The influential
terminationist Senator Arthur Watkins later summarized his "Indian freedom program," writing: "Following in the footsteps of the Emancipation
Proclamation of ninety-four years ago, I see the following words embel-
lished in letters of fire above the heads of the Indians—THESE PEOPLE
SHALL BE FREE." The rhetoric of the ICC debate helped spawn a number of
termination bills in the spring of 1947. For example, in April the House
Subcommittee on Indian Affairs held hearings on "emancipation bills"
sponsored by two prominent terminationists, Francis Case of South Dakota and Wesley D'Ewart of Montana. The advertised intent of the legislation was to free the American Indians—in particular the Indian war
veterans—from property restrictions imposed by federal trust status by
providing them with a "certificate of emancipation" and a patent in fee to
their land, which they could then sell or mortgage to raise capital. The
legislation was intended to revive the competency commissions inaugu-
rated by Commissioner of Indian Affairs Cato Sells in the 1910s. As Commissioner Brophy saw it in 1945, what congressional terminationists

sought to emancipate was trust land, not the Indian. Yet the lifting of property restrictions was not solely the domain of white politicians. Native Americans were hampered by their inability to secure mortgages or other forms of credit because the government held their land in trust. Many Native veterans returned to reservations which faced a declining pool of government credit or lacked adequate tribal revenue to allow for proprietary loans. But making fee patenting possible, and thus exposing landowners with little income to real estate taxes, was not a cure for economic ills if reservation development programs did not follow. And given the fraud and failures of previous emancipation campaigns, it was not unreasonable for critics to label such bills coercive and regressive. Assistant Commissioner of Indian Affairs William Zimmerman testified to the Subcommittee on Indian Affairs of the Committee on Public Lands that he was "troubled by the probable loss of Indian land which might result from the wholesale removal of restrictions." Such "emancipation" bills were unnecessary, he argued, and jeopardized the progress made by constitutionally empowered IRA governments.[12]

Joseph Brown, chairman of the Blackfeet Tribal Business Council of Montana, echoed Zimmerman in contending that the IRA had given the Blackfeet the tools they needed to adapt to modern conditions. Under the emancipation bill, he told the same committee, "you are emancipated whether you like it or not"; under the IRA, he maintained, Native American leaders "have a way to make citizens of them [the Indians]." For Brown and other Native Americans, the question of emancipation or termination was best left to American Indians themselves. Such protests against "emancipation bills" reflect a second important impact of the ICC debate—the ways in which it helped Native American politicians both understand emerging termination pressures and seek legal and political representation to contain them. The legal mandate of the ICC engendered new strategies to pursue specific claims related to the Gordian knot of treaties that lay like memory in Native activists' blood and to use those claims to expand their national sovereignty. Thus the ICC helped to facilitate Indian nationalism, which in turn exacerbated termination pressures.[13]

Third, the ICC debate embedded Native American issues firmly in an international context. During the Cold War, U.S. presidents and federal officials had to pay close attention to the way their resolution of domestic policies played internationally. The passage of the ICC bill sent a message to the world that the United States did in fact show "respect for the rights of little peoples," as Truman put in his statement announcing his signing. "Little peoples" at home and abroad could take note that the United States was acting in fidelity to its principles of fair play for all peoples at home, in effect promising those "little peoples" abroad that they too could share in the material and moral goods of America's "march of progress." The ICC debate was the opening act of the dramatic struggle to define a "new era" for Indians, but it was just one of a number of situations in which domestic racial issues overlapped with the new global implications of American leadership and was thus part of a larger national debate on the importance of resolving race relations to ensure a "new era" for all minorities in America and, by extension, in the world.[14]

"A Prejudice against Color"

Following on the heels of the ICC debate, in December 1946 Truman charged the President's Committee on Civil Rights with studying what Gunnar Myrdal had called the American dilemma—the disjunction between America's democratic ideals and its visible failure to uphold them. The American dilemma had taken on a new prominence because of the U.S. commitment to and hosting of the United Nations and because of rising postwar tensions between the United States and the Soviet Union. The committee's final report, "Civil Rights of American Indians," released in October 1947, argued that the nation's "civil rights record has growing international implications. These cannot safely be disregarded by the government at the national level which is responsible for our relations with the world . . . The subject of human rights, itself, has been made a major concern of the United Nations." In fact, in the U.S. government's battle for hearts and minds worldwide, America's "domestic civil rights shortcomings are a serious obstacle." The section of the report headed "The International Reason" charged: "Those with competing philosophies have stressed and are shamelessly distorting our shortcomings. They have not only tried to create hostility toward us among specific nations, races and religious groups. They have tried to prove our democracy an empty fraud, and our nation a consistent oppressor of underprivileged people." Indeed the Soviet Union and its satellites distributed a steady stream of criticism of American race relations from the 1940s into the 1980s, condemning the United States for denying equal rights to African Americans and Native Americans in particular. As historian Thomas Borstelmann has argued, "There was no greater weakness for the United States in waging the Cold War than inequality and discrimination." As federal officials had done during World War II, the committee pointed out that although the Native population of the United States was only half a million, there were 30 million Indians in South America, further highlighting the international significance of the issue.[15]

The report emphasized that American Indians faced "public prejudice and discrimination," especially in "areas surrounding reservations." It drew on the statements of Assistant Commissioner Zimmerman, who stated that in white communities bordering reservations nothing had changed in the thirty-five years he had been working to advance American Indians' rights. Native Americans were still called "bucks, squaws, and blankets" and "denied access to all but the most unsanitary and undesirable eating, lodging and restroom facilities." As a result, he contended, Jim Crow laws, especially in the American West, presented numerous obstacles to "Indian participation in American life and citizenship." D'Arcy McNickle, representing the National Congress of American Indians, the nation's largest Native American organization, also testified to the President's Committee that American Indians faced discrimination, documenting the denial of adequate housing, GI benefits, and voting rights in several states, as well as racial violence that white authorities routinely ignored. McNickle told committee members that although American Indians did not encounter discrimination "as bad as the Negroes" endured, they still had to contend with "a prejudice against color." But McNickle also addressed a "special" discrimination that Native Americans faced: terminationist attitudes that displayed a prejudice against different cultural orientations toward space. Denied access to the physical spaces of "American life and citizenship" because of white racism, whose virulence in western states mirrored that in the South, American Indians retreated to the welcoming space of the reservation. McNickle felt justified in condemning termination, he said,

because people constantly talk in Congress, and in the press, about freeing the Indians, emancipating Indians. In view of what I have said, the emancipation which is spoken of—it would mean emancipating the Indian away from this little property he has left, relieving

him of the last bit of wealth that he has. When people speak of abolishing reservations, they . . . mean that this piece of home land, that
last that the Indians have, would be destroyed and opened up for exploiters who would like a chance to get at Indian timber, Indian oil,
and so on.

In short, McNickle argued, "on reservations or off reservations," not only
were American Indians "subject to deprivation of civil rights," but also
termination threatened to deprive American Indians of their treaty
rights.[16]

McNickle echoed Brophy's and Zimmerman's contentions that termination amounted to just another land grab and that the federal government had abjured its obligations to facilitate self-government under the
IRA. As Joseph Brown had argued, the IRA made American Indians productive "citizens," but it did so without "abolishing reservations." Mc-
Nickle, a driving force in the NCAI in the 1940s, became in the 1950s the
leading Native voice for reservation development modeled after foreign
aid programs. In this way he connected contemporary civil rights for
American Indians to historical treaty rights in an international matrix
that emphasized the U.S. commitment to nation building and thus the
right of Indian people to live on and develop their pieces of "home land."

"The Plight of the Navajos"

NCAI officials such as McNickle worked assiduously in Congress, in the
press, and in Native communities to contain the spread of termination
ideology and thus to defend their identities and their homelands, both
American and Indian. They employed the rhetoric of World War II and
the Cold War in these campaigns. NCAI president Napoleon B. Johnson
(Cherokee) claimed the mantle of patriotism in protesting federal cuts in
Native American education and health programs after the war; following
the civil rights hearings, Johnson, an Oklahoma Supreme Court justice,
reminded members of Congress in October 1947 that "Indian people sent
more than 30,000 of their boys and girls to the Colors in World War II to
fight for our institutions and American way of life." Native Americans'
national service loomed large in postwar conversations about Indian-white
relations and became an important instrument in galvanizing opposition

to termination. Native Americans considered their collective sacrifices for the United States worthy of basic privileges, not the least of which were GI benefits and voting rights, denied in New Mexico, Arizona, Utah, and North Carolina.[17]

Native Americans outside the NCAI also championed civil rights and treaty obligations in various forums. In one important exposition of these views, Native activists weighed in on the question of postwar race relations during an August 1947 debate aired on radio. Representatives of Navajo and Pueblo groups pointed out that fairness was not present "so long as an Indian cannot vote for the government they must pay taxes to support and give their lives to defend." After the broadcast of "Are Indians Getting a Square Deal?" one Native activist asked, in a statement reprinted in the *Washington Post*: "Why do we propagate democracy abroad and suppress it at home? Why do we give millions in Europe while on an arid western desert in our own country 55,000 of our own people—though of different colored skins from those who conquered them—are slowly starving to death, because we have not kept faith with them?" Lilly Neil, the first woman elected to the Navajo tribal government, complained to a federal official a month later: "The government is making all these big loans to foreign countries, and bragging about what they are doing so fine and noble, for the countries who tried to ruin us . . . I doubt very much if there's a European or Asiatic country who are very much if any poorer than our own Navajo Indian tribe and none of them who need help any worse, and they owe their obligations to us North American Indians first." These statements, echoed by others across the United States, gave voice to a central critique made by Native Americans: rather than fulfill promises made to people who had shed blood for America and for the preservation of freedom around the world, the United States was instead bestowing on European nations, including former enemies, millions of dollars in relief funds and proposing to give billions more in the form of the European Recovery Program, or Marshall Plan, which was at the time under review by the U.S. Congress.[18]

Neil's comments also reflected a growing material crisis in Navajo communities reeling from a disastrous combination of drought and blizzards, a crisis that intersected in the Cold War context with rising anticommunism and the contentious debate on the Marshall Plan program. Unfolding in this ideologically charged environment—and while Truman's study of American civil rights circulated in the national press—the Navajo crisis illustrates clearly the ways in which the national battle over "the reservation" and other Native American issues merged with and mirrored the international battles of the Cold War. The Reverend James Douthitt from Arizona wrote a letter to Truman that echoed over one thousand similar letters and telegrams sent to the president in saying: "No problem you face is more urgent or more important than the plight of the Navajos. It is insignificant in scope compared to many other problems, but its implications are so far-reaching that our country cannot face the world in moral integrity while it continues to shamefully break a sacred treaty obligation with part of our own people."[19]

The Navajo Nation was the largest Indian nation in the United States in terms of territory and one of the largest in terms of population, second only to the Cherokee. During the 1930s the Navajo had a strained relationship with the Bureau of Indian Affairs after the BIA imposed strict grazing regulations that forced many Navajo to slaughter sheep in the name of protecting the reservation ecosystem along scientific principles of conservation. This mandated livestock reduction program produced great anger, directed at John Collier and his BIA employees, because sheep were central to the Navajo economy and culture. The bureau's failure to secure their consent led one Navajo to call the reduction program "something akin to the dictatorial systems of government across the sea." This anger led to the Navajo Nation's rejection of the Indian Reorganization Act in 1935, though it was a close vote of 8,197–7,679, in an election in which 98 percent of Navajo citizens voted. Despite this resentment the Navajo made significant contributions to the United States during World War II, sending more than 3,500 of their people to fight and nearly 15,000 to work in defense industries off the reservation. But most Navajo never forgave Collier for his mandatory sheep-killing program, and the experience engendered an activism that blossomed into Navajo nationalism after World War II and the passage of the ICC in 1946. The material crisis of 1947 resulted from this controversy of the 1930s, the return of veterans and defense workers to the reservation and the subsequent decline of wage income in the mid-1940s, and drought conditions not uncommon in the American Southwest combined with the unusually hard winter of 1947 that brought a series of blizzards to Navajo country. The winter of 1948 exacerbated the crisis; blizzards bringing three to five feet of snow carried what the BIA called "the Navajo Blizzard Emergency" into 1949.[20]

The crisis of Navajo suffering became publicized in various forums between 1947 and 1949, including an expanding national media network, mass circulation magazines such as *Life,* and reports published by the American Red Cross. News of the Navajo's plight generated a national response that had far-reaching consequences for the Navajo and implications for U.S. foreign policy. The responses of white Americans in general, Native Americans, and U.S. politicians made the Navajo Nation the site of an important Cold War drama, casting Native American issues more fully into a rapidly changing international context. By 1949 a newspaper description of the Navajo rescue missions as "a domestic Berlin airlift" brought this point home.[21]

The American people were primed to help the Navajo for several reasons. Federal officials, private Indian rights groups, and local and national media had championed the patriotic wartime service of Native Americans. In addition, the Navajo crisis was unfolding at the same time that Truman's Committee on Civil Rights released its provocative report highlighting the mistreatment of America's minority groups. As Laurent Frantz, a member of the committee, put it: "The Second World War made Americans far more conscious than they are ordinarily of the national ideals of democracy and fair play. The increasing instances of racial tension since the war have dramatized the contrast between the national ideal and the grim realities of the status of racial minorities, especially the Negro, in America." And because the Navajo crisis evolved as the debate over Marshall Plan aid was becoming increasingly public and contentious, many Americans also situated the crisis in an international frame, first by pointing to federal aid for needy Europeans to justify federal aid for needy Indian "citizens" such as the Navajo, and second by organizing Navajo charity drives modeled after European Freedom Trains. A February 1948 *Collier's* article quantified the crisis in international terms: "The United States is seeing that an average German gets 1,500 calories a day, and average Japanese 1,300. The average Navajo gets just over 1,000."[22]

American newspapers provided provocative news coverage of the Navajo relief efforts. A November 1947 *Los Angeles Examiner* article, part of a series called "The Citizens America Forgot," stated that "while the United States is sending billions for the relief of stricken Europe, Navajo Indians face slow starvation in the vast 'concentration camp' of the desert." The *Examiner* article cut both ways, however, painting the Navajo as passive victims confined against their will while capturing a difficult truth about their material conditions. The *Examiner* series used the trope and the trauma of Native American poverty to criticize not just the European focus of the Marshall Plan but the Marshall Plan itself. But the articles, detailed in their coverage of Navajo privations and reprinted in various newspapers and magazines across the country, helped to generate widespread support for federal aid to the Navajo in the form of letters and telegrams to Truman and other public officials. Some of the letters sent to the president made reference to the *Examiner* series, which included articles with titles such as "Navajos Starving in Barren Areas" and photos of Navajo veterans "in silent tribute" at the "War Memorial Cemetery," in which lay "Navajos who were returned to their arid native soil after they shouldered the full responsibilities of American citizens."[23]

Americans actually began sending letters about Navajo conditions before news of the winter crisis spread. In April 1947 Mrs. LaFell Dickinson, president of the General Federation of Women's Clubs, asked President Truman and the BIA to help American Indians, arguing, "I do not see how we can hold up our heads in the United Nations if conditions among these minority groups of original Americans are as bad as pictured to me." Dickinson included a Flagstaff Women's Club resolution that read, "WHEREAS, the American people do not at any time condone the violation or the ignoring of treaties," the Flagstaff Women's Club "does hereby condemn the failure of our national government to observe its obligation" under the Navajo treaty of 1868. The letters poured into the White House mailroom after the winter crisis deepened. The Inman family of California told Truman, "We are horrified and ashamed to learn that such an injustice is being inflicted upon any citizen of the U.S.A. U.S. has just sent an enormous amount of food and money overseas to the starving people there—which we were so happy to do, but now surely we must do as much for our own citizens in the same kind of distress." S. J. Little, Jr. of California was less deferential: "I have been reading and hearing propaganda of the help we as Americans will have to give to the needy people of the world, while we are constantly surrounded by poverty, and greed in our own great country." Expressing hostility to the very idea of extensive foreign aid, Little added, "I am sure we will all be better off, if more head lines of your statements appeared over our country, about bettering America, instead of trying to appease all the foreign nations." Bob Engler of New York City wrote Truman after the *New York Journal American* republished part of the *Los Ange-*

les Examiner series, asking: "Don't you agree that assistance should go to the Navajo Indians even before Europeans? The Indians, after all, were the first Americans." Similar letters came from Missouri, Michigan, Maryland, Illinois, Pennsylvania, Washington, D.C., and throughout the country, from men, women, and children, including one sent to "Mr. Trueman" from seven-year-old Patricia Moffitt of Shelby, North Carolina. Clearly the American Indian problem was, like "the Negro Problem," according to Gunnar Myrdal, "a problem in the heart of the American," young and old.[24]

A number of letter writers supported sending money to Europe but thought that Navajos and Europeans should be treated equally in the foreign aid calculus. Fredericka Mett, a fifth-grader from Milwaukee, told President Truman that she and her classmates "do not feel that you, the government, should *not* help Europe. We think you should help the Navajos and Europe at the same time." Jeannette Jewell of Washington, D.C., wrote Truman after visiting a New Mexico Indian reservation: "I am in accord with all the help which we are sending to Europe and the Far East but does not 'Charity *begin* at Home'?" In Davenport, Iowa, Mrs. S. L. Shain implored Truman to provide Navajo aid: "I feel very deeply the distress of the people of Europe and have done and will do all I can to help them. But I also am sorely distressed over the condition of the Indians of the Southwest. That is a very dark blot on the name of our fair Country." Mrs. J. M. Acosta of California saw the issue of Europeans' getting aid before Native Americans in dark terms, angrily asking Truman: "Why do [Europeans] have to have all of those billions of dollars? It is because they are white and the Indians dark? Black people feel as deeply as any humans. 'If' you can call some white people human! Yes you guessed it I'm plenty dark."[25]

The letters did not make explicit reference to the "Cold War"; the term, first used in a postwar context by George Orwell in 1945, did not gain currency until late 1947 or early 1948, in part the result of journalist Walter Lippman's attacks on the U.S. containment policy. Nor, with few exceptions, did the letters mention the Soviet Union. In one letter that did bring together these key themes, the Reverend Lillian Frey made reference to news accounts of "shipments to Russia" and asked Truman: "How is it possible for you to permit these shipments to Russia, while we have starving natives in our own land? . . . I appeal to you as a Christian to personally see to it, that our moral obligations for the physical and educational welfare of the American Indians is fully discharged." It was still early for many Americans, tired of war, to imagine the world engaged in a new one and the United States at the center of it. Yet some writers saw the big picture. Antonia Wiegand of St. Louis conflated Americans and European fascists in telling Truman that "the Navajos have been treated almost as badly, cumulatively by the white people, as the conquered people of Europe by our enemies during the war." Wiegand expressed clearly the crisis of the American dilemma in saying that she and her fellow St. Louisans "doubt whether this nation's ideals are being carried out on the home front." Her use of the term "home front" may have been a carryover of World War II rhetoric, but given that she was writing over two years after the war ended, it points to the fact that some U.S. citizens recognized that their country was involved in a new kind of struggle in which both American ideals and practices mattered, an international war of public relations in which Navajo poverty would weaken the nation's influence unless Truman acted to ameliorate it. Vera Jeanne Walker of Los Angeles put forward this argument in her December 1947 letter to Truman, writing that "if the Americans are to be the next world leaders," they "had better begin now to treat the Indians as citizens. For this black mark can ruin [America] in the teachings of democracy. People of other countries will see the treatment we give our own people, and they will wonder if they should live by our democratic principles." Conscious of America's growing imperial presence in the world and the associated risks, Walker noted, "Spain, Greece, and Rome through mistreatment of a certain class of people lost their power, and we are no better than [them] with the Navajo problem." In closing she expressed a theme of many other letter writers, saying of the Indians, "For I believe they are more American than we." Praising Native Americans' hybrid patriotism, these citizens understood that if the United States could not honor treaty obligations with people they considered "true Americans" and "American citizens," then people around the world would expect the United States to treat non-Americans in an "un-American" way.[26]

Truman's predecessor, Franklin D. Roosevelt, had encouraged Americans to communicate with him by sending letters addressing their concerns to the White House. Americans young and old, male and female, Indian and non-Indian, religious and nonreligious, in large cities and small towns from coast to coast and in between continued to communicate their outrage and embarrassment over the Navajo situation and to air their concerns about a new foreign policy that situated America firmly as the world's leading humanitarian nation. The letters to Truman articulated two main themes. First, their authors argued that Native Americans had sacrificed to help save Europe during World War II and thus deserved the same aid as Europeans, some of whom, especially Germans and Russians, did not deserve that aid. Many of the letters described the Navajo specifically and Native Americans generally as "original Americans," "first Americans," "forgotten Americans," "American citizens," "100 percent Americans," and "true Americans." As Joan Hall noted to Truman, because "the Indians fought for America along with other Americans . . . they should be treated like Americans." Hall was therefore writing to protest the "un-American way they are being treated." Second, the letters illustrate Americans' understanding of what was at stake in the new phenomenon of postwar U.S. leadership, connecting the international material context of American aid programs with the domestic moral context of government treaty obligations to Native peoples. The letters thus reveal the ways in which Americans imagined themselves as part of a global power that could reshape the world as it reshaped the cultural space of the Navajo reservation with its honorable and compassionate commitment. Valorizing American Indians as "true Americans" contributed to the construction of a new national identity of Americans as cosmopolitan citizens as they traversed the intellectual, racial, and physical boundaries of the postwar global frontier.[27]

Truman's recognition of the significance of the American dilemma, reinforced by the views of senior administration officials and by protests from American citizens, as well as those of Navajo citizens, led him to act on behalf of the Navajo, another example of his own conflation of domestic and foreign policy. Moving to head off criticism of the Marshall Plan, still under review in Congress, the administration asked legislators to provide $500,000 in emergency relief to the Navajo and to the Hopi, a separate Native community whose land lay within the boundaries of the vast Navajo reservation. Addressing politicians and the public, whose letters continued to flow into his office as the Navajo crisis deepened, Truman issued a statement on December 2, 1947, announcing both the short-term relief and his intention to pass a long-term rehabilitation program through which the federal government would "meet the obligation of our democracy to this group of our citizens." He hoped that such aid "forecloses those who would criticize [his] foreign aid program on the ground that we are letting our First Americans starve." Significantly, the House of Representatives fashioned this emergency relief bill in the middle of a debate on foreign aid, embedding the question of the Navajo and Hopi in the larger context of international assistance programs. And it is also important to note that Truman and the Congress responded to the Navajo crisis less than one month after the release of the President's Committee on Civil Rights report, which highlighted both the "moral" and the "international" reasons for addressing U.S. treatment of "underprivileged people."[28]

Roadblocks to Relief

Complicating the Navajos' material crisis, a political crisis arose in the spring of 1948 when the Navajo Council, the Navajo Nation's government, acted on Interior Department consultant Max Drefkoff's recommendations that it fund reservation development by taxing religious missions, levying fees against the white traders who controlled much of the commerce inside reservation boundaries, and instituting price controls. Dretkoff's plan, which he devised after witnessing the Navajo's well-publicized poverty, was supported by Interior Secretary Krug, who also felt impelled to ameliorate the Navajo's distressing conditions, and by the Navajo Nation's attorney Norman Littell, whom the Navajo hired after the passage of the ICC in 1946. Used to getting their way for decades, the white traders protested to any newspaper or politician that would listen. And they played the trump card of anticommunism, which by 1948 was a useful card to play. A trader, William Lippincott, led the charge by telling a joint Senate-House Indian affairs subcommittee that the Navajo Council's resolution would "discourage and eliminate further private enterprise of any sort on the reservation."[29]

The *Los Angeles Times*, perhaps noting the success the rival *Los Angeles Examiner* had in selling stories about Native Americans, published a six-part series on the trader controversy, explaining to its readers that it had sent a team of reporters to the Navajo Nation after it was "informed that an attempt was being made to 'sovietize' the Navajo tribesmen . . . and thus fasten the first Moscow-type control on a vast area in the United States." The articles never failed to remind readers that Max Drefkoff was

"Russian-born" (he was born in Poland, actually) and contended that he had pressured the Navajo Council to pass the resolutions in the name of setting up a Soviet-style "cooperative-state"; it did not help that Drefkoff had once lived in Moscow, Idaho. The *Los Angeles Times* series also defended the traders' magnanimity while claiming that the Navajo enjoyed "relatively great prosperity"; the caption on one picture of a Navajo dwelling read, "This house is elegant, for among its other features it can boast a window." In addition, the *Times* argued that the accounts of "starvation" that led to federal aid had been fabricated as part of the plan to convert the Navajo reservation "into a little Siberia," as one local non-Navajo man put it. The *Times* series employed all the right terms, charging "extermination" of "free trade" and "private enterprise," and "socialism" or "collectivism" or "share-the-wealth" schemes that would "cripple the industrious and well-to-do." John Collier had assured Native American leaders in 1934 that "white people all over the United States own land in partnerships and companies and corporations. It is not communism to allow Indians to do the same if they want to," encouraging them to "assert their rights" in protecting resources from "local interests" who would cry "communism." But by 1948 it was easier to accuse someone of communist-type activity, especially someone with a name such as Max Dretkoff, than it was to defend a "cooperative" activity that was, as a Dretkoff defender put it, "a well-established part of our democracy." With Cold War tensions more mature in 1948 than in 1934, such anticommunist rhetoric now carried the weight of a cudgel.[30]

In the end the BIA nixed the Navajo Council's revenue program on the basis of a decision by Interior Department solicitor Mastin White, who ruled that the council had encroached on the BIA's authority. A compromise plan left traders and Navajo leaders equally unhappy. Despite the fact that some Navajo, likely encouraged by the traders to whom they owed money, opposed the council's decision to regulate businesses operating on its territory, the resolution of the case politicized Navajo leaders, who saw their failed attempt to gain some measure of control over an integral economic component of reservation life as another example of BIA intervention, a 1940s version of the BIA sheep-killing edict of the 1930s.[31]

The rhetorical battle waged by the Navajo traders and their off-reservation champions made the Navajo Nation an even more significant site of Cold War concerns. What if Soviet agents tried to infiltrate poverty-stricken reservations, as the Nazis had? These fears played out as they had during World War II, with communists replacing Nazis as the possible subversive interlopers on Native American soil. A senior BIA official sent the new commissioner of Indian affairs, John Nichols, a July 1949 article titled "A Program to Rescue the American Indian," written by the chairman of the Arizona Communist Party and printed in its organ, *Our Times*. The article stated, "We Communists believe the real long-range program . . . can only come when the Indian people, together with the great mass of workers, small farmers and professionals, will have established socialism common ownership [sic] of all the great resources for the benefit of the vast majority." Nichols responded to the BIA official that the article provided "very good evidence for more generous support of rehabilitation bills for the Indians in Arizona and elsewhere" because it was significant "that the Communists in America, as well as those at the United Nations, are pointing to the plight of the Indians as an example of the failure of capitalism."[32]

Citing anticommunist concerns proved functional for both proponents and opponents of rehabilitation bills. Some politicians found cause to link the very nature of tribal governments to socialism or to Soviet communism, resuscitating the nineteenth-century rhetoric of the reservation as un-American space. In its Navajo series the *Los Angeles Times* reported that Senator Harlan J. Bushfield, a South Dakota Republican, had claimed "he had reports [that] Communists are trying to win over Indians on South Dakota reservations," citing as his evidence a Sioux protest "charging white merchants with price-gouging." Representative E. Y. Berry, another South Dakota Republican and a vocal terminationist, used anticommunist rhetoric in attacking the Indian Reorganization Act, claiming that it "Communizes the Indian Reservations just as completely and just as fairly and just as ungodly as Communist Russia can hope to do." Senator George Malone, Republican of Nevada, broadened the scope of that charge, complaining that the United States was "spending billions of dollars fighting Communism" while it was "perpetuating the systems of Indian reservations and tribal governments, which are natural Socialistic environments." During the 1880s, white reformers had exploited anticommunist concerns to further the socialistic allotment agenda of state-mandated land and wealth redistribution that violated the sacred covenant of the contract known as the treaty. Like them, terminationists of the 1940s and 1950s promoted similarly radical land expropriation schemes using the trope of the socialistic or communistic Indian: American Indians were either already communists because of their tribal loyalties or potential dupes for communist agents who could persuade them to practice the apparently un-American act of protesting high prices.[33]

The trader controversy and the anticommunist rhetoric that sustained it blew into public view just days after Secretary Krug released his recommendation that Congress fund a $90 million long-range Navajo rehabilitation program designed to improve reservation roads, employment opportunities, educational facilities, and public health services. Krug's recommendation came at a difficult moment of growing political pressures, pinning members of Congress between two positions. On the one hand, Congress sought to restrain through termination policies the expansion of federal aid to American Indians as part of its broader imperative to terminate federal programs smelling of welfare statism. On the other, by not acting, Congress would produce a vacuum of moral authority, into which foreign criticism and perhaps foreign agents would pour. The implications of doing nothing were more powerful than those of doing something, the fear of anti-American attacks more compelling than the shrill anticommunist attacks of Malone and Bushfield. Krug made this point clear in his April 1949 testimony to Congress, in which he outlined the bill's "broad significance." He favored the proposed Navajo-Hopi Rehabilitation Bill because it helped the Navajo and Hopi but also because "the plight of the Navajos has been used by the anti-American foreign press in an effort to derogate the treatment received by minority groups in the United States. The approval by the Congress of a comprehensive program for improving the Navajo situation would consequently strengthen this Nation's international prestige and moral position." Such a powerful argument, which joined the other arguments for Navajo aid previously outlined, led the Senate to pass the bill in the form of S. 1407, which allocated funding of over $88 million.[34]

During and after the war Native Americans extended whatever aid they could muster to help people overseas. Inspired by their veterans' stories of suffering in Europe and Asia, leaders of nine Pueblo communities offered to donate part of their store of grain and corn in a letter to Fiorello La-Guardia, director general of the UN Relief and Rehabilitation Administration, explaining that "peoples and children over there got emergency.

Our peoples proud of their sons and so glad they back home again to forget
the war and live the right way for peace. Pretty hard for peoples and children to forget the war and live the right way for peace with empty bellies."
The Navajo emergency soon shifted Native Americans' focus to their own
homelands. The situation dominated the 1947 annual convention of the
National Congress of American Indians, leading delegates to pass a resolution that stated, "We find conditions among our Aboriginal Americans for
whom the United States Government is by treaty bound to protect and
care for, not only deplorable, but a disgrace to the greatest and most humanitarian nation in the world today." Responding to the publicity about
Navajo poverty by framing the United States as the "most humanitarian"
of nations, Native Americans themselves made significant contributions
to the Navajo, reflecting their growing pan-tribal consciousness. Perhaps
the most notable contribution came from Will Rogers Jr., the son of the
famous performer, who had also supported American Indian rights on the
basis of his part-Cherokee heritage. During World War II the younger
Rogers had served with General George Patton at the Battle of the Bulge,
earning a Purple Heart and Bronze Star. After the war Rogers organized
charity drives for the Navajo as president of the American Indian Citizens
League of California. NCAI president N. B. Johnson wrote Rogers in January 1948 to thank him for his help, complaining that the United States
had "spent more than twenty-four billion dollars since V-J day to aid the
destitute and starving people of Europe, and the President is asking for billions more, yet, in our own country we find this deplorable condition existing among our first Americans."[35]

Moved by governmental indifference to Native Americans' broader
economic and social problems and motivated by his own patriotic service,
Rogers assumed an active role in the NCAI. In a stirring speech at the
1948 NCAI Annual Convention, Rogers demanded an end to "racial discrimination" and promoted the Navajo Rehabilitation Bill. He argued
that the BIA "should be an active champion and not a passive guardian of
Indian rights. Most important of all, there should be Indian participation
and agreement at every step of the policy and program." Rogers punctu-
ated his speech with a statement that elicited applause from the audience:
"Today the world looks to America—and, American relations with her
Indians, once a purely domestic matter, is now an international matter. If
we treat our Indians with dignity and honor and fairness, we can answer
every charge thrown at us by communistic, totalitarian Russia." His pas-

sionate and patriotic assertion of Native American rights as a matter of
national security helped lead to his election to the NCAI Executive Committee and his (unsuccessful) nomination for the position of commissioner
of Indian affairs in 1949. The speech and the NCAI's attention to broader
developments in U.S. foreign aid provide additional evidence of Native
Americans' internationalist perspective, as the Navajo crisis engendered
new ways of reimagining Native American space in a Cold War context.
Here too, Rogers's wartime service shaped his argument that Native
Americans deserved the right of "participation and agreement," as he
added his voice to those promoting the need for the United States to demonstrate democratic behavior to distinguish itself from its totalitarian ad-
versaries.[36]

Driven in part by Cold War concerns, Native Americans, white politicians, and reformers represented a consensus that the Navajo deserved
federal aid. But the passage of the Navajo-Hopi bill became complicated
by the other powerful force of the postwar era: termination. The U.S.
House of Representatives submitted its version of the bill with a contro-
versial rider attached, the so-called Section 9 rider, promoted by Antonio
M. Fernandez of New Mexico. The rider proposed extending New Mexico's jurisdiction over the Navajo and Hopi reservations, a clear infringe-
ment of the federal prerogative to manage Indian affairs and an obvious
effort to advance a terminationist agenda of limiting rather than expanding Indians' national sovereignty. Truman, eager to complete the Navajo
legislation as he set his sights on similar but broader goals in the Point
Four foreign aid program announced months earlier in his January 1949
inaugural address, delayed signing the bill to evaluate this new controversy, into which waded prominent American Indian rights supporters as
well as Americans across the country.

Eleanor Roosevelt, who championed American Indian causes in her
weekly newspaper column "My Day," publicized the inequities of Section
9 in an October 1949 article titled "To Arms, Indians!" Roosevelt connected the Navajo controversy to a proliferation of Soviet propaganda:
"One of the Soviet attacks on the democracies, particularly in the United
States, centers on racial policies," she claimed:

> In recent months the Russians have been particularly watching our
> attitude toward native Indians of our country. So the question of
> what we do about our Indians, important as it used to be for the sake

of justice, is enhanced in importance now because it is part of the
fight which we and other democracies must wage, day in and day out
in perfecting our governmental household so that it will not be vulnerable to attack by the Communists.

Calling on Truman to veto the bill, Roosevelt compared the Section 9
"plot" to the Bursum Bill controversy that raged in Pueblo country in
1922–23. In a long telegram former commissioner of Indian affairs John
Collier, now representing the Institute of Ethnic Affairs, told Truman that
the world would judge how he responded to Section 9: "Your veto of this
wicked bill will serve notice to Congress and the world that our national
commitment and honor are not going to be betrayed." National newspapers, attuned to the Navajo story, publicized the controversy. The *New
York Times* opined that the United States had proclaimed its foreign policy
campaign "to be just to minorities the world over. We should begin by being just to those in our own door-yard."[37]

Alerted by such articles and by Indian rights groups such as the National Congress of American Indians and the Association on American
Indian Affairs, Americans from across the country responded with a flood
of letters imploring President Truman to veto the bill because of the Section 9 rider. A group of eighteen teachers and administrators from Mus-
kegon, Michigan, protested, as did Fredericka Martin, who called Section
9 "a most nefarious means of destroying our treaty obligations to these
sorely neglected Americans." Sherwood Moran reminded Truman of his
commitment to civil rights generally, linking that commitment to treaty
stipulations that prohibited state control of Indian affairs. Other letters
expressed more clearly than previous ones the functional nature of giving
American Indians a "fair deal." Sophia Mumford, Lewis Mumford's wife,
told Truman that "the practice of democracy is the best answer to subversive ideologies" and that Section 9 would "nullify the importance of the
bill." Charles Haskell was more explicit in his protest of Section 9, ad-
monishing Truman to resolve the American dilemma because "improvement of our treatment of racial minorities is crucial in [the] struggle with
Cominform both here and abroad." Wilda MacKenzie of Rhode Island
wrote to protest the "Jim Crow" rider, reminding Truman that "there are
about 30 million Indians in the Americas—With us they are a minority
dependent nation—or nations—Our treatment of the Indian—respect for

his sovereignty—his way of life—his religion—affects our international goodwill—with all small nations and groups." MacKenzie's reference to "30 million Indians" may have stemmed from her reading of the President's Committee on Civil Rights report, which had noted the importance of America's treatment of its indigenous people in terms of hemispheric security. Citing the broader context of civil rights, which Truman's administration had championed in late 1947, and the specific context of Indian treaty rights, which required U.S. officials to deal honorably with "small nations and groups" such as the Navajo, these letters reveal Americans uneasily stepping into the new international sphere, unsure of their country's readiness to assume such an important role abroad while still trying to resolve its racial tensions at home.[38]

A Columbia University anthropologist made a different argument to Truman, contending that a Navajo-Hopi rehabilitation bill with Section 9 attached to it would destroy the "home rule responsibility" of the Navajo and "duplicate tragic results familiar to anthropologists in India and Africa," suggesting that if Truman allowed this bill to move forward, then he would be promoting European-style colonialism, a condition which the United States found itself mediating through new Cold War programs such as Point Four. Whether Truman read this particular telegram or any others is hard to determine. The public response to the Navajo crisis was nevertheless clearly visible to federal officials. Interior Secretary Krug had reported to Truman the "numerous references to the Navajo situation in the press and on the radio, as well as a large volume of mail from members of the public urging that all possible aid be given to the Indians." Editorials calling on the president to veto the bill appeared in prominent newspapers such as the *New York Times,* the *Christian Science Monitor,* the *Washington Post,* and the *Baltimore Sun.* Truman evaluated the Section 9 controversy in a Cold War frame, understanding that the boundaries between domestic affairs and international affairs had been, for the most part, erased. Even if he did not read the telegram likening Section 9 to colonialism, he knew that others around the world would make that connection. Thus a hastily added and coercive rider to a broad economic development program was jeopardizing the potential public relations bonanza of both his Point Four program and the Navajo-Hopi Bill, two related agendas that could serve to solidify America's moral standing in the contested space of the developing world.[39]

That the Navajo themselves condemned Section 9 added to the impetus for vetoing the bill. In addition, the U.S. attorney general's office found
Section 9 a "departure" from previous policy asserting federal control of
Indian affairs. In his veto letter to the U.S. Senate, Truman therefore contended that "Section 9 is heavily weighted with possibilities of grave in-
jury to the very people who are intended to be the beneficiaries of the bill"
and contained "serious threats to the basic rights of these Indians"; it
would extend state laws to the two reservations and thus conflict with
"one of the fundamental principles of Indian law accepted by our Nation,
namely, the principle of respect for tribal self-determination in matters of
local government." The bill with Section 9 attached had its supporters,
which included various Chamber of Commerce officials, white traders,
and white editors of local New Mexico newspapers, as well as Senator
Barry Goldwater of Arizona, who argued that it was unwise to reject a bill
merely because of a "provision that we are going to have to have eventually anyway." Unwilling, however, to contest not only Truman but also an
attentive American public that backed his support of Navajo relief, Congress went back to work to revise the bill. On April 1, 1950, Congress rejected Section 9 and passed the Navajo-Hopi Long Range Rehabilitation
Act (Public Law 81–174), which President Truman found acceptable. The
act, which allocated $89,946,240 in development aid for infrastructure
projects on the Navajo and Hopi reservations, represented the financial
and rhetorical equivalent of a domestic Point Four program for the underdeveloped Navajo and Hopi nations.[40]

Point Four and American Indians

Truman first announced the idea of the Point Four (or Point IV) program
in his January 1949 inaugural speech. In the fourth point of the foreign
policy section of his address he pledged America's commitment to "making the benefits of our scientific advances and industrial progress available
for the improvement and growth of underdeveloped areas," in particular
those in Asia and Africa, emerging Cold War battlegrounds. The program
combined humanitarian impulses, global economic imperatives, and national security objectives. And it linked civil rights at home and human
rights abroad. A State Department official emphasized this connection in
early 1950, arguing that the Point Four program "seeks at home to widen

and deepen its own conceptions of civil rights and duties, as the argument that speaks the loudest abroad."[41]

The theoretical and programmatic roots of Point Four had emerged during World War II. According to Secretary of State Dean Acheson, "the inspiration and the proving ground" for the program was the Institute of Inter-American Affairs, which managed technical assistance and diplomatic initiatives in Latin America during the war; Nelson Rockefeller, who launched the IIAA, became the Point Four program's chief administrator. A model for a Point Four–type program also emerged during the war from the Institute of Ethnic Democracy, which comprised officials from the Bureau of Indian Affairs, the Department of the Interior, the Office of War Information, and the Institute of Inter-American Affairs as well as anthropologists from Harvard University and the University of Chicago. Originally called the Society for Total and Local Democracy, the group worked to "shape policies and [educate] American administrators and other specialists who might go to [nonindustrialized] areas" to resolve postwar racial tensions. Emphasizing the perceived value of having the democratic character of the American Indian serve as a basis for such policies, the group intended to study colonialism in an effort to ameliorate the "extreme danger that after the war [the United States] shall attempt to play God with the world ruthlessly." John Collier in particular expounded on this idea in various forums, writing in 1943, "Our Indians today are furnishing a laboratory and a demonstration ground in behalf of the world's reorganization ahead." The U.S. Congress failed to support such enterprises and their cross-border interactions during the war, the result of philosophical differences with Collier and Interior Secretary Harold Ickes as well as its general hostility to the internationalization of the New Deal. When Cold War pressures expanded, however, Congress grudgingly approved massive funding for the Marshall Plan and then for Point Four.[42]

The Marshall Plan benefited from the Navajo crisis, even if only in a small way, because it helped to disarm critics of Truman's proposed budget for the program; and Point Four was shaped by the discourse and the details of the Navajo crisis, which served as a kind of preview of the rehabilitation of "under-developed areas." Private reformers and state politicians drew explicit connections between Point Four and Navajo aid programs. Congratulating him for vetoing the Section 9–tainted Navajo-Hopi bill, Collier told Truman: "At this time in the world, the Navajo-Hopi bill was no big issue, viewed in one way. Viewed in the light of your Point 4 and Civil Liberties programmes, it was an issue of world-wide significance." Edwin Mechem, the governor of Arizona, made a similar connection in a September 1951 letter to Truman in which he argued that the Navajo's poor health, education, and economic situation made "Navajo country" suitable as "an area to be supplemented by Federal funds, under the Point Four Program, designed to assist the unfortunate peoples and the undeveloped areas throughout the world." It would, he felt, "seem strange indeed should an ethnic group comprising America's first citizens fail to qualify, when at the same time this assistance is being received by peoples of practically all parts of the globe." In his opinion, "participation in the Point Four Program is necessary for the Navajo." What was "strange indeed" was that the governor of Arizona should request such assistance when the Navajo had been granted just that in the form of the Navajo-Hopi Rehabilitation Bill. In composing a response for the president, a member of Truman's staff advised calling to Mechem's attention "something he does not seem to know—that we have what amounts to a Point Four Program already in operation for the Navajos." Truman's letter to Mechem makes this point: "It would appear to me that your reference to the Point Four Program does not apply so far as our domestic problems are concerned. The legislative means to do what is needed for the Navajo Indians is already at hand." Mechem's letter is interesting for his apparent lack of understanding of a bill that had implications for Navajo living in his state and that had been at the center of local and state controversies for several years. More interesting, he also spoke of the idea of improving Navajo conditions not for its own value alone but to break down what he called "an important integration barrier," a comment that reveals a central dynamic of Cold War nation-building programs abroad and a portent of changes to come in Indian-white relations at home.[43]

As the debate over the Rehabilitation Bill intensified, BIA officials promoted this connection between BIA activities at home and Point Four programs abroad. In a memo to Philleo Nash, special assistant to President Truman, a BIA official (probably Assistant Commissioner of Indian Affairs John Provinse) recommended a bold agenda consisting of three points that reflected the international and domestic implications of the Navajo Nation relief program: first, the agenda recognized that "reservations are a depressed area according to the President's Point 4"; second, it urged that a secretary for minority affairs should "inform the President on the Indian problem," thus identifying "the Indian people as an American minority of conspicuous problems"; and third, to address the "Indian problem" and its international consequences, the agenda sought "an over-all statement by the President on a half billion dollar rehabilitation plan for all reservations." Provinse outlined the reasons for BIA participation in the Point Four program in a September 1949 memo to Commissioner of Indian Affairs John Nichols, explaining that he supported "a projection of [BIA] experience and 'know how' into the Point Four program" because "most of the under-developed areas of the world are populated by groups of people unfamiliar with western science and its material values, with simple cultures comparable to those of the American Indian." Provinse emphasized the "human factor" in making Point Four work: "If there was ever a program which needed to be 'people-minded,' understanding of cultural differences and aware of conflicts and resistances, it is the Point Four program." Provinse thus stressed the value of Point Four administrators' understanding the history of federal efforts to transform American Indian societies, noting that "even if everything the Indian Service has done in the past 100 years has been wrong, as some of our critics sometimes infer, the mere negative value of the experience on what not to do should be utilized." Given the BIA's hundred-year history of negotiating with Native Americans and its "long experience in the affairs of non-Western groups," it could prove useful "in dealing with preliterate, non-Industrial and non-Christian groups" such as those in Asia and Africa.[44]

Provinse himself embraced the Point Four vision, running BIA seminars for the Department of Agriculture that covered the "human factors" shaping Point Four agricultural programs and later serving as deputy assistant administrator for South Asia in the Technical Cooperation Administration (TCA), Point Four's administrative arm. Numerous other BIA officials migrated to the TCA in the 1950s. E. R. Fryer, a long-standing BIA official, served as an assistant administrator for Near East and Africa TCA activities. William Warne directed Point Four activities in Iran, along with former United Pueblo superintendent John Evans. John Nichols would serve as TCA country director for Egypt after leaving the position of commissioner of Indian affairs. Other BIA officials applied their experiences working with Native Americans to Point Four programs in Libya, Brazil, Peru, the Philippines, Ecuador, and Indonesia. Writing from Indonesia, a former BIA official told his former boss William Zimmerman Jr., who had served in the BIA since the early 1930s, that the "[Point Four] phase of our foreign policy will make an impression that will go down in Histroy [sic] as the greatest movement in our history as a country . . . My training in the Indian Service was about perfect for this [Point Four] work . . . So many things you . . . used to tell me are now coming into real and effective use." He stressed to Zimmerman the need for the United States, in battling the "commies" in Indonesia, to "understand this concept of self-government and self-determination," a notion that Zimmerman had assiduously championed during the Indian New Deal and beyond. Zimmerman himself promoted the "opportunity to show the similarity between the Federal government's special services to Indians and the Point Four Program."[45]

But collaboration between the BIA and Point Four went undeveloped for several reasons, the most important of which is that federal Point Four and BIA goals diverged at nearly the same point in time. Like the Marshall Plan, the Point Four program functioned as a Cold War device to secure alliances in developing countries believed ripe for Soviet intervention. It also sought to integrate those countries into a global free-market economy shaped by American prerogatives. "To increase the output and the national income of the less developed regions," Truman told Congress in June 1949, "is to increase our own economic stability." Yet the Point Four program vested authority in the peoples of those developing countries with the aim of solidifying their political and economic sovereignty. U.S. administrators, Secretary of State Acheson cautioned in a 1952 speech, had to strive to ensure that Point Four recipients understood that "there is nothing of imperialism" in the concept of the program. "We do not propose to dominate other people, or exploit them, or force them to change their ways of life. The two ideas that guide Point IV are first, cooperation, freely sought and freely given, and second, help to those who want to help themselves." Marrying "the concept of Point IV" to the American Indian context, however, did not stand a chance, because cooperation between federal officials and Native leaders began to wane in 1949 and coercion began to wax.[46]

BIA and Interior Department officials understood the value of applying the Point Four "concept of self-government and self-determination" abroad but refused to apply it at home because it would have served as "an important integration barrier," to use Governor Mechem's phrase. Commissioner Nichols himself represented the vanguard of the termination movement within the BIA, a movement that sought to eliminate every "integration barrier." In his August 1949 letter to all BIA staff, written as the Navajo crisis reached its zenith in the Section 9 controversy, Nichols outlined the BIA's new agenda of "integration of the Indian citizens into the social, economic, and political life of the Nation" through various measures, including "the termination of Federal supervision and control special to Indians." Point Four aid programs, with the exception of the Navajo-Hopi program, remained overseas. BIA administrators would work to implement the "concept" of termination at home instead.[47]

The Significance of the Navajo Nation Aid Program

The Navajo Nation serves as a useful site to view emerging Cold War politics and pressures within the United States. But it is important to consider whether Congress's passage of the Navajo-Hopi Rehabilitation Act was a victory for Navajo treaty rights specifically and Native American self-determination generally or a Pyrrhic victory that carried within it the seeds of a coercive trajectory for U.S. Indian policy. The Navajo case raises two key questions. The first is whether it became a precedent for federal aid to other Indian nations or remained an anomalous relief program that served as international public relations. The second question is whether the passage of the act represented continuity with the Indian New Deal and its support of cultural pluralism or with nineteenth-century allotment policy and its imperatives of incorporation.

NCAI cofounder D'Arcy McNickle, for one, complained about the limited reach of Truman's domestic aid program: "Possibly the other tribes did not get enough newspaper publicity; perhaps they were not near enough to starvation—though they might dispute this." Congressmen representing states with sizable American Indian populations made a similar argument in objecting to the Navajo-centric focus of the domestic aid program. Representative Karl Stefan of Nebraska asked his colleagues if they weren't "discriminating against the other tribes" experiencing similar conditions. In Nebraska he had seen unemployment among Native war veterans of the Santee Sioux, Ponca, and Winnebago get "no attention whatsoever." During congressional hearings on the bill, Interior Secretary Krug acknowledged that the Navajo and Hopi were not alone in needing federal aid, describing various other Indian nations also facing dire conditions. At the same time he warned of spreading relief aid too thinly and advocated a new policy of concentrating "on the related problems of a specific area and then [hitting] hard at that one spot." Concerned with cooling down a Cold War "hotspot," Krug argued that Congress's adoption of the Navajo-Hopi program would also send a message to other Native Americans that the federal government intended to help them as well. The Navajo aid package did indeed raise expectations among other Native communities.[48]

The Cold War, for many Native Americans, started on the reservation, in their own underdeveloped countries. Facing difficult conditions in northern Montana, leaders of the Blackfeet Nation called for a domestic version of the Marshall Plan in Indian America. While acknowledging the need for European aid, Peter Vielle, a member of the Blackfeet Tribal Business Council, asked BIA officials: "How about our own people? I believe relief should begin at home." Blackfeet leaders proposed a comprehensive Blackfeet rehabilitation program along the lines of the Navajo-Hopi bill, observing: "The Blackfeet Nation is poorer than any nation of Europe aided by the Marshall Plan, poorer than any of the nations that our boys helped to free from dictatorship. Yet, we ask no charity. We ask only a chance to build our own future." For patriotic Native Americans fresh from the killing fields of Europe or still grieving the loss of someone who died there, the federal government's failure to address their needs amounted to racial discrimination.[49]

In the end the Navajo (and Hopi) alone benefited from the Cold War imperative to improve the international image of the United States. The Navajo had advantages other Indian nations did not. The Navajo Nation, given its large population and expansive lands, had the literal and figurative shape of a nation; its land area approximated that of West Virginia. A March 1948 *Life* magazine article called the Navajo reservation a "foreign land inhabited by an alien people. It is a country within a country." Wesley D'Ewart, chair of the subcommittee of the House Committee on Indian Affairs that sanctioned the first round of federal aid, used similar language in telling a congressional colleague that "this is a Nation within our borders, recognized by treaty, that is actually in need of relief." In addition, private charity groups saw the Navajo as especially deserving because of their prominent wartime service. As we have seen, the press coverage of Navajo suffering made the Navajo crisis a vehicle for Truman to "foreclose" criticism of his Marshall Plan agenda by providing aid. Finally, discoveries of uranium ore in the Colorado plateau of the Four Corners area of Arizona, Colorado, New Mexico, and Utah solidified the federal commitment to relief, marking the Navajo reservation as an important Cold War site for material as well as moral reasons. In October 1949 the Navajo Tribal Council unanimously approved a resolution liberalizing uranium mining operations on the grounds that the U.S. government needed "development of atomic energy whether for weapons of war or for peaceful and beneficial purposes." Navajo prospectors thus became an element of what federal officials called the country's "secret weapon": American Indian uranium miners. Using the language of hybrid patriotism, the Navajo Tribal Council resolved to assist the Atomic Energy Commission "in the interest of the nation and the Navajo Reservation."[50]

The second salient question is whether the Navajo-Hopi Rehabilitation Act represented success or failure for Native American self-determination. While storms raged on the Navajo reservation, a political storm swirled in Washington, D.C., in the fall of 1948 as the federal government began overhauling its bureaucratic structure and philosophy through the Commission on Organization of the Executive Branch of the Government, known as the Hoover Commission for former president Herbert Hoover's oversight of the study. In its final report to the commission, the Committee on Indian Affairs outlined a mission statement that harked back to the late-nineteenth-century Lake Mohonk civilizing mission of incorporation. The committee's statement is quoted at length because it serves as the ideological basis of the federal termination policy that had such important consequences for Native Americans in the 1950s and beyond:

> Assimilation is recognized as the dominant goal within the Bureau of Indian Affairs . . . The feeling is as near unanimity as is possible on any issues of domestic policy. The sentiment of Congress also is solidly behind the goal of assimilation. But if Indians, officials and legislators were all opposed to assimilation, it would still have to be accepted as a controlling policy. The basis for historic Indian culture has been swept away. Traditional tribal organization was smashed a generation ago. Americans of Indian descent who are still thought of

as "Indian" are a handful of people, not three-tenths of one percent
of the total population. Assimilation cannot be prevented. The only
questions are: What kind of assimilation, and how fast?

These "questions" frame the cultural and political struggles of the termination era of the 1950s and 1960s. The Hoover Commission subsequently
recommended that "Indians be integrated into the rest of the population,"
that "Indian social programs be progressively transferred to State governments," and that "cultured, young employable Indians be encouraged and
assisted to leave the reservations and set themselves up on the land or in
business." The coercive and Darwinistic tone of the Hoover Commission
philosophy clashed with the principle of consent that defined, with some
exceptions, the Indian New Deal era. Taken as a whole, the Hoover Commission provided a programmatic and philosophical blueprint for the termination of Native sovereignty.[51]

Not all members of the Hoover Commission supported these recommendations. Secretary of State Dean Acheson, serving as vice chairman,
dissented, arguing that the commission had "neither the right nor the duty
to enter this field. Recollections of the painful history . . . make a novice
in this field pause before endorsing a recommendation to assimilate the
Indian and to turn him, and his culture, and his means of livelihood over
to State control." By 1949 Acheson was a prominent promoter of minority
civil rights for Cold War reasons; he had supported Truman's Committee
on Civil Rights in 1947, believing that "discrimination against minority
groups in this country has an adverse effect upon our relations with other
countries." For Acheson, a policy of forced integration of Native Americans was as detrimental to the nation's image abroad as a policy of forced
segregation of African Americans. Secretary of Defense James Forrestal
joined Acheson in repudiating the commission's authority to "adopt the
policy that assimilation is the first step in the solution of 'the Indian problem.'"[52]

The Hoover Commission mandate forced federal officials, private reformers, and Native American leaders alike to consider the domestic and
international implications of the policy of "integration" through termination. Three basic ideological positions on Native American integration
had emerged by the late 1940s, those of radical terminationists, who
sought the immediate foreclosure of tribal sovereignty, a vocal minority

group which included Senator Barry Goldwater and Senator Arthur Watkins of Utah; gradual or voluntary terminationists, who championed an accretion of Indian sovereignty through federal assistance rather than federal coercion; and anti-terminationists, a large group that included many Native Americans opposed to any kind of mandatory federal assimilation program.

Radical terminationists espoused the notion that termination meant Native Americans' "emancipation" from their reservation "prisons." President Truman articulated the position of gradual terminationists, promoting Navajo relief as a temporary solution on the road to the complete integration of Native Americans into mainstream American society. In his Section 9 veto letter to the U.S. Senate, Truman elucidated both his short-term and long-term views on Native Americans. He rejected Section 9 of the Navajo-Hopi Bill, he argued, because it represented a "broadscale extension of State laws" to reservations and thus jeopardized "the principle of respect for tribal self-determination in matters of local government." Despite his support for that principle, Truman also argued that state jurisdiction over Indian space was inevitable because "in the long run, [the] process of adjustment to our culture can be expected to result in the *complete merger* of all Indian groups into the general body of our population." But because Native Americans' consent represented the moral foundation of such a merger, Truman could accept "no reason for compelling the Navajos and Hopis to accept legal integration long before they have been prepared for such a consequence through the orderly course of social and economic integration." Truman articulated a common view of federal officials, non-Indian reform groups, and some Native Americans, namely, that Native Americans' "legal integration," "economic integration," and "social integration" into the American mainstream was both "inevitable" and desired. The difference between gradual terminationists and radical terminationists was that the latter sanctioned the immediate "economic integration" of Indians' natural resources into American society on the basis of prerogatives of market capitalism rather than the political or moral prerogatives of Native self-determination and national honor.[53]

Secretary of the Interior Julius Krug, perhaps the most vocal supporter of Navajo aid, combined these two themes in his argument for Navajo relief and rehabilitation, which linked the moral dimension of Native

American space with the material dimension of Native American place, particular geographies containing particular resources. While championing the international public relations benefits as well as the "human aspect" of addressing the Navajos' plight, Krug also called for Navajo aid on the basis of the imperatives of national economic integration. "The Nation cannot, from a strictly economic view, afford to permit the present conditions among the Navajos to continue," he told members of Congress. "Certainly we can ill afford to have more than 60,000 persons occupying an area larger than many of our states with almost no purchasing power." He linked Navajo development to the important issue of expansion of the American West, saying: "Nor can we afford to permit continued soil erosion on the Navajo range which not only devastates its productive capacity, but also endangers the huge Federal investment in Hoover Dam, not to mention the untold private and public investment in the many communities which depend upon the Colorado River for domestic water, irrigation, and electric power." World War II had transformed the American West from an undeveloped colonial region into an engine of the postwar economy, generating enormous demand for land, energy resources, and labor forces. Krug also supported Section 6 of the new Navajo-Hopi Rehabilitation Act, which allocated $5.75 million for the "relocation and resettlement of Navajo and Hopi Indians," serving as the foundation of the BIA's Voluntary Relocation Program (VRP), which promoted American Indians' movement from reservations to cities in the 1950s and 1960s. As Krug explained to Truman, population increases on the Navajo reservation had exacerbated the material crisis and thus necessitated the "resettlement" of Navajos for employment opportunities "outside the reservation."[54]

The Rehabilitation Act's goal of building roads not only served to improve travel inside the reservation but also facilitated traveling and living "outside the reservation." Section 6 thus reflected the aims of radical terminationists, those Jim Marshall described in his February 1948 *Collier's* magazine article on the Navajo crisis as "take-'em-off-the-reservation advocates." Such advocates included Representative Richard F. Harless of Arizona, who maintained that the Navajo's "salvation lies in escaping the confines of the reservation. It's like a prison to them." The Navajo story of reservation rehabilitation, then, also contains the broader story of reservation relocation, which became the most influential and corrosive element of the federal government's termination program. And it reveals the literal and figurative terrain of the increasingly contentious public struggle to determine the place of "the reservation" in American society and in American Indians' future.[55]

Contesting Termination

Truman's and Krug's views mirrored those held by private reformers ostensibly devoted to protecting Native American rights. Integrationist (or assimilationist) discourse defined the agendas of a constellation of academic, public policy, and philanthropic enterprises concerned with the place of American Indians in American society. To cite one example among many, Maxwell Hahn, executive vice president of the Field Foundation, which supported research on American Indian policy, told several top BIA officials that "ultimate integration of the Indian is inevitable. It is just a question of how soon, how constructively and how systematically integration can be brought about." Using terminationist language, he complained that American Indians' "cultural acceptance of our values has not been completed."[56]

Terminationists' rhetoric and policies created tensions within white reform groups such as the Association on American Indian Affairs, forcing them to define their positions as the federal government moved to implement programmatic expressions of the official assimilation policy articulated in the Hoover Commission report. The AIAA was the nation's most prominent non-Indian reform group. But its effectiveness was limited for several reasons. It was headquartered on Madison Avenue in New York City, led by a New Mexico anthropologist, Oliver LaFarge, and governed by a board of white philanthropists and anthropologists who were for the most part detached from Native America culturally, politically, and geographically. Most important, LaFarge and the organization that reflected his leadership did not defend the principle of Native self-determination. LaFarge's 1948 "Proposed Program of the AAIA" stated its central goal as facilitating "the mutually beneficial assimilation of the Indians into our general population." LaFarge's February 1950 "Restatement of Program and Policy in Indian Affairs," reading like the Hoover Commission statement, made more explicit his embrace of assimilation:

> Our basic over-all theory or policy is that Indians must become absorbed into the general population. In being thus absorbed, they may

or may not be able to retain enriching elements of their own culture. We do know, as an inescapable fact, that no minority of 400,000 can survive among 150,000,000 of another culture, and retain its identity forever. Our problem is to guide and protect the process of amalgamation, that it will be carried through with benefit to both groups, with justice, and with humanity.

LaFarge's views were similar to those of other AAIA members, in particular its anthropologists. For the core association leadership, then, as it was for Truman and other federal officials, termination of reservation sovereignty represented a natural and inevitable evolution toward a state of American Indians' complete cultural, economic, legal, and social integration into American society.[57]

Such views did not go unchallenged within the AAIA. Association legal counsel Felix Cohen considered LaFarge's phrase "assimilation of the Indians into our general population" to mean the "wiping out of all distinctive Indian traits of character or culture, in line with the 'melting pot' idea of wiping out all non-Anglo-Saxon traits in immigrants." As a "Jew of Russian descent," Cohen found the idea unpalatable and "un-American"; if someone suggested that he assimilate into the Anglo-Saxon mainstream, he would "punch [his] would-be reformer in the nose." More important, Cohen believed that the AAIA's embrace of assimilation provided fuel to "enemies of the Indian seeking to wipe out Indian reservations." He situated the origins of Indianness on Native Americans' land base, identifying termination as a battle over sacred spaces that helped to nourish and sustain Indian cultural identity. He feared that the AAIA's assimilationist agenda would "alienate Indians . . . who have any pride in their own heritage and personality." Cohen was especially concerned with the question of Native Americans' agency, writing that "perhaps it comes down to a question of whether the Indian is mentioned as an object of a process or as a prime mover in a process."[58]

Cohen had played an important role in constructing IRA constitutions for the Interior Department in the 1930s before serving as an attorney for the Blackfeet, Sioux, and other Indian nations in the late 1940s and beyond. Well versed in actual reservation conditions, Cohen warned against the attenuation of American Indian sovereignty. In a provocative 1949 essay he maintained that the American Indian "is to America what the

Jew was to the Russian czars and Hitler's Germany. For us the Indian tribe is the miners' canary, and when it flutters and droops we know that the poison gasses of intolerance threaten all other minorities in our land. And who of us is not a member of some minority." Cohen's work with the American Jewish Congress, the NAACP, and the NCAI sharpened his sensitivity to racial and religious discrimination and to attendant infringements of civil liberties. Empathetic to minority groups' efforts to survive, Cohen contested LaFarge's statement that "no minority of 400,000 can retain its identity forever," arguing instead, "My guess is that it will be easier to find an Indian community fifty years from now that is relatively indistinguishable from what it is today than it will be to find a great city of which the same might be said." Here again he championed what Native Americans were thinking rather than what white politicians or social scientists asserted as gospel. "My political views," he claimed, "are closer to those of the Indians."[59]

Cohen's political views eventually influenced LaFarge's position on the related goals of termination and assimilation, moving LaFarge to reject his earlier premise of "'merger' or 'full acculturation,' since it clearly is possible, and should be a matter of free choice, for Indian groups to retain their own patterns of life . . . while making a successful adaptation to our patterns insofar as ability to compete, to assert and maintain their rights." But LaFarge could not abide Cohen's June 1950 essay "Colonial Administration in the Indian Country," which called the BIA's corruption "like the corruption of prisons, insane asylums, concentration camps, fascist and communist states, and other places where men cannot 'talk back' to officials." Calling the article the association's "declaration of war" on the BIA, AAIA secretary Alden Stevens asked his colleagues, "At this particular time do we want to declare war?" LaFarge did not, objecting to Cohen's conflation of the BIA and Soviet communism. The AAIA leadership refused to publish the essay in the AAIA journal *The American Indian*. Undaunted, Cohen published the essay under the title "Colonialism: U.S. Style" in *The Progressive* instead.[60]

Cohen saw Indian-white relations in 1950 as a form of cold war, a view that the AAIA soon adopted. Cohen's fears of a coercive BIA undermining newfound American Indian sovereignty crystallized in early 1950 when Truman appointed Dillon Myer commissioner of Indian Affairs rather than Will Rogers Jr., whom the NCAI and the Navajo Veterans

League had recommended. Instead of a popular Native American figure who was active in the NCAI and experienced in congressional politics, Truman chose a career bureaucrat with no experience in Indian affairs. Myer had worked with the Department of Agriculture from 1916 until 1942, when President Roosevelt appointed him director of the War Relocation Authority (WRA), which was charged with sending Japanese American citizens to concentration camps in the desert. In a letter to the Omaha Tribal Council, Cohen described Myer as an "expert administrator," explaining that in Washington, D.C., "a would-be dictator is always called an 'expert administrator' by people who admire the capacity of dictators to 'make trains run on time'—even if the trains carry men, women, and children to concentration camps." Equally troubling to Cohen and other Indian rights supporters was Myer's purging of Indian New Dealers from the BIA and replacing them with WRA associates. In his first eight months in office Myer replaced key Indian New Deal personnel with eleven ex-WRA bureaucrats, none of whom had experience working with Native Americans.[61]

BIA veterans of the Indian New Deal era as well as Native American politicians frequently used terms such as "Gestapo," "totalitarian," and "dictatorship" to describe the bureau's new policies under Myer's leadership. A public dispute with Commissioner Myer over American Indians' right to hire attorneys fueled this rhetoric and galvanized supporters of Native sovereignty. In another throwback to nineteenth-century Indian-white relations, Myer used an archaic 1872 law giving the commissioner of Indian affairs the right to veto tribal attorney contracts to justify his right to do so in 1950. Myers attempted to contain the expansion of Indian governments' employment of white attorneys, the legacy of the Indian Reorganization Act and the Indian Claims Commission bill of 1946, which gave American Indian nations incentive to hire attorneys to prosecute claims for compensation or for the return of land. The Navajo hired Norman Littell, who helped to spark political and economic development. Felix Cohen represented the Blackfeet, Sioux, and other Indian nations in their efforts to pursue land claims and secure federal funding for reservation development. And James Curry represented the Pyramid Lake Paiute, at the time fighting to protect their reservation from white squatters, and served as the general counsel of the National Congress of American Indians. In his November 2, 1952, radio address broadcast on Chicago's WFJL,

Curry told his listeners that American politicians "have been telling you how we ought to help . . . democratic peoples of the world in order to keep them on our side in the struggle with world communism. They have told you what must be done to help the great teeming masses of India . . . We ought to say: We approve of your helping these Indians in Asia. But what about a little decency and justice for American Indians here in the U.S.?" Declaring that "Indians were our comrades in arms in every war that we have fought," he called on listeners to support the "national obligation" to extend "home rule" to American Indians. Framing Native American issues as a Cold War matter, these attorneys—especially Curry and Cohen, who represented the nation's most influential Native rights groups, the NCAI and AAIA, respectively—monitored congressional bills threatening Native lands and mobilized their various constituencies to block them, facilitating a countervailing power that checked the momentum of Myer's termination agenda.[62]

As the attorney contracts controversy raged, Myer bravely attended the NCAI annual convention in July 1951 to "clear the air." He first addressed the charges that his behavior had been, in his words, "dictatorial" and "Stalinistic," mounting a rhetorical counteroffensive by asserting that the criticism of Collier, Cohen, and Native American politicians reminded him "of some of the all-too-familiar propaganda efforts in other parts of the world which try to persuade people that white is black and day is night." He claimed that he sought to "diminish" the BIA's supervision of Indian affairs, not to employ a "Machiavellian attempt to enlarge and expand its control and supervision," as his critics charged. And he championed his agenda of relocation as a solution to reservation poverty. Myer claimed that his "Number One objective" was "looking to complete Indian independence and [the] elimination of the need for a Bureau of Indian Affairs," in principle a worthy goal of furthering Native self-determination. But the process by which he attempted to implement this objective was not. His efforts to impose new regulations and expand BIA funding ran counter to his public pronouncements; the paradox of Myer's regime was that during his tenure he doubled the BIA's budget and tried to triple it, while pursuing the most regressive policies of any commissioner since the late nineteenth century. Using the visceral language of the Cold War, Felix Cohen compared Myer's expansion of the BIA to "the vast enlargement of state powers in the Soviet Union, which is officially justified as a necessary means to bring about 'the withering of the state.' An example of the same process closer to home and easier to observe is the intensive power drive which the Bureau of Indian Affairs has been carrying on under the slogan of 'winding up the Indian Bureau.'"[63]

In January 1952 Secretary of the Interior Oscar Chapman ruled against Myer's proposed regulation of the Indian governments' hiring attorneys, largely the result of a coordinated public outcry against Myer that marked a dramatic collective protest against an increasingly repressive federal government. During hearings held in Washington, D.C., in early January 1952, representatives of twenty-four Indian nations testified against the regulations. They emphasized two main themes: first, that Native Americans had served their country during World War II and deserved to be treated as "men" rather than as "savages"; and second, that Native people, as the Pueblo politician Popovi Da put it simply, had "lost faith in the Indian bureau [BIA] and want private attorneys to protect our rights." Representatives of numerous groups offered support: the American Bar Association, American Civil Liberties Union, National Council of Negro Women, National Jewish Welfare Board, B'nai B'rith, American Jewish Congress, Japanese-American Citizens League, American Veterans Committee, Women's International League for Peace and Freedom, National Association for the Advancement of Colored People, and United Automobile Workers–Congress of Industrial Organizations. A coalition of minority and labor groups concerned about the federal government's rollback of civil rights and labor rights in McCarthy-era America came to the aid of a similarly beleaguered group of "original Americans" seeking a fair deal, another example of the ways in which the Native context provides a window into the troubled character of Cold War America.[64]

A Cold War on Indians

Détente rested in the spring of 1952, when Myer's BIA proposed "A Bill to Authorize the Indian Bureau to Make Arrests without Warrant for Violation of Indian Bureau Regulations, etc." This bold language reflects the level of tension that emerged under Myer's regime as well as Congress's willingness to put his ideas into practice. The legislation led to a noisy public attack that both revisited American and German treatment of ethnic minorities during World War II and mirrored the rhetoric of the ongoing Cold War. Representing the AAIA, Felix Cohen protested to the House Interior Committee that the bill "would apply to American citizens of the Indian race the same coercive measures that were applied during wartime to American citizens of Japanese descent in the concentration camps operated by War Relocation Administrator Dillon Myer." The campaign against Myer's regulations led the *Houston Post* to imagine Indian affairs replicating a different aspect of World War II in an April 22, 1952, headline: "Indian Bureau Asks Gestapo Power." And in a phrase that American newspapers repeated in their headlines, the AAIA claimed that the proposed bill "is likely to be viewed by the Indians as a declaration of a Cold War by the Indian bureau against the men and women it is supposed to be serving." The phrase appeared, for example, in an April 17, 1952, *Philadelphia Inquirer* headline, "No 'Cold War' on Indians," and in an April 14, 1952, *New York Post* headline, "New Control Bill Branded 'Cold War on Indians.'" An editorial in *The Nation* put matters in starker terms and assessed the international consequences, opining: "If present policies continue, it is only a question of time before the cold war now smoldering on our Indian frontier bursts into some sort of flame. The blaze is not likely to reveal United States relations with non-white people in a very favorable light."[65]

It is difficult to assess the extent to which Native Americans across the country consumed and repeated such news and such phrases. The National Congress of American Indians, for example, reprinted in its September–October 1952 issue of the *NCAI News Bulletin* the aforementioned editorial from *The Nation* as well as a *St. Louis Dispatch* editorial titled "The Forgotten People: Mirror of World Opinion" that called the Navajo rehabilitation plan "a kind of Point IV for the first Americans." Native Americans were using the term "cold war" to describe their conflict with the federal government by at least the late 1950s, and likely earlier than that. They understood as well as most Americans what was at stake in the international Cold War. A 1950 editorial published in the Navajo journal *Adahooniligii* had called on all Navajo to "register for the draft right now" because of tensions in Korea, arguing that "Russia has a way that they call Communism, and Russia wants all the rest of the people in the world to live as the Russians do." By 1952 many American Indians believed that U.S. officials were trying to force the peoples of the world to live as Americans did. At the very least, the increasingly coercive BIA policies and the use of wartime rhetoric to describe them sowed a climate of fear among Native Americans that triggered family or community memories of U.S. Army violence against them, as well as extralegal violence. For example, the *Shannon County News*, "The Voice of the Sioux Nation," published a statement by an Oklahoma Native American who believed that "if the [arrest] bill becomes law, an Indian could be seized, searched, arrested, imprisoned, or even shot if he had violated no law but only a 'regulation' of the Indian Bureau."[66]

Myer's police powers bill quickly disappeared. But it simply represented a manifestation of BIA policies that found expression in the bureau's less publicized but official "Withdrawal Program," a Myer-designed blueprint for the withdrawal of federal protections of reservation sovereignty. Soviet propagandists may have shared Myer's view that Indian reservations were camps of slow death, but for different reasons. Soviet officials would also have approved of the coercive ways in which BIA officials pushed for the termination of those reservations. The BIA's recommended procedure to "overcome obstacles" to termination on a number of reservations read in part: "Issue certificates of ownership to each individual for their proportionate share of tribal assets. Help to prepare necessary legislation. Insist that such legislation be mandatory and not subject to approval of local and state authorities or of Indian council and Tribes." Here was an updated form of state-mandated allotment writ large, jammed down the throats of Native citizens. Myer's regime generated such visceral criticism because it rejected the principle of self-determination championed by Presidents Roosevelt and Truman and substituted federal control by fiat on reservations governed under the Indian Reorganization Act. In 1947 Commissioner of Indian Affairs William Brophy had applauded Truman for signing the Indian Claims Commission bill because it "distinguishes our Government from the totalitarians." By the end of the Truman era, observers of Indian-white relations, Indian and non-Indian, had trouble distinguishing between their government and that of "the totalitarians."[67]

The rhetorical battle between terminationists and self-determinationists began before Myer assumed office but intensified afterwards because of Myer's aggressive promotion of termination policies, including his plan to strip Native Americans of their right to hire attorneys. To wage their counteroffensive, Indian New Dealers, including Cohen, former commissioner of Indian affairs John Collier, and former secretary of the interior

Harold Ickes employed the language of World War II while modeling their struggle as similar to the Cold War with the Soviet Union. Calling Myer the "Fuhrer of Indian Affairs," Ickes complained to Interior Secretary Oscar Chapman:

> It is unfortunate that those dictators who rule the countries behind the iron curtain should have access to this "charter of Indian liberty." It is not difficult to imagine the use that the Soviets will make of this ill-starred and badly timed notice to the oppressed everywhere, especially those of darker skins than our own, as to just what we, at least within the jurisdiction of the "Commisar" of Indian Affairs, mean when we point with pride to the liberty to do what they are told— that has been bestowed upon the worst-treated minority that has ever existed in America.

Several Indian New Deal officials connected termination to the important Cold War Point Four aid program promoting American values among "those of darker skins." Calling Myer's agenda "totalitarian" in a letter to the *New York Times*, Collier claimed that "the 'pilot projects' of Point Four, now our world-wide enterprise, were the Indian projects of the Hoover and Roosevelt administrations; and they were hugely successful. The concentrated unilateral assault against the trusteeship obligation . . . concerns every citizen, and must be disturbing to every supporter of the United Nations charter." Other former BIA officials warned that U.S. officials' treatment of American Indians sabotaged the international rhetorical claims of Point Four. William Zimmerman Jr. protested to Assistant Secretary of the Interior Joel Wolfson that "the termination of Federal supervision is not only unwise, but is doing great harm. All over the world the United States is saying to dependent and underprivileged people that it will provide assistance under the Point Four Program. Yet, the one possible domestic example of the Point Four Program, the services to the Indians, is threatened with extinction long before it has achieved its objectives."[68]

These Indian New Dealers had spent over a decade working to secure American Indians' rights. Their legacy threatened, they worked now to protect those rights, in part because their experiences became refracted through the lens of the Cold War. Walter Woehlke, another important

Indian New Deal official, saw firsthand how domestic policies complicated U.S. foreign policy. Writing from Vienna, Woehlke described to Collier and to Zimmerman the "Red propaganda concerning American treatment of colored people" and his efforts to get State Department officials in Vienna to pay attention to Native American issues. He compared American termination programs with Soviet campaigns to "eradicate all cultural, spiritual, linguistic and religious manifestations [of ethnic minorities] which do not conform with the 'Marxian ethos.'" Capturing both the continuity of the federal government's assimilation policy and the ways in which the Cold War had changed Americans' understanding of that policy, Woehlke offered a disturbing conflation of Russian and American history: "The Trail of Tears has been traversed by scores of [Russian] groups ranging up to 400,000, and the task of destroying the ethnic loyalties, the cultures, the organizations, the religions of those minorities is being pushed ruthlessly . . . All the more reason why we must not revert to the policy of forcible assimilation by impoverishment and despair which we pursued during the Century of Dishonor," the nineteenth century.[69]

Most important, "forcible assimilation" policies that made mandatory Native Americans' legal, social, and economic integration into "mainstream" American society fostered nationalism among Native politicians. To contain the spread of termination policies, Native American leaders also used the language of World War II and the Cold War to protect their democratic rights. The Blackfeet, for example, contrasted the BIA's dictatorial actions with their own democratic aspirations. George Pambrun, the chairman of the Blackfeet Tribal Business Council, contended in 1952 that the BIA was using "methods of Communist dictatorship against our people . . . Stalin could learn a lot about how to run a dictatorship just by watching the Indian Bureau." Walter Wetzel, Pambrun's successor, protested BIA manipulation of Blackfeet elections, telling the Secretary of the Interior later that year: "Our knowledge of the principles of our Government, and our love of freedom is as great as that of any other citizen of the United States. We have proven our loyalty to the Government of the United States time and time again and we refuse to permit your employees to treat us so shamefully as to attempt to hold and run our elections for us." These voices of protest joined those of the Navajo, Iroquois, Pueblo, Sioux, and other Native people who understood that the coercive behavior of the federal government not only rolled back gains of sovereignty from the Indian New Deal era but also represented a form of total war against Native Americans' right, embedded in instruments of international law called treaties, to preserve their Indianness and their "reserved" homelands.[70]

George Pambrun's provocative comments—and Harold Ickes's and Felix Cohen's for that matter—may be considered rhetorically extreme. Yet such comments, repeated elsewhere by other Native leaders, capture the contentiousness of termination discourse that in large measure stemmed from the contradictions during the Cold War in the behavior of the U.S. government, which on the one hand proclaimed that Americans were containing the antidemocratic forces threatening the freedom-loving citizens of the world, while on the other it pursued antidemocratic policies in other "colored" spaces of the world. During the 1950s the United States undermined the governments of nations such as Iran and Guatemala, whose citizens had chosen their political leaders in democratic elections, because they failed to demonstrate proper respect for the needs of America's free market–loving corporations. The Blackfeet Nation and Guatemala, both equidistant from Washington, D.C., demonstrated the resolve to defend their national sovereignty, however different in nature. Among American Cold Warriors were men and women associated with the Department of the Interior, whose purview included the BIA and the country's natural resources, deemed critical for the prosecution of a war against the Soviet Union and its allies. Speaking in 1949 about Indians of South America as well as of North America, Assistant Secretary of the Interior William Warne asserted that federal officials "can see no well-being for [Indians] unless they be persuaded to mingle with us and to share with us the riches yielded by the good American earth . . . We believe deeply that ours is a true and lasting way of life and we believe that the Indian way, valid though it may have been for the times in which it flourished unchallenged, will not suffice." Such an integrationist attitude erased not only the boundaries between American Indian nations and the United States but also the boundaries between the United States and the rest of the Western Hemisphere. In American officials' conception of Cold War geography, shaped by a rejuvenated Monroe Doctrine, all land served America's purposes. When Guatemala's president Jacobo Arbenz began redistributing that land to small farmers, many of them Indian, U.S. Cold

Warriors terminated Arbenz's agrarian revolution to preserve U.S. hegemony over what Warne had called "the good American earth."[71]

Given the increasingly nationalistic rhetoric of Native American leaders and the resources they controlled, it is not surprising that the BIA, especially under Myer's direction, could adopt in the early 1950s a similar position toward American Indian governments it considered recalcitrant. If the "Cold War was as much about creating an economically, politically, and militarily integrated 'free world,' as it was about waging a war of attrition against the Soviets," to use Christina Klein's assessment of revisionist Cold War historiography, then Native Americans' experiences of containing this integrationist impulse give us additional evidence of the complicated intersections at home and abroad in a dynamic context of Cold War civil rights.[72]

Between 1945 and 1952 the country's movement toward the termination of Native sovereignty gained tremendous momentum, powered by this integrationist Cold War discourse and the demographic expansion of the American West that created enormous pressure for Native Americans' natural resources, some of the new "bright nuggets of gold," as Henry Miller put it. Miller argued in his 1947 book *Remember to Remember* that Native Americans prayed for America's "destruction." But by 1947 Native America and the United States of America were inseparable even as they were divided by tenuous physical, legal, and cultural boundaries. Instead Native Americans prayed and fought to prevent American authorities from destroying *their* homelands, calling on American citizens and politicians to remember their service to the nation in the name of freedom and democracy and to reward them with Cold War aid programs to improve their own underdeveloped nations within the nation. When those calls went unanswered, resistance to termination by Native Americans and their non-Native supporters created a cold war of tensions that took place on multiple fronts, on local, national, and international levels. During the Eisenhower era this cold war got hotter, forcing American Indians to develop new containment strategies to protect both their right to be Indian and their ancestral homelands which sustained that identity. In doing so, American Indians acted patriotically to reify the notions expressed by their fellow American citizens who saw them as "more American than we," as the "true Americans."[73]

5 Nation Building at Home and Abroad

If the Indian would only complete his job of civilizing the white Americans, Point Four would get along faster and more successfully. Then if the white American learned the Indian lesson completely, he would discover that African and Asian and Pacific cultures have perhaps as much to teach as the Indians had to teach. Out of the knowledge could come a meaningful world democracy from which would certainly come a meaningful peace.

—"Civilizing the White Savages: How the Indians Tried and Failed to Civilize the White Man," *Ammunition* (UAW–CIO), June 1952

In September 1961 Helen Peterson, the dynamic executive director of the National Congress of American Indians (NCAI), related to members of a subcommittee of the Senate Judiciary Committee several dramatic cases of racial discrimination experienced by Native Americans during the 1950s: a Winnebago Korean War soldier was denied burial in a white cemetery in Iowa; a fifteen-year-old Native American girl died after two white men threw her from a moving car, a crime for which the men spent three months in jail; an unarmed Sioux veteran of World War II was shot in the back by a white police officer, who served no jail time. Peterson expressed the anger and the angst of Native Americans who had seen President Truman's support of civil rights and Navajo reservation development in the late 1940s devolve in the 1950s into racist crimes and coercive federal termination policies designed to dismantle rather than develop their ancestral homelands. Claiming that American Indians' culture "could lend much to our increasingly materialistic national society," Peterson called on Congress to improve the conditions of American Indians, not only because they "nag at the conscience of thoughtful Americans" but also because "the whole world watches the United States of America and it may soon look much more closely to its relations with its native peoples. These relations may very well be of vital importance in winning the confidence of emerging native peoples and other nations all over the world." Throughout the 1950s and into the 1960s a broad spectrum of Americans, from citizens to politicians, expressed this panoptical and introspective notion of "the world" watching how the United States treated its people of color. To cite two examples among many: in his essay "The 'Inconvenient' American Indian," Representative George McGovern of South Dakota maintained, "Our handling of our minorities is, in the eyes of world populations increasingly critical of our moral stance, a measure of our sincerity"; and the Mays family of Oakland, California, anguishing over a photo of an impoverished American Indian woman that appeared in *Arizona Highways* magazine, wrote to Eleanor Roosevelt: "This case is doubtless for the United Nations. Russia and the rest of the world is watching everything we do and don't do."[1]

Native Americans contested the federal government's termination agenda by defending the place of the "reservation" in maintaining Indian culture. This effort to define and to defend Indianness intersected with Cold War pressures in multiple ways, generating a patriotic response by NCAI officials in an effort to preserve their autonomy in McCarthy-era America even as they called for "foreign aid" programs to further the development of reservations at home. It was during this period that Native Americans' struggles against coercive assimilation most closely mirrored cultural struggles between the Soviet Union and the United States; that Native Americans' hybrid patriotism shaped their conceptions of themselves as Cold War citizens uniquely suited to recognize the extent to which America's domestic policies threatened its foreign policies; and that the struggles of Native Americans to defend their "homelands" helped non-Indian citizens and government officials comprehend what the Cold War meant and what was at stake in it. Native Americans served, as did African Americans, as visible symbols of the other America searching for justice during a time when newly independent nations were trying to understand what America stood for as Cold War boundaries expanded around the world.

The Contours of Termination

By the end of Truman's presidency the conflict over sovereignty between Native Americans and the federal government represented, as *The Nation* had put it, a "simmering cold war." This cold war got hotter when Dwight D. Eisenhower assumed the presidency and Republicans gained control of both houses of Congress. In August 1953 Congress adopted House Concurrent Resolution 108 (HCR 108), signaling its intent to terminate federal supervision and control of Indian affairs by making American Indians "subject to the same laws and entitled to the same privileges and responsibilities" as other American citizens. HCR 108 served as an expression of Congress's legislative commitment to the Hoover Commission's agenda of full assimilation. That August, Congress also passed Public Law 280 (PL 280), which replicated the infamous Section 9 of the Navajo-Hopi Rehabilitation Act by extending state jurisdiction over reservation territory in five states. Eisenhower signed PL 280 claiming that it represented "still another step in granting complete political equality to all Indians in our nation," disingenuously asserting that in the five states affected by the legislation—California, Minnesota, Nebraska, Oregon, and Wisconsin—"Indians have enthusiastically endorsed this bill." He signed it into law, however, despite "grave doubts" about provisions in Sections 6 and 7 because they set a precedent allowing other states to assume jurisdiction over other Indian nations' affairs and thus eliminate Native Americans' "self-government." Eisenhower deemed "unfortunate" and "un-Christian" the law's failure to "ascertain the wishes and desires of the Indians" and called on Congress to amend the legislation during its next session to require consultation with Native groups. Unlike Truman, who stood his ground against Section 9 of the Navajo-Hopi Rehabilitation Act, Eisenhower relented in the hope that Congress would see fit to correct its "unfortunate" and "un-Christian" mistake. But it did not.[2]

PL 280 was passed by Congress during the dog days of August—"mysteriously sneaked through . . . in the adjournment rush," as the *New York Times* put it. Emboldened by Eisenhower's failure to repudiate HCR 108 or to veto PL 280, Congress passed legislation the following year that unilaterally stripped specific Indian nations of their sovereignty, terminating the tribal status of the Klamath in Oregon, the Menominee in Wisconsin, the Uintah and Ouray Utes and four Paiute groups in Utah, the Alabamas and Coushattas of Texas, and several Native groups in Oregon. Energized by HCR 108 and by the "hydra-headed monster" of terminationist legislation that it spawned, the BIA resuscitated its competency program in 1955 and thus liberalized its land sales criteria. The bureau argued that the old policy was "unfair and undemocratic," as it made it difficult for individuals to sell their land, a fundamental American right; critics of the policy countered that it undermined collective holdings of land and workable timber or grazing units and thus destabilized reservation economies. Between 1953 and 1957 Native Americans' land base declined by 1,790,649 acres; during a similar period from 1948 to 1952, their land base had declined by 804,763 acres.[3]

Native Americans also faced what the NCAI called methods of "backdoor termination," which included the taking of Native land for federal energy projects, which resulted in the forced relocation of thousands of Native Americans. In addition, Indians wrestled with the goals and the effects of the Voluntary Relocation Program. By the mid-1950s the BIA's Branch of Relocation Services was operating in cities from St. Louis, Chicago, and Denver to San Jose, San Francisco, and Los Angeles; ultimately, nearly 160,000 Native Americans left reservations under the aegis of the VRP between 1950 and 1970. The program took shape during the Navajo relief crisis, the result of ongoing concerns about the carrying capacity of the Navajo Reservation. The BIA initiated an "off-reservation employment program" in early 1948. During the summer and fall of that year more than thirteen thousand Navajo found railroad, mining, and agricultural jobs; a similar number were working in such jobs during the summer and fall of 1949. The BIA expanded the program to help Navajos "resettle away from the reservation on a permanent basis," but poor housing, education, and health programs and "the disinclination of most Navajos to leave their homeland for more than a few months" hindered its progress. Nevertheless, the idea of permanent resettlement found expression in Section 6 of the Navajo-Hopi Rehabilitation Act, which allocated $5.75 million for the "relocation and resettlement of Navajo and Hopi Indians."[4]

Handicapped by limited financial resources as federal and private relief aid streamed overseas or was dammed up on the Navajo reservation, some federal officials believed that the only way to raise the living standards of Native Americans was to relocate them from reservations to American cities. These officials, facing a distressing panorama of poverty on many Indian reservations, supported a hybrid program of reservation rehabilitation and relocation. Toby Morris, the chairman of the House Indian Affairs Subcommittee, appealed to President Truman for more funding for Native American programs "on and off reservations." Making reference to the money spent on the "rehabilitation of foreign peoples," Morris promoted increased funding for relocation of "forty to fifty percent" of the

American Indian population so as to "integrate them into the overall economy" and allow them to "take their proper place in our American society." But he also supported funding for resource development on Indian lands to assure American Indians committed to reservation life "a decent standard of living in their present location." What, exactly, their "proper place" in Cold War America was became the central question for Native Americans during the 1950s as the domestic pressures of termination increased, even as their ability to define and to defend "their present location," the reservation, became shaped by the international pressures of the Cold War.[5]

Defending Indianness

The Hoover Commission's assertion of assimilation as national Indian policy in 1949 forced the National Congress of American Indians to assess the integrationist ideology driving the termination movement. The commission's statement, the NCAI reported in its March 1949 *Washington Bulletin*, "throws Indians back into a dark era in which they must face once again the doctrine of forced assimilation. We thought that ended with the fighting of a war we were told was to defend the right of little people to 'self-determination.'" The editorial noted that American Indians did not oppose assimilation so much as the forced nature of it as well as the denigration of the reservation as a legitimate cultural space:

> It seems a throw-back, too, to read an all-embracing recommendation that the employable and the progressive be encouraged and assisted to leave the reservations. This puts a stigma of inferiority on those who might choose to stay on the reservations to make their way . . . What is an Indian reservation, anyway, except a rural area settled by Indians . . . Indian rural communities need intelligence and initiative to develop an abundant life, and any program which looks toward the systematic draining away of the best leadership will only continue the sub-standard conditions prevailing on so many Indian reservations today.

This attitude became the kernel of Native Americans' defense of their sovereignty, the repositioning of the reservation as a fundamentally American rural space, though one protected by treaties. In a gendered descrip-

tion the NCAI opined that "Indians want a well-balanced program with
room for individual decision as to whether their young men go or stay,
whether they become farmers, or factory workers, cattle-raisers, or professional men." Preserving choice, preserving consent, lay at the heart of the
NCAI's campaigns during the 1950s and beyond, the reclamation of the ,
foundational principle of "self-determination" for which these NCAI politicians and their family members and friends had fought in the wars of the
world.[6]

The Navajo relief and rehabilitation story of the late 1940s spurred
NCAI officials to seek a broader aid program for Native Americans across
the country. Galvanized by the extensive national and international coverage of the Navajo crisis, officials of the NCAI waged an extensive public
relations campaign to establish its legitimacy as a national organization
capable of speaking for all Native Americans. It directed sophisticated appeals to the American public, to BIA officials and U.S. politicians, and to
Native people themselves, many of whom were unaware of the NCAI's
efforts to defend Native Americans' right to live on reservations protected
by national/international treaties.

Because the NCAI was a political organization it could not offer tax
exemptions to its contributors, and this limited its fund-raising appeal. To
gain support for reservation development along the lines of the Navajo aid
plan, Will Rogers Jr. and other NCAI officials established a "Committee
to Rehabilitate These Indian Nations." Though it was originally called
the NCAI Fund, the organization's trustees deleted the reference to the
NCAI and called it ARROW—American Restitution and Righting of
Old Wrongs—an interesting acronym that speaks to organizers' hybridity
as well as to their cleverness in appealing to a nation enamored with
nineteenth-century images of Indian life. Rogers led the campaign, which
was supported by a sponsoring committee that included Tallulah Bank-
head, Oscar Hammerstein, Lewis Mumford, Paul Muni, Phillip Murray,
Walter White, and other prominent Americans. In his October 10, 1949,
statement announcing the new organization, Rogers described thousands
of Native Americans as "actually displaced persons." The United States,
he urged, had "solved far more complex problems abroad; there is no reason why we should not seek a speedy end to this shocking Indian problem
right in our own back yard." ARROW produced a series of radio broadcasts in 1950, narrated by the actor Gregory Peck, a member of the sponsoring committee. First aired on KEWB, Los Angeles, "The Only Good

Indian" was subsequently distributed in transcript to other radio stations across the country. The title referred to the phrase "The only good Indian is a dead Indian," a motto dating from the nineteenth-century Indian wars in the American West. The broadcast opened with a description of the 1890 Wounded Knee massacre, then referred to the nineteenth-century conquest of Native America as a wholesale massacre which created 550,000 "good" (that is, dead) Indians. "Survivors" were left with no education, diminished sheep herds, and widespread illness. "These are our conquered enemies," Peck intoned, "the people of the sovereign nations with whom we made treaties." The broadcast suggested that the U.S. treated conquered enemies of Germany and Japan better than American Indians after World War II. Closing with a challenge to Americans living "in the freest nation on earth, symbol of hope for the downtrodden everywhere," Peck asked: "Shall we rehabilitate [the Indians], free them as we are doing to peoples everywhere, and right our old wrongs? Or shall we stand by until time has forever erased the question, and the 400,000 survivors have also become GOOD Indians?"[7]

ARROW helped the NCAI expand during the 1950s, fueling its public relations efforts to redefine the space of the reservation as both American and Indian. NCAI officials also sought to educate BIA officials about the meaning of Indianness as the termination crisis intensified in the early 1950s. In a 1951 address to officials attending a BIA summer school, NCAI executive secretary John C. Rainier (Pueblo) connected the organization's goals to the Cold War goals of the United States. "In a larger sense the solution of the Indian problem could well be a key to the success or failure of this government's attempt to win the so-called backward peoples in the other parts of the world," he contended, while warning his audience, "It is logical to assume that if the government fails to please, win, and teach the principles of democracy to the other parts of the world, it is because it has failed to solve its minority problem, including the Indian problem." Employing the panoptical metaphor, he reminded BIA officials that "the eyes of the world are focused upon this government in its treatment of the minority groups." Addressing the ongoing public relations crisis of the international Cold War while highlighting Native Americans' patriotism, he concluded, "It is our obligation to disprove the communist charge that the Indian reservations are no better than Nazi concentration camps."[8]

Native Americans' own public relations campaigns also engaged the ways in which American Indians were symbolically represented in Washington, D.C., the critical political space where Native politicians had to confront congressional terminationists. Whenever members of Congress entered the U.S. Capitol building, they passed by Horatio Greenough's 1853 statue *The Rescue*, which depicted a towering white figure restraining a tomahawk-wielding Indian, who threatened a cowering white woman and her child. The image it presented and its title also argued that white Americans' enlightened intervention rescued Indians from themselves. The argument of terminationists followed along those lines, that Native Americans needed whites to rescue them from the primitive and un-American conditions of reservation life, in this case through legislation and relocation.

Since 1945 the NCAI had complained that the statue presented an offensive image of the American Indian, but the protests against it had begun earlier and included those of white politicians. In 1939 Representative Clark Burdick of Rhode Island introduced a resolution calling for the removal of the statue on the grounds that it insulted American Indians, who are "as patriotic as any other race in our complex civilization." David Lynn, the architect of the Capitol, defended the statue, however, and the resolution died in committee. Two years later Representative James O'Connor of Montana introduced a similar resolution, arguing that the statue represented "an atrocious distortion of the facts of American history." Noting Native Americans' contributions during World War I and their willingness to serve in the army after Pearl Harbor, O'Connor called the statue a "slander on the Indian race," which had become "an integral part of the American Nation."[9]

After World War II, inspired by their wartime contributions and by their belief that they were in fact part of the American nation, Native American activists picked up the mantle of protest. In advance of the November 1952 NCAI convention, Leta Myers Smart (Omaha), a member of the Los Angeles–based California Indian Federation, initiated a petition and letter-writing campaign to persuade Lynn to retire both *The Rescue* and its partner statue *Discovery*, which featured a half-naked Indian woman crouching before a European explorer. In a letter to Lynn, Smart complained that *The Rescue* humiliated American Indians visiting Washington, D.C. But she shrewdly framed the issue in international terms, contending that she and her group acted "for the country at large" in seeking a replacement statue "in better keeping for the right kind of propa-

5.1 Horatio Greenough's sculpture *The Rescue* adorned the East Front entrance of the U.S. Capitol from 1853 until 1958, when the Capitol architect ordered its removal. Groups such as the National Congress of American Indians and some members of Congress objected to its depiction of Indian savagery. Courtesy of Architect of the Capitol.

ganda for Americanism." Smart sounded this theme in subsequent petitions and letters; for example, she explained to the National Sculpture Society in September 1953 that she was acting "for all of us here in the United States, no matter whether we are Indian or something else, to have it so that we are in sooth actually in that enviable position of being a good example to the rest of the world." Linking termination to the Cold War context, Smart spoke the language of hybrid patriotism, representing all American Indians who objected to such images at a time when termination policies threatened Native rights, while justifying the campaign as one waged on behalf of all Americans, "because these statues are bad propaganda for America and would make excellent fodder for our enemies." Presenting the act of removing the sculpture as an ethical obligation to a people whose loyalty to the principles of Americanism had been demonstrated in three major wars in fifty years, Smart also linked material and moral concerns in noting that the United States "has plenty of money to cast upon the waters of many foreign countries, countries that haven't even taken the time to say 'Thank you!' Let Congress do something now in the name of the Indians for a change." In 1958 a new architect of the Capitol, J. George Stewart, had the two statues removed, claiming that they were decaying. But it was Smart's campaign, with support from members of Congress, that impelled Stewart to remove them. She kept her campaign alive to ensure that the statues would never return, chronicling two decades of protest against the statue in a 1959 *Harper's* magazine article that featured an evocative image of an American Indian dressed in a business suit but wearing feathers on his head, walking away from the wrecked statues carrying a sledgehammer. Here was the hybrid American Indian that Eastman, Parker, Bronson, and Smart had championed: the body Americanized but the head still Indian in its thinking and values.[10]

Making a Stand in Washington, D.C.

The sculptor Greenough had wanted to show in *The Rescue* "the "superiority of the white-man, and why and how civilization crowded the Indian from his soil." In the 1950s members of Congress were still debating Indian policy in the same terms. Congressional terminationists, as Senator Arthur Watkins of Utah put it, "sought to return to the historic principles of much earlier decades," meaning the nineteenth-century programs of forced assimilation. But the world, and Native Americans' engagement with it, had changed dramatically since then. Native activists and politicians increasingly viewed themselves as leaders of nations—domestic and dependent, but nations nonetheless. The use of patriotic rhetoric and the framing of American Indian issues as international issues to counter an antidemocratic and interventionist federal government became an especially important strategy for Native American politicians in early 1954, when Congress began to consider a spate of bills that proposed terminating individual Indian nations' sovereignty, using HCR 108 as its justification. These politicians traveled to the nation's capital to demand a different kind of rescue, a rescue not from an enlightened sage but from a federal bully they contended was behaving like the Soviet Union. As they understood it, they were thus acting patriotically in defending the interests not just of Native America but of America itself.[11]

In late February the NCAI staged the "Emergency Conference" in Washington, D.C., to attract public scrutiny to the legislative blitz. New NCAI president Joseph Garry (Coeur d'Alene), a veteran of World War II and Korea, invited Native Americans across the country to "rally an organized protest on a national basis against legislation which, if passed, would endanger the tribal existence of the American Indian people." Native leaders, many of them visiting Washington for the first time, represented forty-three Native communities from twenty-one states. In addition, nineteen non-Indian groups such as the American Legion, the Japanese American Citizens League, and the Montana Farmers Union joined traditional allies from the Association on American Indian Affairs and congressional allies such as Senator Henry C. Dworshak of Idaho, who told delegates that the U.S. government should provide "a Marshall Plan for Native Americans as well as for people in foreign lands." Native Americans' discussions among themselves and in confrontations with congressional terminationists such as Senator Watkins reveal key themes of Native Americans' political and ethnic consciousness in the heat of the termination crisis.[12]

Native politicians first had to address the idea that reservations perpetuated an anachronistic Indianness and to attack the notion, carved in stone in *The Rescue*, that Indianness was un-American and therefore dangerous. In "A Declaration of Indian Rights," the NCAI's official response to the suite of proposed termination bills, NCAI president Garry contested the prevailing belief held by many non-Indian politicians that reservations were similar to concentration camps. "Some of our fellow Americans," he observed, "think that our reservations are places of confinement. Nothing could be farther from the truth. Reservations do not imprison us. They are ancestral homelands, retained by us for our perpetual use and enjoyment. We feel we must assert our right to maintain ownership in our own way, and to terminate it only by our consent." Garry summed up the hybrid patriotism of American Indians in claiming that their goal was to discharge their "full responsibilities as citizens, and yet remain faithful to the Indian way of life." Addressing his "fellow Americans," Garry championed "those things that are promised to every citizen by our national charters, the Constitution and the Declaration of Independence." Other speakers at the Emergency Conference employed the same patriotic rhetoric. Thomas Segundo (Papago) maintained that "cultural diversity is one of the long-accepted traditions of American life." And in a written statement Zuni veterans of World War II and the Korean War reminded members of Congress that Native Americans had "fought for democracy." Now "we would like to have you show us this democratic way of life," read their statement. "We have served [overseas] in order to save our country, our people, our religion, our freedom of press and our freedom of speech from destruction . . . We, now in the land of freedom as Americans[,] are faced with [termination policies] which will mean total destruction of all tribes." Native Americans embraced national service as a vehicle to strengthen both Native identity and the "democratic way of life" that protected it. To them, "our country" meant both the United States and the tribes; "our people" meant both the American people and the Indian people. Once again Native Americans were promoting the view that they were in fact "the real Americans," a theme that had resonated during the Pueblo crisis of the early 1920s and in numerous letters sent to Truman during the Navajo crisis of the late 1940s.[13]

Garry's leadership heralded a new direction in American Indian politics. His service in World War II and the Korean War shaped his approach to resisting what he called Congress's "first wave of attack" and framed the NCAI's sharp responses to white politicians. Garry and other Emergency Conference delegates used the rhetoric of war in calling termination bills "liquidation legislation" and "extermination bills," and branding termination more generally the "annihilation of a culture," a "financial invasion

5.2 The leadership of the National Congress of American Indians pictured here (ca. 1954) reflected the increasingly important role that Native American women played in defending Native sovereignty during the termination era. Left to right: Helen Peterson, D'Arcy McNickle, Joseph Garry, Louis Bruce, and Ruth Bronson. Courtesy of National Museum of the American Indian, Smithsonian Institution, Photo No. 98-10200.

by white people," a grab of "uranium land," and a "battle for survival." On the defensive, terminationists had to defuse comparisons with Soviet-style violence as well as Soviet propaganda critical of U.S Indian policy. In addressing Emergency Conference delegates, George Abbott, the counsel for the House Committee on Interior and Insular Affairs, "urged fairness" in describing HCR 108 as "'terminal' legislation rather than 'liquidation legislation.'"[14]

Native American politicians spoke of their struggle as a Cold War struggle, constantly emphasizing that people around the world paid attention to the United States' treatment of Native people and thus reminding Congress what was at stake in preserving Native Americans' treaty rights. The council of the Isleta Pueblo employed the panoptical metaphor in a written statement: "We regret that we have to become aware of these [termination bills] when the eyes of the world are upon our nation, depending upon its integrity, its honor and its sense of intolerance and when we too seek friends among other peoples." NCAI leaders echoed this internationalist perspective in their report, "What Does Termination of Federal Trusteeship Mean to the Indian Peoples?" They posed the central question that animated postwar Indian nationalism: "Shouldn't Indians have the same right of self-determination that our government has stated, often and officially, is the inalienable right of peoples in far parts of the world? Do we apply a different set of principles, of ethics, to the people within our own borders?" This perspective drew upon bedrock notions of American foreign policy, first expressed by Woodrow Wilson and Franklin Roosevelt and then repeated in various guises as the Cold War evolved, while revealing an awareness of how people in Europe and other parts of the world evaluated the U.S. commitment to these ideals. Situating the struggle of Native Americans in the larger international struggle for the liberation of colonized peoples, the NCAI claimed the ideological and moral high ground in the termination debate.[15]

Like the 1954 U.S. Supreme Court decision in *Brown v. Board of Education*, the Emergency Conference represented a milestone in American race relations. These two events marked the federal government's failure to honor its constitutional obligations to protect minority groups' interests, one mediating white Americans' containment of African Americans' access to white space, the other containing white Americans' encroachment on treaty-protected Indian space. For Native Americans, the Emergency Conference of 1954 marked a turning point in their resistance to congressional termination. Assisted by the legal staff of the Association on American Indian Affairs, the NCAI used the conference to mobilize support from Indian and non-Indian groups and to publicize the antidemocratic nature of Congress's termination agenda in national and international media. Jim Hayes of the American Friends Service Committee estimated that nearly four thousand newspapers, radio stations, and television stations, including the British Broadcasting Company, covered the event, and British and European newspapers provided coverage to their readers. American newspaper reports noted the dignity with which Native Americans presented themselves at the conference. For example, a United Press reporter wrote that "there were no tomahawks, no feathers, no interpreting," but rather "educated Indians" using the "weapons" of "logical explanations, some impassioned pleading, and unadorned facts." Here was the "new Indian" at work, reversing the narrative of *The Rescue* to one in which Native Americans rescued the United States from itself as the world watched. As Joseph Garry put it in his official NCAI press release, the purpose of the Emergency Conference was to "develop constructive programs which will conserve Indian values and serve the best interests of the nation by protecting its national honor."[16]

Proving Their Patriotism

The Emergency Conference sustained a patriotic discourse that emerged as Cold War and termination events evolved simultaneously. The NCAI increasingly employed patriotic language at its annual conventions and in its constitution. At the group's 1949 convention, NCAI officials adopted Resolution 13, a statement of "Loyalty of Indians to U.S. Government": despite ongoing tensions between American Indians and the federal government, which had failed to keep "promises made in good faith," NCAI officials pledged their "allegiance" to that government and stated their "unequivocal objection to any type of government or any type of subversive activity which seeks to undermine or overthrow the present form of government of the United States." A 1953 resolution condemned "organizations, groups, and individuals affiliated with subversive movements and un-American activities designed to undermine American institutions." Detailing the ways in which American Indians had displayed their patriotism, ranging from buying war bonds to providing soldiers for both world wars and the Korean War, this resolution reaffirmed the NCAI's "faith in America and loyalty to its institutions" and offered the organization's help in waging war against subversives at home. The NCAI amended its constitution in 1955 to reflect these changes, adding Section F: "No individual or organization with known subversive activities or affiliation shall be admitted to membership."[17]

NCAI officials worked hard to protect their image as the virus of McCarthyism infected America in the 1950s. In April 1950 NCAI official Ruth Bronson forwarded to NCAI president Napoleon Johnson an edition of the American Communist Party newspaper *Our Times* sent to her by a BIA official on the Uintah and Ouray reservation in Utah. An article in the paper had urged the Uintah and Ouray Ute to join the NCAI, implying that the NCAI's interests were similar to those of the American Communist Party. Bronson recommended sending the article to Attorney General J. Howard McGrath and asserting that the NCAI did not want "the Communist party or any of its sympathizers helping our organization." Bronson believed that the NCAI could use such a letter as a prophylactic in response to "any hostile Congressional Committee or to any McCarthy-like member of Congress." But Johnson disagreed, telling Bronson that it would put the NCAI "in a defensive attitude" and suggested letting "a sleeping giant sleep and not disturb him until he starts something," referring either to Senator Joseph McCarthy, who had recently burst into the spotlight with his accusations about subversives in the State Department, or to the federal anticommunism machinery that he hijacked. Johnson did recommend that Bronson assure the BIA official in Utah that "there is nothing in our program, policy or philosophy that in any way leans towards the communistic theory of government."[18]

The NCAI gained national prominence as a result of the Emergency Conference. Facing increasing scrutiny from both NCAI members and government officials sensitive to un-American activities, NCAI staff went on the offensive to quell any notion that the organization subscribed to "the communistic theory of government." In August 1956 executive director Helen Peterson, a Cheyenne who grew up with Oglala Sioux on the Pine Ridge Reservation, promoted the idea of suing for libel a member of the Yakima Nation of Washington State who had testified during Department of the Interior hearings that "all ideas of the National Congress of American Indians are borne out of a communist front." Peterson told Washington state attorney Charles Luce that the NCAI would likely prevail in such a lawsuit, which she called "particularly appealing to me, since false suggestions of left-wing tendencies existing in this organization have been repeated irresponsibly for the last few years." Peterson considered charges of communism "acutely damaging to this organization." NCAI attorney John Cragun, making reference to previous charges that "the N.C.A.I. were pinko," reassured Luce that NCAI officials "have always checked with the Attorney General's list [of subversive organizations]; and they have repeatedly checked any other source of funds to make certain that they did not take funds from groups which might be questionable from a subversive point of view." The following year Peterson employed a different kind of panoptical metaphor in asking Louis Bruce Jr., the chairman of the NCAI membership committee, to investigate several pending applications because "the time has come when we must be very careful in accepting memberships, so that we can show we are being as watchful as possible."[19]

Acting on this conviction, Peterson rebuffed an effort by a representative of Farm Research to secure a report on the 1957 NCAI annual convention because Farm Research's journal, *Facts for Farmers*, had been listed in the 1944 "Guide to Subversive Organizations and Publications" published by the House Un-American Activities Committee. The *Facts for Farmers* editor, Charles Coe, had expressed interest in "the efforts made by the Indians and their friends to protect their rights." Coe included a copy of the May 1954 *Facts for Farmers*, which carried an article covering the NCAI's February 1954 Emergency Conference and an article titled "Indians Protest Land-Grab" that attacked termination policies for not only threatening American Indian lands but also "open[ing] the way for greedy, land-grabbing interests to plunder the lands of small and family-type farms generally." As they had during the allotment crisis of the 1880s, non-Indian farmers now connected their troubles to those of Indian landowners during the termination crisis of the 1950s.[20]

Peterson explained to Coe that "since our membership is justly very proud of its record of loyalty and our Constitution is specific in its emphasis on this aspect of our policy and operation," the NCAI was "unable and unwilling" to provide materials; she asked him to remove the NCAI from its lists. What is especially interesting about her reaction, other than that the NCAI could not abide the populist rhetoric of *Facts for Farmers*, is that Peterson sent carbon copies of her letter to HUAC, the National Republic, the American Legion, and Veterans of Foreign Wars. The same day, Peterson wrote Letitia Shankle, a Native American from Tulsa, to reassure her that the NCAI received no funds from the Robert Marshall Foundation, which was listed in the "Guide to Subversive Organizations and Publications," but rather from the Robert Marshall Civil Liberties Trust Fund, which was not. Peterson promised Shankle that the NCAI was "scrupulously careful . . . in trying to avoid involvement with questionable groups or persons," noting that NCAI leaders routinely checked the HUAC "Guide" as well as consulted with "three other groups in Washington which make it their business to keep track of un-American organizations and publications."[21]

Peterson's correspondence was not unusual. In January 1958 NCAI office manager Hilda Cragun notified Charles Skippon of the Department of

State's Division of Security that when the NCAI received correspondence from "individuals and organizations which we question," the organization hesitated to respond to ensure that the NCAI did not get involved in any "questionable activity." Cragun forwarded a December 1957 letter sent to the NCAI by a pan-German group called Interressengemeinschaft Deutschsprechender Indianerfreunde (Interest Group for German-Speaking Friends of the Indian), which listed members in Germany, Austria, Switzerland, and the Netherlands. The letter, reflecting Germans' heightened sensitivity to state-sponsored racial violence, noted Europeans' awareness of the "horrible wrong done to your people during centuries and we are ashamed of it . . . [W]e learn that the wrong is continued today by the intention of the American Government to terminate the reservations . . . Termination of the Reservations means, we understand, the extermination of your race, for when your lands are gone, your identity is lost, the Indian will be no more." Demonstrating the NCAI's sensitivity to Cold War propaganda battles, Cragun told Skippon that NCAI officials were "concerned that there may be a group of individuals in Frankfurt/Main who could further hurt the U.S. internationally by stirring up the 'Indian question'" and thus thought it best to bring the letter "to the attention of 'responsible authorities.'" In closing Cragun wrote: "Best wishes to you, Miriam, and the girls. Hope we can get together soon." This personal tone underscores the extent of their relationship.[22]

Three years after stirring up the Indian question with the February 1954 Emergency Conference, the NCAI was now informing on groups supportive of Native American rights to the Department of State, making it its business to "keep track of un-American organizations and publications." Its association with hyperpatriotic groups, its apparently regular contact with the Department of State and HUAC, and its rejection of international critiques of federal policy similar to its own speak both to its patriotic character and to the modus vivendi with federal officials that had developed largely as a result of its aggressive stand at the 1954 Emergency Conference. The NCAI leadership also employed this tactic to preserve the group's autonomy, fearful of itself being watched by the eyes of the FBI and labeled a subversive organization and thus made vulnerable to federal harassment from HUAC and the consequent loss of support from Native American and white supporters alike. As did their counterparts in the NAACP, NCAI officials and other Native American leaders had to negotiate with national Cold War institutions such as the State Department

5.3 West German citizens from the "Heidelberg Ogalala Tribe" and an American GI smoked a peace pipe and "played Indian" at an Indian Jamboree in Mannheim, West Germany, in 1956. Sustaining a long-standing fascination with American Indian culture, Indianist groups in Germany and other European countries protested termination policies during the 1950s and 1960s. Courtesy of National Archives and Records Administration, Central Plains Region (Kansas City).

and HUAC to preserve political efficacy in other areas. The NCAI remained active in fighting for Native sovereignty, but in ways circumscribed by Cold War pressures.[23]

Behind the Buckskin Curtain

Cold War pressures also required tribal politicians to negotiate with local institutions of power. The case of the Colville in Washington State illustrates the emerging divisions among Native Americans over the meaning of the Cold War. As the termination movement gathered steam in the late

1940s, the elected members of the Colville Business Council had voted to send delegations to both the NCAI and the U.S. Congress after deciding that Native Americans "would have to enter [national] politics." Using Cold War rhetoric, both local politicians and mining companies attacked the council's efforts to protect and even to expand reservation sovereignty. So too did off-reservation Colville, who championed the terminationist agenda of dividing reservation assets on a pro rata basis. Lucy Swan, one of the most vocal opponents of reservation sovereignty, complained to the secretary of the interior in "hopes of breaking down this communistic situation." Stella Leach criticized the Colville tribe's membership in the NCAI, calling it "an organization definitely on the 'pink side.'" Colville opponents of tribal sovereignty eventually formed the Colville Indian Association (CIA) and the Colville Indian Commercial Club (CICC) to protest the Business Council's agenda, in particular its efforts to restore land to the reservation. The CICC used the rhetorical cudgel of anticommunism in claiming that the council's proposed land restoration legislation "would relegate the Colville Tribe to a communist type of regimentation." And in an editorial titled "Behind the Buckskin Curtain," CIA president Frank Moore, contending that "the sovereign government under which Indians are forced to live does not differ from that of Russia and its satellite countries," asked, "Can we afford to fight against this form of dictatorship in foreign countries while allowing [it] to develop among Americans at home?" Moore's goal, radically different from the NCAI's, was to *liquidate* rather than *strengthen* tribal government and its control of reservation resources.[24]

Elected Colville politicians were forced to defend their actions using the language of patriotism and democracy. Frank George, an NCAI vice president and a Colville Business Council adviser, maintained that the NCAI "was not associated with any subversive groups and all its members were good Americans." George had warned Colville politicians to be wary of the "ideologies" of "emancipation" and "termination," telling the council, "The fact that people were not all alike in their views was the strength of our way of life." The council's efforts to preserve the Colville reservation came at a time when "the national government was involved in a global war," as Colville councilman Pete Gunn put it. As "loyal citizens," Gunn declared, the Colville "would help their country." In doing so, they situated patriotism within the boundaries of reservations as much as outside them, in effect erasing those boundaries.[25]

The anti-reservation CICC had argued that "liquidation would be the American way," by which it meant that the American end of converting assets into cash—in this case converting reservation resources into pro rata payments—justified the means with which it was accomplished, even by the "communistic" means of political liquidation. The efforts of non-Indians and some Indians as well to force the liquidation of tribal corporate assets in the name of American values highlight this central contradiction of U.S. Cold War behavior: the use of undemocratic means to further an "American" end. This campaign resonated with the federal government's late-nineteenth-century allotment campaign, which also employed anticommunist rhetoric to "mandate a measure unimaginable in U.S. society—the wholesale redistribution of property."[26]

Colville terminationists' views mirrored those of other Native Americans opposed to the maintenance of reservations. Politicians on the Klamath reservation in Oregon and the Menominee reservation in Wisconsin used anticommunist rhetoric in pursuing congressional termination of their reservations, both of which contained valuable timber assets. These intratribal battles complicated the NCAI's efforts to halt congressional termination. And they illustrate the protean nature of Native American identity. Not all Native Americans agreed with NCAI president Joseph Garry, who told an NCAI audience in 1954, "The preservation of your reservation, the retention of your lands . . . are those things that keeps [sic] your identity." Migrations during World War II and through the federal relocation program had created powerful off-reservation constituencies that worked with reservation factions and non-Indian groups to push for the dissolution of tribal estates, in part to liquidate valuable reservation assets into cash and in part to liquidate their tribal identity. In the two most prominent cases of termination, Congress passed legislation terminating the Klamath and the Menominee in 1954, leading to per capita distributions of the land and timber sales and the effective end of the two reservations. Termination represented, for some "elite-acculturated" Native Americans, an opportunity not only to liquidate their reservation's wealth but also to dissociate themselves from "native-oriented" tribal members and thus complete their process of assimilation through a legalistic liquidation of Indianness. The campaign of off-reservation Colville to terminate the Colville reservation along the lines of the Klamath and Menominee terminations, however, dragged on into the early 1970s, ultimately failing.[27]

The Klamath and Menominee terminations and the unresolved Colville case became potent symbols for other Native groups fighting to prevent the termination of their reservations. Indeed the struggle between Colville terminationists and anti-terminationists became associated with an important metaphor of the Cold War: the domino theory. It is difficult to pinpoint American Indians' original application of the image, which President Eisenhower first used in April 1954 in response to a reporter's question about Indochina's strategic importance. Eisenhower had argued that if the first communist "domino" in Indochina fell, then others would fall "very quickly" and trigger "a disintegration that would have the most profound influences." Native students attending the American Indian Development workshop in 1970, and likely before then, faced a final exam containing the following true-false question: "Colville termination expresses the 'domino theory' of eliminating Indian reservations in the United States." The exam question and its correct answer, "true," reveal the extent to which Native activists on the front lines of a struggle to maintain reservation and cultural boundaries saw it as a Cold War struggle and recognized the need to develop strategies to contain the spread of termination ideology and the policies it spawned. If Native Americans did not actually use the term "domino theory" in the 1950s, they at least framed their collective struggle within that context. In the 1950s, and into the 1970s, Native leaders viewed the termination of any American Indian reservation as the "disintegration" of Native sovereignty writ small.[28]

An American Indian in Indochina

Even as they waged Cold War battles at home, Native Americans became involved in resolving the crisis of falling dominos abroad, especially in Indochina, helping U.S. officials to counteract Soviet propaganda by putting a positive spin on American race relations. The government's foreign information campaigns focused on "impressing the peoples of the world with the reliability, consistency and seriousness of the U.S. and its policies; contributing to the prestige of the U.S. in the eyes of the world . . . and influencing the peoples of the world to look toward the U.S. rather than the Soviet Union." Propaganda about racial discrimination in the United States proved the most difficult to counteract, as the problem was endemic and well publicized. A State Department report on the impact of racial discrimination on U.S. foreign relations noted that "commercial press and radio outside the United States, as well as within the United States, dramatize these incidents in headline treatment . . . Hence, Moscow seems to consider it more effective propaganda to avoid competing with non-Communist channels to carry the stories. In fact, Moscow quotes from the non-Communist publications in order to increase the credibility of its stories." For example, a 1951 *Pravda* article, titled "Answers to Readers' Questions: Tragedy of Indians in U.S.A.," combined data on American Indians' poverty published in the *Journal of the American Medical Association* with statements that compared BIA officials to "the raving Führer and the other fascist hangmen, with their jabbering about 'pure-blooded' Aryans and 'inferior' Slavs! The difference between Hitler Germany's racists and U.S. racists is not great—more accurately, there is none at all." To cite one other example, an article in the East German magazine *USA in Wort und Bild* (USA in Words and Pictures), a publication geared toward young readers, featured a photograph of a Native American named Chief Rising Sun protesting treaty violations during congressional hearings, *Life* magazine's "Picture of the Week." And the article used Rising Sun's words as quoted in *Life* to assert that "the history of national minorities in the United States is, as everyone knows, written with blood. The crime that the white men commit against the black Americans every day is monstrous. No less monstrous is their injustice against the red Americans." The article catalogued that bloody history from the 1600s to the contemporary situation of American Indians, "deprived, despised and like a dying-out animal species locked up in a reservation." In short, the article concluded, "the so-called American democracy revealed itself then and made a bloody mockery of its victims."[29]

Drawing on increasing tensions between whites and blacks in the American South, Soviet propagandists published a series of articles in the summer of 1957 condemning U.S. racial discrimination, which a *Krasnaya zvezda* article called "one manifestation of the true nature of the American 'democracy' that the United States is trying to foist on other countries and peoples." A section on American Indians castigated "the 'freedom' zealots across the Atlantic" for denying American Indians "all political rights," including the right to form their own social and political organizations. This heightened propaganda reflected increasing tensions between the United States and the Soviet Union on various fronts, including outer space with the launching of *Sputnik*, and in the contested space of the developing world, in which the "proper place" of Indians in American society became a salient issue.[30]

Shortly after President Truman announced the Point Four program in January 1949, the U.S. government expanded its efforts to promote cultural bonds in underdeveloped areas of the world. A 1949 State Department report stressed that U.S. projects faced barriers related to

> increasing knowledge of the American color bar, by what appear to be genuine fears of American "big business," and by the suspicion, not confined to communist circles, that colonial territories are being increasingly viewed by the United States as sources of materials, bases, and manpower for a future war with Russia . . . If the Point IV program is to serve the long-term foreign policy interests of the United States, it is important that this Government do what it can to meet and overcome these suspicions.

To cite one example among many, a May 1949 article in the *Ceylon Observer* called America's "color bar" the "greatest propaganda gift any country could give the Kremlin in its persistent bid for the affections of the colored races of the world." The State Department proposed ameliorating this public relations crisis in regions served by the Point Four program by employing members of "American cultural or minority groups" who could create connections with the "psychology or cultural patterns of the peoples to be assisted." Thus began what one State Department official called a "cultural offensive," a phrase that captures the contradictions of American Cold War activities abroad.[31]

The importance of this cultural offensive became especially clear after leaders of twenty-nine Third World nations, including India, Vietnam, China, and Pakistan, met in Bandung, Indonesia, in 1955. Speakers at the Bandung Conference, hosted by Indonesia's president Sukarno, championed the rehabilitation of their native cultures, their solidarity in the face of continuing Western imperialism, and their neutrality in the midst of the Cold War between the United States, the Soviet Union, and their respective allies. The State Department reported that when Sukarno visited the United States after the conference, he emphasized to U.S. officials that "educational and cultural interchange between sovereign equals for mutual social, economic and cultural benefits . . . would win friends and influence people in the underdeveloped nations rather than any ostentatious display of might and wealth." The report stressed that "the President of Indonesia was speaking for most of the other underdeveloped countries of the world."[32]

Native Americans participated in this cultural offensive to "win friends and influence people in the underdeveloped nations." The State Department organized five international exhibits of Indian arts and crafts—two in Europe and one each in North Africa, Latin America, and Asia. A Native American named Sun Bear told Interior Department officials that such exhibits would "build good will for this country." The State Department's International Educational Exchange Program (IEEP) sponsored the tour of Native artist Solomon McCombs (Creek) to Syria, Lebanon, Jordan, India, Burma, Libya, and the Belgian Congo. IEEP officials had originally planned to send McCombs to Iran as well, but State Department public relations officer C. Edward Wells argued against it. Wells reported that Iranians gained information about American Indians from films and books distributed by an "unfriendly power," in particular a low-cost Persian-language version of *The Last Frontier* by Howard Fast. First published in 1941, *The Last Frontier* documents the 1878 campaign of the Northern Cheyenne to regain their ancestral homeland in Montana; for Fast, whose works were banned from distribution by the U.S. State Department, American Indians remained a persecuted minority in the twentieth century. Yet Wells thought it unwise for McCombs to tour Iran in conjunction with a visit by an African American athlete "since too much emphasis on our minorities would probably be misconstrued." The State Department, he argued, had to be careful not to draw so much attention to minority representatives and risk reinforcing perceptions of racial discrimination. It was a different story in South Asia, where Soviet propagandists were working hard to forge cultural connections between Soviet ethnic minorities and the peoples of the region. South Asia was especially fertile ground for Cold War propaganda battles given that this was where President Eisenhower situated the crisis of the "domino theory," and given the central role South Asian leaders played in the Bandung Conference. An American attaché reported from Assam, India, that the United States was "losing the propaganda war against the totalitarian powers, particularly in the area of intercultural relations," largely because their representatives appealed not only to elites but also to "people on the village level" through their cultural programming.[33]

The State Department had had hopes of sending American icons like Danny Kaye and William Faulkner to India, Pakistan, and other emerging nations in the developing world. But it was the American Indian artist and dancer Tom Two Arrows (also known as Thomas Dorsey) who became, in the words of a Karachi-based State Department official, "without a doubt the most successful performer that has come out to this area." Two Arrows became an important part of the State Department's efforts to meet the goals outlined by Sukarno and to engage the critical area of "intercultural relations." In some places he competed directly against Soviet or Chinese dance troupes taking part in indigenous festivals. As comfortable in a business suit as in the traditional clothes of his American Indian ancestors, Two Arrows appealed to elites and to "people on the village level," connecting with Pakistanis, Indians (in India), and other nonwhites in demonstrating similarities between their dances, jewelry, and physical features and those of American Indians.[34]

Born in Albany, New York, Two Arrows was a member of the Delaware (Lenni-Lenape) Nation but was adopted by the Onondaga after spending six weeks studying their culture. In his program Two Arrows danced, played Native instruments, told American Indian legends, discussed his costumes, and gave brief talks on Indian games, songs, and dances. In two separate tours between 1955 and 1957 he traveled throughout Malaysia, Vietnam, South Korea, Japan, India, Pakistan, Taiwan, Cambodia, Thailand, and Burma. Wherever he traveled his performances drew huge crowds. In Malaysia he performed before an estimated audience of 25,500. In Vietnam he addressed crowds ranging between 1,500 and 5,000 in six performances in Cholon and Saigon; in addition, the U.S. Information Service Films Production Division prepared a twenty-minute film of his performance for later distribution by USIS mobile units in rural Vietnam. In South Korea he performed before 10,000 Republic of Korea troops, 1,200 ROK personnel, 500 ROK Air Force members, and a full house of 1,200 at the Municipal Theater. According to the State Department, Two Arrows "gave Koreans, who are as sensitive as any Asian people to the [American] race problem, a new insight into the opportunities for success present in the United States for a member of a minority group." He toured Burma in April 1956 and again in January 1957. During his second visit he traveled out of Rangoon and Mandalay on an "up-country trip" to perform before 25,000 Burmese children, army personnel, and villagers. As in Korea and elsewhere, the American race problem received "disproportionate and uninformed criticism," according to the State Department, and thus Two Arrows's program "served as an excellent refutation and clarification." Like Navajo uranium miners, Two Arrows was a "secret weapon" of the Cold War. Rather than mining uranium, however, he mined for hearts and minds "up-country."[35]

Using President Sukarno's definition of success, the State Department reported that Two Arrows "won friends for America" throughout his tours, especially in India and Pakistan. There he faced the most explicit challenge to his tour from Soviet agents asking "obviously 'loaded' questions" and planting "misinformation" about American Indians and reservation life. Given this "Communist penetration" in India and Pakistan, a State Department official somehow thought it "appropriate that it took an American Indian to open up pioneer territory." Like "cultural offensive," the use of the term "pioneer territory" reveals the imperial thrust of American Cold War programming.[36]

During several trips through Pakistan in March and April 1956, Two Arrows gave ten performances, appearing before tens of thousands of Pakistanis. In the remote Hill Tracts of East Pakistan he performed before crowds of ten thousand on two occasions as well as to smaller crowds before he staged his finale at Dacca Stadium in front of eighteen thousand spectators. He was the most valuable IEEP performer, according to a State Department official, because his "educational approach in dispelling Hollywood or Russian inspired misconceptions about the American Indian" enabled him to reach "the educated as well as the illiterate segments of the population." One State Department official wrote of his securing an "entente cordiale" with the people of East Pakistan, an extraordinary appellation for one individual's impact. Perhaps as the result of Two Arrows's visits to Pakistan, two members of the Pakistan Supreme Court asked to visit an Indian reservation during their State Department–sponsored trip to the United States in August 1956.[37]

Two Arrows was equally successful in India. During his January 1956 tour, Consul General R. Borden Reams wrote of "Indians' interest in a minority group, and the similarities in culture which the Indians felt they found" in Two Arrows's presentations. He gave eleven performances before crowds as large as ten thousand, including several appearances as part of the popular All India Children's Festival and the Children's Little Theatre Festival. He established common cultural ground with "unusually interested, sympathetic and attentive audiences" that included local artists who discovered "similarities of themes and techniques between American Indian art and the art of India."[38]

Two Arrows's tours received widespread newspaper coverage that reinforced these cultural connections. The *Statesman* of Calcutta ran a photograph of his performance in a front-page headline. A report in the *Hindustan Times* included a picture demonstrating the physical resemblance between Two Arrows and a member of the Naga ethnic group of India. The reporter claimed that Two Arrows's tour would "rouse more interest in America than a chartered plane full of dollar laden diplomats," in part because "Red Indian Tom Two Arrows looks Nepali, or Naga, or Malayan, or Indonesian." A discussion with Two Arrows, the reporter said, provided "the missing pieces in my imaginative jigsaw of America." He now saw Indian reservations as "just ordinary American villages and countryside demarcated by a road-sign, nothing more." Demonstrating a familiarity with the Navajo aid crisis of the late 1940s, the reporter remarked on the "grimness of the Navajo reservation" but also noted that the Navajo had adapted to difficult conditions. "Ambassador" Tom Two Arrows helped people in India "get to know and like" the "original American" who lived alongside white Americans, the "New Americans." Another observer, Burhanuddin Hassan of the *Pakistan Times*, saw Two Arrows as a hybrid American who "combines in himself the tribal simplicity and modern American elegance."[39]

Two Arrows the "ambassador" explicitly refuted Soviet propaganda by maintaining that, in Hassan's paraphrase, "American Indians live equally well as others in the United States. There is no prejudice against them whatsoever and they are loved and respected all over the country." According to another reporter from the *Pakistan Times*, Two Arrows "denied that there was any colour bar against the Indians. They were loved and liked by all Americans." Speaking to reporters in Taipei, Two Arrows noted that the American Indian population was "increasing even faster than those Americans of European descent," challenging Soviet arguments that American Indians were dying off because of white oppression. Two Arrows, wrote one State Department official, "was able to show . . .

that an American Indian can and does occupy an important place in American society and at the same time has been allowed to preserve his cultural heritage." Two Arrows's propaganda value extended to his traveling partner, his wife, Stella. Secretary of State John Foster Dulles enthusiastically promoted Two Arrows's tours to skeptical personnel in South Asian embassies by pointing out that Two Arrows and Stella, a white anthropologist, "present themselves as typical young Americans who maintain family, home and a place in contemporary society," a model of Cold War domesticity, "while continuing a lively interest" in American Indian culture. When audiences asked if an American Indian could marry a white woman, Tom presented Stella in answer to that question. Dulles justified the additional expense of transporting Stella all over South Asia because she "adds interest to the project as a living proof that successful mixed marriages are possible in the United States." Interestingly, the *Pakistan Times* article on Two Arrows included a photo of Stella, describing her as his "American wife," suggesting that while the couple may have provided a model of Cold War ethnic integration in America, Tom himself could not be fully American, but remained a hybrid bridging East and West.[40]

For U.S. officials trying to counter widespread Soviet propaganda, the Two Arrows team became roving reminders of the possibilities of racial integration and thus of American social progress more broadly, even as the United States sought to integrate South Asia into its Cold War sphere of influence. Why did Two Arrows participate in this campaign, which involved traveling to the most remote regions and under the most difficult conditions for any American performer? Two Arrows was familiar with the cultural and geographical terrain of the area. During World War II he had served with the U.S. Air Transport Command in Southeast Asia, where he learned Bengali and participated in native celebrations. According to Consul General Reams, Two Arrows wanted to lecture against "the warped opinion of Indian life," largely shaped by Hollywood; "his underlying desire is to contradict the movie conception of Indians" dressed in stereotypical garb. Married to a professional white woman, celebrated for his indigenous art by white critics and curators, and living between two Indian communities, the Lenni-Lenape and Onondaga, Two Arrows likely avoided the termination pressures that squeezed much of Native America. Like the African American "Jazz Ambassadors" whom the State Department marketed to the Third World in the 1950s and 1960s as a more hu-

mane face of U.S. race relations than that found in segregated America,
Two Arrows offered an image as problematic as those presented in Soviet
propaganda or Hollywood films recycling stock images of the Noble Sav-
age or the ignorant Plains Indian on horseback. For many Indians in 1950s
America, real integration remained either undesirable or, as it was for most
African Americans, unattainable.[41]

The State Department continued to ameliorate foreign criticism of the
poverty and anger of American Indians by distributing abroad a 1959 report on Indian life that was part of a series called "Discussion Papers on
Minorities." The report was circulated in South Africa, for example, where
State Department officials had noted "an increasing number of instances
where speakers and writers of South Africa refer to the United States Indians." The report countered Soviet charges that reservations functioned as
American concentration camps. One Moscow radio broadcast in February
1958 had declared that Indians, "the most underprivileged people in the
United States," were forced to live in "huge concentration camps . . . Today, gradual extinction is the fate of the people in these reservations." The
Soviet use of "concentration camp" no doubt stemmed from its appeal as a
visceral propaganda term, but it may also have been drawn from U.S. officials' own use of the term to describe Indian reservations, which became
more common after 1945. Another possible influence for both U.S. and
Soviet officials' use of the term in the late 1950s was the American author
Carlos Embry, who argued in his 1956 book *America's Concentration
Camps: The Facts about Our Indian Reservations Today* that reservations
"were set aside as concentration camps for the Indians, much the same as
we have set aside wild life refuges on public lands." The 1959 State Department report countered that "reservations definitely are not 'concentration camps.' They are areas of land reserved by treaty, statute, or executive order by the use and benefit of a specific Indian tribe or tribes . . .
Whether an individual wishes to remain on or leave a reservation is exclu-
sively a question for that Indian to decide." But even as it proclaimed the
reservation sovereign space protected by national treaties, the report, written by a BIA official, denigrated the concept of the reservation and Indian
culture more generally, concluding that "the reservation all too often remains a place where Indians merely continue to exist." The paternalistic
tone illustrates the extent to which federal officials failed to comprehend
the special meaning of the reservation in Native American life, a weakness that heralded other failures of intercultural relations in the 1960s.[42]

The report also condemned the idea of an indigenous Point Four program to develop Indian reservations, criticizing groups which "oppose foreign aid . . . because 'charity begins at home.'" The report thus also reflected the strenuous resistance of federal officials to any program that conflated the interests of American Indians with those of people in regions benefiting from Point Four aid. As Tom Two Arrows traveled abroad through those regions trying to win friends for America, Native American activists waged a campaign at home for a domestic Point Four program that they believed would secure for the United States, as the Shoshone-Bannock of Idaho put it in 1957, "the hearts and minds of the [American] Indian people."[43]

A Point Four Program for Indian America

In a speech to the International Development Conference in April 1952, Secretary of State Dean Acheson described the recipients of Point Four foreign aid funds as people

> determined to share as equals in the benefits of modern progress. They are determined that their resources will no longer be developed in the interest of foreigners on the pattern of the old imperialism . . . They insist that these resources be developed for their own benefit. They are determined to establish their own free political and economic institutions—institutions which will make use of the best of our experience and will, at the same time, retain the best of their own cultures, and their own great traditions. This, I believe is the mood and the temper that has come to Africa and Asia in my lifetime.

During Acheson's lifetime such a mood also prevailed in Native America, whose leaders watched the money from foreign aid programs travel first to Europe and then to the underdeveloped areas of the world. Native Americans were determined to establish their own political and economic institutions, use their own natural resources, and retain their own cultures and traditions. But they sought to accomplish those goals within the boundaries of the United States.[44]

In the early 1950s American Indian activists conceived of an indigenous Point Four program from the intersection of the Navajo aid program at home and the Point Four aid program abroad after Congress failed to advance similar reservation rehabilitation bills for over a dozen other Indian nations along the same lines. D'Arcy McNickle, a founding member of the NCAI, was especially embittered by Congress's refusal to extend Navajo-scale rehabilitation funds to the rest of Native America. He contended that Native Americans deserved Point Four funding because it would vest in them the responsibility to administer development aid, a Point Four imperative, rather than relegate them to being the objects of BIA programs designed and implemented by non-Indians. McNickle proposed the first version of an American Indian Point Four program in his address to the 1951 NCAI annual conference, calling it "A Ten-Point Program for American Indians." In his speech he criticized the BIA for spending the bulk of its funds on salaries for white BIA personnel rather than on developing Native resources, which, he said, would constitute "a fundamental attack on the poverty and lack of opportunity which now confront our Indian people. Admittedly, it would cost money to bring these developments about; let us say it would require staggering amounts of money . . . WHAT I HAVE BEEN SUGGESTING IS, IN EFFECT, A DOMESTIC POINT 4 PROGRAM FOR OUR INDIAN RESERVATIONS, OUR UNDEVELOPED AREAS." He repeated his message in various forums, including an article in *América Indígena*, a monthly journal published in English and Spanish, in which he argued, "Surely the United States, which would like to see undeveloped and under-developed areas of the World brought into more fruitful functioning, is capable of achieving the development of its own native population."[45]

The NCAI adopted a modified version of McNickle's program at its November 1954 convention, championing the creation of what McNickle called a "master plan" for each reservation and the expansion of federal aid to develop each reservation's resources. The NCAI introduced its "Point Nine program" to Congress in February 1955. In presenting the document to Senator James E. Murray, a Montana Democrat who chaired the powerful Senate Committee on Interior and Insular Affairs, NCAI executive director Helen Peterson stated that the program attempted "to persuade the U.S. Government to apply within its own borders those principles which the United States has found to be sound for under-developed countries in other parts of the world . . . The Indian Point Nine Program, in other words, is a kind of domestic Point 4 program of technical assistance." The NCAI's program also reflected, Peterson noted, a broader goal of making officials recognize Native people "as they are" and not as the government wished them to be.[46]

It is important to note that NCAI officials did not oppose either the idea of relocation or the Voluntary Relocation Program. Indeed the NCAI sanctioned the VRP, but only if it served as a "minor and supplementary program" of a broader rehabilitation plan such as Point Four. But NCAI president Joseph Garry detected among BIA officials no "enthusiasm and support" for such aid programs and argued that the VRP had become *the* BIA program; widely promoted and expanded in the mid-1950s, the program now engendered "unrest and fear" among Native Americans. NCAI vice president Carl Whitman (Mandan) explained that he condemned not the VRP but the "tendency of the BIA to ride the 'relocation' horse to the exclusion of all else." In a meeting with BIA officials in Aberdeen, South Dakota, Whitman's efforts to "justify reservation programs were practically ridiculed." As he reported, "We were brow beaten." BIA officials, he complained, praised the relocation program "with almost fanatic ecstasy." Thus, he said, the BIA's policy could be summed up: "If there are no Indians on reservations, then there is no reservation problem."[47]

The Association on American Indian Affairs, the nation's leading non-Indian reform group, promoted its own "American Indian Point IV Program" through an extensive public relations campaign. Over three dozen newspapers, including the *Baltimore Evening Sun*, the *New York Times*, and the *Portland Oregonian*, ran stories on the AAIA plan. These articles echoed the themes that emerged during the Navajo crisis of the late 1940s: the claim that Christian charity begins at home, the argument that American Indians needed substantial federal aid, and the conflation of domestic and foreign contexts. The *Boston Herald* editorialized that Congress should extend a Point Four program to Native Americans because "they are worse off than most of the countries we are now giving Point Four aid to." In Lewiston, Idaho, the *Tribune* remarked that "the United States could learn much about dealing with underdeveloped nations across the globe by working at home in a Point 4 program for Indians." But the *New York Daily News* predicted that Congress would not support the plan because "our Indians live in the wrong country. If they lived, say, in Pakistan or India or Malaya or Timbuctoo—well, sir, there'd be no limit to the U.S. taxpayers' dough our squandermaniacs would shower upon them." Whether the *Tribune* or the *Daily News* had it right remained to be seen.

5.4 These images appeared in the Tekea, Washington, *Sentinel* in March 1956 as part of an NCAI fund-raising campaign promoting a domestic Point Four program of reservation rehabilitation to counter relocation pressures. "Doug" refers to Secretary of the Interior Douglas MacKay. Another slogan of the campaign was "Remind our government that many solemn obligations still remain unfilled at home." Tekea, Washington, *Sentinel* (March 1956). William Zimmerman Jr. Papers (MSS 517), Box 16, Folder 6, Center for Southwest Research, University Libraries, University of New Mexico.

Supporters of a domestic aid program for American Indians were seeking the repeal of HCR 108, the congressional statement of intent to terminate Native sovereignty. As during the Navajo aid debates of the late 1940s, American Indian Point Four advocates were forced to sell their aid program as a Cold War program.[48]

In January 1957 Senator Murray introduced to the Committee on Interior and Insular Affairs Senate Concurrent Resolution 3 (SCR 3), "An American Indian Point Four Program"; Representative Lee Metcalf of Montana introduced a House version, House Concurrent Resolution 155, in March 1957. SCR 3 stated that the "American 'Point 4 program,' as it has been applied successfully in underdeveloped areas of the world, reveals tested techniques whereby American Indian communities may be so developed." It required the BIA to create and manage an American Indian Point Four program that rejected termination policies, protected Indian culture and identity, respected "older, revered values," and provided assistance for vocational, technical, and professional education programs devised by American Indians themselves. The Subcommittee on Indian Affairs of the Committee on Interior and Insular Affairs pushed SCR 3 forward to the Senate Committee on Interior and Insular Affairs. But there it died.[49]

Failing to effect a philosophical reorientation toward Indian-white relations by replacing HCR 108 with SCR 3, congressional supporters then developed concrete legislation in the form of S. 809, "A Bill to provide economic assistance to the American Indians." The bill called for the rehabilitation of reservations with a $200 million fund to establish Native and non-Native industries that would create employment on the reservations. S. 809 was a hybrid bill in that it sanctioned industrializing parts of Native America and integrating them into the national economy even as it furthered a self-determinationist agenda by promoting reservation rehabilitation and thus strengthening Native sovereignty. Indeed the Pine Ridge Sioux championed the American Indian Point Four program as a "new middle way" between "premature termination" that exacerbated social problems and a "paternalism" that perpetuated dependency on federal programs.[50]

Senate hearings on S. 809, held by the Subcommittee on Indian Affairs of the Committee on Interior and Insular Affairs, began on March 27, 1957. Introduced by Senator William Langer, a North Dakota Republican whose purview included several of the poorest reservations in the country, the bill was co-sponsored by twenty U.S. senators, many of them representing American Indian constituencies. Langer's extensive survey of Native America as part of a Juvenile Delinquency Subcommittee investigation persuaded him that increased employment was the answer to that problem and to larger problems of Native health, education, and welfare. As representatives of a group of forty Indian nations put it, Native Americans simply wanted to "obtain stable and gainful employment so that they might become a self-sustaining people." Supporters of S. 809 sounded other key themes: relocation was not the sole answer to the problem of poverty; the termination agenda had failed to advance Native interests while forcing Native Americans to sustain defensive measures rather than develop new programs; Native Americans wanted the opportunity to shape their programs along the lines of the Point Four program abroad; and supporting the program was good Cold War policy.[51]

Senator Langer promoted the international dimensions of S. 809 by arguing that in light of its giving billions in aid abroad, it was critical for the United States to take care of its own citizens, in part "because of the impact that it will have on peoples on foreign lands." He cited the case of an official of an unidentified Asian country who had asked a U.S. official, "How do you expect to solve the plight of the many people in depressed areas around the world when you cannot solve the plight of the few hundred thousand Indians in your own country?" Other key supporters included George McGovern, who asked his colleagues, "Is it not self-evident that if the Indian people of Bolivia or Guatemala qualify for our economic and technical assistance, the Indian people of the United States, our own citizens, should have the same benefits?" McGovern sought to advance a program that reflected the cultural and economic reality of Native life, as many Native Americans were going to remain on the reservation "both because many Indians want it that way, and because there is no realistic alternative," given the failure of relocation programs.[52]

To help make their Cold War case, S. 809 sponsors included Europeans' perspectives in the proceedings, as Senator Paul Douglas, an Illinois Democrat, did in introducing into the *Congressional Record* several letters submitted by foreign organizations supportive of Indian rights. One, signed by a group of Austrians, urged Congress to adopt a Point Four program for American Indians, whom they deemed "these famous and all over the world well-known peoples," explaining that since similar American aid programs had helped to rebuild their own communities, they felt "all the more sensitive that the natives of America should receive less from . . . the United States. Today after the end of the colonial period of the world it is a matter of honor of the great powers to treat the oldest inhabitants of their countries honorably, and to respect their native rights, and also the rights guaranteed by the international rights, above all their self-determination." A second letter, from the Interessengemeinschaft Deutsch-Sprechender Indianerfreunde, which the NCAI had referred to the State Department, was less conciliatory in asserting that the Indian had been "robbed of his country" and in calling termination a form of "extermination." The group claimed that American Indians were "a neglected minority, the worst fed, the worst housed, the poorest of all Americans, as poverty stricken as the poor of Asia and Africa." The group, composed of Germans, Austrians, Swiss, and Dutch, urged Congress to adopt S. 809 in the name of "Christianity, humanity, and of justice . . . in accordance with the laws of the U.N." The Veterans of Foreign Wars, the American Friends Service Committee, and the Board of Home Missions of the Congregational Christian Churches expressed the same themes; the representative of the Board of Home Missions, highlighting the international repercussions of American Indians' poverty, argued that S. 809 represented an "economical program from the standpoint of our foreign relations." Private citizens echoed this point, as Clara Johnson of California did by arguing for an American Indian Point Four program because it "may partially counteract peoples' ideas of U.S. treatment of Negroes."[53]

Most important, representatives of numerous Indian nations supported S. 809 in writing and during the May 1957 congressional hearings. Most of those who testified or who submitted written statements framed the issue in international as well as domestic terms. Linking the nineteenth-century context of treaties with the twentieth-century context of international aid programs, the Shoshone-Bannock of Idaho resolved that the adoption of SCR 3 and S. 809 would "erase that mistrust in the hearts and minds of the Indian people" because the federal government would thereby "fulfill its obligation to carry out the purposes and intent of the original treaties and agreements." Native American women testified or submitted statements to a greater degree than in previous Indian rights campaigns. NCAI executive director Helen Peterson testified, as did Vestana Cadue, chairwoman of the Kickapoo tribe in Kansas, who stated that the Kickapoo "have the same needs as people in underdeveloped countries overseas . . . We have read that it would cost one-half of 1 percent of what this Nation spends on foreign aid to help Indian tribes develop their human and natural resources." In his testimony John Rainier, NCAI treasurer and vice chairman of the All-Pueblo Council, which represented twenty thousand Pueblo, sounded similar themes, asserting, "This great country of ours has been pouring billions of dollars to give technical advice and economic assistance to the undeveloped countries abroad with the hope that, with this huge expenditure and expression of good will, the United States would win these countries on the side of democracy." Rainier demonstrated solidarity with African American and Japanese American groups that had shown support for Native American rights during the 1950s, remarking that NCAI officials "believe, too, that when our minority groups are socially and economically secure, our country will be in a much stronger position to say to the rest of the world, 'This is Democracy as it is practiced in the United States.'"[54]

Two additional witnesses took pains to frame the Cold War dimensions of the legislation in especially provocative ways. NCAI attorney John Cragun asked members of Congress to understand American Indians' affairs by imagining what would happen if Americans "were conquered by the Chinese Communists." He continued: "We wouldn't suddenly and happily become either Chinese or Communists. We ultimately might learn the language, but we couldn't, as would our children and our children's children, share our present cultural prejudices." Edward Dozier (Santa Clara Pueblo), representing the Association on American Indian Affairs, provided the sharpest Cold War framing. S. 809, he told committee members, would be "consonant with our country's role in world affairs" because it would offer "the means of successful Indian adjustment to the modern world in an American way, as contrasted with the totalitarian technique of absorption through destruction." Termination policy, he argued, denied American Indians "the simple American right to live in communities of their fellows. It is easy to imagine how a Communist regime which destroys ethnic groups . . . would apply these same principles to every distinctive American group from the Cherokee Nation to the D.A.R."[55]

American newspapers sustained their coverage of the American Indian

Point Four debates during and after the hearings. The *New York Times* opined that "as we [Americans] rightly denounce the injustice that exists abroad it might do us good occasionally to look homeward and thus find a beam in our own eye: our treatment of the American Indian." Opposing termination, the *Times* supported the Point Four program because "there is no sense in trying to pretend that most Indians are ready for immediate integration into the white man's life." Eleanor Roosevelt championed the program in one of her many columns supportive of Native issues, writing a column in response to a letter from a Native American woman who had asked for "land and work, and not relocation off the reservation." Contending that relocation simply shifted the welfare burden to city government, Roosevelt asked, "Why not use [Point Four] here at home?"[56]

Indeed, why not? The Interior Department opposed an Indian Point Four program because it would create the impression that Interior officials and those of the Bureau of Indian Affairs acknowledged that they had been neglecting Native people, and because it would restrict programs rather than expand them, since extant programs helped both Indian nations and "individual Indians" who lived off-reservation. Beyond the programmatic differences, the divide between Interior officials and supporters of SCR 3 and S. 809 remained a philosophical one. In a letter to SCR 3 sponsor Senator Murray, an undersecretary of the interior explained that SCR 3 constituted a "direct reversal" of HCR 108 and thus of Congress's efforts to terminate Native sovereignty, which the Interior Department supported because "the principle of political self-determination . . . has no application to any minority group of American citizens." Without Interior officials' support, the bill had little chance of moving forward. S. 809 did not reach the light of a congressional vote, failing to make it out of the Senate Interior Committee. Senator Langer and his congressional supporters kept trying. In 1959 he introduced a similar bill, S. 953, arguing that "Congress will appropriate billions of dollars to take care of people outside of the United States of America. It is incumbent upon Congress, therefore, to appropriate $200 million to service properly the needs of the American Indians living on reservations throughout the United States." McGovern kept his campaign in the House alive, telling his constituents that "conditions in Indian territories resemble conditions in foreign underdeveloped areas" aided by U.S. Point Four funding. But conflating American Indian nations and foreign nations served by Point Four proved problematic. Not enough members of Congress, not to mention President Eisenhower and Interior Department officials, wanted to invest American Indians with the authority of a sovereign nation. To do so would run counter to the deep-flowing current of assimilationist thinking, revitalized with Cold War integration rhetoric and reified in various termination bills and programs. Besides, Point Four was a Truman program, a Democratic Party program; Republicans had little interest in sanctioning a domestic version of it. Thus no Point Four program for the American Indian ever materialized. In its stead the Bureau of Indian Affairs offered an underfunded Industrial Development Program geared toward luring companies to Indian reservations to support its equally underfunded vocational training programs. The BIA remained committed to the development of individual Indian resources, not national Indian resources.[57]

But the publicity generated from debates over SCR 3 and S. 809 flowed back down to the reservation level and advanced the cause of Indian nationalism, inspiring leaders of the Apache, Colville, Northern Cheyenne, Blackfeet, Sioux, and other domestic dependent nations to reimagine their homeland as one of the world's "underdeveloped areas" and to ask the federal government to recognize them as such by extending to their people Marshall Plan or Point Four funding. By the end of the 1950s a broad spectrum of Native American activists embraced a conception of Cold War civil rights that was based on the assumption that treaties were instruments of sovereignty and thus nationhood, in the process renewing the national space of the reservation, the maintenance of which symbolized a struggle for international human rights as the nations of "colored peoples" expanded in the 1960s. Clarence Wesley, a prominent activist from the San Carlos Apache community and an emerging voice in the NCAI, argued in a 1956 editorial, reprinted in a 1957 issue of *AmerIndian*, that "real Indian issues are not generally understood by the average citizen, even by some public officials. These issues are not assimilation, integration, emancipation, or government control over the Indian person. Or even civil rights in the usual sense. The real issues are the continuing ownership of land." Wesley contended, as activists would emphasize in the 1960s, that Native American civil rights involved simply "the protection of rights solemnly promised by treaty and law." This meant preserving the reservation as a legally "reserved" space as well as restoring usufructuary privileges provided in federal treaties. Wesley situated this historical claim in the contemporary terms of Cold War rhetoric and nation building when he called on the federal government to offer American Indian communities both "an end to bureaucratic dictatorship" and "the same kind of [economic aid] program that is carried on in underdeveloped countries."[58]

Dam Building and Its Discontents

Native Americans' ongoing crisis over the "continuing ownership of land"—ancestral homelands protected, in theory, by treaties—found expression in battles over particular places in Indian country that became invested with great symbolism. The federal government's construction of massive dams, reservoirs, and navigation locks, which displaced thousands of Native Americans beginning in the late 1940s and accelerating in the 1950s, heightened this crisis: the Fort Garrison Dam took 186,000 acres from the Fort Berthold Indian Reservation in North Dakota; the Sioux lost thousands of acres in South Dakota because of the Fort Randall Dam; and the Yellowtail Dam stripped thousands of acres from the Crow Nation in Montana. In the three most contentious battles of the 1950s, the construction of the Dalles Dam on the Columbia River in Oregon ruined an important fishing site for Native nations in Oregon and Washington and required the relocation of several hundred people; the Kinzua Dam destroyed Seneca cultural sites and homes, resulting in the forced removal of roughly seven hundred Seneca in northwestern Pennsylvania and southwestern New York; and the New York State Power Authority claimed 550 valuable acres from the Tuscarora's already small reservation for use as a reservoir. Although Native Americans were compensated financially for their traumas and troubles in all these cases, part of their sacred geography became submerged when they lost important religious or cultural sites, farming, fishing, and mineral resources, and ancestral homes. Their campaigns to halt the construction of dams and related projects illustrate further the tangible impact of terminationist thinking, the functional use of domestic Cold War tensions to promote anti-sovereignty programs, and the extent to which the international Cold War shaped Native Americans' conceptions of hybrid nationalism. This resistance also had a transformative effect on a new generation of Native leaders who channeled their anger into Red Power activism in the 1960s, the dams and reservoirs serving as massive and enduring symbols of the U.S. government's failure to honor its domestic treaty commitments.[59]

The Dalles Dam, first considered in the 1930s, took on increased importance after World War II, when regional boosters in Oregon and Washington sought new sources of electricity to sustain economic growth in the Columbia River valley. The Army Corps of Engineers, envisioning the dam as part of a massive Columbia River project, held hearings on the proposal in 1946, generating concerted resistance from Native Americans who protested that the dam would destroy sacred fishing sites protected by the 1855 Stevens Treaties. Those treaties, which affected Native Americans throughout the Pacific Northwest, stipulated that in ceding land to the United States, Native Americans retained the right to fish at traditional sites such as Celilo Falls, where Nez Perce, Umatilla, Warm Springs, Yakima, and smaller Native communities had fished for centuries. Despite the treaties, Indian fishermen had seen their access to traditional fishing sites decline each decade, but the Dalles Dam threatened their most important site at Celilo Falls. Boosters situated their claims for the dam within the powerful historical narrative of the "progress" of the American "empire" and within the compelling contemporary frame of Cold War national security, linking the ongoing construction of empire at home with a rapidly expanding U.S. empire abroad. After World War II, boosters demanded construction of the dam to ensure the success of the nation's new "river highway," which replaced the railroad, the nineteenth-century "highway to the Pacific," as the symbol of industrial and national progress. As Native Americans' resistance to the dam stiffened in the 1950s, part of their broader response to the national termination movement, boosters linked the dam to what one called the "national emergency created by naked aggression in Korea and the international threat of [Soviet] imperialism."[60]

In congressional hearings in 1951 both sides employed Cold War rhetoric to make their case. The principal supporters of the dam project included executives of the Inland Empire Waterways Association (IEWA) and the U.S. Army Corps of Engineers (USACE). Using apocalyptic language, IEWA president Charles Baker testified that "the demands of national defense, in trying to avert World War III, make this program imperative." Colonel Ralph Tudor of USACE proclaimed that the dam and its associated navigation lock would become "the gateway of the Empire," while another USACE official testified that electricity from the dam was needed to serve defense industries producing essential materials such as titanium, aluminum, and magnesium. In their testimony Native American opponents employed the patriotic rhetoric common to Native activists of the termination era. Umatilla delegate William Minthorne, a World War II veteran and boarding school graduate, argued that the service of Native Americans in World War II had earned them the protection of the government. Minthorne, a civil engineering student, told committee members that Native Americans also "believe in national defense" and had died to prove it, but he asked whether it was "necessary for national defense to destroy our centuries-old salmon fishery at Celilo." A member of the Yakima delegation added that Congress should "let it be known that the United States lives up to its promises." Such testimony failed to stave off defeat. Congress found industrial boosters and USACE officials more convincing and approved construction funds in 1952. Hoping to find a savior in newly elected President Eisenhower, Native and non-Native opponents sent angry letters to him and to other elected officials. One writer argued that building the dam would give the Soviet Union "true grounds for destroying our reputation throughout the world." In his letter to Eisenhower protesting the dam, Jimmie James, a Native artist who painted scenes of the Columbia River, lamented that Native soldiers fighting in Korea would return home to find that "they have lost what they thought they were fighting for," and urged Eisenhower to stop "squandering our National Honor at such a time when it is so badly needed to face the world in our plea for freedom." Allen Chisholm, a Portland engineer, asked Eisenhower: "WHY should the American government, at this time, so critical, proclaim to the rest of the world, who's [sic] esteem we badly need, that we are a nation of dishonest hypocrites, and that our integrity for honoring a solemn covenant is nil? WHY do we profess to condemn communism, if we adhere to the doctrine that the State is paramount to the Individual?" Chisholm pleaded with Eisenhower to prove "to the whole world, that we are a nation that honors its obligations." Eisenhower, however, deferred to the Corps of Engineers, declining to intervene in a case that had gained considerable momentum before his election. But he faced a similar fight and similar arguments later in his presidency when the Kinzua Dam debate blew up thousands of miles away in Iroquois country.[61]

The fight over the construction of the Kinzua Dam in northern Pennsylvania became, after a decade of traumatic dam building in Native America, a symbol of remaining termination pressures, in large measure because it threatened the Pickering Treaty of 1794, the nation's oldest treaty still in effect. The two chief arguments employed in the Dalles Dam case—that the United States should honor its treaty obligations and save face with the world during the Cold War, and that dam construction would further the nation's ability to wage that Cold War—manifested themselves during the Kinzua Dam battle, reflecting the degree to which many Americans understood their struggles in Cold War terms. Kinzua proponents emphasized the material imperative of the Cold War, the need to maintain industrial production at whatever cost, while Native Americans and their supporters emphasized the moral imperative of America appearing before the world as the defender of minority peoples and their treaty rights.

Pittsburgh business interests had proposed for decades that the federal government fund a large-scale dam to minimize flooding in the city's growing downtown district; resistance from the Seneca Nation and neighboring white communities delayed congressional funding for such a project until July 1956, when Congress appropriated funds in Public Law 641. The Corps of Engineers, by way of the Department of Justice, condemned Seneca Nation lands for the project; the District Court for the Western District of New York held on January 11, 1957, that the Pickering Treaty "could not rise above the power of Congress to legislate with regard to public projects." President Eisenhower, hardly a civil rights champion, did not relish breaking promises with Native groups but was reluctant to intervene in the Kinzua controversy. He deferred to the attorney general, who had already approved the project from a "strictly legalistic viewpoint."[62]

Pittsburgh industrial interests and their congressional sponsors, wanting more water, not less, intended to use the dam to facilitate expanded river traffic in the Ohio Valley and to flush out the pollutants that had become more noticeable in Pittsburgh's rivers during the 1950s defense buildup. But they had to resort to Cold War rhetoric to justify the hugely expensive taxpayer-funded Kinzua plan and its associated reservoir, since engineers had developed an alternate dam system that would preclude the forced relocation of the Seneca and thus preserve the nation's oldest treaty still in force. As during the Dalles Dam fight, Kinzua proponents argued for the project in the name of national security. A Pennsylvania congressman testified in 1958 that "Pittsburgh's safety from floods is one of America's best guarantees for the survival of our democracy, for the Pittsburgh area is one of the greatest of our arsenals of defense." A Pittsburgh businessman asserted that the government's failure to build the Kinzua Dam would imperil "the tomahawks of defense." Such claims helped Eisenhower accept the "legalistic" justifications for abrogating the Pickering Treaty. But ideological and historical currents flowed beneath public rationales for building the dam. Revealing the extent to which terminationist discourse mirrored nineteenth-century American imperial discourse, Eisenhower's executive assistant John Hamlin legitimized the Kinzua Dam on the grounds that it represented a "manifestation of that harsh law of nature, the survival of the fittest," arguing that "a few savages could not stand in the way of the progressive development of this country."[63]

The Seneca, for their part, considered "the reservation as a nation within a nation." Seneca Nation president Cornelius Seneca protested to President Eisenhower that the proposed dam would deprive his people of nearly "two-thirds of their ancestral homelands." Referring to "the promises given to them by the first President of these United States, George Washington," Seneca reminded Eisenhower that the forced relocation of hundreds of Seneca would be "a direct violation of [their] treaty rights." President Seneca sought an audience with Eisenhower to plead his people's case, which the 1794 treaty required. Supporters of the Seneca included George Alexander, chairman of the Republican Committee of Clarion County, Pennsylvania, who wrote Eisenhower to promote President Seneca's visit. Noting that Eisenhower held "many conferences with representatives of foreign nations," Alexander urged the president, "It is my hope and prayer that you can arrange a fifteen minute meeting with representatives of an original American Nation." But Eisenhower declined, embracing the Cold War material imperative of shoring up "the tomahawks of defense" rather than asserting the moral imperative of keeping the promises of his distant presidential predecessor and recognizing the Seneca as a nation within the nation.[64]

The Kinzua Dam controversy, like the Navajo blizzard crisis of the late 1940s, became a cause célèbre and galvanized Indian rights supporters, who conflated the domestic context of termination and the international context of the Cold War to further the conception of the Seneca as a nation within a nation. Opponents of the Kinzua Dam included a coalition of Native American groups led by the National Congress of American Indians, the Association on American Indian Affairs, the American Civil Liberties Union, the American Legion, the American Friends Service Committee (a Quaker group with long-standing ties to the Seneca), and prominent citizens such as Eleanor Roosevelt. Johnny Cash, persuaded that he had Cherokee blood, released an album titled *Bitter Tears: Ballads of the American Indian* that included a song about the Kinzua Dam, "As Long as the Grass Shall Grow," the lyrics of which read in part: "It will flood the Indian country, a proud day for Uncle Sam; It has broke the ancient treaty with a politician's grin." Carl Carmer, chairman of the AAIA's Committee for the Seneca Nation, argued in a statement distributed to politicians and AAIA members that "at a time when United States foreign policy must be judged by our sincerity and fair dealing our government would cut a sorry figure indeed were it cavalierly to disregard a pledge given to a small nation within its borders." William Zimmerman, serving as AAIA field director, asserted a similar position in August 1957, writing in the *Washington Post:* "The United States in its international relations has recently taken a high moral tone, not only with its potential opponents but even with its trusted and tried friends. In the court of world opinion, shall we be condemned for breaking a promise because we have the power to do so?"[65]

Supporters of the Seneca kept up their attacks on the dam project into 1961, bolstered by President John F. Kennedy's campaign promises that his administration "would make a sharp break with the policies of the Republican Party" and therefore would not change "treaty or contractual relationships without the consent of the tribes concerned." Such promises and the visceral nature of another controversy over Iroquois lands on the Tuscarora reservation led to a barrage of publicity for the Seneca's cause. An April 1961 editorial in the *Washington Post* stated:

> Free men rightly are indignant when the Soviet government pushes around its ethnic minorities. But to many people it looks as if the United States is doing the same thing when the Corps of Engineers or the Niagara Power Authority dislodges Seneca or Tuscarora Indians from their homes . . . Therefore we hope that President Kennedy will make clear that the case of the Seneca Indians cannot be brushed aside so simply. Instead, there ought to be a clear indication that the United States will . . . treat its own minorities with the same scrupulous respect that it repeatedly urges on Mr. Khrushchev.

The Seneca also placed their crisis in a Cold War frame. Sparky Watt, a member of the Seneca Council, pointed to the hypocrisy of U.S. foreign policy in arguing that "the United States takes the position that if it's to their benefit to break a treaty then that makes it all right. That's just what Castro is saying about Guantanamo Bay, but the U.S. government doesn't seem to agree about that." Eleanor Roosevelt championed the cause of the Seneca in the *Philadelphia Daily News*, urging federal officials to consider the international consequences of a forced relocation of Native people. Roosevelt wrote that, given Americans'

> preoccupation with world affairs, we sometimes neglect those affairs close at home that may well affect the way people around the world feel about us. For in these days it is the way the non-Communist nations meet their moral and spiritual obligations that best demonstrates the difference between their philosophy and that of the Communists. When we fail to face up to a moral problem, we not only harm ourselves at home but place us in a bad light all over the world.

A *Milwaukee Journal* editorial published the same week criticized dam-building projects such as the Kinzua: "How, the Indians ask themselves, can the United States break treaties and agreements with Indians when it would not dream of doing so with Germans, Laotians or Frenchmen." Similar comments appeared in other newspapers around the country, provoking angry letters from American citizens to their congressional representatives and to President Kennedy.[66]

Such supporters of Indian rights sought to defend the Seneca's homeland but also to preserve the great potential of America's moral thrust in a rapidly changing world of decolonization. Kennedy's inauguration heralded a new phase of U.S. engagement with different cultural groups around the world. Emerging from the 1950s, Americans weary of Cold War tensions embraced Kennedy's "New Frontier," to which they could travel in search of not only new markets but new intercultural relations as well. Walter Taylor, executive director of the American Friends Service Committee, asserted this perspective most clearly after Kennedy assumed office. Taylor urged Sol Tax, the anthropologist who organized the June 1961 American Indian Chicago Conference (AICC), to publicize the Kinzua Dam crisis in its proceedings. Taylor was struck by Tax's rationale for holding the conference: in Tax's words, "The present moment in world history with new nations emerging from colonial experiences provides additional urgency to the task and a significance beyond the desperate needs of American Indians alone." Embracing this internationalist position, Taylor complained to Kennedy's assistant special counsel Lee C. White:

> If the arrogance and lack of cross-cultural understanding exhibited by the United States in the Kinzua controversy should be applied to other small and weak, but hopeful peoples of the world, the "Ugly American" may destroy himself without much help from his enemies. We can ill afford the presumption that the values and ways of American Indians or other people are ridiculous and the sooner they become "like us" the better off they will be.

Like the Seneca, Taylor believed that Kennedy was no Eisenhower and that, given his vision for Latin America as well as his campaign statements supporting Point Four–style programs for Native Americans, he would halt dam construction, given the implications of breaking the nation's oldest treaty. In another letter Taylor cited the "international significance of our permitting the U.S. Army Corps of Engineers to disregard the proper interests of Indians and other Americans at the same time we propose for Latin America: 'Progress, yes—Tyranny, no!'" And he raised the specific context of the new Peace Corps program in a letter to Representative Henry S. Reuss, a Wisconsin Democrat who helped create the Corps: "I do not see how we can send sincere young people to carry a democratic message to young nations freed from colonialism if we continue to deal shamefully with our own 'colonials,' the American Indians." Taylor took his message to various publications, including *The Nation*, which published Taylor's essay "The Treaty We Broke" in September 1961, in which he claimed that "President Kennedy can show American Indians, as well as other 'little people' of the world, that his Administration speaks in deeds as well as words to the rights of an overpowered minority," noting that it would require of Kennedy "an act of courageous statesmanship" to resolve the crisis in the Seneca's favor.[67]

But Kennedy proved no more willing than Eisenhower to mediate the Kinzua Dam dispute. In August 1961 Kennedy explained to newly elected Seneca Nation president Basil Williams that after reviewing the case, he had "concluded that it is not possible to halt the construction of Kinzua

Dam" but promised that the federal government would help the Seneca "make the adjustment as fair and orderly as possible." In his first months in office Kennedy did not prove courageous enough to take on one manifestation of the military-industrial complex that so alarmed his predecessor. Nor did he want to disappoint David Lawrence, a vocal proponent of the Kinzua Dam who, as governor of Pennsylvania, had helped Kennedy win that key state. Thus he kept one campaign promise and broke another, failing to uphold Native Americans' treaty rights and protect their land base. As Chief Clinton Rickard of the Tuscarara Nation wrote of Kennedy's actions, "for a politician who pretended to be a friend of oppressed peoples, this attitude showed his true colors."[68]

"Do You Call This Democracy?"

As the Kinzua Dam fight raged on in the press, the courts, and Congress, another bitter dispute over homelands and national honor in Iroquois country developed when New York State's construction of the St. Lawrence Seaway threatened the land base of the Mohawk and the Tuscarora. On the post–World War II map of the future, as during the great railroad construction era of the late 1800s, Native Americans appeared as natural obstacles to be overcome by legal and engineering systems. Mohawk activist Ernest Benedict noted in a 1941 letter to the ACLU that the St. Lawrence Seaway plans "call for a great canal to be dug through the middle of an island which is part of our reservation. There was no mention of the fact that this was a reservation or of how the land was to be obtained as was done with other affected areas." Animated by their struggles to resist draft conscription during World War II, Benedict and other activists of the Six Nations Confederacy staged a spirited resistance to such development and to associated termination policies that weakened Iroquois sovereignty. Iroquois activists published various newsletters such as *KA-WEH-RAS!* (It Thunders!) and *The Hand* (*That Guided and Protected Your Ancestors Is Now Open to You for Justice!*) to marshal opposition. In 1948, early in the national termination crisis, the publishers of *The Hand* on the St. Regis (Mohawk) reservation bordering Ontario sent members of the U.S. Congress and fellow Indian activists an issue containing several provocative essays that expressed Native Americans' internationalist perspectives. Like the Seneca, the Mohawk promoted the view that George

Washington had signed sacred treaties with the Iroquois that protected the integrity of "our little countries (Reservations you call them)," they told the politicians. The authors employed World War II and Cold War imagery to stake their claim to treaty rights. One essay stated that the "blood of our warriors was shed on the battlefields of France, Germany and Japan for what you then told us was our common cause, DEMOCRACY!" In "Does a Small Nation Have the Right to Exist?" Julius Cook (Sa-Ka-Ron-Hio-Ke-We) made the claim that the Six Nations Confederacy

> has *never* broken any of its treaties and thus it becomes an example to the world. Nowadays, we hear a lot about satellite states being dominated by certain powerful countries wherein any expression of freedom and independent action is ruthlessly squelched and the people become mere subjects of a foreign nation instead of citizens of their own . . . The United States and other so-called western powers have pointed accusing fingers at the countries of Eastern Europe and the Near East. But what is happening there is also taking place here. The Six Nations have every right in the world to exist as a sovereign and independent nation; yet the United States, while it is accusing Russia of dominating its weaker neighbors, itself is forcing the Indians of the Six Nations to accept domination.

Closing his essay by quoting from the Declaration of Independence to justify Iroquois resistance to U.S. imperialism, Cook posed the question at the heart of Native Americans' political struggles: "Will the United States permit a nation to exist within a nation?" Other Iroquois activists similarly framed their protests in international terms. Tillie John of the Seneca reservation protested termination legislation by comparing Iroquois territory to nineteenth-century China: "We have only to behold the sad and bitter experience of China with her unequal treaties, foreign privileges, and foreign jurisdiction over civil and criminal cases on Chinese territory." Maxwell Garrow, a Mohawk official, complained to Senator Herbert Lehman of New York about the 1949 termination acts, saying, "Think how you would react to an alien such as Russia taking away, in the same manner, any of your rights as an American."[69]

Led by the Tuscarora politicians William Rickard and his father, Clinton Rickard, who had served the United States in the American-Filipino

War, representatives of the Six Nations Confederacy expressed their sovereignty in ways that ran counter to gatherings such as the Emergency Conference of 1954, organized by the National Congress of American Indians, and the American Indian Chicago Convention of 1961. The Rickards aided collaborations between the Tuscarora, New York Akwesanse Mohawk, and Canadian Mohawk groups in Ontario through the Indian Defense League of America, holding annual international border-crossing celebrations to mark the anniversary of the Jay Treaty of 1794 and staging parades in New York to assert national sovereignty before the United Nations. Dressed in traditional Iroquois clothing, a delegation of Senecas, Cayugas, Tuscaroras, and Mohawks presented grievances to Soviet Foreign Minister Andrei Vishinsky and to Secretary General Trygve Lie at the UN in 1950. In 1952 and 1957 Clinton Rickard led similar delegations to the UN; during the 1952 visit, one hundred Iroquois marched down Fifth Avenue on American Indian Day to protest treaty violations and what one marcher called American "dictatorship" at home.[70]

The Tuscarora's crisis of sovereignty deepened in the late 1950s when the New York State Power Authority (SPA) claimed by eminent domain over 1,500 acres of their small 6,249-acre reservation for the so-called Tuscarora Reservoir, part of the Niagara Mohawk power company's Niagara Falls hydroelectric project. According to SPA chairman Robert Moses, the architect of urban racial relocation in New York City, "the bulk of the [Tuscarora] land is not used for any purpose at all," repeating the age-old justification for expropriating Indian land used from the 1600s onward. It is important to note that Moses considered uprooting a neighboring white community too complicated. In response, Tuscarora activists posted "No Trespassing" signs, used their cars to block SPA surveyors' access to the reservation, and shot out nighttime surveying lights. Tuscarora clan mothers lay in front of trucks to block SPA surveying teams. With national and international media watching the conflict, nearly two hundred Tuscarora confronted over fifty state troopers and local sheriffs armed with submachine guns and tear gas. Tuscarora armed themselves with signs that read "United States Help Us. We Helped You in 1776 and 1812, 1918 and 1941." When several Tuscarora were arrested, on their own reservation, protesters shouted, "This is Russia!" and "Do you call this democracy?" It was one of the most dramatic acts of resistance to state power at the time, a different kind of Native protest, which to date had not involved such physical turmoil. Some of the Tuscarora's white neighbors were similarly alarmed at the tactics employed to resolve the crisis. In a letter to Governor Averill Harriman published in the *Niagara Falls Gazette*, Roger Millar condemned the use of police power: "Are we going Russian? Are we to permit Moses to brush aside the words of George Washington in 1790?" Moses, too, imagined the confrontation in an international context, ironically calling the construction delays caused by Tuscarora protests an example of "domestic weakness, incompetence and ineptitude in the ruthless, world-wide competition with other systems of government more incisive and less tolerant of obstruction." Angered by the Tuscarora's refusal to embrace his vision of progress, Moses arranged the bugging of their phones, leading the Tuscarora to use their native language while talking on the phone; and he blamed the resistance on "recalcitrants" who ignored the common good. Chief Clinton Rickard retorted that Moses "had spent his career dumping concrete over the landscape" and thus could not "see how people could be using land unless they did likewise."[71]

The U.S. Supreme Court resolved the escalating crisis in 1960 by affirming the right of the United States to take land by eminent domain in spite of national treaties, another painful application of the 1903 *Lone Wolf v. Hitchcock* decision that had affirmed Congress's plenary power at the dawn of the American Century. In the end, the taking of 550 acres of Tuscarora land represented only a partial victory, as the SPA had sought nearly three times that amount. But as Rickard bitterly noted, "the SPA got its reservoir and [the Tuscarora] were left with the scars that will never heal."[72]

During the termination era, as during the removal era and the allotment era, American politicians refused to accept as legitimate Native Americans' conceptions of nation and homeland, equating reservations with communistic forms of social organization or irresponsible land use. The ability of white Americans to pack up and relocate to well-paying jobs and literally new communities like Levittown during the 1950s helps to explain, especially given the conformist atmosphere of Cold War America, the degree to which the reservation remained a symbol of confinement rather than one of culture. Federal officials also ignored the powerful dynamic of racial bigotry that contributed to the failure of the Voluntary Relocation Program. White politicians' indifference to Native land issues was driven by racism, expediency, and a cultural disjunction. In his dissent

5.5 This 1958 photograph documents Tuscarora activists' attempts to demarcate and defend their sovereign territory during their battles with Robert Moses and the New York State Power Authority. From left to right: William Rickard, John Hewitt, and Wallace "Mad Bear" Anderson (kneeling). Courtesy of Buffalo and Erie County Historical Society.

to the 1960 Supreme Court decision on Tuscarora land, Associate Justice Hugo Black opined: "It may be hard for us to understand why these Indians cling so tenaciously to their lands and traditional way of life . . . But this is their home—their ancestral home. There, they, their children and their forebears were born. They, too, have their memories and their loves. Some things are worth more than money and the costs of a new enterprise." Black ended with a sentiment that fit well with the propaganda but not the practice of the period: "Great nations, like great men, should keep their word."[73]

Since the 1910s Native American politicians across the country had seized on this principle—that the United States should protect its growing influence in the world by keeping its word and thus honoring its treaties. Black's eloquent dissent, reprinted in numerous American Indian as well as non-Indian publications, both legitimized these decades of political activity and solidified the rhetorical foundation of a new era of activity. A New Jersey newspaper, noting the Seneca's defeat in the Kinzua Dam case, opined that "the vexing aspect is the fear that these decisions will become precedent for further inroads upon lands occupied by the tribes," bringing to mind notions of a domestic domino theory that galvanized Native Americans to protest new "schemes to take treaty lands and assets."[74]

The American Indian Chicago Conference

The crises in Iroquois country lay like a shadow over Indian-white relations as the 1960s began, engendering new campaigns to prevent the further erosion of Indian country. Native Americans' use of hybrid nationalism to mediate the broader crisis of termination found expression in various forums, the most prominent the American Indian Chicago Conference of June 1961, hosted at the University of Chicago by the white anthropologist Sol Tax. The conference sought to define the contours of what new NCAI president Clarence Wesley called the "Indian Frontier of the Sixties." After attending the December 1960 NCAI annual convention, Tax conceived of the AICC as an opportunity for Native Americans to reach out to the new president; Kennedy had written Wesley in 1960 pledging his support of "the development of the human and natural resources of the Indian Reservations" and promising: "Such a program will indeed be an integral part of the total program of my administration. We must raise the sights of our country. We must exercise world leadership and back up our position through a stronger, more productive America." Tax's final argument for the conference was that "the present moment in world history with new nations emerging from colonial experiences provided additional urgency to the task and a significance beyond the desperate needs of American Indians alone."[75]

Native American participants joined Kennedy and Tax in conflating the domestic and international contexts by linking termination with the Cold War. Several months before the June conference, AICC planners asked Native Americans around the country to articulate their views on the state of Native affairs. The responses, which came from Maine to Texas and from Alabama to the Pacific Northwest, illustrate the extent to which both reservation and off-reservation community leaders had internalized the moral dimensions of the Cold War while associating them with its material dimensions; and they reveal a sharpened identification with the "colored peoples of the earth" and an embrace of self-determination, the operating principle of decolonization. The responses also reflect the diverse nature of Native America at the time. Some respondents championed assimilation in rejecting what one called Indians' "antiquated superannuated way of life," while others considered the struggle against termination a battle for Indians' survival. The perspectives, while heterogeneous, articulated an Indian nationalism that demonstrated Native Americans' widespread engagement with the rhetoric of the Cold War, of decolonization, and of the "War of 1954," as a Montana writer referred to Congress's blitz of termination legislation, a war that had erupted anew in the Seneca and Tuscarora cases.[76]

Many of the responses defending Indian identity drew upon the rhetorical arsenal of freedom and democracy that termination opponents had employed during the "War of 1954." An activist from White Swan, Washington, protested the forced citizenship of American Indians by writing that only "a dictator nation may be able to declare an individual of another power a citizen of that government," a process he compared to the United States making "a RUSSIAN a citizen of this government." During a regional meeting held at Haverford College in Pennsylvania, Red Deer (Mohawk-Cherokee) echoed this spirit of independence, asking that the conference's proposed declaration "safeguard the loss of our lands in what is a de facto occupation of our country." He suggested a broad public relations effort to strengthen the reservation land base, as did Richard Bounding Elk (Penobscot), who supported the development of reservation lands along the lines of the European Recovery Program (the Marshall Plan). Calling on AICC leaders to request an "American Indian Recovery Program . . . a sort of Marshall Plan for Indians," Bounding Elk asked, "Why give [foreign aid] away to the world—give it away here."[77]

5.6 This photograph records one of the regional meetings of the June 1961 American Indian Chicago Conference. Participants in the meeting, held at Haverford College in Haverford, Pennsylvania, in April 1961, included William Rickard (Tuscarora), first row, holding stick; AICC organizer Sol Tax, second row center; Chief Clinton Rickard (Tuscarora), fifth row, right side, in headdress; Tall Oak (Narragansett), fifth row center. Theodore Hetzel Photographs, Group C.2. Courtesy Center of Southwest Studies, Fort Lewis College.

Respondents from Bellflower, California, reflected this nationalist theme and the belief in a domestic "Marshall Plan" as both a panacea for Native American problems and an ethical obligation of the federal government. Presenting their own version of an Indian Point Four program, the Bellflower group maintained that the federal government should "deal with the treaties and the treaty provisions as though they were dealing with foreign nations. We can't help but wish that the United States would treat us as well as they have some of the foreign states in the past decade." Representatives of American Indian communities meeting in Gallup, New Mexico, recommended that the Department of State act as a "buffer organization" to carry out "diplomatic relations" between the United States and what the Bellflower group called "foreign nations." Yet even as they claimed a status of "foreign" people, the Bellflower group asserted a hybrid patriotism common to Native activists; American Indians would contribute to "the All-American society," they argued, if they retained their "cultural heritage." Native Americans from Portland, Oregon, advanced the theme of racial unity in a global context. Believing that discrimination would not disappear for a "great long time," these respondents wrote, "We see it everywhere, and we might as well hold together as a Race . . . because the Chinese, Japanese, Finnish, and most all other races make themselves stronger by a united effort." To do so would be to "step in our rightful place among world people."[78]

Perhaps the most comprehensive response emerged from a gathering in Orono, Maine. Its summary statement recommended that all American Indians "remain separate, independent, autonomous, sovereign nations." Championing "self-determination," it contended that Native Americans ought to be offered "a 'recovery program,' much as the European nations were, in the years following the last World War . . . [T]he American Indian Nations want to manage their own affairs, but need a great deal of aid. A Marshall Plan is only one possible solution. The 'Point Four' Program of aid for underdeveloped countries might be another way of extending this financial assistance to the American Indians." Maintaining that "no one is more deserving than the Indians of *foreign aid* from the U.S. government," the Orono statement linked the Cold War at home and abroad: "One more arguing point that comes to mind is the propaganda value of such a program, particularly as far as the colored peoples of the earth are concerned, and also the existing unfavorable propaganda value of the lack of such a program."[79]

Inspired by conversations with his American Indian friend, a non-Indian respondent took this internationalist perspective one step further. In "An Open Letter to the American Indian Convention," L. A. Lauer of California suggested that Native Americans present their case for sovereignty by securing "a hearing in the United Nations." Failing that, his Indian friend argued, they should seek a hearing "among the Bandung Conference nations, brother nations in colonial areas who also are 'unrecognized.'" These were steps to take "before fighting: violently or disobediently." Comparing American Indians with the people of Tibet, Lauer complained that U.S. officials failed to understand non-Western cultures and traditions. The political and economic dynamics were not identical, yet Native Americans' battle for homeland security evolved alongside those of other "underdeveloped nations" facing similar Cold War pressures.[80]

More than 450 Native Americans from ninety "American Indian Nations" gathered in Chicago the week of June 13–20, 1961. The American Indian Chicago Conference was not a Native American version of the 1955 Bandung Conference, though speeches at both conferences did share common themes: the need to channel precious economic resources into rebuilding postcolonial economies in order to defend political sovereignty, and the importance of rediscovering or retaining individual nations' cultural attributes, which Western values and institutions had submerged in the colonial era and continued to subvert in the Cold War age. After a week of often contentious discussions and negotiations, conference delegates produced the "Declaration of Indian Purpose," a pan-tribal statement that rejected terminationist philosophy and policies and offered a blueprint for ameliorating Native Americans' material crises of poor housing, poor health, unemployment, and inadequate education. The declaration represented an effort to accommodate the great diversity of Native opinions, from those who considered themselves assimilated to those who resisted any form of integration into American social or economic life, and from those who had relocated to American cities to those fixed firmly on reservation ground. Yet even American Indians who considered themselves assimilated took part in the proceedings, suggesting their sustained belief in the primacy of Indianness.

Although it faithfully incorporated the various recommendations from the regional conferences, the final version of the Declaration of Indian Purpose did not reflect the nationalistic statements extolling political and cultural independence. Rather it stayed true to the ethnic patriotism and internationalism that defined the discourse of resistance to termination. Mixing its pan-tribal origins with the ancient language of American freedom, the declaration expressed the AICC delegates' belief in "the future of a greater America . . . where life, liberty, and the pursuit of happiness will be a reality." Yet in asking for federal programs "similar in operation to a Point IV plan," delegates posed "a moral problem which cannot be left answered. For the problem we raise affects the standing which our nation sustains before world opinion." The declaration made clear Native Americans' collective desire to sustain an "Indian" identity, to "hold the scraps and parcels as earnestly as any small nation or ethnic group was ever determined to hold to identity and survival."[81]

For Native Americans in the post–World War II period, "the very meaning of home change[d] with the experience of decolonization and radical-ization," to borrow the words of bell hooks. Cold War and termination pressures of the 1940s and 1950s reinforced Native Americans' "place-based identities." In the May 1961 *NCAI Bulletin*, Marie Potts reported on the work of the AICC steering committee responsible for drafting the final Declaration of Indian Purpose; a great-grandmother from the Maidu community, Potts had learned English at Carlisle Industrial school, then honed her journalistic skills covering Indian affairs for various NCAI publications. She noted that the steering committee had first resolved to address Americans' "considerable ignorance" of Indian affairs: "[One] prevalent idea is that Indian reservations are 'concentration camps'; that Indians ought, somehow, to be 'gotten off the reservations'; that Indian communities or reservations are 'rural slums.'" In this "public relations job" the steering committee felt compelled to defend the very idea of the reservation. In Potts's words:

> To the Indian his reservation is his home; it is his heritage; it is all he has. He feels a part of the land and the people who form the communities on the reservation whereas he sometimes feels unwanted in towns and cities away from the reservation. The Indian's view of the land is different from that of the non-Indian. Indians feel a *social* relationship to the land while the non-Indian regards the land in commercial terms.

For Indians, Potts concluded, the reservation "is the base of their existence, of tribal organizations and Indian identity.[82]

Any public relations campaign would not just have to address the "considerable ignorance" of white Americans, citizens and government officials alike. It would also have to persuade Native Americans to remain on or return to their homelands and fight to develop them rather than leave them for the city. The impetus for relocation stemmed not only from aggressive federal programs but also from the social realities of reservation life. Thus the campaign to defend the reservation worked in two ways: first, to inhibit termination legislation, and second, to limit the appeal of federal relocation programs, which became the equivalent of a slow-moving but equally corrosive termination campaign. By 1961 reservation relocation funding approached twice that for reservation development.[83]

For colonized peoples especially, the "nation fills the void left in the uprooting of communities and kin, and turns that loss into the language of metaphor." By 1961 Indian nationalism had become strengthened in response to the deracination engendered by federal relocation policies and lingering terminationist pressures that came as well from assimilated tribal groups. This new nationalism also evolved as a result of Native American leaders' growing identification with foreign nations struggling to reconstruct themselves in the face of the centripetal forces of the Cold War and of their related claim that the federal government should treat American Indians as members of autonomous nations and thus fight to win *their* hearts and minds amidst a worldwide struggle for the allegiance of "brother nations" everywhere, an incipient consciousness of "a large-scale solidarity," to use Ernest Renan's term. Joining the metaphor of ancestral homelands for which their grandfathers gave their lives with visions of American freedom and democracy for which members of their generation had bled on World War II battlefields, these Native politicians reimagined American Indian nations as a middle ground between the poles of hegemonic American culture and the nascent Third World.[84]

As with African Americans' civil rights campaigns and those of student groups such as Students for a Democratic Society, the 1960s brought a generational and philosophical split in the methods and mentality of Native American activists. In particular, the National Indian Youth Council (NIYC) cut its ideological teeth at the 1961 American Indian Chicago Conference. The NIYC, founded in 1961, rejected the ethnic patriotism of the AICC and the NCAI, their moderate response to coercive assimilation campaigns, to assert an ethnic nationalism. Red Power embodied this ethnic nationalism, embracing the metaphor of war that AICC delegates rejected. The emergence of this new generation of American Indian activists heralded a new stage of the cold war being fought at home.

6   The Last Indian War

A full-blood broadcasts through a microphone planned tribal
    action . . .
We shall learn all the devices of the whiteman
We shall handle his tools for ourselves
We shall master his machinery, his inventions, his skills, his
    medicine, his planning
But we'll retain our beauty
And still be Indian!

—Dave Martin Nez (Navajo), "New Way, Old Way," ca. 1966

During the winter of 1959–60 Louis Schaw and Everett Hagen spent several months on the Pine Ridge and Rosebud Sioux reservations in South Dakota conducting a survey for the Center for International Studies of the Massachusetts Institute of Technology, part of a larger investigation of "underdeveloped" countries. Schaw, a social-clinical psychologist, and Hagen, an economist, intended to use the Sioux context for analyzing the process of social and economic development in those countries. They concluded that the problems of American Indians were "remarkably similar to those faced by 'underdeveloped' colonial or ex-colonial peoples on several continents," calling the two reservations "underdeveloped societies in the midst of our affluent one." In addition, the "suspicion and hostility" expressed by the Sioux toward U.S. officials was similar to what people in "Asia, Africa, and the Middle East feel in some degree toward their former European masters." If American Indians were more numerous, the authors suggested, they would be "rising . . . to demand independence" along the lines of anticolonial counterparts in those non-Western countries.[1]

Yet what Schaw and Hagen found on the Sioux reservations and across Native America was that "Indian tribal leaders of great initiative and imagination are arising[,] . . . the American equivalent of the leaders for independence in colonial countries." This new political activity, they argued, "has probably been stimulated by the independence movement among colonial countries throughout the world. It may reasonably be assumed that the success of colonial peoples in gaining control of their own affairs has resonated in the minds of individuals here and there and everywhere among the American Indian tribes." The "Indian problem" in America, Hagen and Schaw declared, "is not unique; it is only a special case of a world-wide class of problems." They predicted that American Indians' "colonial relationship" to the larger society would "work itself out as similar relationships are doing elsewhere in the world, and without the physical turmoil that accompanies the process in many other places." Sounding the theme of Native Americans' hybrid patriotism, the authors asserted that this resurgence of activity among Indians served "jointly their interests and those of the American people."[2]

Schaw and Hagen also echoed American Indians' emerging political rhetoric, which mirrored the pro-independence, pro-development discourse of decolonization activists abroad. Though similar in some ways to the demands for international decolonization, the call for domestic decolonization by American Indians derived from a particular set of international relationships embedded, as we have seen, in the Gordian knot of treaties signed between the United States and Indian nations in the late eighteenth and nineteenth centuries. Native Americans battled in the 1960s and 1970s to retie that knot and thus strengthen the legal boundaries of a hybrid political space, a "nation within the nation." When Native activists drew upon the language and events of foreign independence movements in waging this struggle for treaty rights, they further intensified American Indian nationalism. This nationalism was manifested in significant protests that did in fact involve "physical turmoil"—in Iroquois country and the Pacific Northwest, in the 1969 occupation of Alcatraz Island in San Francisco Bay, and in particular in the seventy-one-day occupation in early 1973 of the town of Wounded Knee, South Dakota, on the Pine Ridge Reservation itself.

This nationalist consciousness also stemmed from ongoing termination pressures, which had throughout the twentieth century forced Native people both to define their "Indianness" and to defend the idea of the reservation. In the years after World War II Native activists began to collapse the boundaries between the international and the domestic in framing their treaty rights struggles at home as a "cold war" between Indian communities and federal and state officials. In Wisconsin the Bad River Chippewa Tribal Council declared in November 1959 that "a state of cold war" existed between the Chippewa and officials of the Wisconsin Department of Conservation, and that "such state shall exist until such time as the State of Wisconsin shall recognize Federal treaties and statutes affording immunity to the members of this Band from State control over hunting and fishing within the boundaries of this reservation." State officials had claimed jurisdiction over Chippewa land and arrested individuals deemed guilty of violating Wisconsin's fishing and hunting regulations. The Chippewa's statement, "A Declaration of War," like many of the key political documents of twentieth-century American Indian activism, drew from the intellectual bedrock of American political rhetoric: "When, in the course of human events, it becomes necessary to protect the rights and liberties of certain peoples of this great nation from encroachment by other peoples . . ." Mel Thom, who helped found the National Indian Youth Council in 1961, made a similar but broader argument in his essay "Indian War 1963," published in the NIYC newsletter, *American Aborigine*. He contended that Native Americans were involved in "a different kind of war—a cold war, one might say. It's a struggle against destructive forces the Indian cannot sometimes even see, let alone understand."[3]

Native Americans' approaches to resisting termination in the 1960s splintered along generational and ideological lines. In addition to the National Congress of American Indians, which dominated Native American affairs on the national level, termination fostered the growth of numerous other groups organized to fight local and regional battles for sovereignty. According to one such group, the "threat of Termination united the Indians . . . Tribes became better organized and more and more employed their own legal counsel." By 1970 hundreds of Native American interest groups had formed, including the NIYC, representing young activists; the National Tribal Chairmen's Association, which promoted the interests of tribal governments; regional intertribal groups such as the Montana Intertribal Policy Board and the Affiliated Tribes of Northwest Indians; and the urban-based American Indians United, a broad coalition of Native American centers that formed in 1968 to champion the rights of off-reservation Indians, who represented over one-third of the American Indian population. In addition, Indians for National Liberation, the Navajo Liberation Front, and United Native Americans Inc. (UNAI) promoted a liberation theology in publications such as *Rainbow People*, *Black Mesa Fact Sheet*, *Cherokee Examiner*, and *The Warpath*. *Cherokee Examiner* publisher N. Magowan, a U.S. Marines veteran, asserted that "the list of battle zones grows in an ever larger, more aggressive scale throughout the whole of North America." United Native Americans Inc., founded by Lehman Brightman in San Francisco in 1968, published similar rhetoric in *The Warpath*, which Brightman deemed an "International Indian Newspaper" that was a part of a "Liberation News Service." Brightman attacked the relocation policy and "colonialist" BIA officials, exposed the "double system of justice" that discriminated against American Indians, and demanded economic development of reservations. *The Warpath* provided coverage of "Indian liberation struggles" in the United States, Canada, and Latin American countries, including one in Guatemala after the CIA's 1954 overthrow of "a pro-Indian government." Perhaps the most unusual liberation agenda emerged from the socialist National Amerindianist American Redman's Party (NAARP) of South Dakota, which asked the United Nations to divide the state into white territory and the international territory of the "Republic United Tribes of Ameridia."[4]

Native Americans contributed to the making of "the Sixties" in asserting this liberation rhetoric and in staging their own human rights protests while joining those of African Americans and other minority groups. Yet they also worked hard to delineate their causes from those of other groups. While drawing on African Americans' strategy of "sit-in" protests, Native activists and politicians made clear that their particular claims were based on federal treaty obligations that protected their national boundaries. "Treaty rights" was the goal of American Indians, not "civil rights." As militancy increased among young Native activists, however, ideological differences began to divide Native groups committed to that goal. The Affiliated Tribes of Northwest Indians resolved in 1970 that its members sought to "communicate the nature of their needs and problems through legal channels rather than by the militant demonstrations and violence used by other [Native] groups and minorities." The NCAI asserted that it did not seek to solve problems along the lines of young "Red Power" activists, who staged "fish-ins" and occupations of government buildings and sites to defend the literal and figurative space of Indian sovereignty. The

NCAI instead joined President Lyndon Johnson's War on Poverty by employing its various initiatives as a substitute for the American Indian Point Four agenda that Congress had blocked during the Eisenhower years.[5]

Yet the Native American discourse of hybrid patriotism bridged this ideological divide; activists across the political spectrum celebrated Indian values as an important vehicle for solving the nation's political crises abroad as well as its spiritual crisis of materialism at home. Citing U.S. government meddling in "the Congo, Viet Nam, Cuba, South America and other places," which perpetuated the crisis of colonialism, NCAI officials argued that these "failures in foreign policy are a large scale version of the failures in Indian policy made over the last century." Maintaining that Indian values could help heal the "soul of the nation," NCAI leaders stated, "We believe that allowing total development of Indian communities on their own basis will be a major step in providing that variety in American life which is so necessary to a healthy society." Struggling to reconcile their ethnic identity with their national identity, young activists sustained this discourse, using the notion of hybridity to define themselves and their role in modern America. Herbert Blatchford, a young Navajo who helped to found the NIYC in 1961, wrote in *American Aborigine*: "Very few [Indians of his generation] crossed the gap between the two cultures. Those who found it difficult to indulge in the new culture developed into a hybrid group, belonging fully to neither culture." Blatchford believed that an American state that evolved from Indians' ways and mores as much as from whites' would create a more human society, not only at home but abroad as well. "It may be," he contended, "that the Indian people will shed light on *our* international dilemma." Writing in 1971, a Cherokee woman named Juanita Grace also called herself a "hybrid," which she defined as the "living, walking example of the Best of two worlds." The mother of a son serving in the U.S. Marines, she titled her essay "The Fail-Safe Weapon," suggesting, perhaps, that this cultural hybridization could ameliorate the crisis of Americanism, which in 1971 was foundering in the jungles of Vietnam, the hot spot of America's international dilemma.[6]

Solving this "international dilemma" required Americans, Indian and non-Indian alike, to resolve where "Indian country" existed in both time and space. The fluid boundaries of "Indian country" connected rural and urban communities, as American Indians relocated to cities fought new forms of termination by reimagining the sacredness of a reservation space they conceived as an alternative to the anomie of urban America. The fluid boundaries of "Indian country" linked domestic and international contexts during the Vietnam War, producing a disturbing conflation between Indian country and Viet Cong country and between nineteenth-century U.S. imperial expansion and post–World War II U.S. expansion. The fluid boundaries of "Indian country" also forced American courts to revisit the historical context of nineteenth-century treaty making in deciding whether Indian nationhood continued to matter in the realm of law. These various battles over Indian country occurred in real places—on Native American reservations and on American rivers as well as in the courtroom. And they occurred in symbolic spaces—in public discourse, in films from East Berlin, in Soviet propaganda. Taken together, these tensions added up to an ongoing domestic war of culture shaped by the moral and material exigencies of the international Cold War.

A Landmark Dissent

In his dissent to the 1960 Supreme Court decision on Tuscarora land, Associate Justice Hugo Black had argued that "great nations, like great men, should keep their word." Cherokee attorney Earl Boyd Pierce told Justice Black that despite the Court's decision in the *Tuscarora* case, Native Americans would "not be dismayed" thanks to his "'land-mark' Dissent." The ideas animating the dissent, Pierce wrote, "will not only be quoted again and again in future decisions, but eventually carved on monuments erected by Indians themselves," calling Black's closing remarks "as beautifully expressed as the Sermon on the Mount." Native Americans continued to evaluate their treaty rights in a dual international context: first, they viewed them in light of the original international relations embedded in treaty documents, which they read and reread; and second, they evaluated these treaties in a changing global context in which the United States represented the benchmark for democratic aspirations. These contexts evolved simultaneously, reinforcing each other. Robert Yellowtail, the great Crow politician who had battled for treaty rights since the 1910s, called the *Tuscarora* decision "an eye opener to every Indian in America . . . This is autocracy of the Stalin kind."[7]

In spite of these rhetorical continuities, what had changed was the way in which Native activists engaged state and federal officials intent on encroaching upon or fully terminating their treaty rights. Tuscarora activists had physically confronted state officials as they attempted to survey what the Tuscarora deemed a sovereign and sacred place. In March 1959 Tuscarora activist Wallace (Mad Bear) Anderson, who had helped organize resistance to Robert Moses's Niagara Reservoir scheme, led a group of nearly one hundred marchers in picketing the White House after President Eisenhower declined to meet with Tuscarora officials. Anderson and his group then presented a petition to the British embassy, appealing to Britain to intervene and force the U.S. government's fidelity to the 1794 Pickering Treaty. Anderson, a World War II veteran of Saipan and Okinawa, told reporters that the government's failure to address "bitter injustices" made the Tuscarora's grievances "an international problem" and thus required engagement with the United Nations. The group accordingly presented a petition to the UN and appealed to other foreign embassies, though nothing came of the effort. The activists also failed to earn an audience with the National Congress of American Indians, whose executive board was meeting in Washington, D.C. In remarks later introduced into the *Congressional Record*, NCAI president Joseph Garry stated to America and "even the whole world" that the NCAI rejected the "publicity stunt of appealing to foreign nations for settlement of American Indian affairs." Though supportive of the United Nations as a force for world peace, NCAI officials did not regard it as "an appropriate forum for deciding our American Indian questions." The incident heralded a split in the 1960s between NCAI leaders and young Native protesters who scorned their measured patriotism.[8]

In early 1959 Anderson helped create perhaps the most dramatic act of termination resistance to date. The Tuscarora activist encouraged a group of Florida Seminoles, the Miccosukee, to reach out to the new Cuban leader, Fidel Castro, for help in securing a reservation homeland in the undeveloped Everglades, hitherto denied by the state of Florida and the federal Bureau of Indian Affairs. Delighted to reap such a public relations bonanza, Castro invited a Miccosukee delegation to attend July 26 events marking the Cuban Revolution. Eleven Miccosukee activists along with Anderson joined Castro in celebrating his new regime, which extended "recognition" to the Sovereign Miccosukee Nation and expressed to the delegates "hopes that your government will, likewise, be successful in protecting your everglades homeland for your people." Alarmed by the trip and its propaganda benefit to Castro, the BIA, almost certainly prodded by the State Department, set into motion the machinery by which the United States and the state of Florida extended recognition to the Miccosukee Nation and carved out a reservation for it. In return, Miccosukee leader Buffalo Tiger pledged not to return to Cuba. Although this was an anomalous incident, the Miccosukee's campaign represented both the precedent of Native groups moving beyond the boundaries of the United States to seek resolution of bitter land disputes and a preview of the protean ideological boundaries of the 1960s.[9]

John F. Kennedy's presidential campaign statement on American Indian affairs asserted: "Indians have heard fine words and promises long enough. They are right in asking for deeds." By June 1961, when Native leaders gathered at the American Indian Chicago Conference to outline a "New Frontier" in Indian-white relations, many Native Americans, especially those of the Iroquois Confederacy, saw that frontier as a violent place. They had been disappointed by Congress's refusal to fund an American Indian Point Four program, denied access to the United Nations, deprived of justice by the U.S. Supreme Court in the *Tuscarora* case, and demoralized by Kennedy's failure to honor the nation's oldest treaty and thus protect Seneca sovereignty. A new generation of activists, politicized by these bitter defeats and by the implications of decolonization for a Native American nationalism, strove in the 1960s and 1970s to turn Justice Black's moral words into legal deeds using the confrontational tactics practiced by the Tuscarora. In his 1974 book *Behind the Trail of Broken Treaties: An Indian Declaration of Independence*, the influential Sioux activist Vine Deloria Jr. assessed the impact of Anderson's 1959 Washington, D.C., protest on young Native activists, writing: "Indians watched and laughed as the Interior Department tried to pass the incident off as the actions of a few communist-inspired radicals. But they never forgot that the Tuscarora had stood up for Indian treaty rights and the international status of tribes at a time when few men were willing to stand up for any principles at all."[10]

Training Leaders in the "Ways of Indians"

The 1960s generation of Native activists was influenced by several factors, from treaty rights battles such as those of the Seneca and Tuscarora to the international Cold War, Third World nationalism, and the sit-ins staged by young African Americans. Native activists' evolving political consciousness was shaped also by efforts of the World War II generation of Native leaders to provide an intellectual forum for young Native Americans entering an educational system that denied the value of tribal histories and culture. Frustrated by the paternalism of the Bureau of Indian Affairs, his former employer, D'Arcy McNickle founded American Indian Development in 1952 to encourage "self-help" among Native Americans and to expand their "participation in community, state, and national life." The "first step" in Native Americans' development, McNickle argued, "is to get people to see things with their own eyes—to think about them in their own minds." From the beginning McNickle framed this educational process in an international context, animated by his belief that Cold War nation-building programs would invest Native Americans with the economic and political power to define their own communities. A 1952 fundraising letter from his organization to potential donors asked them to "work with us, in spirit as well as in material ways, to help the American Indian achieve their own Point Four program."[11]

AID's educative vehicle was the Workshop on American Indian Affairs, a six-week immersion course designed to teach American Indian college students about Native traditions, the history of colonialism, and the dynamics of social conflict between "folk" and "urban" cultures. Workshop organizers found that most students were "uninformed on broad issues affecting the Indian people as an ethnic group" and in some cases "did not know how to act 'Indian.'" McNickle and other Native leaders recruited students from across Native America to participate. NCAI executive director Helen Peterson encouraged the chairman of the Crow Indian Tribal Council to send Crow students to the AID workshops, maintaining that this would help "Indian college young people to find themselves, gain respect for themselves as Indians." She reminded him, "You know how we all talk in all our meetings about the future generations, but except for rare individuals like yourself, almost no *Indians* are teaching their young people in the ways of Indians or encouraging them to be proud of their INDIANNESS." Restoring "Indianness," then, became the goal of the workshops. But this "Indianness" remained a hybrid construction: Native leaders married the "ways of Indians" to the means of modern American economic development and international nation-building programs in workshops that sought to resolve "the ambiguity of identity" affecting young Native

Americans in an "American society that threatens to engulf them," as one organizer put it."[12]

Beginning in 1956, twenty-five to thirty-five American Indian college students from over twenty different tribal communities met for six weeks each summer in Colorado to revisit their tribal histories, read works on cultural change, and explore the tensions between "major and minor cultures," or "colonialism." Their reading list included Ruth Benedict's *Patterns of Culture*, Everett and Helen Hughes's *When Peoples Meet*, Robert Redfield's *Primitive World and Its Transformations*, and John Collier's *Indians of the Americas*, as well as published articles on American colonialism by Felix Cohen and unpublished essays by Native American intellectuals such as Robert Thomas (Cherokee). Final exams and a required paper posed questions such as "What has been the effect of colonialism on the American Indian?" and "How did [American] Indian Nationalism come about and what are some of the advantages of Nationalism?"[13]

Most workshop participants broadened their understanding of Indians' experiences in this intellectual context. Clyde Warrior (Ponca) noted in his 1962 exam that he had learned that "all over the world tribal peoples are coming in contact with the outside world and basically they all have the same reactions." Frank Dukepoo (Hopi) wrote in his 1962 essay: "I thought colonialism existed only in the older countries like southern Europe or in places such as Africa. It was really quite a shock to find [out] here in America and to the Indians especially that we were under a form of colonialism. I can now see why the Indian leaders of today complain of certain rights and didn't have the power to enact upon them." Angela Russell (Crow) connected "the rise of the Indian Nationalism" to "international nationalism." In provocative essays Sandra Johnson, who grew up on the Makah reservation situated within the boundaries of Washington State, articulated a heightened consciousness shaped by increasingly violent battles between Indians and whites over fishing rights. Johnson documented crises "from Cuba to the Congo" and criticized the United States for exacerbating those crises abroad and at home. Describing "'a clear and present danger' as the white culture extends its influence further and further into the Indian way of life," she contended that "it is not that Indians reject white culture, per se. It is that they reject white culture when they are forced to adapt to it by losing what they are and [what] they value." Referring to white Americans, she wondered what they would do if it became "necessary" for them to live under Russian dominance, where only the political structure is an objectionable difference. Many would cry, "Better dead than Red." And yet, another battle between the Reds and the Whites is being fought within our own borders. Given this different context it may be easier for white citizens to understand our cry which would sound more like, "Better Red than dead."

Like other Native activists, Johnson framed the struggle for Native rights as a cold war while invoking an imagery of indigenous Red Power to define that struggle. Not all Indian participants consumed the workshop with such sanguinary passion; reflecting the heterogeneity of Native America, some students refused to condemn the Bureau of Indian Affairs and rejected the colonialism analogy. But most of them identified lingering termination pressures that necessitated political resistance, some citing the Seneca's Kinzua Dam crisis as clear evidence that federal Indian policy still threatened American Indian homelands and the collective body of treaties that, in theory, protected them.[14]

Workshop students gave voice to the collective angst and anger of this new generation in the workshop's newsletter, *The Indian Progress*; some of the most prominent young activists of the 1960s, including Sandra Johnson, Bruce Wilkie (Makah), and Clyde Warrior, served on its editorial staff. A 1961 editorial issued a clarion call to young Native Americans to "lead the Indians of this continent in tomorrow's world," warning, "If anyone of us . . . turns his back on his people, then he is guilty of helping to destroy his people. Young people, we must, by the fact that we are born American Indians, be dedicated to our people." The most internationalist editorial addressed the lingering problem of termination policies that continued to erode Indian rights. Sustaining an argument that activists had made with regularity in the 1950s, a 1962 editorial opined that treaty rights had to be seen in an international light: "With the stirring of the masses in certain countries abroad, it would be beneficial for our country to uphold and continue to respect federal obligations and treaty rights of the American Indian." The editors believed that "the Tuscarora and Kinzua Dam controversies are sure to be read with wide interest to indigenous peoples throughout the world. The repercussions of the state of Washington's threat to end Indian fishing rights in that state, would have detrimental effects toward good relationships with our indigenous friends abroad. And certainly would not be [in] the national interest." Termination policies such as those driving the Kinzua project, the editorial continued, transmitted fear to "underdeveloped countries" and undermined U.S. foreign aid programs, which were "wasted because of a lack of understanding between different peoples." Speaking the language of hybrid patriotism, the editorial asserted that young Indian leaders in the "Pan Indian movement" intended to educate American society about Indianness and thus "demonstrate to the world that *our country* is still the guardian of self-determination, freedom and the protector of cultures."[15]

This striking call to action reflected an emerging consciousness of pan-Indianism within the United States but also an affinity with "indigenous friends" abroad undergoing similar efforts to protect cultural difference. These student leaders increasingly promoted an Indian nationalism along the lines of Third World nationalism, a development that troubled workshop organizers. McNickle, for his part, did not want to tell participants how to be "Indian" but preferred to let them come to their own conclusions through the readings and discussions. In evaluating the 1963 workshops, McNickle asked Cherokee intellectual Robert Thomas, who provided guidance to the program, "what we might do if it is true, as you suggest, that the Workshop is becoming a focal point for a growing Nationalistic movement in this young group—or whether we need to do anything." In a subsequent letter to McNickle, Thomas described Clyde Warrior, a former workshop participant then active in the National Indian Youth Council, as a "leader of the Red Mau-Mau," referring to the Kenyan nationalist movement. Indeed Warrior predicted on one occasion that "there will be an [Indian] uprising that will make Kenyatta's Mau Mau movement look like a Sunday-school picnic." This inflammatory rhetoric was a harbinger of the emerging split between the NIYC generation of the 1960s and the NCAI generation, which McNickle had helped shape with his ideas and his initiatives during the 1950s.[16]

"A Fighting Generation Is Coming"

Mel Thom, a cofounder of NIYC and its first president, participated in the Workshop on American Indian Affairs in 1963 and found it valuable for helping Indian students "become aware [of Native issues] through history and the social sciences. This is great encouragement to the cause and indicates a fighting generation is coming." But, criticizing organizers' emphasis on theory rather than practice, he suggested in 1964 that McNickle invite NIYC members to address the workshops, maintaining that a knowledge of current affairs as much as study of tribal history and cultures would "educate young Indians to the fact that Indian tribes and treaties are not obligated to go out of existence." Young people such as NIYC members, he told McNickle, "can more directly relate Indian problems to Workshop students."[17]

The first influential organization of this new "fighting generation," the NIYC emerged from the Chicago Conference Youth Group, a youth caucus of the American Indian Chicago Conference held in June 1961. The NIYC held its first meeting in August of that year at the Gallup Indian Community Center, one of a growing number of centers which fostered activism among urban Indian youth. The NIYC initially focused on the ways in which college-educated youth could "find their place in this modern world," as Mel Thom put it. Besides Thom and Warrior, the group's leadership—which included numerous Native women, such as Tuscarora activist Karen Rickard and Mohawk activist Shirley Witt—represented a geographical and cultural cross-section of Native America that encompassed members from the Potawatomi, Winnebago, Chippewa, Shoshone-Bannock, Crow, Mandan, Mohawk, Sioux, Tuscarora, and Navajo communities, among others. Most of these founding members had participated in university Indian clubs in the 1950s. Executive director Herbert Blatchford had served as president of the University of New Mexico Kiva Club of Native students during the mid-1950s, attending the University on the GI Bill after leaving the U.S. Air Force. Thom had been president of the Indian Club of Brigham Young University, where he earned a civil engineering degree; he also served as president of the Southwestern Regional Indian Youth Council (SRIYC) in 1959–60. The SRIYC was one of several regional youth councils supported by the New Mexico Association on Indian Affairs, which promoted the idea of a "national youth council" in the late 1950s; association staff consulted with educators from Europe, Asia, Africa, and South and Central America, developing their vision of youth leadership on an international scale.[18]

The goals of the NIYC included building connections with an "Indian world community" and improving "communications between Indians and other Americans." It also promoted awareness of American Indian issues among foreign citizens, hoping that they would pressure the U.S. government to protect Indian rights. Most important, it opposed termination programs by working to halt the "threat and policy of cultural absorption and oblivion," repeal HCR 108, and advance treaty rights. Through the agency of the NIYC, Thom wrote, American Indians' "'last stand' is in the making." His use of the imagery of Custer's "last stand" increased young activists' sense of crisis and framed that crisis as a survival narrative. NIYC members considered themselves warriors of a new era, using weapons and strategies of public relations in "a struggle for survival, a struggle not only to protect our lands and our civil liberties, but a struggle to regain the minds and hearts of our own people."[19]

Indeed, as Thom wrote in his essay "Indian War 1963," Native Americans were involved in "a cold war, one might say . . . The weakest link in the Indian's defense is his lack of understanding of this modern-type war. Indians have not been able to use political action, propaganda, and power, as well as their opponents. The enemy has made notable gains; they have deployed their forces well. Enemy forces have successfully scattered Indian people and got them divided against themselves." The following year Thom continued this theme in "Indian War 1964," in which he wrote that he and his NIYC colleagues had become convinced that "this is a real war. Indian life is steadily torn apart and Indian integrity is downgraded— all from within a legal framework. Our opposition is out to destroy Indians as a people." Thom called the U.S. Army Corps of Engineers' work a continuation of nineteenth-century violence, but "rather than shooting Indians, it is now more fashionable to drown Indians by building dams."[20]

The Kinzua Dam's flooding of Seneca sacred lands and cultural sites as well as the Tuscarora's loss of reservation land angered NIYC leaders, including Karen Rickard, Chief Clinton Rickard's daughter, in part because the removal of Seneca continued into 1965 and reshaped Seneca society in ways that exacerbated the original trauma of forced relocation. Alvin Josephy Jr., a white historian active in Indian rights campaigns, told Mel Thom in 1965 that the Army Corps of Engineers "are still clubbing [the Seneca]—making the Senecas into Levittown dwellers in tidy, little ranch-house projects all squeezed together like suburbanites! The American Dream!" In addition, the U.S. Congress decided to reduce its compensation to the Seneca from $48 million to $6 million, prompting the NIYC

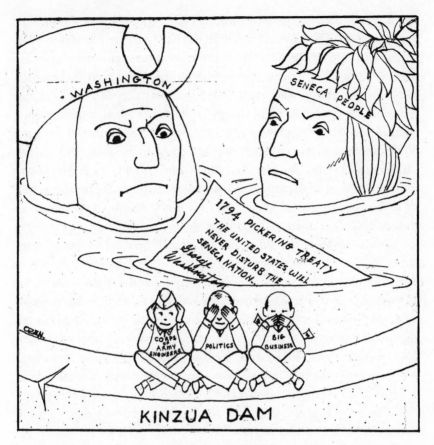

6.1 This political cartoon, published in the newsletter *American Indian Horizon* (April 1964) three years after the Seneca's final court challenge to the Kinzua Dam failed, demonstrates how Kinzua continued to serve as a visceral symbol of broken promises, represented in the Seneca's association with the values of the real America, personified by George Washington. *American Indian Horizon* 11, no. 8 (April 1964). Courtesy of Princeton University Library.

leadership to implore its members and friends to drown Congress with protests that would "have all nations of the world know that by example of the American treaties of the American Indian, every International American Treaty is only pacification."[21]

The NCAI's failure to produce effective resistance to the nightmare that the Kinzua Dam symbolized for many Native Americans represented for NIYC members the faults of the older generation of Indian politicians and activists. Some derisively called the NCAI the "National Council for Aged Indians." The NIYC's break with the NCAI became formal in 1964, when organizers of the NCAI's annual convention refused to let NIYC members join a convention parade because the young activists had written "Red Power" on their cars; NIYC members slipped their cars into the parade anyway. The NIYC asserted a militant approach in promoting "radical and drastic changes in Indian affairs" that contrasted with the NCAI approaches and proposals that had emerged from the 1961 American Indian Chicago Convention. NIYC members embedded this generational frustration in the group's constitution, the preamble to which read: "We, the younger generation, at this time in the history of the American Indian, find it expedient to band together on a national scale in meeting the challenges facing the Indian people. In such banding for mutual assistance, we recognize the future of the Indian people will ultimately rest in the hands of the younger people." Echoing the rhetoric of the Students for a Democratic Society (SDS) manifesto, and prior to young African Americans' employment of "Black Power" rhetoric, the NIYC presented American Indians' struggles as a war against racist colonialism, elaborating a new discourse of Indian "Red Power" despite "knowing full well that there would be some people who would associate the color with Communists."[22]

The NIYC's motto—"a greater Indian America"—was a tenuous proposition, given the heterogeneity of Native Americans, though a greater American Indian identity was not. But the NIYC did not represent a separatist movement. Despite their rhetoric of war, leaders of the group articulated in private and in public a version of the hybrid patriotism that had defined the NCAI generation. Mel Thom explained in a 1964 essay that he neither damned nor disavowed American citizenship. "I value American citizenship very highly, and consider it hard earned by our fathers," he wrote. "I think Indians make their patriotism quite clear with their military record in World War II and the Korean Conflict." Instead Thom promoted a conception of citizenship that embraced rather than elided cultural difference, contending that it was "not contradictory to have full American citizenship and also tribal allegiance. It is consistent with the height of American ideals and principles." He considered American Indian ideals and principles "a real asset to a modern fast-moving America" and maintained that a stable "Indian" identity could allow Native Americans to "contribute to the great American society." Clyde Warrior, a more vocal proponent of "Red Power" than Thom, offered a similar vision of the nation redeeming itself morally by collectively securing Indian culture and furthering Indian economic development. Warrior noted in his testimony at a rural poverty hearing that "America has given a great social and moral message to the world and demonstrated (perhaps not forcefully enough) that freedom and responsibility as an ethic is inseparable from and, in fact, the 'cause' of the fabulous American standard of living. America has not been diligent enough in promulgating this philosophy within her own borders."[23]

The NIYC began as a "movement" and as "an activist organization," according to its own history. In the mid-1960s, however, it faced both an identity crisis and a fiscal crisis, from which it emerged as a "fully tax-exempt charitable and educational agency" based in Berkeley, California, that distributed grant monies and lobbied politicians. The NIYC later joined forces with other pan-Indian groups to protest job discrimination through sit-ins and occupation of federal facilities, promoted Peace Corps programs on Indian reservations, and participated in the Poor People's Campaign that brought together minority groups in a dramatic march on Washington in May 1968 after the assassination of Martin Luther King Jr. A new wave of young Indian activists would build on NIYC Red Power rhetoric, however, in pursuing more "radical and drastic changes in Indian affairs."[24]

"We Have This Treaty Right": The Pacific Northwest Revisited

Perhaps the NIYC's most salient contribution to American Indian activism came in the form of its early support of Indian fishing rights in the Pacific Northwest, which helped to bring that controversy onto a national and even an international stage. Putting into practice its philosophy of highlighting Native material crises that stemmed from the moral failures of the United States to uphold its treaty commitments, the NIYC helped organize support for "Operation Awareness," the March 3, 1964, demonstration by a coalition of forty-seven American Indian communities at the Washington State capitol in Olympia. Clyde Warrior, Hank Adams, and Bruce Wilkie launched the event, which benefited from the charismatic presence of actor Marlon Brando, whom Adams had persuaded to join the cause. After participating in the 1963 March on Washington, Brando had attended the NIYC's August 1963 conference, during which he applauded the group's "dynamic" work. Brando participated in a fish-in in March 1964 and was arrested but quickly released, though he told reporters, "I'll keep on fishing, and if it means going to jail, I'll go to jail." When he participated in another fish-in, police ignored him in the hope of avoiding further publicity. According to journalist Hunter S. Thompson, who covered the fish-in for the *National Observer*, Brando joined American Indians "in three separate assaults against 'the forces of injustice.'" The protest generated publicity and a "new feeling of unity among Indians" and demonstrated the "dynamic leadership" of the NIYC. The NIYC's commitment to Native fishing rights broadened in October 1964, when the nineteen-year-old Adams initiated the Washington State Project to counter what he called "termination plans" in that state. Adams soon left the NIYC to become the executive director of the Survival of American Indians Association (SAIA), the "official voice of the Fishing rights resistance." In addition to Brando, Native Americans found an ally in Dick Gregory, the African American entertainer and civil rights champion, who supported their cause because, he said, Americans needed to start living up to their word "in this country. If we can't do it here," he asked, "where can we?" Invited by the SAIA to join their fish-ins, Gregory was arrested for fishing without a license and sent to jail, where he conducted a hunger strike. Gregory continued to promote Indian rights, as he did in a lecture at Villanova University in March 1969. "We guarantee a foreigner a better way of life than the American Indian," he told faculty and students. "When we become as ashamed of the injustices at home as we are aware of the injustices abroad, America will be truly beautiful."[25]

Thompson noted, "Throughout the country, Indians are doing battle with Federal and state governments over a variety of causes." Indeed, the fishing rights conflict was just one of a number of battles over treaty rights taking place in the 1960s. The Chippewa asserted their treaty right to hunt ducks without having to buy Wisconsin state hunting stamps. Cherokee risked arrest for hunting deer on land regulated by the state of Oklahoma; led by a World War II veteran, they armed themselves with guns as well as lawyers to defend their treaty rights. In all these cases Native activists claimed that the U.S. Constitution supported their cause. But the "fishing war" became the center of the treaty rights conflict because of the ways in which activists connected their struggle to the moral dynamics of the Cold War and the revolutions of decolonization, and because its violence mirrored that of African American civil rights struggles in the South. Most important, the fishing war engendered a contentious legal war that ultimately forced the federal government to decide between states' rights and tribal rights.[26]

The fishing-related protests of American Indians in the Pacific Northwest intensified during the late 1950s in part because they were taking fewer fish from the annual salmon runs as a result of non-Indian commercial fishing operations and the building of numerous dams that inhibited spawning, especially the Dalles Dam, which had destroyed the important Celilo Falls fishing site. Between 1945 and 1957 the number of non-Indian commercial gillnetters in the region rose from 46 to 637, while the expansion of the timber industry and suburbs generated pesticides that damaged the fish population. At the same time, Washington State fish and game officials supportive of termination stepped up harassment of Native fishermen on and off the reservation. In response, activists and their attorneys made a simple argument: Native Americans had been promised the right to fish in their "customary places" by the Stevens Treaties of 1855. Because the federal government controlled all treaty-based relations with American Indians, state governments could not claim jurisdiction over them. Sandra Johnson, a veteran of the Workshop on American Indian Affairs, urged Native Americans in a guest editorial for the journal *Indian Voices* to view that conflict over treaties in the Pacific Northwest as "a legal war that we must enter . . . The State trespasses on Indian land and violates U.S. treaties. They do not honor U.S. Supreme Court decisions or other federal regulations." Native activists pressed the issue just as African-American activists' civil rights campaigns pushed the federal government to uphold their constitutional rights. In the words of Valerie Bridges (Nisqually-Puyallip), arrested at the age of thirteen during a major raid in 1965, she and other activists "set the net and waited for the state . . . to let them know we're not going to stop fishing. We have this treaty right, the supreme law of the land under their Constitution. It's a treaty we're fighting for." Activist Billy Frank Jr. (Nisqually) was arrested over fifty times after 1945, the first time as a fourteen-year-old. After fulfilling a boyhood dream by serving in the U.S. Marines from 1952 to 1954, he fought a different battle to see that military service rewarded, leading his people's resistance to state encroachment.[27]

Jurisdictional struggles over the boundaries of the reservation became especially violent when Washington State officials began conducting more frequent raids of Indian fishing sites beginning in January 1962, creating scenes reminiscent of the American South. After conducting surveillance of Native fishermen, sometimes using spotter airplanes, state and local police and fish and game officials raided fishing sites on the Nisqually River, beating, tear-gassing, and arresting Native men, women, and children and confiscating their fishing equipment. "In time," writes legal historian Charles Wilkinson, "the banks of the Nisqually merged with the school-house steps of Little Rock, the bridge at Selma, and the back of the bus in Montgomery." For American Indian activists, the violence was also reminiscent of frontier America. Janet McCloud (Nisqually), cofounder of the Survival of American Indians Association, compared the equipment con-fiscation policy to "shooting the buffalo in an earlier time." Sandra John-son described legal battles that "flared into hand to hand combat" with Washington State officials who played "the role of a modern day 'cavalry,'" as "motorboats [sprang] from behind bushes" along rivers where Indians fished, "reminding one of the early battle scenes of this country." From the beginning the local press prejudicially called the conflict the "Indian War."[28]

The "fishing war," as other observers called it, was the second major outbreak of violence in a continuing domestic cold war between Ameri-can Indians and American government officials, the first coming in the Tuscarora's defense of their reservation sovereignty against the imperialis-tic schemes of Robert Moses and New York State officials. A Native American television cameraman, Buddy Noonan, telling SAIA members, "It sounds like a hot war up your way," pledged to provide coverage of the fishing wars because "one-sided news networks" were painting Native ac-tivists as radicals rather than as legitimate protesters championing the rule of law. Other activists framed the "fishing war" in familiar Cold War terms of the domino theory. For instance, the SAIA argued that if Washington State officials "can violate a Federal treaty to stop 'off-reservation' fishing, what is to stop them from ending 'on-reservation' fishing whenever they are ready to. When all Indians realize this, perhaps, then a unified front can be formed." This domestic domino theory spurred unified action on the part of Indians all over the country to contain state encroachment in the absence of federal protections. In a fund-raising appeal to its supporters, the SAIA situated its struggle in the larger context of international agreements that cemented Cold War alliances, insisting:

> There can be no compromise whatsoever in this controversy. We reject any and all efforts by anyone to compromise our rights under the [Stevens] Treaty. The United States has not only the legal duty to honor the Indian Treaty, but also has the moral duty to recognize the Treaty just as it does the South East Asia Treaty, the NATO Treaty, all other Treaties that this Government is bound to recognize and uphold.[29]

Activists also situated their struggle in the context of decolonization, imagining themselves part of a growing coalition of postcolonial nations. Because white juries routinely found Native Americans guilty of violating state fishing laws, SAIA member Don Matheson argued that an "international tribunal" would be the only way to secure justice because "other dark-skinned people" would sit on it. Robert Casey, another frequent writer for the SAIA's *Survival News*, promoted this notion that Native Americans' struggles with the federal government were part of a "world wide race war," citing the Algerians kicking out the French and the Indonesians driving out the Dutch, among other acts of decolonization. "Somewhere along the line the white pundits are going to have to analyze these revolutions for what they really are—NOT Communist led conspiracies, but a world wide race war against all the whites outside of Europe."[30]

SAIA activists fueled this Cold War and decolonization rhetoric, which routinely appeared in their public statements, as part of a strategy to bring attention to their embattled corner of the world. Fishing rights activists in the Pacific Northwest cast a wide net in securing aid for their cause. The Nisqually Nation appealed to the United Nations, the Indian European Legion of Europe, and citizens of England and Europe in its campaign to force the government to honor its treaty commitments. The SAIA submitted an essay titled "The Last Indian War" to foreign journals to publicize their resistance. The English journal *New Statesman* published it in 1966, generating letters and donations from England, Scotland, and Germany. But these ideas also percolated throughout activists' personal writings and internal correspondence, expressing a heightened consciousness of Indian nationalism in an international context. Yet SAIA activists also

tempered their rhetoric, using the language of hybrid patriotism to emphasize the justness of their cause. After Washington State officials' violent
arrest of Native men, women, and children at the October 13, 1965, fish-
in, Don Matheson wrote, "This is still the best country in the world," even
though "some of our white citizens have not yet been truly 'Americanized.' Their idea of treaties is very similar to that held by Joseph Stalin."
Highlighting their patriotism, and their expectations of reward for their
military service, in 1965 Nisqually fishermen staged a symbolic protest by
raising the American flag upside down, a military distress signal, using the
funeral flag of a Nisqually who died at the Battle of the Bulge in 1945.[31]

Fundamentally, fishing rights activists had faith in the law. Valerie
Bridges had explained it in simple terms: "We have this treaty right, the
supreme law of the land under their [the U.S.] Constitution." Activists
had their limits, however. Emphasizing the international nature of these
treaties, they threatened to take their case beyond the borders of the
United States. If the country did not accept its obligations, then activists
would appeal the United Nations for protection and "to the governments
and peoples of the world. For it would seem that Hanoi, or Moscow or
London or France should be deeply concerned with United States treaties
and the violation of them." But first they appealed to "good men of conscience with justice in their hearts." SAIA leader Janet McCloud (Tula-
lip) hoped that President Johnson was one of those men, writing him in
September 1965 in recognition of World Law Day: "We are now hearing
today, cries of cultural genocide used within the Soviet Union, also against
the Jewish people. Nevertheless, the very same policy is used today by this
government against the Indian people; yet, one is condemned and the
other justified. Is there any answer to this contradiction?" McCloud once
again brought to the fore the American dilemma at a critical moment in
the Cold War. In September 1965 America's Cold War contradiction between words and deeds worsened when Johnson expanded the nation's
commitments in Vietnam, a war that intersected with the fishing wars in
significant and interesting ways.[32]

To Vietnam and Back

The use of Vietnam War imagery to describe the fishing wars of the Pacific
Northwest became more frequent as both conflicts escalated in the mid-

1960s. For example, Darrell Houston opened his 1966 essay on the "Indian Salmon War" by observing, "Three game wardens padded through the tangled underbrush with a stealth that would have done credit to a Viet Cong combat patrol." Activists conflated these two struggles in moral as well as material terms. While Washington State officials were confiscating the boats and nets belonging to American Indians, the U.S. government was supporting the South Vietnamese fishing industry with motors, fingerlings, equipment, and fishing piers, a "fisheries development program that dwarfs the needs of American Indians," according to one activist. Other fishing rights activists protested the drafting of American Indians "to go to some strange land to fight for United States treaty commitments. While right here on the Indian fished rivers our people have to take up arms to protect themselves against their still aggressive treaty breaking white neighbors." Janet McCloud, editor of the SAIA newsletter *Survival News*, declared that American Indians and "the other colored people and Nations are turning away from the white American Colonists in disgust. They are going to jail rather than help King Cong fight the Viet Cong." McCloud organized the Indian GI Resistance Movement (Hew-Kecaw-Na-Yo) to assist Native soldiers in claiming conscientious objector status and avoid serving King Cong America as it rampaged through Southeast Asia.[33]

On October 13, 1968, in Olympia, Washington, Sidney Mills (Yakima) became the most celebrated American Indian soldier to announce publicly his "decision of conscience" to "RENOUNCE FURTHER OBLIGATION IN SERVICE OR DUTY TO THE UNITED STATES ARMY." After a seven-month hospital stay spent recovering from injuries suffered in Vietnam, Mills returned home to help defend the treaty rights of his fellow Yakimas, saying that he could no longer serve the United States in its "less compelling struggle in Vietnam." Mills now joined "another battle, a cause to which the United States owes its protection, a fight for people who the United States has abandoned." While Indian fishermen in Vietnam were fighting and dying, he said, "Indian fishermen live here without protection and under steady attack" from state police, game wardens, and citizen militias. The drowning of Jimmy Alexander (Yakima) in one such attack weighed heavily on Mills, as did the case of Sergeant Richard Sohappy (Yakima), a Silver Star and Bronze Star honoree recuperating from injuries suffered in Vietnam, who was arrested three times for fishing illegally to feed his family. Mills was driven to act publicly by police clubbings of Native women and children who joined the fish-ins; he later claimed that his paratrooper unit had perpetrated "many My Lais." For "it's not an invading army we're hurting [in Vietnam]," he wrote. "It's the women and especially the children we're outright murdering." Mills, McCloud, and others saw themselves on the front lines of a war for treaty rights and for cultural survival against a United States whose waging of war on the Vietnamese represented an extension of its racism at home.[34]

Given Native activists' and politicians' use of Cold War rhetoric to stage their defense of sovereignty and treaty rights during the 1950s, it is important to consider the ways in which Native American activists linked international and national developments in the 1960s as the Vietnam War assumed such prominence in American life and as the protean boundaries of the Third World began to shape Native Americans' conceptions of nationalism. Beyond its Cold War context, the U.S. war in Vietnam served as both a contemporary mirror of American frontier history and a crucible through which young American Indian activists sharpened their identity as victims of American "colonialism."

Playing Cowboys and Indians in Vietnam

American observers of Vietnam before the 1960s described the Vietnamese much as colonial Americans had described American Indians from the early 1600s, as "very lazy and not prone to be ambitious." When the United States became involved in determining Vietnam's future during the 1950s, Americans used these racial tropes to justify their intervention. And when the number of U.S. troops increased, their use of Indian metaphors to describe the people, the place, and the process in Vietnam became more common and more public. According to American journalist Frances Fitzgerald, who traveled throughout Vietnam in 1966, U.S. military officers described Viet Cong–controlled territory as "Indian Country," the phrase putting the Vietnam War

> into a definite mythological and historical perspective: the Americans were once again embarked upon a heroic and (for themselves) almost painless conquest of an inferior race. To the American settlers the defeat of the Indians had seemed not just a nationalist victory,

but an achievement made in the name of humanity . . . Quite uncon-
sciously, the American officers and officials used a similar language to
describe their war against the NLF [Viet Cong].

The language of U.S. military policies is riddled with references to American Indians. As early as 1962, a U.S. counterinsurgency specialist likened
the concept of "strategic hamlets" to the "old stockade idea our ancestors
used against the Indians." In his 1965 testimony before the Senate Foreign
Relations Committee, General Maxwell Taylor also compared the army's
pacification program in Vietnam to colonial Americans' experiences with
Indians, saying: "It is very hard to plant the corn outside the stockade
when the Indians are still around. We have to get the Indians farther away
in many provinces to make good progress." The U.S. Air Force embedded
heroes of frontier battles in bombing campaigns code-named "Daniel
Boone," "Sam Houston," and "Buffalo Hunter." U.S. Navy personnel ran
patrols through "Indian Country" near the Cambodian border and into
North Vietnam. In a Green Beret training manual, published in comic
book format, the caption for an image of a U.S. soldier killing a Viet Cong
read, "That's one little Indian that won't talk anymore." A Vietnamese
scout training American GIs to "walk point" was called a "Kit Carson
scout." And so on.[35]

Soldiers also used the nineteenth-century trope of George Armstrong
Custer as heroic victim to frame their own experiences. One Navy pilot
described his bombing of a target fifteen miles south of Hanoi by noting, "I
felt like Custer going into Indian country." Colonel Harold Moore rel-
ished the fact that his "airmobile" unit was made part of the Seventh Cavalry, which had gone so far as to adopt Custer's regimental fight song as its
own. It is not surprising, then, that Custer's name appeared in a Kurtz-like
message scrawled in a Saigon latrine: "We'll bring peace to this land if we
have to kill them all—General Custer." White American soldiers used the
Custer legend to imagine themselves caught in a hostile racial space, to
embody his supposed heroism in that space, and to avenge his death, the
killing of an archetypal white hero by savages, a deed that transcended
space and time. In this light the U.S. Army's massacre of Sioux at Wounded
Knee in 1890, conducted by members of Custer's old Seventh Cavalry,
became a prelude to more vengeance. In his 1970 review of two books on
the My Lai massacre, the noted psychiatrist Robert Jay Lifton contended

that GIs' use of the Indian-hating variant "The only good dink is a dead dink" linked the frontier past to the Vietnam present in a way that had helped to trigger the massacre.[36]

The journalism, fiction, and film of the Vietnam era both documented and mirrored the U.S. military's discourse of frontier conquest to link American imperialism of the past with the present conflict. An AP reporter described American soldiers' battles with Viet Cong as like "Custer at the Little Big Horn." While he was conducting interviews during 1967–68, the journalist Michael Herr encountered a captain who volunteered to take him to the jungle "to play Cowboys and Indians." Herr concluded that "Vietnam was where the Trail of Tears was headed all along." Nicholas von Hoffman, writing in the *Washington Post*, contended that My Lai was not an isolated incident but another version of the 1864 Sand Creek massacre and the 1890 Wounded Knee massacre. Tom Hayden, who founded SDS in 1962, provided the most comprehensive comparison of the Indian Wars and the Vietnam War in his 1972 book *The love of possession is a disease with them*, the title of which came from an 1877 statement by the Sioux leader Sitting Bull after U.S. officials abrogated the 1868 Fort Laramie Treaty to take the Sioux's sacred Black Hills. Hayden cast the Vietnam War, and President Nixon's expansion of it into Laos and Cambodia, as a continuation of "a tradition of Western imperialism which, in America, began with the attempted destruction of the Indian," chronicling in twenty pages the "amazingly close" parallels between American violence in Indian America and Indochina.[37]

Such comparisons quickly found their way into novels about Vietnam. The Japanese writer Takeshi Kaiko, a Hiroshima survivor, toured Vietnam as a correspondent during 1964–65 and in 1968 published *Into a Black Sun*, a novel based on those experiences. Describing an archetypal U.S. Army captain, Kaiko wrote that his "insatiate energy . . . made me think of men in covered wagons, those ancestors of his who rode into the great plains and drove the Indians out." In David Halberstam's 1967 novel *One Very Hot Day*, an army captain calls a Viet Cong attack a "massacre," to which his South Vietnamese counterpart Captain Dang responds: "That is the word, massacre. From your Indian films." These connections between the nineteenth-century frontier and the New Frontier of the 1960s quickly emerged in contemporary films about the Vietnam War. In the pro-war film *The Green Berets* (1968), John Wayne migrated easily from his usual location on the Indian frontier to a Vietnamese frontier where the Viet Cong "whoop like marauding Indians." In a different vein, *Little Big Man* (1970) conflated massacres of Native Americans and Vietnamese in high-lighting General Custer's personification of the genocidal madness of U.S. policy in Vietnam. Director Ralph Nelson conceived *Soldier Blue* (1970), his frontier film about the 1864 slaughter of Native Americans at Sand Creek, "in the light of Vietnam . . . The same army. Different victims." According to *New York Times* film critic Dotson Rader, the massacre of Indians in *Soldier Blue*, situated in the nineteenth-century American West, was "a forerunner in a line of American-directed massacres running from before the Civil War (when Sand Creek occurred) to Dresden and Hiroshima into Vietnam." Indeed a Native American woman, Roxanne DeLory, viewed the film in this context, writing in a National Indian Youth Council publication that she was "sickened and disturbed" by the failure of Americans to act after Sand Creek: "Had someone spoken and had someone listened, perhaps the Wounded Knee massacre would not have happened twenty years later. Perhaps, the massacres of innocent women and children in Viet Nam would not be happening now."[38]

National and international cultural contexts intersected in complex ways when this connection between American racism in the frontier era and the Cold War era became embedded in Soviet bloc critiques of American policies in Vietnam. *Pravda*, the official organ of the Central Committee of the Communist Party, kept up its coverage of American Indian affairs to paint the United States as a racist and imperialist country. An April 1965 essay conflated the "planned mass extermination of the local Indians" and American efforts to "strangle the national-liberation movement in South Vietnam and in all of Southeast Asia." When *Little Big Man* played in Moscow in conjunction with the Seventh Moscow International Film Festival in 1971, a reviewer described a vicious massacre of Cheyenne by U.S. Army troops as "what the American military is perpetuating in our time in Indochina!" The film served as a "warning" about contemporary "racism and imperialist aggression" and the "empty phrases of the international murderers." This engagement of Soviet bloc countries with American Indian history had deep roots in East Germany, which married a fascination with Indian culture to Cold War critiques of American expansionism. In 1965, as the United States widened its operations in Vietnam, East Germany's state film studio, Deutsche Film-

Aktiengesellschaft (DEFA), began producing the first of twelve
Indianerfilme, or "Red Westerns," which attacked U.S. expansion in the
American West as an expression of colonial greed and racism. The Yugo-
slav actor Gojko Mitic became the anti–John Wayne, playing Indian roles
such as Osceoloa (Seminole) and Tokei-itho (Sioux), heroic leaders who
try to save their people and their resources from marauding and massacring American capitalists. The films, shot in Russia, Hungary, and Cuba
and shown throughout the Soviet bloc, included *Die Söhne der Grossen
Bärin* (The Sons of Great Mother Bear), which attracted nearly 10 million
viewers, making it and the *Indianerfilme* genre an important Cold War vehicle for delineating the continuities of an American imperial narrative.[39]

American Indians in Vietnam

American Indian soldiers also situated Vietnam in a timeless American
frontier narrative. While serving in Vietnam, Leroy TeCube (Jicarilla
Apache) documented comparisons between enemy territory and "Indian
Territory" as well as "references to the Indian wars of a century ago." A
Seneca soldier recalled that his sergeant told his platoon, "This [base] is
Fort Apache, boys, and out there is Indian Country." In the midst of the
U.S. Army's racist violence, a number of American Indian soldiers identified with the Vietnamese as people of color and with their experiences as a
colonized people. Guy Dull Knife Jr. (Lakota Sioux) remarked: "We kind
of looked alike in some ways and it seemed to make a difference. To me
and them." Dull Knife "often wondered if what we were doing to the Vietnamese wasn't the same as what the army had done to us. We were kicking
them out of their homes, killing all their animals, herding them from one
place to another and trying to force a government and a way of life on
them that they didn't really want." Historian Tom Holm (Cherokee-
Creek), a Vietnam veteran, argued that "the Vietnamese were attempting
to throw off the shackles of colonialism and were, therefore, in the same
kind of struggle to attain human and civil rights that nonwhites in America were striving for." In his memoir, titled *Viet Cong at Wounded Knee:
The Trail of a Blackfeet Activist,* Woody Kipp noted his physical resemblance to the Vietnamese, as well as their interest in his features. He also
connected their experiences to those that his people had suffered in the
past. Watching a machine gun assault on Vietnamese targets helped him,
he said, "more clearly comprehend what my people had faced in the

American West when the whites came with the Gatling guns." The Vietnam War enlarged Native soldiers' understanding of both tribal histories and their internationalist perspective on American Indians' place in a world in which people of color were fighting for independence from their white colonial masters. Just as their experiences accorded with those of African American soldiers, their understanding accorded with African American activists' critiques of the Vietnam War. As the novelist James Baldwin wrote in 1968: "A racist society can't but fight a racist war—this is the bitter truth. The assumptions acted on at home are also acted on abroad, and every American Negro knows this, for he, after the American Indian, was the first 'Viet Cong' victim." Vietnam was not about politics so much as it was about "racial hatred," as Kipp put it.[40]

By 1968 this understanding spurred many Native Americans to oppose the Vietnam War. Native American soldiers, however, had already been politicized before arriving in Vietnam. More than 42,000 Native Americans from over one hundred different tribal communities served in the Vietnam War, their average age roughly twenty. Tom Holm found through his interviews with fellow Native veterans that they had enlisted, or at least not resisted induction, "because they were patriots in the tribal sense of the word. To them, military service was part of an honorable family and/ or tribal tradition. They wanted to be warriors—to protect their land and their people." Some Native Americans linked their personal commitment to treaties their ancestors had signed with the United States pledging their tribe's support in times of crisis such as war. Maintaining, "My people have always honored our treaties, even when the whites haven't," one veteran explained, "I went in because our treaties say that we're allied to the U.S." A twice-wounded Green Beret agreed: "The U.S. has broken its part of the bargain with us, but we are more honorable than that. If we respond in kind, we are no better than they are. The point is, we are better than they; we honor our commitments, always have and always will." As during the 1950s, when Native leaders promoted themselves as "First Americans" more patriotic than government officials, a new generation of Native activists emerging from the crucible of Vietnam took the moral high ground to exemplify American national honor at a time when it was eroding at home and abroad, especially among newly recognized Third World nations, articulating the notion that treaties are sacred international documents that know no temporal or spatial limits.[41]

Native activists at home also used Vietnam to explain their militancy and justify their demands for federal recognition of treaty rights and reservation development. In an April 1966 statement to the press, NIYC leader Mel Thom criticized the federal government's failure to resolve poverty at home, as Martin Luther King would in his April 1967 Riverside Address. Reinforcing the same conception of the reservation as ancestral homeland that NCAI officials used in their attacks on termination legislation during the 1950s, Thom explained: "Indians need help in developing resources on their own reservations. The reservations are our ancestral homes, and we should be allowed to live on them peacefully. There is no sense in fighting for the rights of the South Vietnamese to determine their own future, and at the same time, forcing American Indians from their lands and denying them the right to decide their own future." At the fifth annual Wisconsin Indian Leadership Conference held the following year, Thom told members of the Wisconsin Indian Youth Council (WIYC) and the Great Lakes Inter-Tribal Council that Americans' inability to accept cultural difference "has gotten us into some very serious human problems throughout the world—including Viet Nam." The WIYC repeated this theme but in more provocative terms. The inaugural edition of the group's newsletter, *Indian Council Talk*, included an essay titled "My Lai and Indian Oppression," in which Michael Connors urged his readers to connect the My Lai massacre to American frontier history: "Doesn't this case that the Imperialist Regime finds itself entangled in Vietnam bring back memories of cases that our oppressed Indian brothers the Cheyenne, Kiowas, Arapahoes, Apaches, Hunkpapa and Brule Sioux and the Shoshones found themselves involved in during the 1800's?" Referring to the Vietnamese as *"our fellow Third World Brothers,"* Connors called on the United States to change its approach to American Indians, or else "we radicals within the Indian Movement from the extreme left will change it for you . . . For if you are to live by your Declaration of Independence and your Constitution, then you must account for your actions be they of the present or the past." Only then, he wrote, would the "Third World People of this Land" gain their freedom. Connors's statement reflects the war's radicalizing impact on a broad Indian movement and the extent to which young American Indians imagined themselves part of this burgeoning Third World. Still, Connors, like previous generations of Native activists, continued to believe in the American intellectual heritage as the moral foundation for improved relations between America and Indian America.[42]

Of course not all Native Americans opposed U.S. involvement in Vietnam, especially before the January 1968 Tet Offensive destroyed any illusions that U.S. forces were making material progress and My Lai destroyed any lingering doubts about America's moral mission. Native newspapers, which proliferated during the 1960s, printed announcements about tribal members being sent to Vietnam, dying in Vietnam, or returning home, and sent issues to Native servicemen in Vietnam. PFC Kuntson Chatlin (San Carlos Apache) sent a letter to the editor of the *Apache Drumbeat*, the San Carlos Apache newspaper he read in Vietnam, to provide his perspective on the war. "This is a sad war, too many good people getting killed," he wrote. "The men are paying a high price just to protect freedom and protect the people from communist aggression. People should back up the war instead of protesting against it."[43]

The National Congress of American Indians provided that public backing in January 1967 by asking Secretary of Defense Robert McNamara to send a Native American dance troupe of thirty men and women from fifteen reservations to Vietnam to build morale for U.S. troops, which included thousands of American Indians. Echoing a familiar refrain from the 1950s, NCAI officials told McNamara: "The first Americans are second to none in their loyal patriotism and courage. Whenever danger has threatened, America's Indians have rallied to their country's defense and to protect the freedom all Americans cherish." The Department of Defense declined to sponsor such a trip, explaining that it sent only famous entertainers to Vietnam. Undaunted, the NCAI organized a letter-writing campaign to members of Congress in whose states the Indian entertainers lived; NCAI director Johnny Belindo noted in a letter to a U.S. senator that "many [military] units have taken Indian names or used American Indian slogans to boost their morale. Nothing could be more appropriate than a visit by an American Indian dancing troupe." The NCAI was driven both by patriotism and by anger that the U.S. Army devalued American Indians' culture even as it appropriated its nomenclature in waging the war. NCAI official Henry Hough declared that "of the 135 entertainment units sent to Viet Nam this year, at least one [should be] made up of AMERICAN INDIANS!" Joking to a colleague that the Defense Department should change its mind, Hough remarked, "I don't think they want a Second Front started, at home, by all the Indians and their friends."[44]

As NCAI executive director, Vine Deloria Jr. supported this 1967 cultural mission to Vietnam. But, like most Native Americans, and most Americans in general, he soon soured on the war. In his 1969 book *Custer Died for Your Sins: An Indian Manifesto*, Deloria detailed American Indians' protests against dishonorable American deeds in Indian country and in Vietnam alike that were animating a growing indigenous "Second Front at home." Deloria, who had earned degrees in theology and law, described a trail of broken treaties marking the moral geography of American Indians' domestic cold war. He ridiculed President Lyndon Johnson's contention that "America had to keep her commitments in South Asia or the world would lose faith in the promises of our country" and Richard Nixon's claim that "Russia was bad" because it failed to honor treaties and agreements with the United States. "Indian people laugh themselves sick when they hear these statements," Deloria wrote. "America has yet to keep one Indian treaty or agreement despite the fact that the United States government signed over four hundred such treaties and agreements with Indian tribes. It would take Russia another century to make and break as many treaties as the United States has already violated." A U.S. Marines veteran, Deloria lamented the Seneca's loss of land to the Kinzua Dam, arguing that while the United States justified the "bloody orgy" of Vietnam as "commitment-keeping" it was "busy breaking the oldest Indian treaty," the Pickering Treaty of 1794. The Kinzua Dam symbolized American's perfidy in the early 1960s, but "new incidents involving treaty rights daily remind Indian people that they were betrayed by a government which insists on keeping up the façade of maintaining its commitments in Vietnam." Employing the panoptical metaphor common to Native activists of the post–World War II era, one famously echoed by protesters at the 1968 Democratic Party convention in Chicago, Deloria wrote: "The world is indeed watching the behavior of the United States. Vietnam is merely a symptom of the basic lack of integrity of the government, a side issue in comparison with the great domestic issues which must be faced—and justly faced—before this society destroys itself." The principal question for Deloria was: "Is the word of America good only to support its ventures overseas in Vietnam or does it extend to its own citizens?"[45]

Deloria's book provided an answer to that question and helped to unify a disparate Indian movement through a historical narrative that stressed continuity rather than change. Angrily updating the familiar refrain of Cold War civil rights activists of the 1950s NCAI generation, Deloria both captured the anger of young activists and fueled it, offering a resistance "manifesto" that promoted Indian nationalism and decolonization. He became the most visible spokesperson for American Indians' grievances, publishing a series of books and articles in mainstream forums. In a December 1969 *New York Times Magazine* essay, for example, he connected the Vietnam War with an ongoing "War between the Redskins and the Feds." He documented the ways in which the new secretary of the interior, Walter Hickel, who called the federal government "over-protective" of Indian rights, had galvanized radical Native American groups around the country, fueling the "nationalistic tone" of the National Traditionalist Movement of the Iroquois and animating the "third-world-oriented United Native Americans [who] took up the battle cry." Deloria argued that one of Hickel's proposals employed "logic used by the Army to destroy a Vietnamese village—'We had to destroy the village to save it.'" And so continued Americans' "unilateral war against Indian communities . . . known as 'termination.'"[46]

Vietnam cast into stark relief Indian-white relations of the late 1960s and early 1970s, shaping Native Americans' perception of an ongoing cold war with the federal government, the government's efforts to contain the Indian nationalism which that war furthered, and national and global press coverage of the confrontations that ensued. Two principal narratives running parallel during this period intersected with Vietnam and Cold War pressures: American Indian activists' occupations of Alcatraz Island, BIA headquarters in Washington, D.C., and the Wounded Knee hamlet in South Dakota; and the ongoing "legal war" over fishing rights in the Pacific Northwest. Treaty rights remained at the center of these respective but related struggles to advance American Indian self-determination.

The Occupation of Alcatraz

Alcatraz Island in San Francisco Bay, originally inhabited by the Ohlone Indians before they became extinct during the American conquest of California, served as a federal prison until 1963. The following year Sioux activists from the San Francisco American Indian Center claimed the island under the terms of an 1868 treaty that declared unused federal lands available for Indian possession. Although the group's intent was to highlight the federal government's failure to honor American Indians' land claims

and treaty rights, the protest served as an important act of symbolic reoc-
cupation of former Indian country that inspired a new group of activists
five years later. In early November 1969 the city of San Francisco announced that it would broker the sale of the island from the federal government to the highest bidder. Justifying their actions on the basis of this
earlier Sioux claim, a small group of American Indian students organized
Indians of All Tribes and occupied the island on November 9. A larger
contingent of nearly one hundred American Indians, most of them UCLA
students, began a longer occupation of the island on November 20 for the
purpose of, in the language of hybrid patriotism, "the enrichment of all
Indians and the nation at large." Activists wanted to use the island to
house an academic center for the study of Native American traditional
culture, spirituality, and ecology, to offer job training programs, and to create a museum that would help Americans understand Indian values and
traditions. Lasting eighteen months, the Alcatraz occupation galvanized
young Native Americans across the country. In the words of Patricia Silvas, it represented for Natives of her generation "a chance for us to be Indian, to learn about our people, and to let our children be Indian . . . The
promise of Alcatraz is the first time that *all* Indians have worked for these
things together." Alcatraz became a sacred place to which all Indians could
lay claim, a real and metaphorical place for pan-Indian activity that would
inspire similar acts of protest in the 1970s.[47]

Native activists drew support from Latino and African American communities, while celebrities including Merv Griffin, Anthony Quinn, Ethel
Kennedy, and Jane Fonda visited the island, as did representatives of the
United Auto Workers. Native activists also sought foreign support, situating their actions in an international frame. Journalist William Meyer
(Eastern Cherokee) wrote, "The Indian movement is aware of the international aspect of its struggle," noting that Alcatraz Indians had explored
"the possibility of receiving 'foreign aid' from countries other than the
United States." To generate support for their cause, occupation leaders
started Radio Free Alcatraz, which broadcast its first message on December 22, 1969, on several California and New York stations. Radio Free Alcatraz became a domestic version of Radio Free Europe, which the State
Department operated to persuade people in Soviet bloc countries that the
United States believed in democracy, not dictatorship. Alcatraz intersected in important ways with the Vietnam War, which complicated that

Cold War distinction between democracy and dictatorship. Anthony Garcia (Apache), a Vietnam veteran, helped to organize the first landing on the island in late 1969, joined by a number of other Native veterans who linked their fighting abroad with a new battle at home. Alcatraz organizers claimed that because of local, national, and international support for their cause, "the symbol of the American Indian shined out before the nation and the whole world."[48]

Indeed the world watched the Alcatraz occupation unfold just as U.S. involvement in Vietnam was being viewed through the bloody lens of an army massacre of nearly five hundred Vietnamese civilians at My Lai, a story which journalist Seymour Hersh first reported on November 12, 1969. On November 20, the day the Alcatraz occupation began, *Life*, *Newsweek*, and *Time* all reported on the My Lai story, as did newspapers and television stations; gruesome photographs showed dead elderly women and young children. A ten-month court-martial trial of U.S. Army officers began in March 1970.

This convergence of domestic and international events generated great interest in Alcatraz and American Indians' place in American society more generally. During a trip abroad the mayor of San Francisco fielded numerous questions from Europeans about "Alcatraz and the Indians." The *Times* of London published five articles on the occupation and Indian Red Power between November 1969 and March 1970, including an editorial opining that "only some form of statehood conferring direct representation in Washington would be the real answer" to the problems of the "first Americans." The editorial condemned a "neo-colonial bureau," the BIA, for failing to protect American Indians from fraud and to preserve their resources from "going the way of the buffalo." The editorial writer, and a portion of the British public, likely viewed the Alcatraz occupation in conjunction with the November 19, 1969, BBC broadcast of the documentary *Now That the Buffalo's Gone*, narrated by Marlon Brando, which chronicled white Americans' "callous repression" of American Indians in the nineteenth century and the continuing repression of American Indian fishing activists, and gave a "brutal statistical account" of "what it means to be an American Indian." Domestic and international coverage of the occupation alarmed a Nixon White House staff already trying to defuse the My Lai controversy. General Services Administration official Robert Kunzig had ordered U.S. marshals to remove the occupiers at gunpoint soon after they took control of the island; according to White House staffer Bradley Patterson Jr., the GSA plan was "likely to spill blood and stir up enormous public revulsion." Federal officials began negotiating with Alcatraz occupiers to bring the crisis to a peaceful end, eager to avoid creating a national and international spectacle of U.S. officials carting defenseless Indians off the island in body bags and creating more revulsion toward American violence at home and abroad.[49]

Native Americans' control of Alcatraz ended in June 1971 when federal marshals took fifteen Native activists off the island, without violence. By the end of the eighteen-month occupation reporters and journalists, as well as many Native Americans, had lost interest, in large measure because of the ways in which Alcatraz had shaped Indian-white relations in the months that followed the initial act of occupation. Richard Oakes (Mohawk), a principal organizer of the protest, claimed that he and other activists had occupied Alcatraz "not so much to liberate the island, but to liberate ourselves for the sake of cultural survival." Alcatraz, he believed, had pushed American Indians "in the direction of Indianness" and sparked similar occupations because "Alcatraz is not an island . . . it is an idea." During the eighteen-month period activists staged over fifty "sit-ins" or "occupations" of federal government sites in Chicago, Cleveland, Denver, Alameda (California), and other cities; in solidarity, National Indian Youth Council members staged sit-ins on college campuses in North Dakota, Washington, Arizona, New Mexico, Oklahoma, and Wisconsin. In March 1970 Native activists occupied two U.S. Army centers near Seattle, Fort Lawton and Fort Lewis. Activists wanted to turn Fort Lawton into a cultural center along the lines of Alcatraz; and at Fort Lewis, a jumping-off point for Vietnam-bound soldiers, they were protesting the U.S. Army's treatment of Native Vietnam veterans. Eighty-four Indian activists, along with Jane Fonda, were arrested during the March 8 protest. The United Indians of All Tribes (UIAT), which organized the Alcatraz occupation, staged similar protests on March 15 and April 2. UIAT members claimed, "Alcatraz is the beginning of an idea, and now Fort Lawton has become the continuation of this concept of a United Indians of all Tribes dedicated to all of our people everywhere."[50]

Activists also occupied icons of American liberty. They briefly occupied Ellis Island in New York harbor, and on Thanksgiving Day 1970 members of the American Indian Movement (AIM) boarded a *Mayflower* replica in

Philadelphia harbor. In one other noteworthy protest, on August 29, 1970, Lehman Brightman of the United American Indians, AIM leaders Dennis Banks and Russell Means, and Alcatraz organizer John Truddell led twenty other protesters in occupying Mount Rushmore, situated on formerly Sioux land, where they hung a large banner that read "Sioux Indian Power." AIM had originated in 1968 as an American Indian patrol to act as witnesses to police brutality in Minneapolis, home to thousands of relocated Native Americans. Devoted to confronting paternalistic missionary groups operating on Indian reservations and to protesting employers' discrimination against Native applicants, AIM members viewed their organization, according to Kills Straight (Dakota Sioux), as "first a spiritual movement, a religious rebirth, and then a rebirth of Indian dignity." AIM joined other Native activists in occupying symbolically important places to highlight treaty rights violations. Although AIM members had nothing to do with the planning or leadership of the Alcatraz occupation, several of them traveled to the island in the summer of 1970 and left it with a new sense of purpose. As Kills Straight elaborated, AIM channeled "Indian dignity" into political action by serving as the "shock troops of Indian sovereignty."[51]

Not all American Indians protested in these ways or embraced AIM as a national voice for "Indian sovereignty" during this tumultuous period. Many Sioux opposed the Mount Rushmore protest, and a second one that followed on June 6, 1971, maintaining that the protesters were outsiders who threatened the ongoing campaign for compensation for the U.S. government's theft of the Black Hills in the 1870s. In his 1970 investigation of Taos Pueblo life, *New York Times* reporter Winthrop Griffith "found few hints of Third World awareness and no sweeping denunciations of Western, white, technological, oppressive society—such as those of militant black Americans and an increasing number of Indians of other tribes." But, he noted, the Taos Pueblo were "angrily conscious" of the efforts of U.S. officials to diminish their ancestral lands; Griffith quoted a U.S. Forest Service employee who had said that he would "rather negotiate with the Chinese Communists" than with the Taos in their fight for sovereignty. To claim that sovereignty, moderate American Indian leaders embraced President Johnson's War on Poverty initiatives such as the Office of Economic Opportunity (OEO) programs that increased Native control of education and economic development. And Native American groups continued to promote economic development through Cold War aid programs: a group of leaders representing thirty Native American communities proposed to federal officials in 1967 that the U.S. government "extend to the American Indian people the massive benefits that are now being offered to citizens of the new Nations of Asia, Africa, and Latin America"; another group called for an American Indian "Marshall Plan" at the Republican National Convention in August 1972. These Native leaders persisted in their critiques of federal termination policies, but they did not support occupations or foster liberationist rhetoric.[52]

But as with African American militancy, Indian militancy at Alcatraz and elsewhere made moderate groups such as the NCAI more appealing to federal officials. President Richard Nixon tacked this way when he publicly repudiated federal termination policies. Arguing that Native Americans "should no longer be treated like a colony within a nation," Nixon felt compelled, he said, to resolve "a grave injustice [that] has been worked against them for a century and a half." He found support for abandoning termination from Vice President Spiro Agnew and anti-terminationist officials such as Labor Secretary George Schultz and OEO director Donald Rumsfeld. Significantly, Nixon and his aides crafted a major address on Indian affairs as the Alcatraz occupation wore on, promoting similar acts of sustained protest. In his July 8, 1970, speech to the U.S. Congress Nixon said that the "first Americans" had made "enormous contributions to this country—to its art and culture, to its strength and spirit, to its sense of history and its sense of purpose." It was now time "to break decisively with the past and to create the conditions for a new era in which the Indian future is determined by Indian acts and Indian decisions." He rejected termination, he said, because it abrogated the federal government's "solemn obligations" in treaties that continued to "carry immense moral and legal force." The Nixon administration moved quickly to strengthen Native "self-determination" by introducing over twenty proposals to Congress in 1970, six of which were adopted; Congress extended the life of the Indian Claims Commission, established the Navajo Community College, and passed the Native Alaska Claims Act, which opened the door for Native Americans in Alaska to receive compensation and federal support services. The administration also expanded the BIA's budget, enlarging health, education, and economic development programs. Additionally, the Nixon White House threw its support to the Taos Pueblo (New Mexico) in their long campaign to secure the return of Blue Lake, both a religious site and the source of irrigation water. Nixon's endorsement of the Taos Pueblo's cause helped persuade Congress to pass the land restoration bill in late 1970.[53]

Nixon's undersecretary for health, education, and welfare, Frank Carlucci, later remarked that the president's 1970 speech to Congress demonstrated "a remarkable consistency" with "the Nixon doctrine in foreign affairs." Nixon's 1970 message and his American Indian policies, which drew on the ideas of his presidential predecessor Lyndon Johnson, also represented a domestic form of the policy of détente that he would promote with the Chinese a year later. While these two contexts differ in significant ways, the point is that Nixon's formal rejection of termination was a diplomatic measure designed to thaw deep-rooted cultural tensions between American Indian leaders and U.S. government officials, tensions that amounted to what some Native leaders had called a "cold war." In imagining the opening of diplomatic relations with China, Nixon had written in 1967:

> Dealing with Red China is something like trying to cope with the more explosive ghetto elements in our own country. In each case a potentially destructive force has to be curbed; in each case an outlaw element has to be brought within the law; in each case dialogues have to be opened . . . ; and, not least, in neither case can we afford to let those self-exiled from society stay exiled forever.

Nixon's anti-termination program served as a form of rhetorical and programmatic containment of "explosive" American Indian radicalism shaped by the Alcatraz occupation.[54]

Moderate American Indian leaders hailed his 1970 speech as "the famed Nixon Indian message." But for a new generation of Native activists, Nixon's politicking failed to resolve ongoing battles over treaty rights in Sioux country and in the Pacific Northwest. Furthermore, his dramatic funding increases offered few benefits for urban Indian communities, which produced most of the militant Native activists. His administration spent less than $10 million on urban Indian programs, not sufficient to address the needs of this growing and increasingly vocal constituency; by 1970 nearly half of all Native Americans lived in cities rather than on reservations.

Nixon's proposals also did little to reform the Bureau of Indian Affairs, which continued to resist expanding tribal authority on many reservations.[55]

All Trails Lead to Wounded Knee

President Nixon's support for Native America faltered after activists associated with the American Indian Movement occupied the BIA headquarters in Washington, D.C., on the eve of the 1972 presidential election, the culmination of its Trail of Broken Treaties protest against ongoing treaty violations in the Pacific Northwest and elsewhere. Activists began the protest on the West Coast, picked up caravans of supporters from various Native communities along the way, and rendezvoused in the capital on November 1. Once in Washington the activists, nearly one thousand representing eight Native organizations, became angry when federal officials failed to help them find decent lodging and prevented them from conducting a religious ceremony at the Iwo Jima Memorial in Arlington National Cemetery; World War II, Korean, and Vietnam veterans, who considered Iwo Jima veteran Ira Hayes a symbol of their collective sacrifice to the United States, saw the refusal to honor this request as a betrayal of their service. The group then occupied the BIA building on November 2, renaming it the "Native American Embassy." Claiming this federal space as their own, activists sought diplomatic negotiations along the lines of a sovereign power. AIM leaders issued to federal officials a "20 Point Proposal," which asserted that Native American tribes were "nations unto themselves" and that the U.S. government had failed to honor the international status of its many treaties. The authors of the proposal noted that American Indian nations had been forced to spend nearly $40 million between 1962 and 1972 fighting against treaty violations in court, an expensive and frustrating process that drained Indian communities of precious resources. The proposal included, among other points, recommendations for reforming the BIA; the formation of a federal commission to review treaty commitments and the numerous violations of them; and rapid resolution of such violations to prevent the bankrupting of American Indian plaintiffs forced to wage costly legal battles. The occupation ended after a tense week and with little tangible result apart from media coverage of broken furniture and scattered files in the BIA building. Federal officials provided money to activists to travel to their respective homes and promised that there would be no prosecutions for the occupation or the vandalism of federal property. But they failed to address specific treaty complaints or the organizers' "20 Point Proposal." As Frank Carlucci put it on behalf of the administration, "We avoided a bloody confrontation."[56]

Activists' staging of the Trail of Broken Treaties and the occupation of the BIA building had three broad effects. First, it further estranged younger AIM activists from moderate tribal leaders, who embraced the Nixonian agenda of self-determination; one AIM member put it bluntly in declaring that "anything Nixon says is shit." Second, the events of November 1972 pushed AIM into the national spotlight, strengthening its leaders' resolve to seek bigger public stages on which to air their grievances after the federal government ignored the group's "20 Point Proposal." AIM national director Vernon Bellecourt issued a press statement explaining to the American people that AIM did not endorse the destruction of federal property but wanted Americans to consider the broader context of the BIA occupation and direct their anger instead at the government for "the broken treaties of yesterday, the broken promises of today, and the dim prospects of tomorrow." The statement urged: "Be outraged, that your government is destroying a people in Vietnam, just as they are destroying the Indians. Sand Creek, Wounded Knee, Hanoi, My Lai—this is your government." Addressing President Nixon, AIM warned him not to leave "another 'Trail of Broken Promises.'" The third result of AIM's militancy was that it prompted the FBI to plant informants within the organization, part of the Nixon administration's broader investigation of Native American, African American, Latino, women's liberation, and antiwar activists. The federal government began surveillance of American Indian militant groups after the American Communist Party (ACP) promoted the so-called "American Indian liberation movement" and held a special "National Conference on Indian Liberation" in early November 1969, before the occupation of Alcatraz. Although the FBI did not link AIM to the ACP, it was sufficiently alarmed by AIM's bold offensive within the capital itself—and on the eve of a presidential election—to follow AIM's trail after the protest ended, shifting its attention "from a declining black militancy to a rising American Indian militancy."[57]

That trail led to Native American activists' dramatic occupation of Wounded Knee, South Dakota, which lasted from February 27 to May 8,

1973, the longest armed civil conflict in the United States since the Civil War. The Wounded Knee occupation grew from a violent civil conflict on the Oglala Sioux reservation that pitted tribal president Dickie Wilson and his Guardians of the Oglala Nation militia against the Oglala Sioux Civil Rights Organization (OSCRO), composed of Sioux who lived geographically, culturally, and politically remote from tribal and BIA operations. OSCRO members accused Wilson of election fraud, fiscal corruption, and the use of his Guardians of the Oglala Nation group to stifle dissent, calling it the GOON squad. OSCRO's attempts to impeach Wilson through constitutional measures failed, leading to a series of meetings in late February in which OSCRO members called on AIM to help them mediate Wilson's use of violence to undermine their reform campaign. That specific conflict grew to symbolize Native Americans' larger concerns about treaty violations. On February 27 AIM members joined disaffected Oglala Sioux in forcibly occupying the small village of Wounded Knee, which consisted of several churches, a trading post, and a museum. It also was the site of the 1890 massacre of nearly three hundred Sioux men, women, and children by the U.S. Seventh Cavalry, Custer's old regiment.[58]

Wounded Knee activists transformed this sacred historical site into sovereign space, declaring themselves members of the Independent Oglala Nation and establishing border patrols to demarcate its territory. This act of creating Indian country within Indian country struck some observers as ridiculous, a dramatic performance rather than a desperate measure. A *Time* magazine article complained of "too many theatrical asides aimed at the TV cameras and too many studied parallels to the Viet Nam War, including a 'demilitarized zone' and 'ceasefire observers.'" In one such exposition of this parallel, members of the Wounded Knee Legal Defense/Offense Committee announced that they intended to "launch a massive legal assault against the federal government . . . until South Dakota begins to look more like America and less like war torn South East Asia."[59]

But the occupiers' claim to sovereignty illustrates the depth of the crisis for "traditional" Sioux as well as the internationalist perspectives and experiences of the activists, their perception of the public relations value of framing their protest in international terms, and their belief in the sanctity of international treaties which lay at the heart of the protest. As at Alcatraz, and throughout the Cold War, Native Americans appealed to

international bodies and foreign countries to support their cause. Vine Deloria Jr. argued that the people at Wounded Knee "sought the recognition
by the nations of the world of their rightful status as nations in the community of nations." AIM representatives traveled to the UN on three separate occasions in the most explicit effort to secure that recognition. On
March 2 Vernon Bellecourt, joined by Onondaga (Iroquois Confederacy)
leaders, met with UN Chef de Cabinet (Undersecretary) C. V. Narasimhan.
Bellecourt told Narasimhan of his hope that Wounded Knee would "draw
national and international attention to the popular revolution that was
taking place among the Indians." He asked the UN to recognize the international sovereignty of American Indian people and to send UN observers to Wounded Knee to guard against the federal government's use of
force against the Sioux people. Narasimhan explained to Bellecourt that
the UN Charter prohibited intervening in internal state matters. Bellecourt subsequently addressed the United Nations Correspondents Association, telling its members that Sioux representatives would take their case
to UN delegations to seek their support for Native sovereignty because
Native Americans had never stopped believing that "they were independent people belonging to sovereign independent nations." They were
"willing to lay down their lives" at Wounded Knee in that belief. Iroquois
leaders later demonstrated in UN Plaza in support of the Wounded Knee
occupation and met with an official of the U.S. Mission to the United Nations. Iroquois representatives presented a petition to the United Nations
Human Rights Commission in support of the Sioux; they did so, according
to a U.S. official, "at the request of Oglalas, not as a disloyal act, but as a
matter of representing the case to the international community," describing themselves as "intensely loyal Americans."[60]

Participants in the Wounded Knee occupation embodied this notion of
hybrid patriotism across several generations. In addition to OSCRO members, activists at Wounded Knee included American Indian veterans of
World Wars I and II, Korea, and Vietnam, who were joined by two non-
Indian representatives of Vietnam Veterans Against the War. Facing them
across the demilitarized zone were CIA veterans of Vietnam, Pentagon
representatives, Eighty-second Airborne troops, and law enforcement officers using Vietnam-issue automatic rifles as well as helicopters and over a
dozen U.S. Army armored personnel carriers. U.S. Air Force Phantom jets
flew "reconnaissance" missions to support these ground forces. The stale-

mate turned into a hot war when those forces let loose with machine gun volleys, creating one-sided firefights that reminded Indian and non-Indian observers of Vietnam; one estimate had the government shooting 500,000 rounds during the seventy-one-day conflict, nearly seven thousand per day. It is a miracle that such firepower resulted in only two fatalities, both Native activists, one of them an army veteran. When Webster Poor Bear, a Vietnam veteran, was injured in one of the firefights, his father lamented to reporters, "My son went through Vietnam without getting a scratch, and now he gets shot by the same government that sent him there." Such accounts and the extent to which Americans had turned against the Vietnam War fueled the conflation of Wounded Knee and Vietnam.[61]

For many young Americans of all ethnicities, Wounded Knee replaced Vietnam as a site of protest against what they viewed as America's racist imperialism. Several hundred supporters held a "United People for Wounded Knee" demonstration in San Francisco on March 20, one of a number staged to raise awareness of and money for the occupation. The FBI tracked numerous groups that expressed solidarity with the Wounded Knee activists, including Students for a Democratic Society, the Socialist Workers Party, the Young Socialist Alliance, the Black Panther Party, and the Venceremos Organization, a Maoist group based in California, which sent a group to Wounded Knee to offer medical aid. Wounded Knee also became seen as the site and symbol of a possibly broad Indian uprising, "Indian country" migrating from Vietnam to the American heartland in an atavistic and anachronistic outburst of Indian violence. An instructor for the California Specialized Training Institute, Military Division, who traveled to Wounded Knee to study the "disorder" and glean insights into the federal response, reported to his superiors, "Considering the apparent A.I.M. success we might see this happen in California where there is a large Indian population." For some observers AIM represented more broadly a migration of communists to the heartland. Dickie Wilson, the embattled Nixon-like chairman of the Oglala Sioux tribal government, played the communist card by distributing a leaflet which claimed that Wounded Knee "is all part of a long range plan of the Communist Party." The activists' use of Czech-made AK-47 machine guns, which Native American veterans had brought back from Vietnam as souvenirs, prompted some critics of the occupation to assume that they had been donated by communist governments. A local non-Indian resident complained to a reporter: "There are no Indians out at Wounded Knee. There are nothing but Chicanos, Negroes, Russians and Cherokees. They call themselves the American Indian Movement. It's the American Communist Movement."[62]

Activists' conflation of Wounded Knee with Vietnam highlighted the international nature of this contested ground. William Means (Oglala) later reflected that he and other Native American Vietnam vets "went from being the hunter as an American GI, to being the hunted, as an American Indian Movement Oglala young person trying to stand up for what we believe in." Means considered it an "honor to fight for your own country at Wounded Knee," adding, "When they tell you that you're fighting for America in another indigenous people's country, over in Vietnam, I learned a political education." Native Americans "had become the VC in our own homeland," according to another Vietnam veteran who participated in the occupation, Guy Dull Knife Jr. (Sioux). Veteran Woody Kipp (Blackfeet) embedded this connection in the title of his memoir, *Viet Cong at Wounded Knee*, in which he wrote that he had never appreciated his experience of Vietnam until he participated in the Wounded Knee occupation. As he and other Native American activists followed nighttime flares and dodged bullets, "the entire Vietnamese scenario began to flesh itself out, taking shape slowly, focusing through the haze . . . Vietnam became a wide screen upon which the issues of race and oppression flashed in an increasingly brighter luminescence."[63]

Wounded Knee was the most dramatic in what would become a series of American Indian protests played out on a "wide screen." Lakota Sioux medicine man Wallace Black Elk claimed a larger significance for the protest, saying: "The eyes and the ears of the whole universe are now focused on Wounded Knee. And little Wounded Knee turned into a giant world." Bradley Patterson Jr. of Nixon's White House staff agreed, noting in his assessment of Wounded Knee that "even a distant South Dakota crisis is being watched by the world." But if Wounded Knee collapsed boundaries between historical racial violence in the United States and Cold War racial violence, it was in part because of the emotional resonance of the site and because the occupation intersected with ongoing and new U.S. crises in the world. Although the Paris Peace Accords had ended the Vietnam War several months earlier, the American public was tired of seeing images of the U.S. military and police forces killing people of color. A police assault on Attica Prison in New York State in 1971 had ended with the deaths of twenty-nine prisoners, adding another context for imagining a fresh massacre.[64]

President Nixon agreed with an aide's assessment that the U.S. government did not need "an Indian massacre on our hands." According to Deputy Attorney General Joseph Sneed, who was responsible for day-to-day management of the crisis, officials "were always aware of the dramatic quality of the occupation of Wounded Knee for Indians as well as Americans generally, and it's quite clear that it was necessary to demonstrate to the world as much restraint as we possibly could, while at the same time fulfilling the mission that had been assigned to us." The Nixon White House staff, veterans of two high-stakes events at Alcatraz Island and the AIM occupation of BIA headquarters, maintained this emphasis on restraint; the chief of staff of the Eighty-second Airborne Division argued that his men could, if ordered, overwhelm Wounded Knee with military force. Federal officials wanted no such thing, in part because of the presence of nearly three hundred reporters; the occupation became a long-running drama on television and in newspapers, followed by most Americans, many of whom, according to national polls, supported it. The United Nations received appeals from Americans asking the organization to prevent what they feared was an imminent massacre. A San Francisco–based Indian rights group sent a telegram to Secretary General Kurt Waldheim claiming that American Indians "once again face slaughter at the hands of the United States Government . . . All nations have a responsibility to prevent another massacre. We strongly urge intervention by the United Nations in this international affair." The "use of force would be unconscionable," read a New Jersey man's telegram to Waldheim. A Milwaukee woman pleaded with Waldheim's office to "alleviate the situation so that there is no massacre at dusk tonight as threatened by U.S. Marshalls." But the UN had no authority to intervene.[65]

Adding to pressure on the federal government to resolve the crisis without violence, and to activists' efforts to publicize their grievances, reporters from at least twelve other countries, including Japan and the Soviet Union, covered the conflict, especially during its first month. The Wounded Knee story even found its way onto the front pages of African newspapers. The *Times* of London ran fifteen articles on Wounded Knee between March 2 and May 8, 1973. One article, printed after two Native Americans were shot and killed, opined that the Wounded Knee crisis had helped most Americans understand "that the Indian wars are the most shameful episode in American history." One reader of the *Times*, Dachine Rainer, responded to its coverage by noting that American Indians were reacting against "remarkably aggressive, violent exercises" by the U.S. government, but also against the "mounting suspicion that the pattern of life in the United States is not particularly beneficial to humans, either at home or abroad." The experiences of American Indians thus represented just one element of what she called "the Great American Disenchantment," a broader condemnation of American Cold War leadership centered on the Vietnam debacle and the replication of American racial dynamics at Wounded Knee.[66]

Vine Deloria Jr. contended that the world press and its readers were paying attention to Wounded Knee because of long-standing interest in Indian culture, which had created an expanding network of Indianist clubs in Europe, the Soviet Union, and elsewhere. But on a deeper level, he argued in his 1972 book *Behind the Trail of Broken Treaties*, Europeans in particular

> had become aware, partially because of the collapse of their colonies in other parts of the world, of the deep desire of smaller nations to gain a place in the family of nations . . . They had recognized, where the United States had not, that the world had indeed shrunk and our planet could not afford to place its destiny in the hands of any nation or group of nations . . . Rather, the community of nations had become a community in which even the smallest nation had rights which could not be violated. To see a tiny Indian tribe attempt to cast off the bonds of colonialism and become a free nation fascinated the European journalists who visited the United States and made the journey to Wounded Knee.

Supporters of the Wounded Knee occupation held demonstrations abroad, forcing the State Department to cable its embassies with instructions to deflect criticism of U.S. government treatment of Indians. In addition, the department canceled a goodwill tour of Europe by American Indian dancers for fear of drawing attention to the Wounded Knee crisis. Officials cautioned the Nixon White House: "If Indians are killed, we can surely expect sharp and widespread foreign condemnation of this U.S. Government action. It would come at a particularly unpropitious time, giving Arab governments an excuse to fog up the terrorist issue." Wounded internationally by the violence of the Vietnam War, and on the cusp of a new ideological conflict with Islamic states hostile to American economic and cultural influences, the United States could not allow assertive Arab governments, now banded together in OPEC (Organization of the Petroleum Exporting Countries), to take the moral high ground by labeling the United States a terrorist government.[67]

Press attention became, as one supporter put it, the activists' "best protection against attack." When most reporters left Wounded Knee to cover the unfolding Watergate mess and the compelling return of Vietnam POWs, private citizens maintained vigilant attention. Actor Marlon Brando resurfaced to support the occupation. After he skipped the Academy Awards, Brando explained in a *New York Times* op-ed piece why Sasheen Littlefeather had accepted his Oscar for Best Actor, an event beamed to millions around the world, adding another expression of the Great American Disenchantment:

> What kind of moral schizophrenia is it that allows us to shout at the top of our national voice for all the world to hear that we live up to our commitment when every page of history and when all the thirsty, starving, humiliating days and nights of the last 100 years in the lives of the American Indian contradict that voice? . . . All that we have succeeded in accomplishing with our power is simply annihilating the hopes of the newborn countries in this world, as well as friends and enemies alike, that we're not humane, and that we do not live up to our agreements.

Brando did not attend the award ceremony, he said, because he believed it more important to travel to Wounded Knee "to help forestall . . . a peace which would be dishonorable." He never made it to Wounded Knee, but news of his refusal to attend the ceremony and the speech delivered by Littlefeather in his absence made its way around the world. In another dramatic intervention Bill Zimmerman, a Boston-based antiwar activist who had sent medical supplies to people affected by U.S. bombing in Vietnam, Laos, and Cambodia, helped to arrange an airlift of food supplies requested by Wounded Knee leaders, thus conflating the "children of Viet Nam" and their "awful fate" with the Indians at Wounded Knee. On April 17, 1973, Zimmerman and two other pilots dropped two thousand pounds of food to support the occupation. On May 4 a group of Iroquois leaders appealed to the United Nations Division of Human Rights, on behalf of the "besieged" Oglala Sioux, to "intervene to render some humanitarian measures to our people in Wounded Knee, particularly in allowing the passage of food and medical help, water and fuel."[68]

The UN had no authority to intervene, however, and in any event the occupation ended several days later, on May 8, after a series of negotiations between organizers and federal officials. But what Wounded Knee came to represent—in addition to the site of a communist insurgency, a re-creation of Vietnam, or a new sovereign Indian space—was a new Cold War narrative: the outgunned and desperate indigenous peoples in an occupied zone asserting a moral right against the material might of the United States, a reversal of the compelling narrative of the United States airlifting food to a Berlin besieged by communist forces. While different in many respects, these various narratives emerging from Wounded Knee demonstrate the fluidity of boundaries within and between the international Cold War and the domestic cold war that American Indians both participated in and shaped. The narratives also reflected Native Americans' belief that treaty violations and the attendant national dishonor lay at the heart of these domestic and international tensions. According to Vine Deloria Jr., the occupation influenced other Native American leaders "to examine their own treaties with the United States to determine how they could respond to the general cry for reform of the treaty relationship."[69]

AIM's demise as an influential national Indian rights organization represents the other significant outcome of the Wounded Knee occupation. With most Americans' attention turned to the Watergate scandal, the U.S. government set out to destroy rather than contain AIM. The Department of Justice issued 185 indictments, most of them targeting AIM members, leading one activist to note, "We've been so busy in court fighting these indictments we've had neither the time nor the money to do much of anything." In a high-profile case three AIM leaders—Dennis Banks, Russell Means, and Pedro Bissonette—were tried and acquitted in a St.

Paul, Minnesota, courtroom, during which proceedings the federal trial judge catalogued FBI witness tampering and other illegal activities. "It's hard for me to believe that the FBI, which I have revered for so long, has stooped so low," he lamented. Despite the government's failure to convict AIM leaders, the series of expensive trials ended AIM's legitimacy and effectiveness. For AIM the legal crackdown represented a cruel irony, as "the plight of Indian people has been drowned out by media focus on Watergate and the government's dubious activities," said one supporter. Yet it is in this context that another important legal drama unfolded. While AIM members found themselves dragged into the courts to face federal prosecution, another battle over Native American rights was shaping up across the country in the Pacific Northwest, one in which federal attorneys defended rather than indicted Indian activists.[70]

"This Paper Secures Your Fish"

In her essay "1973 Handbook on Indian Warfare," published in the inaugural issue of *Lummi Squol Quol*, the journal of the Lummi tribe of Washington State, Monica Charles connected the recently ended Wounded Knee occupation with the pending federal court case *U.S. v. Washington*, which would resolve Native Americans' decades-long struggle to secure treaty-based fishing rights in the Pacific Northwest. "The battle between the white and us hasn't changed much in the 500 years that they've been here," she wrote, noting that at Wounded Knee "we were defending ourselves with .22's against their Vietnam tested equipment." But, as Charles put it, a "new style of fighting evolved" during the twentieth century: "Whole Tribes have been wiped out with the pounding of a gavel." The two kinds of "Indian warfare" became linked as Native people across the country shifted their attention from the Vietnam-like battlefield of South Dakota to the legal battlefield of Washington State in a case that had broad implications for Native treaty rights.[71]

Makah activist Sandra Johnson had called the struggles of Native peoples against the repression of state governments "a legal war that we must enter . . . The State trespasses on Indian land and violates U.S. treaties. They do not honor U.S. Supreme Court decisions or other federal regulations." Native Americans' intentional waging of a "legal war" had led to a series of court cases adjudicating fishing rights in the Pacific Northwest. In

6.2 Violence erupted September 9, 1970, as several hundred local police and Washington State troopers attacked fishing rights activists of the Puyallup River Reservation. Using tear gas and shotguns, the police arrested sixty activists, but the violence pushed the U.S. Justice Department to file suit against the state of Washington a week later. Courtesy of Dolores Varela/Maiselle Bridges Collection.

1968 Vietnam veteran Richard Sohappy and his nephew David triggered a test case after their arrests on the Columbia River in 1968. The Department of Justice offered its support in the case, *Sohappy v. Smith*, which evolved into *United States v. Oregon*. In his July 1969 decision in *United States v. Oregon*, federal judge Robert C. Belloni validated the tribes' treaty claims as transcending state laws. Although it proved an important precedent in asserting a judicial commitment to the moral sanctity of treaty documents, the decision laid open the question of how to put that commitment into practice in material terms, as Belloni did not quantify a "fair share" of fish for Indian and non-Indian fishers. A year later federal officials supported fishing rights activists in Washington State by filing *U.S. v. Washington*, a class-action suit on behalf of Native communities that traced their right to fish to the 1855 Stevens Treaties. At that time federal negotiator Isaac Stevens had told Native diplomats, "This paper [the treaty] secures your fish." Native activists had fought throughout the twentieth century to secure their treaty rights in order to secure their fish.[72]

Much was at stake in the *U.S. v. Washington* decision, as it became another "wide screen" on which appeared the intersection of domestic and international politics. Frank Carlucci emphasized this intersection during congressional hearings on Wounded Knee, contending that "the Indian population, though small in number, is quite large in symbolic importance to the Nation. Resolution of the problems of the American Indian is important in itself, bearing as it does upon their well-being as citizens and upon the solemn treaty obligations of the Republic." Americans' failure to provide justice for American Indians, Carlucci claimed, "comes to bear in our dealings with the developing Nations of the Third World. And as a foreign service officer, I have had many occasions to appreciate that it is a matter of no small importance to them in their dealings with us." *U.S. v. Washington* represented U.S. officials' support of minority activists at a time when Wounded Knee had exposed again the contradictions of the "American dilemma" to the world. Indeed, federal officials' simultaneous prosecution of AIM leaders and support of fishing rights activists served as a potent symbol of that dilemma. In a June 1973 essay titled "The Indian Dilemma," likely a reference to Gunnar Myrdal's phrase, an ACLU official highlighted Americans' "obligation to examine the 'Indian question,' and to participate to the extent we can in the bringing about of 'peace with honor' in the new Indian wars."[73]

The *U.S. v. Washington* trial, which began in August 1973, featured poignant testimony from Native American elders involved in those new Indian wars, including some who brought to life the meaning of broken treaties by describing the ways in which state officials' repression of fishing practices restricted the ability of Native people to maintain cultural traditions and perform religious ceremonies. After spending several months listening to such testimony and then several months more studying the treaties, the migratory patterns of the fish, and the history of state regulation, U.S. District Court judge George Boldt released a 203-page opinion that captured the historical and moral dimensions of the fishing wars. Delaying his ruling until February 12, 1974, to accord with Lincoln's birthday, Boldt decided in *U.S. v. Washington* (known thereafter as the Boldt Decision) to uphold the rights of Native Americans in Washington State and Oregon to fish off-reservation sites using whatever methods they chose, regardless of state laws, and to share equally in the commercial catch of "harvestable fish." Boldt's quantification thus required that state governments and their citizens and tribal governments and their citizens each receive 50 percent of the harvest, on the grounds that the treaty involved two separate sovereign parties. Boldt developed several principal themes in his decision. The first, which he derived from ethnographic data presented by academics and by Native people during the trial, was that Native Americans' sustenance and society depended on fishing, as it "provided and still provides an important part of their livelihood, subsistence and cultural identity." And second, despite twentieth-century industrialization and demographics that did not favor Native people, the "mere passage of time could not erode the rights guaranteed by solemn treaties that both the United States and Indian tribes pledged on their honor to uphold." Boldt thus viewed the treaty in two traditional contexts: one an Indian world in which fishing was cultural; and the other a classic white American conception of property rights in which a treaty is a contract and thus must be honored.[74]

Boldt reached his decision within two contemporary contexts as well, one specific to Native Americans' place in America and the other specific to America's place in the world. He noted that in recent legislation the U.S. Congress had made clear that its new "intent and philosophy . . . is to increase rather than diminish or limit the exercise of tribal self-government." Accordingly, the Boldt Decision provided to Native Americans material grounds for expanded economic and cultural self-determination. The larger context was moral, involving nothing less than America's honor in the world. Boldt had no doubt followed the Wounded Knee saga, as he had followed the "fishing wars" throughout the 1960s. The public nature of American Indian activism during a decade of fish-ins and the Wounded Knee occupation had reminded citizens and public officials alike that Native Americans were willing to die to protect or to resurrect their treaty rights. The troubling prosecutions of Wounded Knee activists were taking place as he was preparing his decision. Contemporary observers, including American Indian plaintiffs, made much of the fact that Boldt was a "conservative judge," a law and order judge, who had previously prosecuted union and Mafia leaders and had sentenced Vietnam protesters to six months in jail for contempt of court. In his decision Boldt decried the "provocative, sometimes illegal, conduct of extremists on both sides" of the fishing rights conflict. As the war in Vietnam came to its ig-nominious close abroad and Watergate soiled the honor of American po-litical institutions at home, his "pounding of a gavel" represented "peace with honor" in the "new Indian wars."[75]

Judge Boldt won no friends among non-Indian politicians and fishermen, some of whom burned him in effigy. Writing in a 1976 opinion piece, "In-dian Treaties Cannot Be Ignored," Ralph W. Johnson, professor of law at the University of Washington, criticized opponents of the Boldt Decision, pointing out:

> In the 1950s and 1960s, these same people, with great moral righ-teousness, decried the illegal fish-ins and demonstrations of Indians, and admonished them, as good law-abiding Americans, to resolve their arguments in the courts. They did. Now where are the voices of moral righteousness? Now the Indians' rights have been upheld in the courts (by a legally-conservative and judicially-careful federal judge) . . . The decision is the law of the land, and, popular or not, is here to stay.

During a 1978 banquet held in Judge Boldt's honor, fellow federal judge William Dwyer said that Boldt had demonstrated in his decision "the courage to uphold the law even when it was unpopular to do so." He noted that the story of Boldt's life "tells us a good deal about our country." Born in Montana in 1903 to immigrant parents from Denmark, Boldt began practicing law in 1926 and served his country as a lieutenant colonel in Burma during World War II before President Eisenhower appointed him a U.S. District Court judge in 1953. The Boldt Decision transcended the U.S. Supreme Court's *Lone Wolf v. Hitchcock* decision, handed down the year Boldt was born. Courts and boosters had used *Lone Wolf v. Hitchcock* to justify building the Kinzua Dam and other projects of the Cold War era. In deciding *Lone Wolf* in 1903, the Supreme Court had supported Con-gress's right to abrogate treaties "when circumstances arise which will not only justify the government in disregarding the stipulations of the treaty, but may demand, in the interest of the country and the Indians them-selves, that it should do so." In holding the government to its word, em-bedded in "the stipulations of the treaty," the Boldt Decision worked in the interests of both the country at large and American Indians, creating a new anti-imperial narrative that portrayed America upholding the treaty during a time of such complex conflicts as the Vietnam War and the Watergate constitutional crisis.[76]

Boldt's life and his reading of the law tell us much about the United States' history of ignoring Native Americans' rights. Boldt knew that history well, noting after the trial that "in the early days of our country, the judges who first spoke on Indian rights have always had such a profound sense of guilt in taking away the Indians' livelihood that they made plans for them to have other places to go and fish. It's always been that way, all down through the years." In his decision Boldt presented a narrative that linked the past with the present. Arguing that during the mid-1800s "Congress chose treaties rather than conquest as the means to acquire vast Indian lands," he implied that ignoring those treaties would sustain the history of America's acquisition of Indian property as one of imperialism. In an age of heightened anticolonialism, such a story would indeed say "a good deal about our country." Boldt's decision represented a major victory for Native Americans in their twentieth-century legal war to restore the integrity of treaties with which they could maintain their homelands and their culture in the face of relentless imperial pressure. It codified the sentiment of Justice Hugo Black in his dissent to the 1960 *Tuscarora* decision: "Great nations, like great men, should keep their word."[77]

Throughout the twentieth century, Native Americans from Maine to California and from Florida to Washington State had assiduously and passionately promoted a patriotic belief in the integrity of the U.S. Constitution in particular and in the rule of law more broadly, creating the moral context in which Judge Boldt could "uphold the law" that defined anew Indian-white relations in everyday life, in the discourse of American minority rights, and in the realm of international relations. Believing in an empire of liberty for all, Native American citizens of both the United States and their own Indian communities maintained pressure on the federal government to make the United States a nation that truly honored its obligations at home and abroad, sustaining an internationalism born in the early years of the American Century and matured in the crucible of the 1950s. The product of an indigenous patriotism shaped by national sacrifice, it crafted a version of Americanism designed to make friends among other peoples of the world.

Epilogue: Indian Country in the Twenty-first Century

The frontier has gone restless now.

. . .

We'll ride 'em [Iraqis] down like Cherokee.

—Second lieutenant in Iraq, 2004

In his January 1983 statement on federal Indian policy President Ronald Reagan promised that his administration would negotiate with American Indians on a "government to government basis," thus reinforcing the federal government's commitment to American Indians' treaty rights, hard won during the dark days of the termination era. Reagan pledged to uphold these rights because, as he put it, "the Constitution, treaties, laws, and court decisions have consistently recognized a unique political relationship between Indian tribes and the United States." His statement drew on the long history of international relations embedded in the body of treaties signed between the United States and Indian nations, what the Crow politician Robert Yellowtail has called the "sacred covenants" of American history. And it drew as well on contemporary legislative acts and court decisions such as the 1974 Boldt Decision that affirmed the sanctity of those treaties and reserved to Native governments the powers common to state governments. A year after the Boldt Decision, the U.S. Congress codified self-determination rather than termination as the operating principle of federal Indian policy by passing the Indian Self-Determination and Education Assistance Act, which gave Native governments new power to administer federal funds and develop social and economic programs. Subsequent legislation and court decisions strengthened the legal, social, and financial boundaries of Indian country.

In *United States v. Wheeler* (1978), the U.S. Supreme Court opined that American Indian sovereignty "is of a unique and limited character" but that "until Congress acts, the tribes retain their existing sovereign powers." In the mid-1970s and into the 1980s Congress acted to expand those sovereign powers. For example, ten days before Reagan issued his Indian policy statement, Congress passed the Indian Tribal Governmental Tax Status Act of 1982, which gave Indian nations tax advantages similar to those enjoyed by state governments.[1]

The expansion of these sovereign powers came at a cost for Native Americans. Despite executive, legislative, and judicial support for American Indians' treaty rights, some American citizens and government officials attacked treaty-based privileges in a violent "backlash" movement in Washington, Wisconsin, Montana, Minnesota, Michigan, and other states. These critics opposed tribal sovereignty because it strengthened American Indians' control of natural resources and secured their fishing and hunting rights on and off reservations. In Washington State, non-Indians protested the Boldt Decision by harassing Indian fishers and burning effigies of Judge Boldt. In Wisconsin, where Indians also asserted their treaty rights to hunt and fish, a new discourse of violence was manifested on bumper stickers and picket signs that read "Save a Deer, Shoot an Indian," "Save a Walleye, Spear a Pregnant Squaw," and "Too Bad Custer Ran Out of Bullets." Native Americans also faced financial backlash from Reagan administration officials who cut federal funding for Indian programs from $3.5 billion to $2.5 billion, part of the administration's "new federalism" initiative to deconstruct the New Deal edifice. And the backlash emerged in the form of a new round of rhetoric that attacked Native governments as socialistic. The most disturbing attack came from Secretary of the Interior James Watt, who complained during a January 1983 television broadcast of "Conservative Counterpoint" that "if you want an example of the failures of socialism, don't go to Russia. Come to America and go to the Indian reservations." Watt's remarks followed on the heels of Reagan's policy statement supporting American Indian sovereignty, prompting Indian leaders to call Reagan's true intentions terminationist. Chippewa leader David Lester warned Native Americans to beware when federal officials begin to "use the term 'liberty' or 'freedom,' [because] that's the kind of rhetoric that has been used traditionally to promote the termination of the reservation system." Such termination fears were not unfounded, given that in 1976 Watt had initiated the Mountain States Legal Foundation, a Colorado-based public interest law firm hostile to American Indians' control of land and valuable natural resources worth billions of dollars, an object of white politicians' desires during the 1950s and 1960s. Native American self-determination, then, remained a tenuous prospect, attacked by public officials and private citizens as un-American and dangerous as the Reagan administration renewed a rhetorical and military cold war with perceived enemies in the Soviet Union, Latin America, and the Middle East.[2]

Americans continued to conflate "the Indian" and foreign enemies, a practice fueled by domestic struggles over American Indians' sovereignty and the resources it protected. This rhetorical violence, so common during the Vietnam War, reappeared during U.S. military operations in El Salvador and then more publicly during the 1991 Gulf War, when Brigadier General Richard Neal's description of Iraqi-held territory as "Indian Country" prompted Native Americans across the United States to protest. "It only shows the deep root of prejudice," said army veteran Sam Brushel, one of a number of Native veterans who were offended by Neal's remark. The National Congress of American Indians declared that Neal had insulted the nearly fifteen thousand Native American troops serving in the Persian Gulf. This conflation resurfaced in various forums during post-9/11 military operations in Afghanistan and in the U.S.-Iraq War. One senior U.S. official likened Osama Bin Laden to an Indian chief by calling his followers "Indians." Outside the safe Green Zone in Baghdad lay the "Red Zone," "Indian country," and "the wild, wild West." Sergeant Dan South described his compound in Iraq as "like a little fort in Indian country." Resuscitating a familiar ghost, Sergeant James Riley told reporters during his evacuation from a Red Zone battle: "We were like Custer. We were surrounded." The "Indian Wars" became a lens through which both proponents and opponents of a new round of U.S. expansion by way of imperialism viewed the Iraq War. Republican commentator Pat Buchanan complained that Democrats critical of President George W. Bush had "ridden out a little too far into Indian country and are heading for the Little Big Horn where their daddies disappeared long ago." In a telling remark, foreign policy analyst Stephen Biddle, a former professor at the U.S. Army War College, stated his opposition to a reduction in ground forces in Iraq by warning that it would leave army convoys to "roll through Indian country with no cavalry." More broadly, U.S. officials and analysts linked the frontier of the nineteenth-century American West to the protean frontier of the twenty-first-century war on terror. Documenting the multiple hot spots in "Indian country" where terrorists operated, Robert D. Kaplan argued that the "War on Terror was really about taming the frontier," an action Kaplan supported in the name of advancing the "boundaries of free society and good government into zones of sheer chaos." Rejecting this twenty-first-century version of the "white man's burden," a former U.S. State Department official criticized the Bush administration in an essay whose title said it all: "Our Indian Wars Are Not Over Yet: Ten Ways to Interpret the War on Terror as a Frontier Conflict."[3]

This conflation of Indians and terrorists angered American Indian activists, who felt deeply the violence of 9/11 and the loss of American Indian soldiers who died in the military conflicts that followed. A February 8, 2006, editorial in *Indian Country Today*, the national American Indian newspaper, complained: "Bad analogies from American Indian history are becoming the fad among pundits on the Middle East. We wish they would cut it out. The comparisons don't explain much about the deep and deadly conflicts of that region, but they do show a dangerous level of ignorance about the tribal nations of this continent." Indeed such comparisons elided the intense patriotism of American Indians, patriotism they had demonstrated throughout the twentieth century and after 9/11. As a September 12, 2001, editorial in *Native American Times* put it: "American Indians love this country like no other . . . Today we are all New Yorkers." Other American Indian activists, angered by this renewed use of the trope of the enemy Indian and disturbed by the U.S. military's violence against Iraqi civilians, erased the boundaries of time and space to stress the continuities of American imperialism from the nineteenth-century war on Indians to the twenty-first-century war on terrorism. Scott Starr wrote in his August 2007 editorial "Indian Country" that the comparisons of Iraq to Indian America offended him and yet helped him understand that "after 515 years of conquest—in the minds of Imperial America—the First Nations of the Americas are still regarded as enemies, hostiles, obstacles to progress . . . as terrorists." Floyd Westerman, a former AIM member who helped occupy Wounded Knee in 1973, called the invasion of Iraq "just another land grab," likening it to "Oklahoma and the Mid-West in America. Back then it was about land and gold and now it was about oil."[4]

As during the Cold War, the foreign press publicized Native Americans' dilemmas at home as U.S. foreign policy trumpeted America's democratic aspirations abroad. The Al-Jazeera news service sent a reporter to Nevada to interview Shoshone activist Carrie Dann, who described her long-running campaign to preserve her ancestral homeland by resisting the expansion of the federal government and corporations intent on devouring her people's resources. Echoing the arguments of Cold War era Native activists, Dann told the reporter: "I can't believe that this is happening supposedly in America where everybody talks about democracy, and how good democracy is. As far as the indigenous people go, we have not seen that democracy." The article noted the Shoshone's protests against development projects sought by Halliburton and Bechtel, identified as "a major contractor of the US defence department in Iraq."[5]

This linkage between expansion abroad and expansion at home found expression in other ways that mirrored past cold wars between Native Americans and the United States, from the Indian Wars of the late nineteenth century to the termination era of the 1950s and 1960s. American Indians' own expansion helped to create a new stage of that cold war. Representing a belated Point Four or Marshall Plan program, American Indian casinos generated hundreds of millions of dollars in profit for health, education, and welfare programs; in 2007, 224 of the 562 federally recognized tribes offered casino gambling, though 23 of those tribes accounted for nearly half the revenues generated. The wealthiest gaming nations also moved "beyond the reservation" in establishing additional casinos and in purchasing businesses such as the Hard Rock Casino and hotels. Many of these gaming tribes have bought land bordering their reservations in an effort to restore part of their ancestral homelands. The conflict between Indians and non-Indians over the boundaries of Indian country at home increasingly employs the language of war. The mayor of Shakopee, Minnesota, monitoring the land purchases of the neighboring Mdewakanton Sioux Community, warned that the Sioux were "out to garner as much as they can get, wherever they can get it, and they have the war chest to do that." The Sioux's land manager, contrasting two models of land acquisition, offered a history lesson on nineteenth-century American imperialism while seizing the moral high ground in claiming that his people were buying land that Americans had taken "by the point of a gun—and we are buying it back with American dollars." Reflecting this war rhetoric, the

Minneapolis Star Tribune reporter documenting the controversy noted that the Sioux had "stockpiled" two thousand acres bought with their casino revenues, suggesting a larger conflict to come. A Shakopee town official demonstrated this concern in referring to a Mdewakanton Sioux leader's decade-old comment that he hoped to recover land lost to the states of Wisconsin, Iowa, South Dakota, and Minnesota, implying that the Sioux had a dangerous agenda of territorial expansion.[6]

Visions of such expansion led a Los Angeles humor magazine, *LaLa Times*, to print a story titled "California Indian Tribes Split Casino Profits to Buy Nevada and Arizona," which told of the fictitious multimillionaire Shoshone elder Linda Eaglefeather and her plan to acquire the two states with casino monies. Though amusing, the piece reflected anti-sovereignty opponents' concerns about American Indians' assertiveness in the American West, especially in Nevada and Arizona, where the growth of Las Vegas, Phoenix, and Tucson were generating enormous demand for land, water, and energy. This conflict discourse emerged most clearly in the summer of 2007 in a land use controversy that pitted the small community of Quechan (Yuma) Indians against development advocates in Arizona and California who supported the construction of a $4 billion oil refinery complex. American Clean Fuels had a contract to build the complex on land forty miles distant from the Quechan reservation, but Quechan politicians worked to prevent the complex from desecrating what the Quechan considered sacred ground. The vice president of Arizona Clean Fuels complained that the Quechan were practicing "psychological imperialism" and compared Quechan leader Mike Jackson to Hugo Chávez, the Fidel Castro–like leader of Venezuela, who regularly criticized the United States as an imperial bully. Suggesting a broader conflict, the executive director of the Yuma County (Arizona) Chamber of Commerce maintained that the case raised the "question of how far does [the Quechan] sphere of influence go. Does it go clear to Phoenix? To Las Vegas? The whole West?" Although critics of Quechan sovereignty did not explicitly resurrect the trope of the Indian communist, they trotted out the Cold War version of the Monroe Doctrine shibboleth and argued for a domestic domino theory suggesting that American Indians intended to hinder the march of progress in the West and thus jeopardize the American way of life. For the Quechan's part, Mike Jackson claimed that he was not opposed to the refinery complex itself but opposed developing it without a proper archaeological investigation of its impact on what his people considered sacred ancestral land. Jackson stated that his people have "learned how to play the political game in America that's been played against us in the past . . . [Developers] come, smile, and shake my hand, but they don't like it. Too bad. That is how the process is now." Asserting a sovereign stance not unlike that of foreign nations abroad, Jackson described a diplomatic "process" which guaranteed that his people's voice would be heard in defining the use of space, whether on the reservation or off, thus extending their sphere of influence to land owned before the "Indians wars" of the nineteenth century violently reshaped the social and political geography of the American West.[7]

Writing in 1886, as those wars came to an end, Commissioner of Indian Affairs J. D. C. Atkins called Indians' resistance to American imperial expansion "patriotic and noble," while posing the fundamental question that continues to define modern Indian-white relations: "Is it not asking too much of the American people to permit a political paradox to exist within their midst . . . simply to gratify this sentimentality about a separate nationality?" In the 1880s, as during the 1830s, America was not ready to permit Indian nations to exist within the nation. Americans' willingness to do so in the twenty-first century remains uncertain, even as the boundaries separating Indian America and America have become socially, economically, and politically fluid. But as new international crises engender old patterns of conformity and as new domestic economic, environmental, and demographic pressures re-create old historical tensions over space, especially in the American West, a restless frontier of material and moral challenges may lead to a new era of "Indian wars," a rebirth of termination. If so, Native Americans will once again move to protect their cultural identity and their political sovereignty by promoting their particular version of patriotism, one born of historical memories of imperial violence and of national sacrifice made in the name of a greater America.[8]

Archival Sources

American Indian Periodicals (AIP), Firestone Library, Princeton University.

Archives of the Association on American Indian Affairs (AAIA), Seeley G. Mudd Library, Princeton University.

Carol Sullivan Wounded Knee Papers, Center for Southwest Research, University Libraries, University of New Mexico.

D'Arcy McNickle Papers (DMP), Newberry Library, Chicago.

Department of Interior or Records of the Secretary of the Interior (RG48), National Archives.

Dillon S. Myer Papers (DSMP), Harry S. Truman Library, Independence, Mo.

Dorothy Parker Papers, Newberry Library, Chicago.

Dwight D. Eisenhower Papers (DDEP), Dwight D. Eisenhower Library, Abilene, Kans.

Felix S. Cohen Papers, Beinecke Library, Yale University.

Foreign Newspapers Archive, Library of Congress.

General Records of the Department of State (RG59), National Archives.

Harry S. Truman Papers (HSTP), Harry S. Truman Library, Independence, Mo.

Helen Peterson Papers (HPP), National Museum of the American Indian, Smithsonian Institution.

John Collier Papers (JCP), microfilm, Beinecke Library, Yale University.

Office of the Architect of the Capitol, Washington, D.C.

Papers of the National Indian Youth Council (P-NIYC), Center for Southwest Research, University Libraries, University of New Mexico.

Papers of William A. and Sophia A. Brophy (PWSB), Harry S. Truman Library, Independence, Mo.

Philleo Nash Files (PNF), Harry S. Truman Library, Independence, Mo.

Records of the Bureau of Indian Affairs (RG75), National Archives.

Records of the National Congress of American Indians (R-NCAI), National Museum of the American Indian, Smithsonian Institution.

Records of the President's Committee on Civil Rights (RG220), National
    Archives.
Roger A. Finzel American Indian Movement Papers (RFAIM-P), 1965–1995,
    Center for Southwest Research, University Libraries, University of New
    Mexico.
Shirley Hill Witt Papers, Center for Southwest Research, University Libraries,
    University of New Mexico.
Sol Tax Papers (STP), Smithsonian Institution.
United Nations Archives (UNA).
Western Americana: Frontier History of the TransMississippi West, 1550–1900,
    microfilm, Beinecke Library, Yale University.
William Zimmerman Jr. Papers (WZP), Center for Southwest Research, Univer-
    sity Libraries, University of New Mexico.

Notes

Prologue

1. The controversy is covered in *Fort Apache Scout* 11 (October, November, December 1972), American Indian Periodicals (hereafter AIP), Firestone Library, Princeton University.

2. Vine Deloria Jr., *Behind the Trail of Broken Treaties: An Indian Declaration of Independence* (New York: Dell, 1974), xiv; Arthur N. Gilbert, "The American Indian and United States Diplomatic History," *History Teacher* 8 (February 1975), 231, 240.

3. Lippman quoted in David Ryan, "By Way of Introduction: The United States, Decolonization, and the World System," in *The United States and Decolonization: Power and Freedom*, ed. David Ryan and Victor Pungong (London: Macmillan, 2000), 18–19; Paul A. Carter, *Revolt against Destiny: An Intellectual History of the United States* (New York: Columbia University Press, 1989), 208. See also Charles Maier, *Among Empires: American Ascendancy and Its Predecessors* (Cambridge, Mass.: Harvard University Press, 2007).

4. Emerich de Vattel, *The Law of Nations or the Principles of Natural Law Applied to the Conduct and to the Affairs of Nations and of Sovereigns* (Dublin: L. White, 1792), 165; John Locke, *Two Treatises of Government* (New York: Cambridge University Press, 1963), 113.

5. Knox quoted in Frederick E. Hoxie, "The Curious Story of Reformers and American Indians," in *Indians in American History: An Introduction*, 2nd ed., ed. Frederick E. Hoxie and Peter Iverson (Wheeling, Ill.: Harlan Davidson, 1998), 210; Thomas Jefferson to James Madison, April 27, 1809, in *The Writings of Thomas Jefferson*, vol. 12, ed. Andrew A. Lipscomb and Albert Ellery Bergh (Washington, D.C.: Thomas Jefferson Memorial Association of the United States, 1903), 277. On expansion with honor, see Reginald Horsman, *Expansion and*

American Indian Policy (Norman: University of Oklahoma Press, 1992), in particular 54–59.

6. Mary E. Young, "The Cherokee Nation: Mirror of the Republic," American Quarterly 33 (Winter 1981): 502–524.

7. Andrew Jackson, "Second Annual Message to Congress, 1830," in A Compilation of the Messages and Papers of the Presidents, ed. James D. Richardson (New York, 1897), 1085, http://www.mtholyoke.edu/acad/intrel/andrew.htm; Worcester v. Georgia quoted in Theda Perdue and Michael D. Green, eds., The Cherokee Removal: A Brief History with Documents (Boston: Bedford Books, 1995), 73.

8. Homi Bhabha, "DissemiNation: Time, Narrative, and the Margins of the Modern Nation," in Nation and Narration, ed. Homi Bhabha (London: Routledge, 1990), 310. Maureen Konkle explores early histories of resistance in Writing Indian Nations: Native Intellectuals and the Politics of Historiography, 1827–1863 (Chapel Hill: University of North Carolina Press, 2004); see in particular chap. 1, "The Cherokee Resistance."

9. Christine Kinealy, The Great Irish Famine: Impact, Ideology, and Rebellion (New York: Palgrave, 2006), 80 (my thanks to Sarah Yeh for this reference); Bonnie S. Anderson, "The Lid Comes Off: International Radical Feminism and the Revolutions of 1848," National Women's Studies Association Journal 10 (Summer 1998): 1–12; Edward Said, Representations of the Intellectual: The 1993 Reith Lectures (New York: Pantheon Books, 1993), 44. See also Nancy A. Hewitt, "Origin Stories: Remapping First Wave Feminism," Proceedings of the Third Annual Gilder Lehrman Center International Conference at Yale University, October 25–28, 2001, http://www.yale.edu/glc/conference/hewitt.pdf.

10. Modris Eksteins, Walking since Daybreak: A Story of Eastern Europe, World War II, and the Heart of Our Century (Boston: Houghton Mifflin, 2000), xi; Gunnar Myrdal, An American Dilemma: The Negro Problem and Modern Democracy (New York: Harper & Brothers, 1944); Gary Gerstle, American Crucible: Race and Nation in the Twentieth Century (Princeton: Princeton University Press, 2001).

11. On the intersection of the Cold War and civil rights, see Thomas Borstelmann, The Cold War and the Color Line: American Race Relations in the Global Arena (Cambridge, Mass.: Harvard University Press, 2001); Nikhil Pal Singh, Black Is a Country: Race and the Unfinished Struggle for Democracy (Cambridge, Mass.: Harvard University Press, 2004); Penny M. Von Eschen, Satchmo Blows Up the World: Jazz Ambassadors Play the Cold War (Cambridge, Mass.: Harvard University Press, 2004); Mary L. Dudziak, Cold War Civil Rights: Race and the Image of American Democracy (Princeton: Princeton University Press, 2000); Brenda Gayle Plummer, ed., Window on Freedom: Race, Civil Rights, and Foreign Affairs, 1945–1988 (Chapel Hill: University of North Carolina Press, 2003); Penny M. Von Eschen, Race against Empire: Black Americans and Anticolonialism, 1937–1957 (Ithaca, N.Y.:

Cornell University Press, 1997); and Daniel M. Cobb, "Talking the Language of the Larger World: Politics in Cold War (Native) America," in *Beyond Red Power: American Indian Politics and Activism since 1900*, ed. Daniel M. Cobb and Loretta Fowler (Santa Fe: School for Advanced Research, 2007), 161–177.

12. Susan Schekel, *The Insistence of the Indian: Race and Nationalism in Nineteenth-Century American Culture* (Princeton: Princeton University Press, 1998), 19; Cheever quoted in Mary Hershberger, "Mobilizing Women, Anticipating Abolition: The Struggle against Indian Removal in the 1830s," *Journal of American History* 86 (June 1999), http://www.historycooperative.org/journals /jah/86.1/hershberger.html. For a recent conception of the international Cold War, see Paul Steege, *Black Market, Cold War: Everyday Life in Berlin, 1946–1949* (Cambridge: Cambridge University Press, 2007).

13. On American patriotism, see in particular John Bodnar, *Remaking America: Public Memory, Commemoration, and Patriotism in the Twentieth Century* (Princeton: Princeton University Press, 1992); John Bodnar, ed., *Bonds of Affection: Americans Define Their Patriotism* (Princeton: Princeton University Press, 1996); and Cecilia E. O'Leary, *To Die For: The Paradox of American Patriotism* (Princeton: Princeton University Press, 1999); on hybridity, see Homi K. Bhabha, *The Location of Culture* (New York: Routledge, 1994), 4. Kevin Bruyneel explores the hybrid space of "domestic dependent nations" in *The Third Space of Sovereignty: The Postcolonial Politics of U.S.-Indigenous Relations* (Minneapolis: University of Minnesota Press, 2007); "Honor Spurs Muscogee (Creek) Leonard Gouge 'To His Country's Defense,'" *Cherokee News Path*, September 28, 2001, http://www.the peoplespaths.net/Cherokee/News2001/Sep2001/CNO010928LeonardGouge.htm.

14. Untitled article, *Birney Arrow* (June 1969); and D. Hollowbreast, "July 4, 1963," *Birney Arrow* (July 1963), AIP; Ronnie Lupe, "Chairman's Corner: Why Indians Are Willing to Fight and Die for a Country That Has Been So Cruel to Us," *Fort Apache Scout* 31 (November 31, 1992): 2.

1. Westward the Course of Empire

1. Angie Debo, *Geronimo: The Man, His Time, His Place* (Norman: University of Oklahoma Press, 1976), 419. On the commodification of Geronimo, see Philip Deloria, *Indians in Unexpected Places* (Lawrence: University Press of Kansas, 2004), 136–182. For coverage of the Roman Triumph, see Mary Beard, *The Roman Triumph* (Cambridge, Mass.: Harvard University Press, 2007).

2. Debo, *Geronimo*, 421. In 1905 Geronimo dedicated his autobiography, *Geronimo: His Own Story*, to Roosevelt because he thought the president was "fair-minded and will cause my people to receive justice in the near future." Geronimo died in 1909 without seeing that justice.

3. Roosevelt quoted in Thomas G. Dyer, *Theodore Roosevelt and the Idea of Race* (Baton Rouge: Louisiana State University Press, 1980), 83; and Gail Bederman, *Manliness and Civilization: A Cultural History of Gender and Race in the United States, 1880–1917* (Chicago: University of Chicago Press, 1996), 182; Knox quoted in Frederick Hoxie, "The Curious Story of Reformers and American Indians," in *Indians in American History: An Introduction*, 2nd ed., ed. Frederick Hoxie and Peter Iverson (Wheeling, Ill.: Harlan Davidson, 1998), 210; Ruth Miller Elson, *American Schoolbooks of the Nineteenth Century* (Lincoln: University of Nebraska Press, 1969), 77; Roosevelt quoted in Howard K. Beale, *Theodore Roosevelt and the Rise of America to World Power* (Baltimore: Johns Hopkins University Press, 1989), 68. For the most part historians have maintained this view. For example, in *The United States and Imperialism* (New York: Blackwell Publishers, 2000), Frank Ninkovich begins his analysis with the Philippines conquest, offering no coverage of Native Americans' experience with American imperial expansion or evaluation of the ways in which the Philippines campaign mirrored those in the American West.

4. Treaty of Prairie du Chien, August 19, 1825 (on the 1825 use of "reservation"); Annual Report of the Commissioner of Indian Affairs, November 27, 1850; and Annual Report of the Commissioner of Indian Affairs, November 27, 1851, in *Documents of United States Indian Policy*, 3rd ed., ed. Francis Paul Prucha (Lincoln: University of Nebraska Press, 2000), 42–43, 81–82, and 86. In 1848 Commissioner William Medill argued for the need "to colonize *our* Indian tribes . . . within reasonable and fixed limits" (emphasis added); Annual Report of the Commissioner of Indian Affairs, November 30, 1848, ibid., 76–77. See also Stuart Banner, *How the Indians Lost Their Land: Law and Power on the Frontier* (Cambridge, Mass.: Harvard University Press, 2005), 228–256.

5. Alfred L. Riggs, "What Shall We Do with the Indians?" *The Nation* 67 (October 31, 1867): 356.

6. Craig Miner, *The Corporation and the Indian: Tribal Sovereignty and Industrial Civilization in Indian Territory, 1865–1907* (Columbia: University of Missouri Press, 1976), 48, 87.

7. Ibid., 26, 56; Alan Trachtenberg, *The Incorporation of America: Culture and Society in the Gilded Age* (New York: Hill and Wang, 1982), 30. Bruno Latour examines the "Great Divide" in *We Have Never Been Modern* (Cambridge, Mass: Harvard University Press, 1993), 12.

8. C. J. Hillyer, *Atlantic and Pacific Railroad and the Indian Territory* (Washington, D.C.: McGill and Witherow, 1871), 26, 52, 37; "Western Americana: Frontier History of the TransMississippi West, 1550–1900," Reel 16, Beinecke Library, Yale University. For a crisp summary of Congress's reasons for abandoning treaty

making, which were both procedural and philosophical, see Francis Paul Prucha, *The Great Father: The United States Government and the American Indians* (Lincoln: University of Nebraska Press, 1986), 164–166.

9. Congressmen quoted in Miner, *The Corporation and the Indian*, 84, 108; Emerich de Vattel, *The Law of Nations or the Principles of Natural Law Applied to the Conduct and to the Affairs of Nations and of Sovereigns* (Dublin: L. White, 1792), 165.

10. Philip M. Katz, *From Appomattox to Montmartre: Americans and the Paris Commune* (Cambridge, Mass.: Harvard University Press, 1998), 2, 136, 131; Samuel Smiles, *Thrift*, in *The Human Record: Sources of Global History*, vol. 2, *Since 1500*, 5th ed., ed. Alfred J. Andrea and James H. Overfield (Boston: Houghton Mifflin, 2005), 274–275.

11. Katz, *From Appomattox to Montmartre*, 132; for coverage of boosters' use of the terms "savage" and "communist," see 131–137. Brooklyn, for example, became a figurative and literal urban reservation in need of domesticating. As Richard Slotkin writes of nineteenth-century reformers' attitudes, "The analogy of slum and reservation must therefore be seen as reversible: the lesson of urban concentration teaches us how to deal with Indians; and dealing with Indians may teach us how to deal with uprisings in the urban slums." See Richard Slotkin, *The Fatal Environment: The Myth of the Frontier in the Age of Industrialization, 1800–1890* (New York: Atheneum, 1985), 451.

12. Ronald T. Takaki, *Iron Cages: Race and Culture in Nineteenth-Century America* (New York: Alfred A. Knopf, 1979), 184, 186–188; Protestant minister Lyman Abbott suggested putting recalcitrant Indians "under close surveillance." *Proceedings of the Third Annual Meeting of the Lake Mohonk Conference* (1885), in *Americanizing the American Indians: Writings by the "Friends of the Indian," 1880–1900*, ed. Francis Paul Prucha (Cambridge, Mass.: Harvard University Press, 1973), 36; Michel Foucault, *Discipline and Punish: The Birth of the Prison* (New York: Vintage Books, 1976), 209, 176.

13. Slotkin, *The Fatal Environment*, 463, 481, 484. The conflation of American Irish and American Indians appeared as early as September 1862, when opponents of Irish women labor activists painted them as "savages," likely in reference to the horrific violence between Dakota Sioux and Minnesota settlers which had begun that August. This conflation emerged more fully during the 1863 draft riots in New York City. One account of the riots reports: "A great roaring suddenly burst upon our ears—a howling as of thousands of wild Indians let loose at once . . . The Irish have risen to resist the draft." Ellen Leonard, "Three Days of Terror," *Harper's New Monthly Magazine* 34 (January 1867): 225. Influenced by the anti-Irish rhetoric surrounding the events in New York, the following year the *Banner*

of Ulster, a Presbyterian newspaper in Belfast, described Catholic "rioters" there as destroyers of property and as "a savage horde of American Indians." *Banner of Ulster,* August 16, 1864. I am grateful to Mark Doyle for this reference.

14. Robert Wooster, *The Military and United States Indian Policy, 1865–1903* (Lincoln: University of Nebraska Press, 1988), 58, 59.

15. Francis Paul Prucha, *American Indian Policy in Crisis: Christian Reformers and the Indian,* 1865–1900 (Norman: University of Oklahoma Press, 1976), 3.

16. Commissioner quoted in Prucha, *Americanizing the American Indians,* 3; *Tribune* quoted in John M. Coward, *Native American Identity in the Press, 1820–1890* (Urbana: University of Illinois Press, 1999), 213; Henry L. Dawes, *Fifteenth Annual Report of the Board of Indian Commissioners* (1883), in Prucha, *Americanizing the American Indians,* 28.

17. Carl Schurz, "Present Aspects of the Indian Problem," *North American Review* 133 (July 1881): 6, http://cdl.library.cornell.edu/moa/browse.author/s.35 .html; Charles C. Painter, "Our Indian Policy as Related to the Civilization of the Indian," *Proceedings of the Fourth Annual Meeting of the Lake Mohonk Conference* (1885); *Proceedings of the Eighteenth Annual Meeting of the Lake Mohonk Conference of Friends of the Indian* (1900); and Merrill Gates, "Land and Law as Agents in Educating Indians," *Seventeenth Annual Report of the Board of Indian Commissioners* (1885), in Prucha, *Americanizing the American Indian,* 70, 332, and 50.

18. Dawes, *Fifteenth Annual Report of the Board of Indian Commissioners,* 30, 29; Oberly quoted in David Wallace Adams, *Education for Extinction: American Indians and the Boarding School Experience, 1875–1928* (Lawrence: University Press of Kansas, 1995), 23; *Proceedings of the Fourteenth Annual Meeting of the Lake Mohonk Conference of Friends of the Indian* (1896), and *Proceedings of the Eighteenth Annual Meeting of the Lake Mohonk Conference of Friends of the Indian* (1900), in Prucha, *Americanizing the American Indians.* 334; Michel de Montaigne, "Of Cannibals," in *The Human Record: Sources of Global History,* vol. 2, *Since 1500,* 3rd ed., ed. Alfred J. Andrea and James H. Overfield (Boston: Houghton Mifflin, 2001), 39. See also Matthew Frye Jacobson, *Barbarian Virtues: The United States Encounters Foreign Peoples at Home and Abroad, 1876–1917* (New York: Hill and Wang, 2000), 36–38, 49–54.

19. The history of Ivory Soap is covered in Davis Dyer, Frederick Dalzell, and Rowena Olegario, *Rising Tide: Lessons from 165 Years of Brand Building at Procter and Gamble* (Boston: Harvard Business School Press, 2004), 24–41. The soap was originally branded as "Procter and Gamble's White Soap." An advertisement for Bell's Buffalo Soap embedded in a late-nineteenth-century children's storybook showed how a "little red skinned Indian" would become cleansed by Buffalo Soap. See Juliann Sivulka, *Stronger Than Dirt: A Cultural History of Advertising Personal*

Hygiene in America, 1875 to 1940 (Amherst, N.Y.: Humanity Books, 2001), 100. For images and analysis of the "soap monkey" and of British imperial advertising, see Anne McClintock, *Imperial Leather: Race, Gender and Sexuality in the Colonial Contest* (London: Routledge, 1995), especially 207–231. Timothy Burke examines the discourse of cleanliness and civilization in *Lifebuoy Men, Lux Women: Commodification, Consumption, and Cleanliness in Modern Zimbabwe* (Durham: Duke University Press, 1996).

20. George E. Ellis, *The Red Man and the White Man in North America* (Boston: Little, Brown and Company, 1882), 585; Francis Paul Prucha, *Indian Policy in the United States: Historical Essays* (Lincoln: University of Nebraska Press, 1982), 28. For a good assessment of the allotment policy, see Leonard A. Carlson, *Indians, Bureaucrats, and Land: The Dawes Act and the Decline of Indian Farming* (Westport, Conn.: Greenwood Press, 1981); and David Rich Lewis, *Neither Wolf nor Dog: American Indians, Environment, and Agrarian Change* (New York: Oxford University Press, 1997).

21. U.S. Congress, House Committee on Indian Affairs Minority Report, *House Report No. 1576;* and *Congressional Record,* vol. 11, pt. 1, in Prucha, *Americanizing the American Indians,* 129 and 132, 133, 137.

22. Benjamin Heber Johnson, "Red Populism? T. A. Bland, Agrarian Radicalism, and the Debate over the Dawes Act," in *The Countryside in the Age of the Modern State: Political Histories of Rural America,* ed. Catherine McNicol Stock and Robert D. Johnston (Ithaca: Cornell University Press, 2001), 24, 31, 33. Also see Jo Lea Wetherilt Behrens, "In Defense of 'Poor Lo': National Indian Defense Association and *Council Fire*'s Advocacy for Sioux Land Rights," *South Dakota History* 24 (Fall–Winter 1994): 153–173.

23. Knights of Labor quoted in Trachtenberg, *The Incorporation of America,* 99; Albert Parsons, ed., "The Indians," *The Alarm,* November 8, 1884, in *Haymarket Scrapbook,* ed. Dave Roediger and Franklin Rosemont (Chicago: Charles H. Kerr Publishing Company, 1986), 102. In addition to Friedrich Engels, *The Origin of the Family, Private Property, and the State: In Light of the Researches of Lewis H. Morgan* (Hottingen-Zurich, 1884), see Karl Marx, *The Ethnological Notebooks of Karl Marx: Studies of Morgan, Phear, Maine, Lubbock* (Assen: Van Gorcum, 1972).

24. *Hamlin Garland's Observations on the American Indian, 1895–1905,* ed. Lonnie E. Underhill and Daniel F. Littlefield Jr. (Tucson: University of Arizona Press, 1976), 27, 29, 46.

25. Franklin Rosemont, "Anarchists and the Wild West," in Roediger and Rosemont, *Haymarket Scrapbook,* 101; Gerald F. W. Ronning, "'I Belong in This World': Native Americanisms and the Western Industrial Workers of the World, 1905–1917" (Ph.D. diss., University of Colorado, 2002), 296, 240. Some Wobbly

spokesmen were Native American, including Frank Little, who was lynched in 1917. Little was a literal and a metaphorical hybrid, the Wobbly as noble industrial savage.

26. *House Report No. 1576*, in Prucha, *Americanizing the American Indians*, 125–126; W. B. Vickers, *History of the Arkansas Valley, Colorado* (Chicago: O. L. Baskin & Co., 1881), 35; see 122–178 for his coverage of the "Ute War" of 1879. For an excellent history of the region, see Ned Blackhawk, *Violence over the Land: Indians and Empires in the Early American West* (Cambridge, Mass.: Harvard University Press, 2006).

27. Loring Benson Priest, *Uncle Sam's Stepchildren: The Reformation of United States Indian Policy, 1865–1887* (New Brunswick, N.J.: Rutgers University Press, 1942), 248. Numerous public officials and private reformers employed the trope of the "communist Indian" to justify federal policies. For example, the secretary of the interior contended in his 1881 annual report that "the tribal relation is a hindrance to individualization. It means communism, so far, at least, as land is concerned." See "How to Civilize Indians," *New York Times*, November 16, 1881, 2. As late as 1900 the prominent reformer Merrill Gates defended allotment as a solution to "savage communism." *Proceedings of the Eighteenth Annual Meeting of the Lake Mohonk Conference of Friends of the Indian*, 333.

28. Here I draw on Richard Fried's notion of the functionality of anticommunist rhetoric. See his *Nightmare in Red: The McCarthy Era in Perspective* (New York: Oxford University Press, 1991); "An Act making Appropriations for the current and contingent Expenses of the Indian Department," *U.S. Statutes at Large*, 16:566, in Prucha, *Documents of United States Indian Policy*, 135. Merrill Gates argued that Indian nations were outside of "international law" because he did not feel inspired to recognize treaties as legitimate. *Proceedings of the Eighteenth Annual Meeting of the Lake Mohonk Conference of Friends of the Indian*, 338.

29. Philip C. Garrett, "Indian Citizenship," in *Proceedings of the Fourth Annual Meeting of the Lake Mohonk Conference*, 63–65 (emphasis added); *Proceedings of the Third Annual Meeting of the Lake Mohonk Conference*, 39; *Proceedings of the Fourteenth Annual Meeting of the Lake Mohonk Conference of Friends of the Indian*; and *Proceedings of the Eighteenth Annual Meeting of the Lake Mohonk Conference of Friends of the Indian*. Merrill Gates reiterated this idea in 1900: "To do away with the pretence that each little Indian tribe had the right to be regarded as an organized 'nation,' as a 'state' . . . to do away with this anomaly was a gain. The theory that each Indian tribe . . . was [not] to be regarded as a separate imperium in imperio was a stride in the right direction." *Proceedings of the Eighteenth Annual Meeting of the Lake Mohonk Conference of Friends of the Indian*, 338.

30. Justice minister quoted in Augie Fleras and Jean Leonard Elliott, *The Na-*

tions Within: Aboriginal State Relations in Canada, the United States, and New Zealand (Toronto: Oxford University Press, 1992), 179; judge quoted in Grant Morris, "'The final legal frontier': The Treaty of Waitangi and the Creation of Legal Boundaries between Maori and Pakeha in New Zealand Society," in *Colonial Frontiers: Indigenous-European Encounters in Settler Societies*, ed. Lynette Russell (Manchester: Manchester University Press, 2001), 119.

31. *Lone Wolf v. Hitchcock*, 187 U.S. 553 (1903), http://caselaw.lp.findlaw.com /scripts/getcase.pl?court=US&vol=187&invol=553. For coverage of the case, see Blue Clark, *Lone Wolf v. Hitchcock: Treaty Rights and Indian Law at the End of the Nineteenth Century* (Lincoln: University of Nebraska Press, 1999).

32. *An Act to Amend Section Six of an Act Approved February Eighth, Eighteen Hundred and Eighty-Seven* (Burke Act), *Statutes at Large*, 34, 182–183, Native American Documents Project, http://www.csusm.edu/nadp/a1906.htm; Philip J. Deloria, *Indians in Unexpected Places* (Lawrence: University Press of Kansas, 2006), 151; Sells quoted in Prucha, *The Great Father*, 298.

33. Alexandra Harmon, "American Indians and Land Monopolies in the Gilded Age," *Journal of American History* 90 (June 2003): 109; Janet McDonnell, *The Dispossession of the American Indian* (Bloomington: Indiana University Press, 1991), 120. See also Banner, *How the Indians Lost Their Land*, 257–290.

34. Harmon, "American Indians and Land Monopolies," 123, 112.

35. Max Weber, "A Letter from Indian Territory," *Free Inquiry in Creative Sociology* 16 (November 1988): 133, 135, 136. According to Lawrence Scaff, Weber saw in precapitalist Indian country similarities with eastern German communal land practices; personal correspondence, February 13, 2006. For coverage of Weber's trip through America, see Marianne Weber, *Max Weber: A Biography*, trans. and ed. Harry Zohn (New York: John Wiley & Sons, 1975), 279–304; Wolfgang J. Mommsen, "Max Weber in America," *American Scholar* 69 (Summer 2000): 103–109; Lawrence A. Scaff, "Remnants of Romanticism: Max Weber in Oklahoma and Indian Territory," in *The Protestant Ethic Turns 100: Essays on the Centenary of the Weber Thesis*, ed. William Swatos and Lutz Kaelber (Boulder: Paradigm, 2005), 77–110. For a portrait of the Owen family, see *A Cherokee Woman's America: Memoirs of Narcissa Owen, 1831–1907*, ed. Karen L. Kilcup (Gainesville: University Press of Florida, 2005). Weber may very well have seen Buffalo Bill's traveling show, "Buffalo Bill's Wild West and Congress of Rough Riders of the World," which first played Germany in 1890. See Robert W. Rydell and Rob Kroes, *Buffalo Bill in Bologna: The Americanization of the World, 1869–1922* (Chicago: University of Chicago Press, 2005), 110–116. A number of Native Americans developed an internationalist perspective through their travels to England and Europe with Buffalo Bill's troupe in the late 1800s and early 1900s. The experiences of these

American Indian performers, especially Lakota Sioux, are chronicled in numerous books. In addition to *Buffalo Bill in Bologna,* see James Welch's fictional account, *The Heartsong of Charging Elk: A Novel* (New York: Anchor Books, 2001); Louis S. Warren, *William Cody and the Wild West Show* (New York: Alfred A. Knopf, 2005); *Buffalo Bill's Wild West Warriors: A Photographic History by Gertrude Ksebier,* ed. Michelle Delaney (New York: HarperCollins, 2007); and Christian F. Feest, ed., *Indians and Europe: An Interdisciplinary Collection of Essays* (Lincoln: University of Nebraska Press, 1999).

36. Stewart quoted in Walter L. Williams, "American Imperialism and the Indians," in Hoxie and Iverson, *Indians in American History,* 244–245; soldiers quoted in Stuart Creighton Miller, *Benevolent Assimilation: The American Conquest of the Philippines, 1899–1903* (New Haven: Yale University Press, 1982), 94, 179, 180, 237–238; Richard Drinnon, *Facing West: The Metaphysics of Indian-Hating and Empire-Building* (New York: New American Library, 1980), 288. See also Paul A. Kramer, *The Blood of Government: Race, Empire, the United States, and the Philippines* (Chapel Hill: University of North Carolina Press, 2006). For comparisons between American Indians and Korean "barbarians," see Gordon H. Chang, "Whose 'Barbarism'? Whose 'Treachery'? Race and Civilization in the Unknown United States–Korea War of 1871," *Journal of American History* 89 (March 2003): 1331–65.

37. Lawton quoted in Miller, *Benevolent Assimilation,* 97. Lawton was killed in battle wearing a bright yellow raincoat; see Bonnie Miller, "The Spectacle of War: A Study of Spanish-American War Visual and Popular Culture" (Ph.D. diss., Johns Hopkins University, 2005), 289–290; "New Light on the Traits, Character and Customs of the Warlike Filipinos," *New York Herald,* April 9, 1899, in Miller, "The Spectacle of War," 271.

38. Williams, "American Imperialism and the Indians," 238, 239.

39. *Lone Wolf v. Hitchcock,* 187 U.S. 553; Theodore Roosevelt, *The Strenuous Life; Essays and Addresses* (New York: Century, 1900), sec. 15, http://www.bartleby.com/58/.

2. The Defense of the Reservation

1. Richard Henry Pratt, *Battlefield and Classroom: Four Decades with the American Indian, 1867–1904* (New Haven: Yale University Press, 1964), 214, 284, 283. On life at the boarding schools, see David Wallace Adams, *Education for Extinction: American Indians and the Boarding School Experience, 1875–1928* (Lawrence: University Press of Kansas, 1995); K. Tsianina Lomawaima, *They Called It Prairie Light: The Story of Chilocco Indian School* (Lincoln: University of Nebraska Press, 1994); Brenda J. Child, *Boarding School Seasons: American Indian Families, 1900–*

1940 (Lincoln: University of Nebraska Press, 1998); and Robert A. Trennert, *The Phoenix Indian School: Forced Assimilation in Arizona, 1891–1935* (Norman: University of Oklahoma Press, 1988).

2. Charles Alexander Eastman, M.D. (Ohiyesa), "The North American Indian," July 28, 1911, in *Papers on Inter-racial Problems: Communicated to the First Universal Races Congress,* ed. G. Spiller (New York: Negro Universities Press, 1911), 374; Montezuma quoted in Lucy Maddox, *Citizen Indians: Native American Intellectuals, Race, and Reform* (Ithaca, N.Y.: Cornell University Press, 2005), 112; Arthur C. Parker, "Problems of Race Assimilation in America: With Special Reference to the American Indian," *American Indian Magazine* (October–December 1916): 294, 297, 298. Eastman served as a federal physician for the Pine Ridge Agency in South Dakota from 1890 to 1893, during which time he attended to the dying Sioux of the December 1890 Wounded Knee massacre. On Montezuma's life and times, see Peter Iverson, *Carlos Montezuma and the Changing World of American Indians* (Albuquerque: University of New Mexico Press, 1982). For coverage of Parker's life, see Joy Porter, *To Be Indian: The Life of Iroquois-Seneca Arthur Caswell Parker* (Norman: University of Oklahoma Press, 2001). On the SAI, see Hazel W. Hertzberg, *The Search for an American Indian Identity: Modern Pan-Indian Movements* (Syracuse: Syracuse University Press, 1971), 31–58. Tom Holm explores the progressivism of Native Americans in *The Great Confusion in Indian Affairs: Native Americans and Whites in the Progressive Era* (Austin: University of Texas Press, 2005). Steven Crum documents the less well known efforts of the Brotherhood of American Indians, which also formed in 1911, in "Almost Invisible: The Brotherhood of North American Indians (1911) and the League of North American Indians (1935)," *Wicazo Sa Review* 21 (2006): 43–59.

3. McKenzie quoted in Maddox, *Citizen Indians,* 116; Charles A. Eastman, *From the Deep Woods to Civilization: Chapters in the Autobiography of an Indian* (Boston: Little Brown, 1929), 189, 139. Eastman wrote that he could not "conceive of the extremes of luxury" in "civilized" America, noting that Sioux chiefs had "divided their last kettle of food with a neighbor" and shared their possessions with grieving families (147).

4. Montezuma quoted in Maddox, *Citizen Indians,* 114; Parker, "Problems of Race Assimilation in America," 299; Eastman, "The North American Indian," 376, 195. Eastman examines his 1911 experience in *From the Deep Woods to Civilization,* 189–194. His correspondence included "inspiring letters received . . . from foreign countries," as his books were translated in France, Austria, Bohemia, and Denmark. For a thoughtful examination of this generation of Native intellectuals and activists, see Frederick E. Hoxie, "Exploring a Cultural Borderland: Native American Journeys of Discovery in the Early Twentieth Century, *Journal of American History* 79 (1992): 969–995.

5. "Opening Address by Dr. Charles A. Eastman," *American Indian Magazine* 7 (Fall 1919): 146, 148; Hertzberg, *The Search for an American Indian Identity*, 308.

6. On the tension between civic nationalism and racial nationalism, see Gary Gerstle, *The American Crucible: Race and Nation in the Twentieth Century* (Princeton: Princeton University Press, 2001).

7. Thomas J. Morgan, "Instructions to Indian Agents in Regard to Inculcation of Patriotism in Indian Schools," December 1889, in *Documents of United States Indian Policy*, 3rd ed., ed. Francis Paul Prucha (Lincoln: University of Nebraska Press, 2000), 180.

8. Michael L. Tate, "From Scout to Doughboy: The National Debate over Integrating American Indians into the Military, 1891–1918," *Western Historical Quarterly* 17 (October 1986): 424, 425. Thomas A. Britten evaluates Native Americans' experiences against those of other minorities fighting in the war in *American Indians in World War I: At Home and at War* (Albuquerque: University of New Mexico Press, 1997), 116–131.

9. Britten, *American Indians in World War I*, 39 (Dixon), 43 (Sells); Pratt quoted in Tate, "From Scout to Doughboy," 427. Also see "The American Indian's Part in the World War: Shall He Fight in Segregated Race Units or Side by Side with Other American Soldiers?" *American Indian Magazine* 5 (July–September 1917): 146–50; and Joseph K. Dixon, *The Vanishing Race: The Last Great Indian Council* (Amsterdam: Fredonia Books, 1913).

10. "Extracts from the Second Report of the Provost Marshal General to the Secretary of War on the Operation of the Selective Service System to December 20, 1918," National Defense Program: Correspondence on Selective Service, Box 1, Records of the Bureau of Indian Affairs, Record Group (hereafter RG) 75, National Archives (hereafter NA); Russell Lawrence Barsh, "American Indians in the Great War," *Ethnohistory* 38 (Summer 1991): 277, 278; Barsh estimates the rate of Indian deaths at 5 percent, much higher than the 1 percent estimated for non-Indians (278). Commissioner Sells found Indian patriotism "especially noticeable among the younger generation, largely the product of our Indian schools." Britten, *American Indians in World War I*, 67. William C. Meadows covers the exploits of Choctaw and Cherokee "code talkers" during World War I in *Comanche Code Talkers of World War II* (Austin: University of Texas Press, 2002), 7–34.

11. Sawell quoted in Kirstin Erica Lesak, "Soldiers to Citizens: World War I and the Acceleration of the American Indian Assimilation Process" (M.A. Thesis, University of Maryland, Baltimore County, 2002), 59; Chauncey Yellow Robe, "Indian Patriotism," *American Indian Magazine* 6 (1919): 129, 128.

12. "Declaration of Indian Policy in the Administration of Indian Affairs," April 17, 1917, in Department of the Interior, *Report of the Commissioner of Indian Affairs to the Secretary of the Interior*, FY 1917 (Washington, D.C.: Government

Printing Office [hereafter GPO], 1917), 3. John Finger found that federal officials, because of pressure to fill quota requirements and their unfamiliarity with Indians' status, misrepresented the obligations of service to Cherokee in North Carolina, persuading some that they had no protections against induction. See John Finger, *Cherokee Americans: The Eastern Band of the Cherokee in the Twentieth Century* (Lincoln: University of Nebraska Press, 1991), 35–43.

13. On the Beaulieu brothers' newspaper, see Frederick Hale, "Going on the Great White Father's Warpath: Reactions to World War One on the White Earth Reservation," *Native American Studies* 11 (1997): 43–48 (Clement Beaulieu's comment 48). Also see Melissa Meyer, *The White Earth Tragedy: Ethnicity and Dispossession at a Minnesota Anishinaable Reservation* (Lincoln: University of Nebraska Press, 1994), 88–89. Erik M. Zissu covers Seneca resistance in "Conscription, Sovereignty, and Land: American Indian Resistance during World War I," *Pacific Historical Review* 64 (November 1995): 543–549. Richard N. Ellis examines the Goshute resistance to the draft in "'Indians at Ibapah in Revolt': Goshutes, the Draft, and the Indian Bureau, 1917–1919," *Nevada Historical Society Quarterly* 19 (1976): 163–170.

14. Perryman quoted in Peter Iverson, *We Are Still Here* (Wheeling, Ill.: Harlan Davidson, 1998), 52; Zissu, "Conscription, Sovereignty, and Land," 563; and see 549–555 for resistance to conscription in Oklahoma.

15. CPI quoted in Barsh, "American Indians in the Great War," 287; censor quoted in Robert Rydell and Rob Kroes, *Buffalo Bill in Bologna: The Americanization of the World, 1869–1922* (Chicago: University of Chicago Press, 2005), 139.

16. *New York Evening Herald* quoted in Barsh, "American Indians in the Great War," 289, 288; Arthur C. Parker, "The American Indian in the World Crisis," *American Indian Magazine* 6 (Spring 1918): 15; "Indians with the Allies," *American Indian Magazine* 5 (Spring 1917).

17. Edward Said, *Representations of the Intellectual: The 1993 Reith Lectures* (New York: Pantheon Books, 1993), xiii; Gertrude Bonnin, "Editorial Comment," *American Indian Magazine* 6 (Autumn 1918): 114.

18. Charles A. Eastman, "The Indian's Plea for Freedom," *American Indian Magazine* 6 (Winter 1919): 163; Gertrude Bonnin, "Editorial Comment," *American Indian Magazine* 6 (Winter 1919): 161, 162. Eastman contended that Native Americans had "no right of self-determination. The fourteen points seemingly do not apply to us." Arthur C. Parker made a similar comment in his January 1918 address, "Making Democracy Safe for the Indians," *American Indian Magazine* 6 (Spring 1918): 28, arguing, "If we are consistent in our aim to bring democracy to all the peoples of the earth let us deal with the Indians in a democratic way." David L. Johnson and Raymond Wilson explore Bonnin's views on self-determination in "Gertrude Simmons Bonnin, 1876–1938: 'Americanize the First American,'"

American Indian Quarterly 12 (Winter 1988): 27–40. Frederick Hoxie includes copies of key SAI speeches in *Talking Back to Civilization: Indian Voices from the Progressive Era*, ed. Frederick E. Hoxie (Boston: Houghton Mifflin, 2001). Thomas Britten covers the citizenship debates in *American Indians in World War I*, 176–181.

19. "An Address: In Defense of the Rights of the Crow Indians, and Indians Generally, before the Senate Subcommittee on Indian Affairs, by Robert Yellowtail, September 9, 1919," *American Indian Magazine* 6 (Fall 1919): 134, 133, 136. Erez Manela explores the impact of Wilsonianism on foreign anticolonial movements in *The Wilsonian Moment: Self-Determination and the International Origins of Anticolonial Nationalism* (Oxford: Oxford University Press, 2007).

20. Laura M. C. Kellogg, *Our Democracy and the American Indian: A Comprehensive Presentation of the Indian Situation as It Is Today* (Kansas City: Burton Publishing Company, 1920), 17, 19, 22–25. Kellogg promoted the League of Iroquois Confederacy as a model for international cooperation.

21. "Opening Address by Dr. Charles A. Eastman," *American Indian Magazine* 7 (Fall 1919): 149; "Thomas L. Sloan, Omaha Indian," *American Indian Magazine* 7 (Fall 1919): 162; Mabel Power, "Self-Determination, the War Cry of the Iroquois," *American Indian Magazine* 7 (Summer 1919): 82, 85, 86; Gertrude Bonnin, "Editorial Comment: The Black Hills Council," *American Indian Magazine* 7 (Spring 1919): 3. See also "Editorial Comment: Settle All Tribal Claims," *American Indian Magazine* 4 (Spring 1916): 3.

22. "Opening Address by Dr. Charles A. Eastman," 150, 147; "Indian Rights as Guaranteed by Treaties," *American Indian Magazine* 7 (Winter 1919): 167–170.

23. Melville Kelly quoted in Lawrence C. Kelly, *The Assault on Assimilation: John Collier and the Origins of Indian Policy Reform* (Albuquerque: University of New Mexico Press, 1983), 187; and Britten, *American Indians in World War I*, 181; "The Philadelphia Conference," *American Indian Magazine* 6 (Spring 1918): 12 (emphasis added).

24. Carlos Montezuma, "While the Iron Is Hot, Strike," *Wassaja* 3 (May 1918): 2; Lesak, "Soldiers to Citizens, 118. See also "Indians Are Fighting for Their Freedom, Liberty, and Rights," *Wassaja* 2 (June 1917): 2.

25. "Self-Determination for American Red Man: Native Race Proposed for Full Citizenship in a Bill Now before Congress," *New York Times*, August 10, 1919, 3; Arthur C. Parker, "Making Democracy Safe for the Indians," *American Indian Magazine* 6 (Spring 1918): 29; Kellogg, *Our Democracy and the American Indian*, 41, 33, 32, 30.

26. Parker, "The American Indian in the World Crisis," 17; Frederick Hoxie, "From Prison to Homeland: The Cheyenne River Reservation before World War I," in *The Plains Indians of the Twentieth Century*, ed. Peter Iverson (Norman: Uni-

versity of Oklahoma Press, 1985), 55–75. See also Hoxie's larger work, *A Final Promise: The Campaign to Assimilate the Indians, 1880–1920* (Lincoln: University of Nebraska Press, 1988).

27. "The American Indian's Part in the World War," 146. Hertzberg examines the various ways in which pan-Indian intellectuals viewed the reservation—as prison, community, and refuge—in *The Search for an American Indian Identity*, 313–319.

28. Indian Citizenship Bill, *U.S. Statutes at Large*, 41:350, in Prucha, *Documents of United States Indian Policy*, 215; Tate, "From Scout to Doughboy," 435; Indian Citizenship Act, June 2, 1924, *U.S. Statutes at Large*, 43:253, in Prucha, *Documents of United States Indian Policy*, 218; "Making Indians Citizens," *New York Times*, June 24, 1924, 12. The bill stated that citizenship "shall not in any manner impair or otherwise affect the right of any Indian to tribal or other property."

29. "Meeting of the [Blackfeet] Tribal Business Council," February 25, 1926, File 13256-1926-Blackfeet-054, Central Classified File (hereafter CCF) 1, RG 75, NA.

30. Quoted in Hertzberg, *The Search for an American Indian Identity*, 65; Kellogg, *Our Democracy and the American Indian*, 50, 51, 58, 78, 80; and see 39–40 for her views on "incorporation." Kellogg argued that Indian reservations suffered from lack of credit. Expanding credit facilities became a central feature of the Indian Reorganization Act of 1934.

31. D. H. Lawrence, "Certain Americans and an Englishman," *New York Times Magazine*, December 24, 1922, 9; "The Protest of Artists and Writers against the Bursum Indian Bill," October 1922, in Kelly, *Assault on Assimilation*, 215; see also 380 (statement); for Kelly's coverage of the Bursum Bill controversy, see 213–255. On the impact of southwestern American Indian painting on non-Indian artists and intellectuals, see Bill Anthes, *Native Moderns: American Indian Painting, 1940–1960* (Durham: Duke University Press, 2006).

32. "'Minority Rights' at Home," *New York Times*, January 4, 1923, 18; "Ill-Treated Indians," *New York Times*, February 4, 1923, 28; "Fall Angry Over Pueblos," *New York Times*, January 26, 1923, 9; critics quoted in Kelly, *The Assault on Assimilation*, 343. A compromise reached in June 1924 created the Pueblo Lands Act, which established a Pueblo land board charged with investigating claims and evicting settlers. See Donald Parman, *Indians and the American West in the Twentieth Century* (Bloomington: Indiana University Press, 1994), 78–80.

33. Lewis Meriam et al., *The Problem of Indian Administration: Report of a Survey made at the request of Honorable Hubert Work, Secretary of the Interior, and submitted to him, February 21, 1928* (Baltimore: Johns Hopkins University Press, 1928), 42, 462; *Annual Report of the Secretary of the Interior, 1930* (Washington, D.C.: GPO, 1930), 25–26.

34. For a full review of Collier's long career, see Kenneth R. Philp, *John Collier's Crusade for Indian Reform, 1920–1954* (Tucson: University of Arizona Press, 1977). For a short review, see E. A. Schwartz, "Red Atlantis Revisited: Community and Culture in the Writings of John Collier," *American Indian Quarterly* 18 (Autumn 1994): 507–531.

35. John Collier, "The American Congo," *The Survey* 50 (August 1923): 476; John Collier, "Amerindians," *Pacific Affairs* 2 (March 1929): 119, 118; Collier quoted in Carey McWilliams, *Brothers under the Skin* (Boston: Little, Brown, 1943), 68. Laurence Hauptman explores Collier's attention to European colonial practices in "Africa View: John Collier, the British Colonial Service, and American Indian Policy, 1933–1945," *The Historian* 48 (1986): 359–374.

36. John Collier to Superintendents, Tribal Councils, and Individual Indians, January 20, 1934, Circular Letter, 2, Box 1, Part 1-A, File 4894-34-066, Entry 1011, "Records Concerning the Wheeler-Howard Act, 1933–1937," RG 75, NA (hereafter RCWHA); ibid., 4, 11.

37. Collier misjudged Native America by proposing that tribal members contribute their individual landholdings to an expanded tribal estate, sparking a fierce resistance among Native Americans. For example, Hugh Jackson, a Blackfeet veteran of World War I, objected: "It looks as if we want to be governed under a communistic form of government like in Russia . . . I don't believe we should try any changes." The Blackfeet, Jackson said, "are living in the United States, and the system is that you have to own property by title. We are not in a foreign country." See "Minutes of the Blackfeet Tribal Business Council," February 5, 1934, 13, CCF 9522-E-1936-Blackfeet-054, pt. 1, RG 75, NA. For a review of the congresses and the evolution of the IRA, see Vine Deloria Jr. and Clifford Lytle, *The Nations Within: The Past and Future of American Indian Sovereignty* (New York: Pantheon, 1984).

38. "Minutes of the Plains Congress, Rapid City Indian School, Rapid City, South Dakota, March 2–5, 1934," 7, File 4894-1934-066, Box 3, pt. 2AA, RCWHA. See Box 7, pt. 9, for media coverage of the conferences; ibid., 15, 16, 17.

39. Ibid., 18. See also March 5, afternoon session, 8–9.

40. Deloria and Lytle, *The Nations Within*, 110, 115, 119, 120. Local white newspapers fueled the use of this anticommunist rhetoric, as did some Indian newspapers. See Mary Ann Weston, *Native Americans in the News: Images of Indians in the Twentieth-Century Press* (Westport, Conn.: Greenwood Press, 1996), 67–69.

41. *Statutes at Large of the United States*, 48 Stat. 984 (1934); S. 3645, "A Bill to conserve and develop Indian lands and resources; to extend to Indians the right to form business and other organizations; to establish a credit system for Indians; to

grant certain rights of home rule to Indians; to provide for vocational education for Indians; and for other purposes," Box 7, pt. 11-B, RCWHA. Alarmed by Collier's vision of a stronger Native America, Wheeler introduced a new bill, S. 3645, to replace the original, S. 2755. For a succinct comparison of the original bill and the final product, see Deloria and Lytle, *The Nations Within*, chap. 10 and appendix. For analysis of the Indian New Deal and the Indian Reorganization Act, see Thomas Biolsi, *Organizing the Lakota: The Political Economy of the New Deal on the Pine Ridge and the Rosebud Reservations* (Tucson: University of Arizona Press, 1992); Stephen Cornell, *The Return of the Native: American Indian Political Resurgence* (Oxford: Oxford University Press, 1988), pt. 2; Laurence M. Hauptman, *The Iroquois and the New Deal* (Syracuse: Syracuse University Press, 1981); Graham D. Taylor, *The New Deal and American Indian Tribalism: The Administration of the Indian Reorganization Act, 1934–45* (Lincoln: University of Nebraska Press, 1980); Donald Parman, *The Navajos and the New Deal* (New Haven: Yale University Press, 1976); Elmer Rusco, *A Fateful Time: The Background and Legislative History of the Indian Reorganization Act* (Reno: University of Nevada Press, 2000); Paul C. Rosier, *Rebirth of the Blackfeet Nation, 1912–1954* (Lincoln: University of Nebraska Press, 2001).

42. *Annual Report of the Commissioner of Indian Affairs*, November 27, 1851 (Washington, D.C.: GPO, 1851), 86; Francis Paul Prucha, *The Great Father: The United States Government and the American Indians* (Lincoln: University of Nebraska Press, 1986), 324; "Minutes of the Plains Congress, March 5, 1934," 21. Some of the seventy-seven tribes later voted to adopt the IRA once its credit-lending features became known. Section 18 of the final bill reflected Collier's claim that he and his staff would not "act unless the Indians are willing to go with us." The provision stipulated that the secretary of the interior must call for tribal referendums on the IRA within one year after the passage of the act. The IRA would not affect any tribe whose majority of eligible voters rejected the legislation, but once a tribe did so, it could not claim any benefits provided under the law.

43. Quoted in Rosier, *Rebirth of the Blackfeet Nation*, 98.

3. World War II Battlegrounds

1. Begay chronicles his various journeys in Keats Begay and Broderick H. Johnson, eds., *Navajos and World War II* (Tsaile, Ariz.: Navajo Community College Press, 1977), 40–43. The book is a collection of interviews with Navajo veterans. For an account of Omaha veteran Hollis Stabler's travels during World War II, see his *No One Ever Asked Me: The World War II Memoirs of an Omaha Indian Soldier*, ed. Victoria Smith (Lincoln: University of Nebraska Press, 2005).

2. Corporal James P. O'Neill, "Indian in Iran," *Yank, the Army Weekly*, quoted in *HighRoad* (May 1945): 35, Folder 87, Box 10, D'Arcy McNickle Papers (hereafter DMP), the Newberry Library (*HighRoad* was the publication of the Evening Meeting of the Methodist Youth Fellowship); Marc S. Gallicchio, *The African American Encounter with Japan and China: Black Internationalism in Asia, 1895–1945* (Chapel Hill: University of North Carolina Press, 2000), 2; Ella DeLoria, *Speaking of Indians* (Lincoln: University of Nebraska Press, 1998), 144, 141. Commissioner of Indian Affairs William Brophy, who replaced John Collier in 1945, wrote that "thousands of Indians who had never been far from a reservation had attained widened viewpoints in the military camps and in the factories of this country, and in the far reaches of the earth." William A. Brophy, "Office of Indian Affairs," *Annual Report of the Secretary of the Interior, Fiscal Year Ended June 30, 1946* (Washington, D.C.: GPO, 1946), 351.

3. Flora Warren Seymour, "Trying It on the Indian," *New Outlook* (May 1934), reprinted in *Native Americans: Opposing Viewpoints*, ed. William Dudley (San Diego: Greenhaven Press, 1998), 207. Seymour was a former member of the private assimilationist group Board of Indian Commissioners, which Collier and President Franklin Roosevelt disbanded in 1933.

4. Bruner quoted in Jere Franco, *Crossing the Pond: The Native American Effort in World War II* (Denton: University of North Texas Press, 1999), 6; AIF leaders quoted in John Finger, *Cherokee Americans: The Eastern Band of the Cherokee in the Twentieth Century* (Lincoln: University of Nebraska Press, 1991), 90. Laurence Hauptman covers AIF activities in "The American Indian Federation and the Indian New Deal: A Reinterpretation," *Pacific Historical Review* 52 (November 1983): 378–402.

5. "Highlights of the Roosevelt Record in Indian Affairs," *The First American* (1940): 1, 3, in Records Relating to the National Defense Program, 1940–1945: Correspondence on Selective Service, Box 2, RG 75, NA; Pelley quoted in Geoffrey S. Smith, *To Save a Nation: American Counter-subversives, the New Deal, and the Coming of World War II* (New York: Basic Books, 1973), 143–144. *The First American* was Jemison's short-lived soapbox. Jemison's mother was Seneca, her father Cherokee. Laurence Hauptman chronicles Jemison's life and work in "Alice Jemison: Seneca Political Activist, 1901–1964," *The Indian Historian* 12 (Summer 1979): 15–62.

6. Smith, *To Save a Nation*, 144; Kenneth William Townsend, *World War II and the American Indian* (Albuquerque: University of New Mexico Press, 2000), 51–52. On Pelley's nefarious activities, see Smith, *To Save a Nation*, 53–65. Pelley was convicted of sedition in 1942.

7. Franco, *Crossing the Pond*, 18; Kuhn quoted in Townsend, *World War II and the American Indian*, 55–56.

8. William C. Meadows, *Comanche Code Talkers of World War II* (Austin: University of Texas Press, 2002), 65; on Ross's activities, see Franco, *Crossing the Pond*, 22–24; Townsend, *World War II and the American Indian*, 37–40; and James V. Compton, *The Swastika and the Eagle: Hitler, the United States, and the Origins of World War II* (Boston: Houghton Mifflin, 1967), 11–13.

9. Franco, *Crossing the Pond*, 32.

10. Townsend, *World War II and the American Indian*, 33 (May quote), 36 (*El Alcázar* quote); "Fightingest Americans: In Both World Wars the Indian Has Been the Terror of U.S. Enemies," *PIC*, April 13, 1943, 10, Folder 2, Box 123, AAIA-A; broadcast quoted in Richard L. Neuberger, "The American Indian Enlists: He Feels His Kinship to the Chinese, the East Indians, the Arabs and the Filipinos, and to Colonial Peoples All Over the World," *Asia and the Americas* 42 (1942): 628. Richard Cancroft explores Karl May's influence in "The American West of Karl May," *American Quarterly* 19 (Winter 1967): 249–258. On Germans' fascination with all things American Indian, see Colin G. Calloway, Gerd Gemünden, and Susanne Zantop, eds., *Germans and Indians: Fantasies, Encounters, Projections* (Lincoln: University of Nebraska Press, 2002); and Christian Feest, ed., *Indians and Europeans: An Interdisciplinary Collection of Essays* (Lincoln: University of Nebraska Press, 1999).

11. Analyst quoted in Z. A. B. Zeman, *Nazi Propaganda*, 2nd ed. (Oxford: Oxford University Press, 1973), 61; Max Paul Friedman, *Nazis and Good Neighbors: The United States Campaign against the Germans of Latin America in World War II* (Cambridge: Cambridge University Press, 2003), 2, 1, and 2–8 passim. After investigating further, U.S. officials cut in half the number of Germans scheduled for deportation.

12. Carey McWilliams, *Brothers under the Skin* (Boston: Little, Brown, 1943), 5, 22. Americans, McWilliams urged, had to rid themselves of the "myopia" that made them "think of Western Europe and America as the world" (17–18).

13. "America's Handling of Its Indigenous Minority," speech by John Collier, December 4, 1939, Reel 32, John Collier Papers (hereafter JCP).

14. "Address by John Collier," September 4, 1934, Reel 32, JCP; John Collier, "Indians Come Alive," *Atlantic Monthly* 170 (September 1942): 75; Collier quoted in Gerard Colby (with Charlotte Dennett), *Thy Will Be Done: The Conquest of the Amazon: Nelson Rockefeller and Evangelism in the Age of Oil* (New York: Harper-Collins, 1995), 145.

15. On collaboration between Collier and Sáenz, see Colby, *Thy Will Be Done*, 67.

16. John Collier, "The Indian in a Wartime Nation," *Annals of the American Academy of Political and Social Science* 223 (1942): 32, 33; McWilliams, *Brothers under the Skin*, 24. For a summary of the conference, see John Collier, "Notes on

the First Inter-American Congress on Indian Life," *Indians at Work* (June 1940); and "Governments and Natives of the Americas and of Oceania," *Indians at Work* (August 1941), Reel 32, JCP.

17. *Annual Report of the Secretary of the Interior* (Washington, D.C.: GPO, 1941), xxi; see, for example, "The Greatest Unmet Practical Need in Indian Service," November 21, 1944, Reel 32, JCP. The document is a memorandum prepared for Dr. Pio Jaramillo Alvarado, director of the National Indian Institute of Ecuador. According to Richard Neuberger, Arab leaders also requested engineers from the Bureau of Indian Affairs to help them develop railroads and irrigation systems. See Neuberger, "The American Indian Enlists"; Bain Attwood, *Rights for Aborigines* (Crows Nest, Australia: Allen and Unwin, 2003), 120; see 120–123 for coverage of Thomson's visit and his promotion of the IRA as a vehicle to give Aborigines the same powers as Native Americans. Thomson was one of a number of Australian reformers who were inspired by Collier's Indian New Deal programs. Barrie Pittock championed the IRA in the 1960s (*Annual Report of the Secretary of the Interior*, xxi). See John Collier, "The Future of the Indian," October 27, 1941; and "Radio address on Indian Day," April 19, 1944, Reel 32, JCP.

18. John Collier, *From Every Zenith: A Memoir and Some Essays on Life and Thought* (Denver: Sage, 1963), 300–301, 368. Also see Kenneth Philp, "John Collier and the Indians of the Americas: The Dream and the Reality," *Prologue* 11 (Spring 1979): 5–21.

19. Quoted in Neuberger, "The American Indian Enlists," 629.

20. Collier, "The Indian in a Wartime Nation," 29, 30.

21. Neuberger, "The American Indian Enlists," 630, 628, 629; Orval Ricketts to Morris Burge, Association on American Indian Affairs, Inc., December 13, 1940, Folder 2, Box 123, AAIA-A; "Our Red Indians in the War for Democracy," address by John Collier to the Rotary Club of New York, June 8, 1944, 9, Reel 32, JCP.

22. Proceedings of the Meeting of the Navajo Tribal Council, June 3–6, 1940, CCF 1907–1939-Navajo-54889, Box 11, RG 75, NA.

23. Brown quoted in Begay and Johnson, *Navajos and World War II*, 61; Navajo draftee quoted in Evon Z. Vogt, *Navajo Veterans: A Study of Changing Values* (Cambridge, Mass., 1951), 64; Smith quoted in Townsend, *World War II and the American Indian*, 77.

24. *Annual Report of the Secretary of the Interior* (Washington, D.C.: GPO, 1941), xxii; Ojibwe quoted in Alison Bernstein, *American Indians and World War II* (Norman: University of Oklahoma Press, 1991), 36; John Collier, Commissioner of Indian Affairs, "Indians in the War for Democracy," Circular 181242, March 11, 1942, Records Relating to the National Defense Program, 1940–1945, Box 2, RG 75, NA. For coverage of Native American code talkers, see Meadows, *Comanche Code Talkers of World War II*, 67–72.

25. Bernstein, *American Indians and World War II*, 75. On the Blackfeet victory garden, see "Project—Assisting in the Nation's War Effort," in "Annual Report of Extension Work," 1942, 11, CCF 2, File 1332-1943-Blackfeet-031, RG 75, NA. Ronald Takaki compares the experiences of American ethnic groups in World War II in *A Different Mirror: A History of Multicultural America* (Boston: Houghton Mifflin, 1993), chap. 14. The BIA publication *Indians at Work* offers extensive coverage of Native Americans' wartime contributions. Also see Tom Holm, "Fighting a White Man's War: The Extent and Legacy of American Indian Participation in World War II," in *The Plains Indians of the Twentieth Century*, ed. Peter Iverson (Norman: University of Oklahoma Press, 1985), 69–81.

26. Patty Loew, "The Back of the Homefront: Black and American Indian Women in Wisconsin during World War II," *Wisconsin Magazine of History* 82 (1999): 89; Grace Mary Gouveia, "'Uncle Sam's Priceless Daughters': American Indian Women during the Depression, World War II, and Post-war Era" (Ph.D. diss., Purdue University, 1994), 117, 124; Chippewa woman quoted in Townsend, *World War II and the American Indian*, 176. For a condensed version of Gouveia's coverage of World War II, see "'We Also Serve': American Indian Women's Role in World War II," *Michigan Historical Review* 20 (1994): 153–182.

27. Department of the Interior Information Service press release, October 11, 1940, Records Relating to the National Defense Program, 1940–1945: Education-related, Box 2, RG 75, NA; Clark quoted in Richard L. Neuberger, "American Indians Fight Axis," *New York Times*, August 30, 1942, 7; Coffee quoted in Neuberger, "The American Indian Enlists," 630; *Saturday Evening Post* quoted in Meadows, *Comanche Code Talkers*, 39; "Two Shades of Redmen Found on This Continent," n.d. (ca. October 1940), unidentified newspaper clipping, Records Relating to the National Defense Program, 1940–1945: Correspondence on Selective Service, Box 1, RG 75, NA; Collier quoted in Franco, *Crossing the Pond*, 127.

28. "Mobilization of the Indian Service and Indian Resources for National Defense," June 15, 1940, 10, Records Relating to the National Defense Program, 1940–1945: Correspondence on Selective Service, Box 1, RG 75, NA; J. C. Morgan and Howard Gorman to John Collier, October 15, 1940, Records Relating to the National Defense Program, 1940–1945, Box 2, RG 75, NA; William Snake to Collier, January 1942, Records Relating to the National Defense Program, 1940–1945: Correspondence on Selective Service, Box 1, RG 75, NA; Shedd quoted in Townsend, *World War II and the American Indian*, 71; for Townsend's coverage of the debate on segregated Indian units, see 69–72.

29. Finger, *Cherokee Americans*, 107.

30. Collier to Captain Robert B. Coons, Selective Service Committee, October 17, 1940, Records Relating to the National Defense Program, 1940–1945: Correspondence on Selective Service; and John Collier to Chief of the St. Regis

Mohawk Nation, October 16, 1940, Records Relating to the National Defense Program, 1940–1945, Box 2, RG 75, NA; Collier to William Zimmerman, Assistant Commissioner of Indian Affairs, October 24, 1940, Records Relating to the National Defense Program, 1940–1945: Correspondence on Selective Service, Box 2: Education-Related, RG 75, NA; Collier quoted in *Washington Star*, January 24, 1941, Records Relating to the National Defense Program, 1940–1945: Correspondence on Selective Service, Box 1, RG 75, NA; "St. Regis Mohawk Council," October 8, 1940, Records Relating to the National Defense Program, 1940–1945: Education-related, Box 2, RG 75, NA. Cases of resistance included a group of landless Chippewa-Cree opposing conscription. The U.S. attorney for Montana discovered that the Communist Party of Montana had funded the group's resistance to conscription and provided "a fertile field for the development of Communistic principles." See Louis E. Mueller, Chief Special Officer, to Commissioner of Indian Affairs, October 21, 1940, Records Relating to the National Defense Program, 1940–1945: Correspondence on Selective Service, Box 1, RG 75, NA.

31. Swann quoted in Bernstein, *American Indians and World War II*, 33; see 31–33 for her coverage of the case. For broader coverage of Six Nations' resistance to the draft, see Townsend, *World War II and the American Indian*, 112–124; Decision by C. J. Frank, November 1941, Folder 2, Box 123, AAIA-A.

32. "5 Indians Fight Draft as Threat to Sovereignty," *New York Herald Tribune*, October 21, 1941, Folder 2, Box 123, AAIA-A; Collier quoted in Townsend, *World War II and the American Indian*, 121; Ernest Benedict to American Civil Liberties Union, March 27, 1941, Folder 2, Box 123, AAIA-A.

33. "5 Indians Fight Draft as Threat to Sovereignty."

34. *Annual Report of the Secretary of the Interior* (Washington, D.C.: GPO, 1942), xxii.

35. Sioux quoted in Bernstein, *American Indians and World War II*, 81; Michael L. Lawson, *Little Bighorn: Winning the Battle, Losing the War* (New York: Chelsea House, 2007), 126; "Fightingest Americans,"12. Also see Franco, *Crossing the Pond*, 104. Beard was the last survivor of the Battle of Little Big Horn and purported to be the model for the U.S. Buffalo Nickel minted in 1913.

36. Townsend, *World War II and the American Indian*, 199. In 1942 nearly 1,500 Japanese Americans were transferred to the Navajo-owned Leupp Indian Plant in Winslow, Arizona. For Collier's take on "concentration camps," see *From Every Zenith*, 301–303. Alexander Leighton examines the contributions of BIA personnel to the running of the Poston camp in *The Governing of Men: General Principles and Recommendations Based on Experiences at a Japanese Relocation Camp* (Princeton: Princeton University Press, 1945), 373–374.

37. Bernstein, *American Indians and World War II*, 83–84.

38. Collier, "The Indian in a Wartime Nation," 35; "Our Red Indians in the

War for Democracy," Address by John Collier to the Rotary Club of New York, June 8, 1944, Reel 32, JCP; McWilliams, *Brothers under the Skin*, 67, 74, 75 (Embree quote). McWilliams's arguments drew from Collier's writings, but the journalist in turn helped to shape Collier's larger perspective. See John Collier, "Paper for panel discussion at WRITERS' CONGRESS, Hollywood, Calif.," October 1943; and *"Brothers under the Skin,"* Reel 32, JCP.

39. McWilliams, *Brothers under the Skin*, 78, 7; Gunnar Myrdal, *An American Dilemma: The Negro Problem and Modern Democracy* (New York: Harper & Brothers Publishers, 1944). Myrdal made little mention of Native Americans, noting only that "even the American Indians are now considered as ultimately assimilable," which "speaks against the doctrine that race prejudice under all circumstances is an unchangeable pattern of attitude" (53).

40. Justino Herrera to Mrs. Dietrich, July 27, 1943; Tony Aguilar to Mrs. Dietrich, July 23, 1943, 75; and Joseph Roybal to Mrs. Dietrich, January 21, 1943, 49, all in "Doing Fine and Thanks a Million," comp. Margretta Steward Dietrich, New Mexico Association on Indian Affairs, Folder 3, Box 123, AAIA-A. "Doing Fine" is the collection of letters Dietrich received in exchange for sending the packages and newsletters.

41. Octavio Suina to Mrs. Dietrich, April 30, 1943 51; Lewis Naranjo to Mrs. Dietrich, 11; and Private Pino to Mrs. Dietrich, May 13, 1943, 61–62, in "Doing Fine"; Aguilar to Mrs. Dietrich, 67. Also writing from Iran on August 3, 1943, Private Wilson Guerroro noted the condition of "the Natives" of Iran: "They are really going through a hard life, there [sic] clothes looks a thousand year old, sheep skin jacket not tanned, two hole cut for their arms, no shoes, old ragged pants just comes to their knee . . . Really it's a sorrowful life." "Doing Fine," 72–73.

42. Captain Oliver LaFarge, "The Brothers Big Elk," *The American Indian* 1 (November 1943): 17, Reel 32, JCP.

43. Ibid.; U.S. Congress, Senate, "Partial Report 310, Pursuant to S.R. 17 Extending S.R. 79 in the 70th Cong.," in Senate Committee on Indian Affairs, "Survey of Conditions among the Indians of the United States," 78th Cong., 1st sess., 1943; "S-310," *The American Indian* 1 (November 1943): 26; "American Indians Protect You. Do You Protect Them?" n.d., Folder 3, Box 123, AAIA-A; Collier quoted in Townsend, *World War II and the American Indian*, 204.

44. Naranjo to Mrs. Dietrich, 11.

45. Phinney quoted in John Fahey, *Saving the Reservation: Joe Garry and the Battle to Be Indian* (Seattle: University of Washington Press, 2001), 10. For coverage of the founding of the NCAI, see Thomas W. Cowger, *The National Congress of American Indians: The Founding Years* (Lincoln: University of Nebraska Press, 1999), 31–45. The original name of the organization was the National Council of American Indians, duplicating that of an organization Gertrude Bonnin started

after the Society of American Indians lost influence in the early 1920s. During the NCAI's first convention, delegates changed the name to the National Congress of American Indians to avoid confusion with Bonnin's organization, though the two groups shared common goals.

46. Quoted in Cowger, *National Congress of American Indians*, 43.

47. Ruth Muskrat Bronson, "What Does the Future Hold?" *HighRoad* (May 1945): 42, Folder 87, Box 10, DMP. On Bronson, see Gretchen G. Harvey, "Cherokee American: Ruth Muskrat Bronson, 1897–1982" (Ph.D. diss., Arizona State University, 1996).

48. Ibid., 31, 34; John Collier, "Greetings," *The American Indian* 1 (November 1943): 1, Reel 32, JCP.

4. The Cold War on the Indian Frontier

1. Henry Miller, *The Air-Conditioned Nightmare* (New York: New Directions, 1970), 26, 28, 36–37; Henry Miller, *Remember to Remember*, vol. 2 of *The Air-Conditioned Nightmare* (Norfolk, Conn.: New Directions, 1947), 427.

2. Miller, *Remember to Remember*, 426.

3. Ibid., 213; Miller, *The Air-Conditioned Nightmare*, 36.

4. Greg Robinson, *By Order of the President: FDR and the Internment of Japanese Americans* (Cambridge, Mass.: Harvard University Press, 2000), 2; U.S. Congress, House, *Relief of Needy Indians*, Hearings before the House of Representatives Committee on Indian Affairs, 76th Cong., 3rd sess., H.R. 8937 (Washington, D.C.: GPO, 1940), 13; U.S. Congress, House, *Investigate Indian Affairs*, Hearings before a Subcommittee of the Committee on Indian Affairs, pt. 3, Hearings in the Field, 78th Cong., 2nd sess. (Washington, D.C.: GPO, 1944), 400. Numerous books and articles have covered the relocation of Japanese Americans using the term "concentration camps," including Allan S. Bosworth, *America's Concentration Camps* (New York: W. W. Norton, 1967); Roger Daniels, *Concentration Camps USA: Japanese Americans and World War II* (New York: Holt Rinehart and Winston, 1971); Michi Nishiura Weglyn, *Years of Infamy: The Untold Story of America's Concentration Camps* (Seattle: University of Washington Press, 1976); and Richard S. Nishimoto, *Inside an American Concentration Camp: Japanese American Resistance at Poston, Arizona* (Tucson: University of Arizona Press, 1995). The use of the term to describe Native American reservations persists in various publications. See, for example, Brenda Child, "The Sesquicentennial of Indian Survivance in Minnesota," *2007 OAH Annual Meeting Supplement* (February 2007): A7. In the April 7, 2001, edition of the African American newspaper *New Pittsburgh Courier*, Junius Stanton described "surviving Native Americans" living in "concentration camps euphemistically called 'reservations.'" The comparison of concentration

camps and reservations has also appeared in mainstream academic books such as Anthony F. C. Wallace, *The Long Bitter Trail: Andrew Jackson and the American Indians* (New York: Hill and Wang, 1993). See also Elizabeth Cook-Lynn, *Anti-Indianism in Modern America: A Voice from Tatekeya's Earth* (Urbana: University of Illinois Press, 2001), 191.

5. Oswald Villard, "Wardship and the Indian," *Christian Century*, March 29, 1944, 397, 398; O. K. Armstrong, "Set the American Indians Free," *Reader's Digest* (August 1945): 49, 47. For a balanced analysis of veterans' views on postwar adjustments to reservation life, see "The Problem of the Returned Indian Veterans," *NCAI Bulletin* (October 1947): 5–6, AIP.

6. Henri Lefebvre, *The Production of Space* (Oxford: Blackwell, 1992), 271, 391. Oswald Villard quotes a BIA superintendent as saying, "Wardship and full manhood stature do not go together"; see Villard, "Wardship and the Indian," 397.

7. For Brophy's tenure, see Donald Fixico, *Termination and Relocation: Federal Indian Policy, 1945–1960* (Albuquerque: University of New Mexico Press, 1986), 22–25.

8. "Memorandum for the Association on American Indian Affairs" (ca. late 1945); and John G. Evans, General Superintendent of the United Pueblo Agency, to William A. Brophy, April 9, 1946, Folder: Indian Commissioner (Correspondence 1945–1946), General File—Indians, Papers of William A. and Sophie A. Brophy (hereafter PWSB), Harry S. Truman Library (hereafter HSTL). See also William A. Brophy, "Office of Indian Affairs," *Annual Report of the Secretary of the Interior, Fiscal Year Ended June 30, 1946* (Washington, D.C.: GPO, 1946), 363.

9. For the bill's evolution, see Nancy Oestreich Lurie, "The Indian Claims Commission Act," *Annals of the American Academy of Political and Social Science* 311 (May 1957): 56–70; and Harvey D. Rosenthal, *Their Day in Court: A History of the Indian Claims Commission* (New York: Garland, 1990).

10. On Ira Hayes's fame and its consequences, see Karal Ann Marling and John Wettenhall, *Iwo Jima: Monuments, Memories, and the American Hero* (Cambridge, Mass.: Harvard University Press, 1991), 170–188; Charles E. Grounds to the President, July 27, 1946, Folder OF 6-AA: Indian Claims Commission, Box 75, White House Central Files: Official File (hereafter WHCF:OF), Harry S. Truman Papers (hereafter HSTP), HSTL; Arthur Watkins, "Termination of Federal Supervision: The Removal of Restrictions over Indian Property and Person," *Annals of the American Academy of Political and Social Science* 311 (May 1957), 55; Julius Krug to Truman, April 1, 1946; and Director of the Budget to Harry S. Truman, February 21, 1946, Folder OF 6-AA: Indian Claims Commission, Box 75, WHCF:OF, HSTP; William Brophy to Harry S. Truman, December 31, 1947, Folder OF 6-C: Office of Indian Affairs (1945–1949), Box 68, WHCF:OF, HSTP.

11. Truman to Director of the Budget, February 25, 1946; and "Statement by the President," August 13, 1946, Folder OF 6-AA: Indian Claims Commission, Box 75, WHCF:OF, HSTP. When the ICC disbanded in 1978 it had distributed roughly $657 million to Indian nations, though attorney fees took, in some cases, one-third of the awards. The average award, according to Alison Bernstein, was about $3 million; see Bernstein, *American Indians and World War II*, 162–163.

12. Stigler quoted in Fixico, *Termination and Relocation*, 30; Watkins, "Termination of Federal Supervision," 55. On Watkins's role in the termination movement, see R. Warren Metcalf, *Termination's Legacy: The Discarded Indians of Utah* (Lincoln: University of Nebraska Press, 2002), 21–48, 234–43; U.S. Congress, House, *Emancipation of Indians*, Hearings before the Subcommittee on Indian Affairs of the Committee on Public Lands, 80th Cong., 1st sess., H.R. 2958, H.R. 2165, and H.R. 1113 (Washington, D.C.: GPO, 1947), 42.

13. U.S. Congress, House, *Emancipation of Indians*, 137–139. I borrow here from N. Scott Momaday: "The immense landscape of the continental interior lay like memory in her blood"; see *The Way to Rainy Mountain* (Albuquerque: University of New Mexico Press, 1969), 7.

14. See Mary L. Dudziak, *Cold War Civil Rights: Race and the Image of American Democracy* (Princeton: Princeton University Press, 2000), 250.

15. "To Secure These Rights: The Report of the President's Committee on Civil Rights" (Washington, D.C.: GPO, 1947), 100, 146–147; Thomas Borstelmann, *The Cold War and the Color Line: American Race Relations in the Global Arena* (Cambridge, Mass.: Harvard University Press, 2001), 268.

16. "To Secure These Rights," 147; Robert Carr to Members of the President's Committee on Civil Rights, June 6, 1947, Folder: American Indians, Civil Rights of, Box 16, Records of the President's Committee on Civil Rights: RG220, HSTL; "Statement of D'Arcy McNickle, National Congress of American Indians," May 15, 1947, Box 12, Folder: National Congress of American Indians, Records of the President's Committee on Civil Rights, RG220, HSTL.

17. Judge N. B. Johnson to Hon. Styles Bridges, Chairman, Senate Appropriations Committee, n.d., National Congress of American Indians, *Sentinel Bulletin* (October 1947), AIP.

18. "Are Indians Getting a Square Deal?" radio broadcast, August 21, 1947, National Congress of American Indians, *Sentinel Bulletin* (October 1947), AIP; Lilly J. Neil to Mr. Beatty, General Director of Indian Education, September 8, 1947, in *"For Our Navajo People": Diné Letters, Speeches, and Petitions, 1900–1960*, ed. Peter Iverson (Albuquerque: University of New Mexico Press, 2002), 103. Native Americans whose reservation lands lay within New Mexico and Arizona gained the vote in 1948; Native Americans in Utah did so in 1953. See Peter Iverson, *Diné: A History of the Navajos* (Albuquerque: University of New Mexico Press, 2002), 203.

19. James B. Douthitt to Honorable Harry S. Truman, November 21, 1948, Folder 296 (1948–June 1949): Indians, Legislation Pertaining to, Box 937, WHCF:OF, HSTP.

20. Iverson, Diné, 134, 155; "The Navajo Blizzard Emergency," Report of J. M. Stewart, United States Indian Service, Folder: Commissioner John Nichols 1949–1950, Office of the Commissioner of Indian Affairs, Box 1, RG 75, NA.

21. Quoted in Bernstein, American Indians and World War II, 157.

22. Laurent Frantz, "Statement of Plan of Work," 8, Folder: Philleo Nash, Box 9, Records of the President's Committee on Civil Rights, RG220, HSTL; "Twilight on the Navajo Trail," Collier's, February 7, 1948, 21.

23. Los Angeles Examiner, November 25, 1947, Folder 296 Legislation re Navajo-Hopi Tribes, Box 938, WHCF:OF, HSTP. Newsmagazines such as Collier's and American Magazine published additional articles on the Navajo situation. In September 1948 the Watchtower Bible and Tract Society (Jehovah's Witnesses) in Brooklyn published in its magazine Despertad (Awake), "The Whites Fleece the Indians." The article, printed in Spanish and distributed in parts of Latin America, quoted from the Examiner's coverage of the Navajo crisis in arguing that "the condition of the Indian is worse than a national disgrace, it is an international scandal." Documenting the Navajo sheep-killing episode of the 1930s and the theft of the Sioux Nation's Black Hills, it claimed that the condition of the Navajo was the fault of "a hostile and egoistic people full of racial prejudice, people too occupied with the problems of world domination to give much consideration to this 'forgotten people.'" See "The Whites Fleece the Indians," September 8, 1948, in "Translation of Excerpts from DESPERTAD (AWAKE)," File 811.4016/8-2449, Box 4685, Central Decimal File, 1955–1959, Records of the Department of State, RG 59,NA, Suitland, Md. An American doing business in Latin America translated the article and sent it to Senator J. W. Fulbright as evidence of "the effective propaganda the Communists are spreading in Latin America." See J. W. Fulbright to George Allen, Assistant Secretary of State, August 24, 1949, File 811.4016/8-2449, NA.

24. Dickinson to Truman and Dickinson to Commissioner of Indian Affairs, April 12, 1947; Mr. and Mrs. D. Inman to President Harry S. Truman, November 27, 1947; and Engler to President Harry Truman, November 26, 1947, Folder 296 (1945–November 1947): Indians, Legislation Pertaining to, Box 937, WHCF:OF, HSTP; Patricia Moffitt to President Trueman, December 5, 1947, Folder 296 (December 1947): Indians, Legislation Pertaining to, Box 937, WHCF:OF, HSTP; Gunnar Myrdal, An American Dilemma: The Negro Problem and Modern Democracy (New York: Harper & Brothers, 1944), lxxi. In response to Mrs. Dickinson's letter, William Hassett, secretary to the president, responded that President Truman and his staff recognized that "the Navajo problem . . . is probably the most serious situation in the whole field of Indian administration," explaining that the secretary of

the interior was working on a comprehensive development program to ameliorate the crisis. Hassett to Dickinson, May 8, 1947, Folder 296 (1945–November 1947): Indians, Legislation Pertaining to, Box 937, WHCF:OF, HSTP.

25. Fredericka Mett to President Truman, December 4, 1947; Mrs. S. L. Shain to President Truman, December 2, 1947; and Mrs. J. M. Acosta to President Harry S. Truman, n.d., Folder 296 (December 1947): Indians, Legislation Pertaining to, Box 937, WHCF:OF, HSTP.

26. Lillian Frey to President Truman, December 1, 1947; Antonia B. Wiegand to Mr. Truman, December 3, 1947;; and Vera Jeanne Walker to President Harry Truman, December 10, 1947, Folder 296 (December 1947): Indians, Legislation Pertaining to, Box 937, WHCF:OF, HSTP. Exercising his "privileges as an American to criticize anyone I see fit," which included the president, Louis Samu of Pennsylvania told Truman that he should suspend aid shipments to Europeans until the government helped the "only true Americans," the Navajo. He took issue with Truman's contention that "the Communistic hordes will sweep over all of Europe . . . because we won't aid them they'll turn to Communism. Then why haven't the Navajo turned Communist?" Louis Samu to Mr. President, February 7, 1948, Folder 296 (1948–June 1949): Indians, Legislation Pertaining to, Box 937, WHCF:OF, HSTP. Paul Boyer explores Americans' conceptions of the postwar order in *By the Bomb's Early Light: American Thought and Culture at the Dawn of the Atomic Age* (Chapel Hill: University of North Carolina Press, 1994).

27. Joan Hall to President Truman, December 9, 1947, Folder 296 (December 1947): Indians, Legislation Pertaining to, Box 937, WHCF:OF, HSTP. Christina Klein explores a similar construction in *Cold War Orientalism: Asia in the Middlebrow Imagination, 1945–1961* (Berkeley: University of California Press, 2003), 9.

28. "Statement by the President, December 2, 1947, Folder 296 (December 1947): Indians, Legislation Pertaining to, Box 937, WHCF:OF, HSTP. In addition to the Friendship Trains of aid for Native Americans that U.S. citizens and Red Cross officials organized, the Departments of Defense and Agriculture and the War Assets Administration assisted in the relief effort, adding to the impression of a foreign aid campaign. See, for example, Truman to Clinton Anderson, n.d., Folder 296 (December 1947): Indians, Legislation Pertaining to, Box 937, WHCF:OF, HSTP; "House Approves Aid for Navajos and Hopis: Bill for $2,000,000 Is Rushed to Senate," *New York Times,* December 10, 1947, 64.

29. Lorania Francis, "Indian Bureau Official Accused," *Los Angeles Times,* April 23, 1948, 17.

30. Ed Ainsworth, "Indian Directors in Peculiar Role," *Los Angeles Times,* April 29, 1948, 2; Ed Ainsworth, "Attempt to 'Sovietize' Navajo Tribes Told," *Los Angeles Times,* April 28, 1948; Ed Ainsworth, "Navajo Destiny Hinges on Decision of Tribal Council on Soviet System," *Los Angeles Times,* May 4, 1948, 2; "Minutes of the Plains Congress, Rapid City Indian School, Rapid City, S.D., March 2–5,

1934," afternoon session, March 5, 9, File 4894-1934-066, Box 3, pt. 2AA, RCWHA; Charles Clifford Wilson, "Navajo Co-operatives Plan Defended," *Los Angeles Times*, May 24, 1948.

31. On the controversy, see Iverson, *Diné*, 216–218.

32. Morris Graham, "A Program to Rescue the American Indian," *Our Times*, July 1, 1949, 8; and John R. Nichols to Paul Fickinger, September 15, 1949, Folder: Commissioner John Nichols 1949–1950, Office of the Commissioner of Indian Affairs, Box 1, RG 75, NA.

33. "Senator Says Indians Are Targets of Reds," Associated Press report, *Los Angeles Times*, May 1, 1948, 2; Berry quoted in Edward Charles Valandra, *Not Without Our Consent: Lakota Resistance to Termination, 1950–1959* (Urbana: University of Illinois Press, 2006), 24; Malone quoted in Stephen Cornell, *The Return of the Native: American Indian Political Resurgence* (Oxford: Oxford University Press, 1988), 121. Congressman George Schwabe had earlier supported the elimination of the BIA because it encouraged "socialistic and . . . communistic thinking" among American Indians; quoted in Fixico, *Termination and Relocation*, 18.

34. "Statement of Secretary of the Interior J. A. Krug before the Subcommittee on Indian Affairs of the House Public Lands Committee, April 18, 1949," Navajo-Hopi Rehabilitation, 1947–1948 folder, Box 313, AAIA-A.

35. See *Annual Report of the Secretary of the Interior, Fiscal Year Ended June 30, 1946* (Washington, D.C.: GPO, 1946), 354, 368; "Minutes of the NCAI Convention in Santa Fe, 1947," 40, Folder: Proceedings 1947, Box 2, Records of the National Congress of American Indians (hereafter R-NCAI), National Museum of the American Indian, Smithsonian Institution, Suitland, Md.; N. B. Johnson to Will Rogers Jr., January 8, 1948, Will Rogers folder, Box 68, R-NCAI. Other Native communities pledged food or monetary assistance. For example, the UN Relief and Rehabilitation Administration received a check for $40 from Native schoolchildren in Alaska, the proceeds of a sale held to help starving people in Europe.

36. "Address of Will Rogers, Jr., before the Fifth Annual Convention of the National Congress of American Indians," December 13–16, 1948, NCAI Publications folder, Box 11, Helen Peterson Papers (hereafter HPP), National Museum of the American Indian.

37. Eleanor Roosevelt, "To Arms, Indians! The Congressmen Are Coming!," October 5, 1949, My Day Project, http://www.gwu.edu/~erpapers/myday/display doc.cfm?_y=1949&_f=md001402; John Collier to Truman, October 12, 1949, Folder 296 (1951): Legislation re Navajo-Hopi Tribes, Box 938, WHCF:OF, HSTP; "An Ancient Minority," *New York Times*, September 27, 1949, 26.

38. Fredericka Martin to Truman, October 13, 1949; Sherwood Moran to Truman, October 20, 1949; Sophia Mumford to Truman, November 1, 1949; Charles Haskell to Truman, October 12, 1949; Wilda MacKenzie to Truman, October 12,

1949, Folder 296 (1951): Legislation re Navajo-Hopi Tribes, Box 938, WHCF:OF, HSTP.

39. Marion W. Smith to Truman, October 12, 1949, Folder 296 (1951): Legislation re Navajo-Hopi Tribes, Box 938, WHCF:OF, HSTP; Secretary of the Interior, "Report to the President on Conditions of the Navajo Indians," 8, Folder 296 (December 1947): Indians, Legislation Pertaining to, Box 937, WHCF:OF, HSTP.

40. Peter Campbell Brown, Acting Assistant to the Attorney General, to Stephen Spingarn, the White House, n.d., Folder: Navajo Hopi Indian file [1 of 2], Box 32, Staff Member and Office Files (hereafter SMOF): Philleo Nash Files (hereafter PNF)—President's Committee on Equality of Treatment and Opportunity, HSTP; Harry S. Truman, To the Senate of the United States, October 17, 1949, Folder: Commissioner John Nichols 1949–1950, Office of the Commissioner of Indian Affairs, Box 1, RG 75, NA; Barry Goldwater to the President, October 13, 1949, Folder 296 (1951): Legislation re Navajo-Hopi Tribes, Box 938, WHCF:OF, HSTP. On the Rehabilitation Act, see Peter Iverson, *The Navajo Nation* (Westport, Conn.: Greenwood Press, 1981), 56–61. The Navajo monthly *Adahooniligii*, printed in English and Navajo, published the details of the bill so that all Navajo could understand its implications for reservation development. See "The Long Range Bill," *Adahooniligii* 5 (August 1950): 5.

41. *Public Papers of the Presidents, Harry S. Truman, 1949* (Washington, D.C.: GPO, 1964), 114; Samuel P. Hayes Jr., "Point Four in United States Foreign Policy," *Annals of the American Academy of Political and Social Science* 268 (March 1950): 29. Rebekah C. Beatty Davis explores the connection between the management of American Indian lands and foreign policy objectives in "Development as a Tool of Diplomacy: The Domestic Models for U.S. Policy in the Jordan River Valley, 1939–1956" (Ph.D. diss., Georgetown University, 1999).

42. Acheson quoted in Claude C. Erb, "Prelude to Point Four: The Institute of Inter-American Affairs," *Diplomatic History* 9 (Summer 1985): 249; "Some Notes Taken at New York Meeting, December 30, 1942," Reel 32, JCP. See also "Minutes of Meeting of January 30, 1943"; "Suggested Work Flow of Society for Total and Local Democracy, January 30, 1943"; "Why an Institute of Native or Ethnic Affairs Should Be established," February 24, 1943; and "An Institute of Ethnic Democracy," November 3, 1943, Reel 32, JCP; "What the AMERICAN INDIANS Will Do in the Future for Themselves and For Us," Predictions of Things to Come: Forecasts by Experts, Summer 1943, Reel 32, JCP.

43. Collier to Harry S. Truman, October 26, 1949, Folder 296: Legislation re Navajo-Hopi Tribes, Box 938, WHCF:OF, HSTP; Edwin Mechem to President Harry S. Truman, September 24, 1951; P.N. to Charles S. Murphy, October 2, 1951; and Truman to Gov. Edwin Mechem, October 3, 1951, Folder 296 (1951–1953), Box 938, WHCF:OF, HSTP.

44. "Memo to Philleo Nash," n.d.; and Provinse to John Nichols, "The Indian Service Experience in Its Relationship to the Point-Four Program," September 6, 1949, Folder: Memoranda, Box 25, SMOF:PNF.

45. "Inter-relationship of Point Four and Indian Administration," Association on American Indian Affairs, n.d., Folder 6, Box 151, AAIA-A; Eric [no last name provided] to William Zimmerman Jr., May 26, 1952, Folder 9, Box 1, William Zimmerman Jr. Papers (hereafter WZP), Center for Southwest Research, University Libraries, University of New Mexico; William Zimmerman Jr. to Assistant Secretary of the Interior Joel Wolfson, September 3, 1952, Folder 9, Box 1, WZP. The Department of the Interior, whose purview included the Bureau of Indian Affairs, lent its expertise in minerals exploration and development to the Technical Cooperation Administration. For a brief survey of this cooperation, see Stanley Andrews, TCA administrator, to Secretary of the Interior Oscar Chapman, October 13, 1952, File 1-111: Point Four (Part 3), Box 2639, Records of the Department of the Interior (RG 48), NA.

46. "To the Congress of the United States," June 24, 1949, Folder: Point Four Program, Box 115, President's Secretary's File (hereafter PSF): General File, 1945–1953, HSTP; "1952: April 8: Point Four—Read by Secretary Dean Acheson," Presidential Addresses, Letters and Messages folder, Box 200, PSF: Historical File, 1945–1953, HSTP. On Point Four as a Cold War program, see "Point Four Program in Relation to Dependent Areas," in *Documentary History of the Truman Presidency*, vol. 27, *The Point Four Program*, general ed. Dennis Merrill (Bethesda, Md.: University Publications of America, 1999), 137–147.

47. John Nichols, "Circular 3704," August 15, 1949, Folder: Commissioner John Nichols 1949–1950, Office of the Commissioner of Indian Affairs, Box 1, RG 75, NA.

48. Harold Edward Fey and D'Arcy McNickle, *Indians and Other Americans: Two Ways of Life Meet* (New York: Harper & Brothers, 1959), 186; *Congressional Record, House*, February 21, 1950, 2130, 2131; "Statement of Secretary of the Interior J. A. Krug before the Subcommittee on Indian Affairs of the House Public Lands Committee, April 18, 1949," Navajo-Hopi Rehabilitation, 1947–1948 folder, Box 313, AAIA. For an example of the use of Cold War "hotspot," see Penny M. Von Eschen, *Satchmo Blows Up the World: Jazz Ambassadors Play the Cold War* (Cambridge, Mass.: Harvard University Press, 2004), 146.

49. Peter Vielle, Blackfeet Tribal Business Council Secretary, to Commissioner of Indian Affairs, November 25, 1947, CCF File 50403-1941-Blackfeet-720, RG 75, NA; Henry Magee et al. to William Zimmerman, April 11, 1949, CCF File 7056-1944-BF-071, RG 75, NA. The council proposed legislation to be titled "A bill to promote the economic recovery of the Blackfeet Indians and better utilization of the resources of the Blackfeet Reservation and for other purposes." Lone Eagle (Sioux) wrote President Truman after reading of his request for 2 million

tons of grain for India's "starving millions." Asking Truman to support the "Original Americans," Lone Eagle vouched for his patriotism, telling Truman that he had served during World War I, his son served during World War II, and his son-in-law had just returned from Korea: "all enlisted volunteers—all good loyal Americans." Lone Eagle to Truman, February 5, 1951, Folder 296 (1951–1953): Indians, Legislation pertaining to, Box 937, WHCF:OF, HSTP.

50. "The Navajos: Fenced in by Alien World, They Struggle to Exist on Land That Cannot Support Them," *Life*, March 1, 1948, 75; Wesley D'Ewart, Chairman, Subcommittee on Indian Affairs, to Richard Welch, Chairman, Public Lands Committee of the House, November 24, 1947, Folder 7: Navajo-Hopi Rehabilitation, 1947–1948, Box 313, AAIA-A; "Resolution of the Navajo Tribal Council" (CJ-7-49), October 14, 1949, author's files (my thanks to William Chenoweth, research associate for the New Mexico Bureau of Mines and Mineral Resources, for sending me this document); Thomas E. Mullaney, "U.S. Now Ranks Second in Uranium Mining as Government Lends Aid to Prospectors," *New York Times*, February 24, 1952, F1; "Resolution of the Navajo Tribal Council: Advisory Committee to Draft Mining Regulations," March 22, 1951, author's files. D'Ewart's statement also appeared in "House Unit Urged to Back Navajo Aid," *New York Times*, November 30, 1947, 21. That 80 percent of its people did not speak English also highlighted for some politicians the Navajo Nation's foreign character; for coverage, see Doug Bruge et al., *The Navajo People and Uranium Mining* (Albuquerque: University of New Mexico Press, 2006). Peter H. Eichstadt examines Navajo mining and its devastating health consequences in *If You Poison Us: Uranium and Native Americans* (Santa Fe: Red Crane Books, 1994), 33–79. The Spokane and Laguna Pueblo also contributed uranium to national defense programs, but their experiences are not well documented. For coverage of Laguna Pueblo, see Valerie Kuletz, *The Tainted Desert: Environmental Ruin in the American West* (New York: Routledge, 1998); see also Ward Churchill, "A Breach of Trust: The Radioactive Colonization of Native North America," *American Indian Culture and Research Journal* 23 (1999): 23–69.

51. Charles J. Rhoads et al. "Report of the Committee on Indian Affairs to the Commission on Organization of the Executive Branch of the Government," October 1948, 54, Box 83, AAIA-A; U.S. Senate, 81st Cong. 1st sess. "Progress on Hoover Commission Recommendations," *Report of the Committee on Expenditures in the Executive Departments*, October 12, 1949 (Washington, D.C.: GPO, 1949), 310.

52. For Acheson's and Forrestal's comments, see White House "Memorandum for the Files," March 4, 1949, Memoranda folder, Box 25, SMOF:PNF. For coverage of Acheson's activities promoting civil rights in a Cold War context, see Dudziak, *Cold War Civil Rights*, 80–81, 100 (Acheson quoted 80).

53. Harry S. Truman to the Senate of the United States, October 17, 1949,

Folder: Commissioner John Nichols 1949–1950, Office of the Commissioner of Indian Affairs, Box 1, RG 75, NA (emphasis added).

54. "Statement of Secretary of the Interior J. A. Krug before the Subcommittee on Indian Affairs of the House Public Lands Committee, April 18, 1949," 3, Folder 8: Navajo-Hopi Rehabilitation, 1947–1948, Box 313, AAIA-A; Gerald D. Nash, *World War II and the West: Reshaping the Economy* (Lincoln: University of Nebraska Press, 1990), xii; *Congressional Record, House*, February 21, 1950, 2131; Secretary of the Interior, "Report to the President on Conditions of the Navajo Indians," 6, Folder 296 (December 1947): Indians, Legislation Pertaining to, Box 937, WHCF:OF, HSTP. The resettlement plan included the "proposed colonization of 1,000 families on irrigated land of the Colorado River Reservation."

55. Jim Marshall, "Twilight on the Navajo Trail," *Collier's*, February 7, 1948, 21.

56. Hahn also wrote: "Many Indians stay on the reservation when they shouldn't be there. We are not sure why." "Notes on Conference with Dillon S. Myer and John H. Provinse," Folder: Correspondence, Box 24, SMOF:PNF.

57. "Proposed Program of the Association on American Indian Affairs for Use of the American Indian Fund," May 3, 1948; and "Association on American Indian Affairs Restatement of Program and Policy in Indian Affairs," February 8, 1950, Folder 31, Box 4, AAIA-A. See also, for example, Clyde Kluckhohn to Alexander Lesser, February 24, 1950, Folder 1, Box 44, AAIA-A.

58. Felix Cohen to Alexander Lesser, May 18, 1948, Folder 5, Box 36, AAIA-A. For a comprehensive collection of Cohen's writings, see *The Legal Conscience: Selected Papers of Felix S. Cohen*, ed. Lucy Kramer Cohen (New Haven: Yale University Press, 1960).

59. "Indian Self-Government," *The American Indian* (September 1949), reprinted in Cohen, *The Legal Conscience*, 313–314; Cohen to Lesser, March 1, 1950, Folder 6, Box 36, AAIA-A. For a broader view of the miner's canary as racial barometer, see Lani Guinier and Gerald Torres, *The Miner's Canary: Enlisting Race, Resisting Power, Transforming Democracy* (Cambridge, Mass.: Harvard University Press, 2002).

60. Oliver LaFarge, "Proposal for a Study of Fundamentals of the Indian Problem" (First Discussion Draft), July 21, 1950, Folder 13, Box 402, AAIA-A; "Colonial Administration in the Indian Country," 12 (n.d.), Folder 6, Box 36, AAIA-A; LaFarge to Lesser, August 8, 1950, Folder 1, Box 44, AAIA-A. Cohen's article appeared as "Colonialism: U.S. Style," *The Progressive* 15 (1951): 16–18.

61. Secretary of the Interior Oscar Chapman to President Truman, March 18, 1950, Folder OF 6-C: Office of Indian Affairs (1950–1953), Box 68, WHCF:OF, HSTP; Cohen to Amos Lamson, May 12, 1950, Folder 6, Box 13, AAIA-A; "A Partial List of Personnel Changes—Final Draft," October 1, 1952, Box 1, Folder 11, Dorothy Parker Papers, Newberry Library, Chicago. The list appears to be the

appendix to John Collier's report, "On Why Dillon S. Myer Should Not Be Reappointed as Commissioner of Indian Affairs," October 18, 1952, Folder 11, Box 1,
Dorothy Parker Papers. On Myer's regime, see Felix Cohen, "The Erosion of Indian Rights, 1950–1953: A Case Study in Bureaucracy," *Yale Law Journal* 62 (February 1953): 348–390; and Richard Drinnon, *Keeper of Concentration Camps: Dillon Myer and American Racism* (Berkeley: University of California Press, 1987),
163–248.

62. Iverson, *The Navajo Nation*, 55; radio address by James E. Curry, "More
about Indians and Their Lawyers," November 2, 1952, Folder 9, Box 1, WZP.
Curry gave three speeches on Chicago radio station WFJL to defend his law practice and to attack Myer's policies. He sent copies of the transcripts to Milton
Eisenhower in the hope that Eisenhower's brother Dwight, newly elected to the
presidency, would fire Myer.

63. NCAI Annual Convention, July 25, 1951, Folder: 1950–1953 Commissioner of Indian Affairs: Notes and Talks, Box 2, Dillon S. Myer Papers (hereafter
DSMP), HSTL; "Statement by Dillon S. Myer, Commissioner of Indian Affairs,
before a Subcommittee of the Senate Committee on Interior and Insular Affairs,"
January 21, 1952, Folder 1950–1953: Commissioner of Indian Affairs Memoranda
and Reports, Box 4, DSMP. The BIA budget grew from $44 million in FY 1949 to
$85 million in FY 1953. Myer requested $122.35 million for FY 1954. Figures cited
in Collier, "On Why Dillon S. Myer Should Not Be Reappointed."

64. "Chapman Decides Attorney Contract Issued," press release, Department
of the Interior, January 24, 1952, Attorney Contracts, 2 of 2, Box 24, SMOF:PNF;
"Indians Tell Interior Department 'In War We Were Men; Now They Think We
Are Savages,'" *Washington Daily News*, January 4, 1952; "Navajo Describes Indian
Service as a 'Liability,'" *Albuquerque Journal*, January 4, 1952, Folder Attorney
Contracts, 2 of 2, Box 24, SMOF:PNF.

65. Cohen quoted in "Indian Bureau under Attack," *Portland Oregonian*, March
2, 1952 ; "Indian Bureau Asks Gestapo Power," *Houston Post*, April 22, 1952; "No
'Cold War' on Indians," *Philadelphia Inquirer*, April 17, 1952; and "New Control
Bill Branded 'Cold War on Indians,'" *New York Post*, April 14, 1952, "Press Com-
ment on Indian Bureau Police Bill," Folder: Personal Correspondence File, Box 4,
DSMP; "Experiment in Immorality," *The Nation*, July 26, 1952, 61. The *New York
Times* reported the AAIA's comment about the bill's creating a "cold war" in its
front-page coverage of the controversy; see Kenneth Campbell, "Bill on American
Indians Decried as Threatening Unfair Arrests," *New York Times*, April 14, 1952.

66. *NCAI News Bulletin* (September–October 1952): 4, 7; "The War," *Ada-
hooniligii* 5 (September 1950): 2; "Bill S. 2543 Is a Threat to Indians, Oklahoma
Man Warns," *Shannon County News*, March 20, 1952, "Press Comment on Indian
Bureau Police Bill," Folder: Personal Correspondence File, Box 4, DSMP.

67. "Listing and Description of Tasks Remaining to be Done to Effect Com-

plete Withdrawal of Bureau Services by Termination or Transfer to Other Auspices," 16–17, "Withdrawal Programming, Schedule C, Blackfeet Agency," File 17091-1952-Blackfeet-077, pt. 1, RG 75, NA; Brophy to Truman, December 31, 1947.

68. Ickes to Chapman, August 30, 1951, Folder: Harold L. Ickes, Box 47, Papers of Oscar L. Chapman, Correspondence File, 1949–1953, HSTP; John Collier, "Striking at Indians: Directive Viewed as Aimed at Destruction of Trusteeship," *New York Times*, October 19, 1952, E10; Zimmerman to Assistant Secretary of the Interior Joel Wolfson, September 3, 1952, Folder 9, Box 1, WZP.

69. Walter Woehlke to John [Collier], December 9, 1952, Folder 9, Box 1, WZP. Woehlke sent a copy of the letter to Zimmerman.

70. U.S. Congress, Senate, Subcommittee of the Committee on Appropriation, "Statement by George Pambrun," *Interior Department Appropriations for 1952: Hearings before the Subcommittee of the Committee on Appropriations*, 82nd Cong., 1 sess., pt. 1 (1951), 1228–29; Walter Wetzel to Secretary of the Interior, May 1, 1952, File 1141-1946-Blackfeet-068, Pt. 2, RG 75, NA.

71. Gerard Colby (with Charlotte Dennett), *Thy Will Be Done: The Conquest of the Amazon: Nelson Rockefeller and Evangelism in the Age of Oil* (New York: HarperCollins, 1995), 207. The best account of Arbenz and the CIA is Piero Gleijeses, *Shattered Hope: The Guatemalan Revolution and the United States, 1944–1954* (Princeton: Princeton University Press, 1991). Also see Stephen Schlesinger and Stephen Kinzer, *Bitter Fruit: The Untold Story of the American Coup in Guatemala* (Garden City, N.Y.: Doubleday, 1982).

72. Klein, *Cold War Orientalism*, 16.

73. On social containment, see Elaine Tyler May, *Homeward Bound: American Families in the Cold War Era* (New York: Basic Books, 1988); Jane Sherron de Hart, "Containment at Home: Gender, Sexuality, and National Identity in Cold War America," in *Rethinking Cold War Culture*, ed. Peter Kuznick and James Gilbert (Washington, D.C.: Smithsonian Institution Press, February, 2001), 124–155; Donna Penn, "The Sexualized Woman: The Lesbian, the Prostitute, and the Containment of Female Sexuality in Postwar America," in *Not June Cleaver: Women and Gender in Postwar America*, ed. Joanne Meyerowitz (Philadelphia: Temple University Press, 1994), 358–381; and A. Yvette Huginnie, "Containment and Emancipation: Race, Class, and Gender in the Cold War West," in *The Cold War American West, 1945–1989*, ed. Kevin J. Fernlund (Albuquerque: University of New Mexico Press, 1998).

5. Nation Building at Home and Abroad

1. Statement of Helen L. Peterson before the Constitutional Rights Subcommittee, September 1, 1961, Helen Peterson Correspondence Folder, Box 67, R-

NCAI; George McGovern, "The 'Inconvenient' Indian," unpublished ms., Folder 14, Box 134, AAIA-A; H. S. Mays family to Mrs. Franklin D. Roosevelt, July 14, 1961, Folder 12, Box 157, AAIA-A.

2. House Concurrent Resolution 108, August 1, 1953, U.S. *Statutes at Large*, 67 (1953), in *Documents of United States Indian Policy*, 3rd ed., ed. Francis Paul Prucha (Lincoln: University of Nebraska Press, 2000), 234; "Statement by the President," August 15, 1953, OF 121 (1) Indians, Box 618, OF 120-C, Official File, Central File, Dwight D. Eisenhower Papers (hereafter DDEP), Dwight D. Eisenhower Library, Abilene, Kans. In a phone conversation with Senator Arthur Watkins, Eisenhower noted that the "failure to consult with the Indians would be in effect forcing the Indians to accept something which might be entirely contrary to their own desires." Eisenhower wanted assurances that future legislation would not proceed "without consultation," a principle Watkins rejected. See transcript of Eisenhower's phone call with Watkins, August 14, 1953, File: Phone Calls, July–December 1953 (2), Box 5, DDE Diary Series, Ann Whitman File, 1953–1961, DDEP. The Democratic Party emphasized in its 1952 platform statement that "the American Indian should be completely integrated into the social, economic, and political life of the nation." See "Text of Democratic Party Platform for 1952 Race as Adopted by the Convention," *New York Times*, July 24, 1952, 16.

3. "In Fairness to the Indian," *New York Times*, August 12, 1953, 30; Oliver La Farge to William Zimmerman, October 16, 1953, Folder 5, Box 16, WZP; "Indian Land Sale Is Eased by U.S.," *New York Times*, June 27, 1955, 21; "Statement of Hon. Lee Metcalf before the Subcommittee on Indian Affairs of the House Interior and Insular Affairs Committee, 15 May 1959," Lee Metcalf Correspondence, Box 67, R-NCAI. On the passage and meaning of HCR 108, see Donald L. Fixico, *Termination and Relocation: Federal Indian Policy, 1945–1960* (Albuquerque: University of New Mexico Press, 1986), 91–102; Kenneth R. Philp, *Termination Revisited* (Lincoln: University of Nebraska Press, 2000), 168–75; and Larry W. Burt, *Tribalism in Crisis: Federal Indian Policy, 1953–1961* (Albuquerque: University of New Mexico Press, 1982), 19–47. In the end, roughly thirteen thousand Native Americans were "terminated" and 1,365,801 acres of trust land withdrawn from government supervision, representing about 3 percent of the Native American land base. See Paul Prucha, *The Great Father: The United States Government and the American Indians* (Lincoln: University of Nebraska Press, 1986), 348.

4. "NCAI Leaders Hold Meeting in Washington," *NCAI Bulletin* 5 (March 1959): 1, Folder 8, Box 141, AAIA-A; "Summary of Navajo Developments," February 1, 1950, U.S. Department of the Interior, Bureau of Indian Affairs, Navajo-Hopi File, RG 75, NA; *Congressional Record, House*, February 21, 1950, 2131.

5. Toby Morris to President Truman, October 19, 1951, Folder OF 6-C: Office of Indian Affairs (1950–1953), HSTP.

6. "Hoover Report Recommends Indian Office Transfer," *Washington Bulletin* (March 1949), AIP.

7. "Launching of 'Arrow,'" October 10, 1949, ARROW folder, Box 24, SMOF:PNF; Arnold Marquis, *Hollywood Quarterly* 4 (Summer 1950): 416, 418, 419. Tensions between ARROW and the NCAI led to a division in 1957, with the NCAI creating the NCAI Fund as its own fund.

8. John C. Rainier, "The National Congress of American Indians," June 16, 1951, reprinted in *Friends Intelligencer,* March 8, 1952, Folder 4, Box 16, WZP.

9. U.S. Congress, House, 76th Cong., 1st sess., April 26, 1939, House Joint Resolution 276, Submitted by Clark Burdick, Record Group Correspondence, Office of the Architect of the Capitol (hereafter RGC-OAC); U.S. Congress, House, 77th Cong., 1st sess., April 14, 1941, House Joint Resolution 176, Submitted by James O'Connor, RGC-OAC.

10. Leta Myers Smart to David Lynn, Capitol Architect, November 3, 1952, RGC-OAC. A year later Smart joked to Lynn that some of her associates were intent on getting rid of the statues "even if we have to get the communists to do it." Smart to Lynn, November 1, 1953, RGC-OAC; Leta Myers Smart to Joseph Morris, Managing Editor, *National Sculpture Review,* September 9, 1953, RGC-OAC; Leta Myers Smart, "Hold That Man!—Stay His Hand!" unpublished ms., RGC-OAC; Leta Myers Smart, "The Last Rescue," *Harper's* 219 (October 1959): 92. Representative August Johansen told Stewart, after he replaced Lynn as Capitol architect, that it was best to keep the statues out of the public eye, noting, "Maybe this is a good time to make peace with the Indians"; Johansen to Stewart, October 5, 1959, RGC-OAC. Vivien Green Fryd examines the rise and fall of *The Rescue* in *Art and Empire: The Politics of Ethnicity in the United States Capitol, 1815– 1860* (New Haven: Yale University Press, 1992), 94–105. See also Susan Schekel, *The Insistence of the Indian: Race and Nationalism in Nineteenth-Century American Culture* (Princeton: Princeton University Press, 1998), chap. 6.

11. Greenough quoted in Richard Drinnon, *Facing West: The Metaphysics of Indian-Hating and Empire-Building* (Minneapolis: University of Minnesota Press, 1980), 20 (for Drinnon's analysis of *The Rescue,* see 119–121); Arthur V. Watkins, "Termination of Federal Supervision: The Removal of Restrictions over Indian Property and Person," *Annals of the American Academy of Political and Social Science* 311 (May 1957): 55.

12. "Resume of the Emergency Conference of American Indians on Legislation"; and Banquet Meeting, February 26, 1954, Emergency Conference folder, Box 257, R-NCAI.

13. Joseph Garry, "A Declaration of Indian Rights," Emergency Conference Bulletin folder, Box 257, R-NCAI; Banquet Meeting, February 26, 1954; "Statement of Zuni Indian Veterans of World War II and the Korean Conflict," February 17, 1954, Emergency Conference Bulletin folder, Box 257, R-NCAI.

14. "Resume of the Emergency Conference of American Indians on Legislation"; Emergency Conference Session, February 27, 1954; "Address of Martin Vigil," February 27, 1954; "'Give It Back to the Indians' Aim of Chiefs' Parley Here," *Times-Herald*, February 26, 1954, Special Issues, Emergency Conference, General Materials folder; Address of Clarence Wesley, Emergency Conference Bulletin folder; and "Address by George Abbot, counsel for the House Committee on Interior and Insular Affairs," February 28, 1954, Emergency Conference Bulletin folder, Box 257, R-NCAI. On Garry's life and times, see John Fahey, *Saving the Reservation: Joe Garry and the Battle to Be Indian* (Seattle: University of Washington Press, 2001).

15. "Statement of the Council of the Pueblo of Isleta," January 27, 1954, Emergency Conference Bulletin folder; and "What Does Termination of Federal Trusteeship Mean to the Indian Peoples?" n.d., 2, General Material folder, Box 257, R-NCAI.

16. Jim Hayes to Lawrence Lindley, General Secretary, Indian Rights Association, Hayes Correspondence folder, Box 257, R-NCAI; Emergency Conference—Press Releases folder, Box 257, R-NCAI (UPI reporter, Garry statement).

17. Resolution No. 13: "Loyalty of Indians to U.S. Government," Proceedings 1949 folder, Box 2, R-NCAI; Resolution No. 20: "Condemning Un-American Activities and Movements," Resolutions and Policy Statements folder, 1954, Box 5, R-NCAI; NCAI Constitution, 1955, Constitution and By-laws folder, Box 1, Helen Peterson Papers (hereafter HPP), National Museum of the American Indian, Smithsonian Institution.

18. Ruth Bronson to Napoleon Johnson, April 10, 1950; and Napoleon Johnson to Ruth Bronson, April 13, 1950, Judge Johnson Correspondence folder, Box 65, R-NCAI.

19. John Cragun to Charles Luce, Esq., August 16, 1956; and Helen Peterson to Charles F. Luce, Esq., August 10, 1956, Libel Matter folder, Box 11, HPP; Helen Peterson to Louis Bruce Jr., January 25, 1957, NCAI Membership and Financial Documents folder, Box 13, HPP.

20. Charles Coe to National Congress of American Indians, November 14, 1957; and *Facts for Farmers* (May 1954), Subversive Organizations: Attorney General's List, 1957–1958, 1960 folder, Box 166, R-NCAI.

21. Helen Peterson to Charles Coe, Editor, November 19, 1957; and Peterson to Letitia Shankle, November 19, 1957, Subversive Organizations: Attorney General's List, 1957–1958, 1960 folder, Box 166, R-NCAI.

22. Hilda Cragun to Charles Skippon, January 22, 1958, Subversive Organizations: Attorney General's List, 1957–1958, 1960 folder, Box 166, R-NCAI; M. Muller-Fricken et al. to National Congress of American Indians, December 12, 1957, ibid. The group sent a similar letter to the U.S. Congress. Skippon for-

warded Cragun's letter and the German group's letter to the State Department's Bureau of German Affairs; see Department of State Reference Slip, January 28, 1958, ibid. Cragun suggested that the European group might have learned about the NCAI from a United States Information Agency film shot in Utah in 1956. Cragun continued to forward to government officials material the NCAI considered subversive. For example, she forwarded a letter from a member of Youth against the House Un-American Activities Committee to a HUAC representative in 1960; Hilda Cragun to Steve Kopunek, February 1, 1960, Subversive Organizations: Attorney General's List, 1957–1958, 1960 folder, Box 166, R-NCAI.

23. For coverage of the NAACP and the Cold War, see Mary L. Dudziak, *Cold War Civil Rights: Race and the Image of American Democracy* (Princeton: Princeton University Press, 2000), 29, 67; Penny M. Von Eschen, *Race against Empire: Black Americans and Anticolonialism, 1937–1957* (Ithaca, N.Y.: Cornell University Press, 1997); and Manning Marable, *Race, Reform, and Rebellion: The Second Reconstruction in Black America, 1945–1990* (Jackson: University of Mississippi Press, 1991), 24, 28, 30, 58.

24. "Minutes of the Special Meeting of the Colville Business Council," November 14, 1947; Lucy Seymour Swan to Secretary of the Interior, February 23, 1953; "Minutes of Meeting, Nespelem," March 21, 1953; and "Minutes of the Special Meeting of the Colville Business Council," August 21, 1950, file 8026-1946-Colville-054, pt. 1, Box 12, RG75, NA; Frank Moore, "Behind the Buckskin Curtain, Part 2," *Republic Independent,* April 25, 1957, file 14300-1948-Colville-054, Box 18, RG75, NA.

25. "Frank George Talk to the Colville Business Council," August 14, 1953, file 6555-1952-Colville-053, Box 9; and "Minutes of the Regular Meeting of the Colville Business Council," January 11, 1951, file 8026-1946-Colville-054, pt. 2, Box 12, RG75, NA.

26. "Indians Working Towards Independent Status," *Republic Independent,* n.d. (ca. 1957), file 14300-1948-Colville-054, Box 18, RG75, NA; Alexandra Harmon, "American Indians and Land Monopolies in the Gilded Age," *Journal of American History* 90 (June 2003): 109.

27. Joe Garry speech, November 21, 1954, Dictabelt Transcripts of Proceedings, 1954 folder, Box 5, R-NCAI. The termination acts were passed in 1954, though they did not take effect until 1961. On Klamath termination, see Theodore Stern, *The Klamath Tribe: A People and Their Reservation* (Seattle: University of Washington Press, 1965). On Menominee termination, see Nicholas C. Peroff, *Menominee DRUMS: Tribal Termination and Restoration, 1954–1974* (Norman: University of Oklahoma Press, 1982). On Menominee sociological divisions, see George and Louise Spindler, *Dreamers without Power: The Menomini Indians* (New York: Holt, Rinehart and Winston, 1971). The Colville termination case prompted

Ruth Packwood Scofield to publish a book in 1972 supportive of termination, *Americans behind the Buckskin Curtain* (New York: Carlton Press, 1972). The book attacked John Collier and Native traditions as communistic.

28. President's Press Conference, April 7, 1954, Dwight D. Eisenhower Library, http://www.nps.gov/archive/eise/quotes2.htm; Question 36, Final Exam, American Indian Development Workshop, 1970, Teaching materials/workshops folder, Box 30, HPP.

29. "U.S. Information Policy with Regard to Anti-American Propaganda," November 13, 1947, Records Relating to International Information Activities, 1938–1953, Box 121, General Records of the State Department (RG59), National Archives, College Park, Md.; "Summary Review: III. Communist Bloc propaganda," Box 4159, Central Decimal File (hereafter CDF), 1955–1959, RG 59, NA; "Answers to Readers' Questions: TRAGEDY OF INDIANS IN U.S.A.," *Current Digest of the Soviet Press* (Joint Committee on Slavic Studies) 3 (September 22, 1951): 28. See also "A Review by A. Pushkin of John Tanner's Narrative," *Pravda*, June 6, 1949, 2, reprinted in *Current Digest of the Soviet Press* 1 (July 5, 1949): 25; "'Geht die Sonne nicht mehr auf?' fragt Häuptling 'Aufgehende Sonne,'" *USA in Wort und Bild* 5 (1954), Folder 10, Box 134, AAIA-A. Chief Rising Sun's real name, it seems, was Alzamon Ira Lucas I; whether he had American Indian heritage remains a subject of debate.

30. "Army Paper's Views on American History—Concluded," *Krasnaya zvezda*, June 27, 1957, reprinted in *Current Digest of the Soviet Press* (August 28, 1957): 35, 15.

31. "Point Four Program in Relation to Dependent Areas," in *Documentary History of the Truman Presidency*, vol. 27, *The Point Four Program*, general ed. Dennis Merrill (Bethesda, Md.: University Publications of America, 1999), 143, 146; Lakshman Senevivatne, "Washington's Color Bar," *Ceylon Observer*, May 21, 1949, File 811.4016 5–2549, Box 4685, CDF, 1945–1949, RG 59, NA; J. Graham Parsons to Department of State, February 8, 1957, File 592.51J/2-857, Box 2263, CDF, 1955–1959, RG 59, NA. A. D. Mani, who reported on American race relations for readers in Bombay from New York City, summarized the efforts of Truman's Committee on Civil Rights, noting the denial of suffrage to "(American) Indian residents of the states of Arizona and New Mexico." See "The U.S.A. Is Fighting Racialism," enclosure no. 4 to despatch no. 575, John J. MacDonald, American Consul General, Bombay, India, to Secretary of State, November 5, 1947, File 811.4016/11-547, Box 4685, CDF, 1945–1949, RG 59, NA.

32. "Semi-Annual Report on the International Educational Exchange Program," American Embassy, Karachi, to the Department of State, September 14, 1956, File 511.90D3/9-1456, Box 2227, RG 59, NA.

33. Raymond Davis, Assistant to the Secretary of the Interior, to White House Staff Secretary, January 27, 1955, File: Bureau of Indian Affairs—Information and Public Relations, pt. 1, Box 313, CCF, 1954–1958, Records of the Office of the Secretary of the Interior (RG48), NA; C. Edward Wells to the Department of State, May 20, 1954, File 511.883/5-2054, Box 2216, CDF, 1955–1959, RG 59, NA; "Cultural Programs," in "A Preliminary Fact Book on India," August 19, 1957, Special Reports 1957, Box 14, Records of the United States Information Agency (RG306), NA. For a brief description of McCombs's travels to Lebanon, see Armin H. Meyer to the Department of State, January 17, 1955, File 511.83a3/1-1755, Box 2216, CDF, 1955–1959, RG 59, NA. Meyer wrote that "curiosity about American Indians in general, and the opportunity to see one, were perhaps as important as drawing cards as were the paintings themselves." Frances Saunders briefly discusses U.S. efforts to ban Fast's work in *The Cultural Cold War: The CIA and the World of Arts and Letters* (New York: New Press, 1999), 191, 194.

34. Alexander B. Daspit to the Department of State, Washington, D.C., April 4, 1956, File 511.90D3/4-456, Box 2227, CDF, 1955–1959, RG 59, NA. The State Department singled out three members of the IEEP as "resoundingly successful": Dr. Jan Karski, who lectured on communism and democracy; Bob Mathias, the Olympic decathlon champion; and Two Arrows. See "Semi-Annual Report on the International Educational Exchange Program," American Embassy, Karachi, to the Department of State, September 14, 1956, File 511.90D3/9-1456, Box 2227, CDF, 1955–1959, RG 59, NA. Congress hesitated to spend "entertainment money" on Two Arrows's tours, but State Department officials explained to House Appropriations Committee members that his first tour had succeeded in "an area where the [diplomatic] missions are practically nonexistent," justifying the expenditure because of "a great interest abroad in the American Indian." See "American Indian Culture," *Congressional Record, House*, July 12, 1956, 11389.

35. "Report from Kuala Lumpur," May 3, 1957, Daniel V. Anderson to Department of State, January 21, 1957, File 032-Tucson, Two Arrows, Tom/1-2157, RG 59, NA; John P. McKnight to Department of State, Washington, D.C., December 21, 1956, File 032 Two Arrows, Tom/12-21 56, CDF, 1955–1959, RG 59, NA; Paul Neilson to the Department of State, June 7, 1957, File 032 Two Arrows, Tom/6-757, CDF, 1955–1959, RG 59, NA. The Tehran embassy requested that Two Arrows visit Iran, but he did not.

36. Alexander B. Daspit to the Department of State, Washington, D.C., April 4, 1956, File 511.90D3/4-456, Box 2227, CDF, 1955–1959, RG 59, NA.

37. James C. Flint, USIS-Lahore, to USIA-Washington, D.C., May 7, 1956, File 032 Two Arrows, Tom/5-756, CDF, 1955–1959, RG 59, NA; William L. S. Williams to the Department of State, Washington, D.C., May 28, 1956, File

511.90D3/5-2856, Box 2227, CDF, 1955–1959, RG 59, NA; Arthur Z. Gardiner to the Department of State, Washington, D.C., August 25, 1956, File 511.90D3/8-2556, Box 2227, CDF, 1955–1959, RG 59, NA.

38. R. Borden Reams to the Department of State, March 8, 1956, File 032 Two Arrows, Tom/3-856 CS/N, CDF, 1955–1959, RG 59, NA.

39. *Calcutta Statesman*, January 24, 1956, 1; "On the Trail of Tom Two Arrows: 'Red Indians,'" *Hindustan Times*, January 29, 1956, 5; Burhanuddin Hassan, "Tom Two Arrows: Man and His Art," *Pakistan Times*, April 1, 1956, 8. Hassan's comment stemmed in part from the fact that Two Arrows performed in "the most modern of American suits" since his traditional clothes had been lost en route. Two Arrows's exposure to Muslim and Hindu artists shaped his own art, as he created hybrid expressions drawn from the two similar styles. It is interesting to note that for some in India, the American Indian represented a step backward. Ten years earlier, on the eve of independence, Syud Hoosein, an Indian nationalist who promoted Westernization, called B. G. Horniman, a nationalist crusader along with Mahatma Gandhi, "the last of the Mohicans," suggesting that it was the task of Indian journalists to adopt and promote a new, modern outlook. See "Working Journalists in Danger of Being Hirelings," *Bombay Sentinel*, June 18, 1946, File 811.4016 6-2046, Box 4685, CDF, 1945–1949, RG 59, NA.

40. Hassan, "Tom Two Arrows," 8; "Tom Two Arrows in Lahore," *Pakistan Times*, March 25, 1956, 7; Donald Webster to the Department of State, December 19, 1956, File 032 Two Arrows, Tom/12-1956, RG 59, NA; Thomas E. Flanagan to the Department of State, March 22, 1956, File 032 Two Arrows, Tom/3–2256, RG59, NA; Dulles to Bombay et al., December 19, 1955, File 511.003/12-1955 CSBM, RG 59, NA; Dulles to Bangkok et al., August 28, 1956, File 032 Two Arrows, Tom/8-2856, RG 59, NA.

41. Dulles to Bombay et al., December 19, 1955; Reams to Department of State. For an excellent study of the Jazz Ambassadors, or Jambassadors, see Penny M. Von Eschen, *Satchmo Blows Up the World: Jazz Ambassadors Play the Cold War* (Cambridge, Mass.: Harvard University Press, 2004).

42. Glenn G. Wolfe to Department of State, October 5, 1959, "South African Comments on American Indian," file 811.411/10-559, Box 4159, CDF, 1955–1959, RG 59, NA; "Soviet Mourns Indians: Tribesmen in U.S. Facing Extinction, Radio Says," *New York Times*, February 16, 1958, 22; Carlos B. Embry, *America's Concentration Camps: The Facts about Our Indian Reservations Today* (New York: David McKay, 1956), 93, 137; Leonard Ware, "The American Indians: In Profile," Discussion Paper on Minorities no. 5, n.d. (ca. 1958), file 811.411/12-458, Box 4159, CDF, 1955–1959, RG 59, NA. For a "Summary Review" of racism's "Impact on Foreign Relations," see John A. Calhoun to Gerald D. Morgan, "Request from

the Civil Rights Commission," December 31, 1958, file 811.411/12–458, Box 4159, CDF, 1955–1959, RG 59, NA. The State Department generated an enormous archive of material relating to the impact of race on the U.S. government's efforts to address domestic racism. The archive contains much less material on "the Indian problem" than the voluminous material on "the Negro problem." Tom Two Arrows's campaign dominates these files. Other records report on complaints or warnings sent from citizens abroad. Dr. Emily Babb of Massachusetts, for example, forwarded to the State Department a letter from an American friend writing from Ahmednagar, India, commenting on the need for the U.S. government to change its policies toward American Indians because of international concerns. See Acting Secretary to Dr. Emily A. Babb, October 22, 1958, Box 4159, File 811.411/10-2358, CDF, 1955–1959, RG 59, NA.

43. Ware, "The American Indians: In Profile"; "Senate Concurrent Resolution 3: Statement of the Shoshone-Bannock Tribes, Inc.," May 10, 1957, Folder 2, Box 315, AAIA-A. Frank Parker of the Fort Hall Tribal Council repeated these themes to a congressional committee visiting the Fort Hall Reservation in October 1957; see "Further Statement of Frank W. Parker, Chairman, Fort Hall Tribal Council," Hearings before a Special Indian Subcommittee of the Committee on Interior and Insular Affairs, House of Representatives, 85th Cong., 1st sess., October 15, 1957 (Washington, D.C.: GPO, 1957), 92.

44. "1952: April 8: Point Four—Read by Secretary Dean Acheson," Folder: Presidential Addresses, Letters and Messages, Box 200, PSF: Historical File, 1945–1953, HSTP.

45. "A Ten-Point Program for American Indians," July 1951, Speeches 1951 folder, Box 3, R-NCAI; D'Arcy McNickle, "U.S. Indian Affairs—1953," America Indigena 13 (October 1953): 273 (published in English, summarized in Spanish), Folder 85, Box 10, D'Arcy McNickle Papers (hereafter DMP), Newberry Library, Chicago. McNickle based his American Indian Point Four program on the federal government's Point Four program, but he also studied other countries' experiences with economic development. See McNickle to Delbert Clark, Fund for Adult Education, March 16, 1953, 1953 Workshop correspondence: Folder 198, Box 23, DMP. On McNickle's Point Four inspirations, see Harold Edward Fey and D'Arcy McNickle, Indians and Other Americans: Two Ways of Life Meet (New York: Harper & Brothers, 1959), 197–200; Dorothy R. Parker, Singing an Indian Song: A Biography of D'Arcy McNickle (Lincoln: University of Nebraska Press, 1992), 175–176; and Thomas Cowger, The National Congress of American Indians: The Founding Years (Lincoln: University of Nebraska Press, 1999), 108–109, 117–118. The NCAI took note of U.S. congressmen who supported rehabilitation, as one did in arguing that "Indians need just the kind of help that is being given by U.S. money

to backward nations, that the Indian program would cost far less than we are spending on strangers, and that the Indians are deserving of help"; quoted in NCAI *Washington Bulletin* (October–November 1951), Folder 3, Box 16, WZP.

46. "Proposal for Elements to Be Included in a 'Point Four Program for American Indians,'" Reports, Reprints, News Releases and Clippings, 1955 folder, Box 6, R-NCAI; National Congress of American Indians press release, February 23, 1955, Press Releases folder, Box 11, HPP. In her speech at the convention Peterson argued that the United States should "begin to apply, at least on a small scale at home, what we have learned to be essential for our wellbeing as a nation among nations. Let us encourage an attitude and a program very much in the nature of a domestic point-four program with America's own conquered people"; HLP, 11-14-54, Speeches 1954 folder, Box 5, R-NCAI.

47. Joseph Garry to LaVerne Madigan, Executive Director, Association on American Indian Affairs, December 28, 1956, Folder 8, Box 141, AAIA-A; Carl Whitman, speech draft, March 15, 1956, Carl Whitman Correspondence folder, Box 69, R-NCAI.

48. "Aid for (American) Indians," *Boston Herald*, March 22, 1956, Folder 6, Box 151, AAIA-A; "A Point Four Program for American Indians?" *Tribune* (Lewiston, Idaho), April 26, 1956; and "Our Misplaced Indians," *New York Daily News*, April 21, 1956, Folder 2, Box 315, AAIA-A.

49. Senate Concurrent Resolution 3 (SCR 3), "An American Indian Point Four Program," Folder 2, Box 315, AAIA-A. Murray introduced an earlier version, SCR 85, on July 6, 1956.

50. Richard Schifter (attorney for the Sioux) to Senator Richard L. Neuberger, July 29, 1957, Folder 2, Box 315, AAIA-A.

51. Hearings before the Subcommittee on Indian Affairs of the Committee on Interior and Insular Affairs, United States Senate, 85th Cong., 1st sess., on S. 809, S. Con. Res. 3, and S. 331 (Washington, D.C.: GPO, 1957), 3.

52. "Statement by William Langer in Support of S. 809" and "Statement by George McGovern, a representative in Congress from the State of South Dakota," ibid. McGovern sponsored a "companion resolution," House Concurrent Resolution 160. S. 809 earned bipartisan support, with eight Republican and twelve Democratic cosponsors, mostly from western states. Representatives of numerous chambers of commerce and state legislators supported S. 809, eager to get their hands on part of the proposed $200 million in funds.

53. "The So-Called Indian Point 4 Program—Letters" and "To the Congress of the United States of America," December 21, 1957, *Congressional Record, Senate*, 85th Cong. 2nd sess., 104, pt. 2, February 10, 1958, 1894–95; "Statement by Frank S. Ketcham, Attorney for the Board of Home Missions," Hearings before the Subcommittee on Indian Affairs of the Committee on Interior and Insular Affairs,

United States Senate, 85th Cong., 1st sess., on S. 809, S. Con. Res. 3, and S. 331, 149; Johnson quoted in "Point 4 Program for American Indians—Petition," *Congressional Record, House,* 85th Cong. 1st sess., 103, pt. 7, June 19, 1957, 9839. Senator Douglas introduced the letters only after the AAIA attorney attested that they were not "Communist-inspired." See Richard Schifter to LaVerne Madigan, February 13, 1958 Folder 2, Box 315, AAIA-A. Father Peter Powell, who worked with relocated American Indians in the Chicago Indian Center, passed them on to Senator Douglas saying they "reveal the international concern" about U.S. treatment of American Indians. "The So-Called Indian Point 4 Program—Letters."

54. "Senate Concurrent Resolution 3: Statement of the Shoshone-Bannock Tribes, Inc."; "Statement of Mrs. Vestana Cadue, Chairman, and Mrs. Minerva Spoone, Secretary, Kickapoo Tribe, Horton, Kans.," and "Statement by John Rainier, Vice Chairman, All-Pueblo Council of New Mexico," Hearings before the Subcommittee on Indian Affairs of the Committee on Interior and Insular Affairs, United States Senate, 85th Cong., 1st sess., on S. 809, S. Con. Res. 3, and S. 331, 101. See also "Further Statement of Frank W. Parker, Chairman, Fort Hall Tribal Council," Hearings before a Special Indian Subcommittee of the Committee on Interior and Insular Affairs, House of Representatives, 85th Cong., 1st sess., October 15, 1957 (Washington, D.C.: GPO, 1957), 92; and D'Arcy McNickle, "It's Almost Never Too Late," *Christian Century,* February 20, 1957, 229. In addition, Mrs. R. I. C. Prout, president of the General Federation of Women's Clubs, supported SCR 3 because "we are doing so much for the underprivileged of other nations while the plight of a group of our own people is so deplorable in many instances." See "Statement of Mrs. R. I. C. Prout, President, General Federation of Women's Clubs," Hearings before the Subcommittee on Indian Affairs of the Committee on Interior and Insular Affairs, United States Senate, 85th Cong., 1st sess., on S. 809, S. Con. Res. 3, and S. 331, 183.

55. "Statements of John W. Rainier, Attorney, National Congress of American Indians; and Mrs. Helen Peterson, Executive Director, National Congress of American Indians," Hearings before the Subcommittee on Indian Affairs of the Committee on Interior and Insular Affairs, United States Senate, 85th Cong., 1st sess., on S. 809, S. Con. Res. 3, and S. 331, 150; "Statement of Association on American Indian Affairs, Inc., on Senate Concurrent Resolution 3, presented to the Senate Subcommittee on Indian Affairs," May 13, 1957, Folder 2, Box 315, AAIA-A.

56. "Beam in Our Eye," *New York Times,* February 24, 1957, 178; Eleanor Roosevelt, "Point 4 Program for U.S. Indians Might Solve Their Problems," March 26, 1956, My Day Project: http://www.gwu.edu/~erpapers/myday/display doc.cfm?_y=1956&_f=md003441. Kimmis Hendrick, writing in the *Christian*

Science Monitor, called SCR 3 "an opportunity [for Americans] to prove to them-selves and the world that they can cure a great historical injustice"; Kimmis Hen-drick, "A Program for the First Americans," *Christian Science Monitor,* February 1, 1958, Folder 2, Box 315, AAIA-A.

57. Undersecretary of the Interior to Senator James E. Murray, July 1, 1957, Folder 2, Box 315, AAIA-A; "Economic Assistance to American Indians," *Con-gressional Record,* February 5, 1959, 1790; "Point Four for Indians Needed, Says McGovern," *Yankton Press and Dakotan,* June 17, 1959, Folder 2, Box 315, AAIA-A. See Larry Burt, "Factories on Reservations: The Industrial Development of Commissioner Glenn Emmons, 1953–1960," *Arizona and the West* 19 (Winter 1977): 317–332.

58. Clarence Wesley, "Guest Editorial," *AmerIndian: American Indian Review* (September–October 1957): 2. The editorial first appeared in the June 23, 1956, edition of the *Arizona Republic;* it was reprinted in the June 26, 1956, *Congres-sional Record* at the request of Senator Barry Goldwater.

59. See Michael L. Lawson, *Dammed Indians: The Pick-Sloan Plan and the Mis-souri River Sioux, 1944–1980* (Norman: University of Oklahoma Press, 1994).

60. Katrine Barber, *Death of Celilo Falls* (Seattle: University of Washington Press, 2005), 65, 32.

61. U.S. Congress, House Appropriations Committee, *Civil Functions, Depart-ment of the Army, Appropriations for 1952 Hearings, Part 1,* 82nd Cong., 1st and 2nd sess., 1951, 310, 178, 374, 682; quoted in Barber, *Death of Celilo Falls,* 91; Jim-mie James, "THINGS WE MUST REMEMBER," n.d. (ca. March 1953); Jimmie James to President Eisenhower, June 2, 1953; and Allen Chisholm, "???????????? SOME QUES-TIONS A DEMOCRACY MUST ANSWER," n.d. (ca. March 1953), DDEP, Central Files, General File, GF17-B-1, Box 311, Endorsement Chief Rising Sun. See also Jim-mie James to President Eisenhower, June 5, 1953. James asked Eisenhower to ap-point a Native American commissioner of Indian affairs "because through the world we are being watched, because we have gone out of our way to preach Lib-erty and Justice for all, and there can be no question but we are now in the real test, and here at home." Jimmie James to Hon. Dwight D. Eisenhower, March 17, 1953, DDE Papers, Central Files, General File, GF17-B-1, Box 311, Endorsement Chief Rising Sun.

62. Harold H. Healy Jr. (Executive Assistant to the U.S. Attorney General) to Bernard Shanley, Secretary to the President, May 8, 1957, Fred A. Seaton Papers (hereafter Seaton Papers), 1946–1972, Box 17, Kinzua Dam (Seneca Indians), Dwight D. Eisenhower Presidential Library; "Memorandum of Conference with the President," July 22, 1957, Ann Whitman File, DDE Diary Series, Box 25, Staff Memos, DDEP. On the Kinzua Dam controversy, see Joy A. Bilharz, *The Allegany Senecas and Kinzua Dam* (Lincoln: University of Nebraska Press, 2000).

63. U.S. Congress, House, Committee on Appropriations, *Public Works Appropriations for 1958* (Washington, D.C.: GPO, 1957), 1036, 1049–50; Hamlin quoted in Laurence Hauptman, *The Iroquois Struggle for Survival: World War II to Red Power* (Syracuse University Press, 1986), 102, 104.

64. "Seneca Indians Protest Huge Kinzua Dam Plan," *AmerIndian* 5 (May–June 1957), 1; Cornelius V. Seneca to Honorable Dwight D. Eisenhower, March 26, 1957; and George W. Alexander to the Honorable Dwight D. Eisenhower, March 27, 1957, Kinzua Dam (Seneca Indians), Box 17, Seaton Papers, 1946–1972.

65. Johnny Cash, *Bitter Tears: Ballads of the American Indian* (Columbia Records, 1964); "Sent to Various Politicians and Members," April 1957; and William Zimmerman, comment, *Washington Post*, August 12, 1957, Folder 29, Box 3, WZP.

66. "Candidates Speak Out on Indian Affairs," Association on American Indian Affairs, n.d. (ca. 1960), Folder: Clippings, Articles, General Indian, Box 12, Sol Tax Papers (hereafter STP), National Anthropological Archives, Smithsonian Institution, Suitland, Md.; *Washington Post* editorial, April 8, 1961, Folder: Clippings, Box 12, STP; Watt quoted in Edward Linn, "Rape of the Senecas," *SAGA Magazine*, Folder: Articles, Box 27, STP; Eleanor Roosevelt, "Moral Issue at Stake, in Senecas' Land-for-Dam Fight," *Philadelphia Daily News*, June 8, 1961, Box 91, PWSB; "Indians Working on Bill of Rights," *Milwaukee Journal*, June 15, 1961, Folder: Clippings, Box 12, STP. The 1960 Democratic platform stated, "Free consent of the Indian tribes concerned shall be required before the Federal Government makes any change in any Federal-Indian treaty or other contractual relationship." See http://presidency.ucsb.edu/ws/index.php?pid=29602.

67. Walter Taylor to Friends, re: American Indian Charter Convention, January 1961; Walter Taylor to Lee C. White, Assistant Special Counsel, August 24, 1961; Walter Taylor to Burt Aginsky et al., March 17, 1961, "Kinzua Dam: Operation Goliath"; and Walter Taylor to Honorable Henry S. Reuss, July 29, 1961, Kinzua Dam folder, STP; Walter Taylor, "The Treaty We Broke," *The Nation*, September 2, 1961, 121. Michael E. Latham examines American academics' sense of the promise of the New Frontier in *Modernization as Ideology: American Social Science and "Nation Building" in the Kennedy Era* (Chapel Hill: University of North Carolina Press, 2000).

68. John F. Kennedy to Basil Williams, August 9, 1961, Kinzua Dam folder, STP; *Fighting Tuscarora: The Autobiography of Chief Clinton Rickard*, ed. Barbara Graymont (Syracuse: Syracuse University Press, 1973), 154.

69. Ernest Benedict to American Civil Liberties Union, March 27, 1941, Folder 2, Box 123, A-AAIA; Ron-Aren-Kaien-Kwi, "An Appeal for Justice," *The Hand That Guided and Protected Your Ancestors Is Now Open to You for Justice!* (hereafter *The Hand*) (January 1948); and Julius Cook, "Does a Small Nation

Have the Right to Exist?" *The Hand* (January 1948), Six Nations Confederacy folder, Box 140, R-NCAI; Garrow quoted in Hauptman, *The Iroquois Struggle for Survival*, 58, 60.

70. "Fifth Avenue Trail Trod by Iroquois," *New York Times*, September 28, 1952, 29. On the delegation's visits to the United Nations, see "Iroquois See Vishinsky in Annual U.N. Protest," *New York Times*, October 24, 1950, 9; "Iroquois Draw U.N. Veto When They Call to Dance," *New York Times*, September 27, 1952, 19; "Iroquois at U.N. 'House of Peace,'" *New York Times*, January 31, 1957, 10. Clinton Rickard was the first commander of the VFW post established on the Tuscarora reservation in 1955.

71. Rickard, *Fighting Tuscarora*, 147; Edmund Wilson, *Apologies to the Iroquois* (New York: Farrar, Straus and Cudahy, 1960), 142–147, 150, 154. For Moses's and Rickard's comments, see Hauptman, *The Iroquois Struggle for Survival*, 167–168.

72. *SPA v. Tuscarora Indian Nation*, 80 S. Ct. 543 (1960); Rickard, *Fighting Tuscarora*, 152. Also see "Tuscaroras Vote to Yield Land to State, Ending 2-Year Fight," *New York Times*, August 14, 1960, 1.

73. *SPA v. Tuscarora Indian Nation*, 80 S. Ct. 543 (1960), reprinted in "Tuscarora's Lose Fight for Reservation," *Race of Sorrows* 5 (April 1960): 4, AIP.

74. "Redskins Bite the Dust Again," *Elizabeth Journal*, March 9, 1960, Tuscarora folder, Box 133, R-NCAI.

75. Clarence Wesley to Tribal Officials, n.d. (ca. March 1961), Folder 6, Box 59, AAIA-A; John F. Kennedy to Clarence Wesley, November 16, 1960, American Indian Charter Convention folder, Box 36, R-NCAI; Tax quoted in Walter Taylor, re: *American Indian Charter Convention*, January 1961, Folder 6, Box 59, AAIA-A. On the American Indian Chicago Conference, see James B. LaGrand, *Indian Metropolis: Native Americans in Chicago, 1945–1975* (Urbana: University of Illinois Press, 2002), 168–185; Parker, *Singing an Indian Song*, 187–193; Cowger, *The National Congress of American Indians*, 133–140; Laurence Hauptman and Jack Campisi, "The Voice of the Eastern Indians: The American Indian Chicago Conference of 1961 and the Movement for Federal Recognition," *Proceedings of the American Philosophical Society* 132 (November 1988): 316–329. Nancy Lurie, who attended the AICC, reprints some of the conference documents in "The Voice of the American Indian: Report on the American Indian Chicago Conference," *Current Anthropology* 2 (December 1961): 478–500.

76. Progress Report no. 4, "American Indian Chicago Conference 'Charter Convention'" folder, Box 148, R-NCAI.

77. Ibid.

78. Progress Report no. 6, June 7, 1961, "American Indian Chicago Conference 'Charter Convention'" folder, Box 148, R-NCAI; "Gallup, New Mexico, February 25, 1961," Progress Report no. 4, April 26, 1961; Progress Report no. 6.

79. Progress Report no. 4 (emphasis added).

80. L. A. Lauer, "An Open Letter to the American Indian Charter Convention," February 15, 1961, "Letters and Other Contributors to AICC from Non-Indians, Reference Material 1961" folder, Box 148, R-NCAI.

81. "Declaration of Indian Purpose: The Voice of the American Indian," 19–20, American Indian Chicago Conference, June 13–20, 1961, AICC Reports and Clippings folder, Box 10, HPP.

82. Hooks quoted in David Harvey, *Justice, Nature, and the Geography of Difference* (Malden, Mass.: Blackwell Publishing, 1996), 104; Devon Gerardo Pena, "Endangered Landscapes and Disappearing Peoples? Identity, Place, and Community in Ecological Politics," in *The Environmental Justice Reader: Politics, Poetics, and Pedagogy*, ed. Joni Adamson et al. (Tucson: University of Arizona Press, 2002), 72–73; Marie Potts, "AICC Steering Committee Meets in Chicago, April 26–30," *NCAI Bulletin*, May 1961, AIP.

83. For relocation figures, see Stephen Cornell, *The Return of the Native: American Indian Political Resurgence* (Oxford: Oxford University Press, 1988), 131.

84. Homi K. Bhabha, "DissemiNation: Time, Narrative, and the Margins of the Modern Nation," in *Nation and Narration*, ed. Homi K. Bhabha (London: Routledge, 1990), 291; Ernest Renan, "What Is a Nation," ibid., 19.

6. The Last Indian War

1. E. E. Hagen and Louis C. Schaw, *The Sioux on the Reservation: the American Colonial Problem*, preliminary ed. (Cambridge: Massachusetts Institute of Technology Center for International Studies, 1960), i, 2–18.

2. Ibid., ii, 6–38.

3. Bad River Band of Chippewa Indians, "A Declaration of War," November 10, 1959, Records of the Wisconsin Conservation Commission, Box 419, Folder 4, Wisconsin Historical Society, Madison (my thanks to Jim Oberly for the citation); Mel Thom, "Indian War 1963," *American Aborigine* 3 (n.d. [ca. 1963]): 2, AIP.

4. Affiliated Tribes of Northwest Indians Annual Convention, Senate Sub-Committee, 2, Folder: Affiliated Tribes of Northwest Indians, 1957–1975, Box 139, R-NCAI; "Editorial Comment RPAE" and "CE Bust," *Rainbow People* 1 (1971), AIP; "Some of the Efforts of United Native Americans," *The Warpath* 1 (Fall 1969): 2, AIP; "U.S. Suppresses Indians," *The Warpath* 1 (n.d.), AIP; Alexis Wolf to U.N. Undersecretary C. V. Nrasimhan, July 14, 1973, Wounded Knee, S.D., File 4, Series 271, Box 1, United Nations Archives (hereafter UNA). The *Cherokee Examiner* supported the "Arab Liberation Movement" and promoted the idea that "everyone has a right to their nationality, and to the lands of their forefa-

thers"; "Indians for National Liberation," *Rainbow People* 1 (July 28, 1971): 18, AIP.

5. Affiliated Tribes of Northwest Indians Executive Council Meeting Resolution no. 2, May 16, 1970, Folder: Affiliated Tribes of Northwest Indians, 1957–1975, Box 139, R-NCAI.

6. "Editorial," *NCAI Sentinel* 11 (Winter 1966), NCAI Sentinel, Box 37, HPP; Blatchford quoted in Stan Steiner, *The New Indians* (New York: Dell, 1968), 30; Juanita Grace, "The Fail-Safe Weapon," *The Raven Speaks* 4 (July 7, 1971), AIP.

7. *SPA v. Tuscarora Indian Nation*, 80 S. Ct. 543 (1960), reprinted in "Tuscarora's Lose Fight for Reservation," *Race of Sorrows* 5 (April 1960): 4, AIP; Earl Boyd Pierce to Honorable Hugo L. Black, March 16, 1960; and Robert Yellowtail, "The Tuscarora Decision," n.d., Tuscarora folder, Box 133, R-NCAI.

8. "N.Y. Indians March before White House," *New York Herald-American*, March 20, 1959, Box 91, PWSB; "NCAI Criticizes Indian March on White House," *NCAI Bulletin* 5 (March 1959): 3–4, Folder 8, Box 141, A-AAIA; "National Congress of American Indians: Extension of Remarks of Hon. Quentin Burdick," March, 20, 1959, *Congressional Record*, Appendix (1959), A2473.

9. Harry A. Kersey Jr., "The Havana Connection: Buffalo Tiger, Fidel Castro, and the Origins of Miccosukee Tribal Sovereignty, 1959–1962," *American Indian Quarterly* 25 (Fall 2001): 499. Kersey found no direct connection between the BIA's actions and State Department promptings, but it seems likely that the department would have tried to contain Cuba's influence in Native American affairs.

10. "Candidates Speak Out on Indian Affairs," Association on American Indian Affairs, n.d. (ca. 1960), Folder: Clippings, Articles, General Indian, STP; Vine Deloria Jr., *Behind the Trail of Broken Treaties: An Indian Declaration of Independence* (Austin: University of Texas Press, 1974), 21.

11. "Articles of Incorporation," American Indian Development, Inc., Folder 188, DMP; D'Arcy McNickle, AID Report, 1952, Folder 191, DMP; American Indian Development brochure, 1952, Folder 195, DMP. McNickle received financial support from the Marshall Field Foundation, the Bureau of Catholic Indian Missions, and the Daughters of the American Revolution and various other women's groups. AID's management team included Viola Pfrommer, who had worked with indigenous groups in El Salvador and with Mexican Indian leadership programs.

12. "Leadership Training," n.d., Folder 192, DMP; Helen Peterson to Edward Posey Whiteman, October 10, 1958, Folder: Crow, 1957–1958, Box 105, R-NCAI; "Aims and Policies of the Workshop," *American Indian Workshop Bulletin* (December 1959), Folder 194, DMP. The Workshop on American Indian Affairs began in

1956 under the direction of Sol Tax, professor of anthropology at the University of Chicago; AID staff assumed responsibility in 1960.

13. "College Workshop on American Indian Affairs, Reading List and Course Outline, 1965," Workshops, 1965 Reading List and Course Outline, Box 30, HPP.

14. Clyde Warrior, "Where Peoples Meet," 4; Frank Dukepoo, "7/15/62," 1; Angela Russell, "Indian Nationalism," 3; and Sandra Johnson, "Heredity, Race and Society," 2, Workshops, Student Papers 1962, HPP; Sandra Johnson, "Final Conclusions," 2, AID Workshops, Box 30, Workshops 1964, Miscellaneous Papers and Exams, HPP. Gloria Keliiaa complained that too many students condemned the BIA and rejected the colonialism argument, which she called "an argument that is too old" (2); Workshops, Student Papers 1962, HPP.

15. Editorial, *The Indian Progress* 4 (July 17, 1961): 2; and Editorial, *The Indian Progress* 7 (July 23, 1962): 2 (emphasis added), Folder 194, DMP.

16. D'Arcy McNickle to David Aberle, February 8, 1966, Folder 207, DMP; D'Arcy McNickle to Robert K. Thomas, November 14, 1963, Folder 204, DMP; Robert K. Thomas to D'Arcy McNickle, April 22, 1964, Folder 205, DMP; Warrior quoted in Steiner, *New Indians*, 16.

17. Mel Thom, "Future of Indian America," 1964, Folder 30, Box 5, Papers of the National Indian Youth Council (hereafter P-NIYC), Center for Southwest Research, University Libraries, University of New Mexico; Mel Thom to D'Arcy McNickle, May 15, 1964, Folder 205, DMP.

18. Mel Thom, "Indian Youth Councils," *Indian Voices* (September 1963), AIP; "All in the Day's Work," newsletter of the Southwestern Association on Indian Affairs (January 1959); "Report of the Executive Secretary for 1958," Folder 19, Box 19, P-NIYC. The New Mexico Association on Indian Affairs changed its name to the Southwestern Association on Indian Affairs in 1959.

19. NIYC public relations brochure, n.d., Folder 16, Box 1, P-NIYC; Mel Thom, "Future of Indian America," 1964, Folder 30, Box 5, P-NIYC; "National Indian Youth Council ABC Publication Project," n.d., P-NIYC Box 1, Folder 44, Box 1, P-NIYC.

20. Mel Thom, "Indian War 1963," *Aborigine* (n.d. [ca. 1963]): 2, AIP (the NIYC changed the name to *American Aborigine* in 1964); Mel Thom, "Indian War 1964," *Aborigine* (n.d. [ca. 1964]): 5, 7, AIP.

21. Alvin Josephy Jr. to Mel Thom, June 10, 1965, Folder 19, Box 2, P-NIYC; To Directors, Members, and Subscribers," May 26, 1964, Folder 19, Box 4, P-NIYC. One finds numerous mentions of Kinzua and the Seneca in a range of writings. An unpublished essay drew the lesson from Kinzua that "the old boogieman, termination, is after us again"; C. Thundercloud, "1964—So Far," Shirley Hill Witt Papers, University of New Mexico, Box 3, Folder 5, Center for Southwest Research, University Libraries, University of New Mexico. A poem published in

1968 read in part: "The word of cornplanter and washington is run thru by the unfeathered lance of progress and lake perfidy rises higher"; Chiron Khanshendel, poem dated January 10, 1967, *Many Smokes* (3rd Quarter 1967): 3, Carol Sullivan Wounded Knee Papers, Center for Southwest Research, University Libraries, University of New Mexico.

22. *Indian Voices* (November 1965): 13, Box 3, Folder 37, Shirley Hill Witt Papers, University of New Mexico; "National Indian Youth Council, Inc. 1961–1975," n.d., Folder 16, Box 1, P-NIYC; "Indian Youth Council Chooses New Officers," 1966, Folder 30, Box 3, P-NIYC; "Certificate of Incorporation of the National Indian Youth Council," 1962, Folder 1, Box 1, P-NIYC; "Uses of Red Power," *Kansas City Star,* March 1968, Folder 28, Box 2, P-NIYC.

23. Thom, "Indian War 1963," 4; Mel Thom, "Future of Indian America," 1964, Folder 30, Box 3, P-NIYC; "Warrior Testifies at Rural Poverty Hearing," *Americans before Columbus* (May 1967), Folder 5, Box 30, P-NIYC.

24. To: Members and Friends of N.I.Y.C., January 18, 1968, Folder 38, Box 1, P-NIYC.

25. Brando quoted in *Vernal Express,* n.d., Folder 15, Box 1, P-NIYC; Hunter S. Thompson, "The Catch Is Limited in Indians' Fish-In," *National Observer* (March 9, 1964): 13; "Washington State Indian Fishing Rights," ca. 1964, Folder: NIYC, Box 152, R-NCAI; William Meyer ('yonv'ut'sisla), *Native Americans: The New Indian Resistance* (New York: International Publishers, 1971), 72; Robert C. Lee, "Dick Gregory Goes Fishing," *The Nation,* April 25, 1966, 487; Carol Underwood, "Dick Gregory Blasts CIA in Lecture at Villanova," *Main Line Times,* March 20, 1969. See also Hank Adams, "The Washington State Project," October 15, 1964, Folder: NIYC, Box 152, R-NCAI. Sherry Smith examines non-Indians' contributions to treaty rights campaigns in the Pacific Northwest in "Indians, the Counterculture, and the New Left," in *Beyond Red Power: American Indian Politics and Activism since 1900,* ed. Daniel M. Cobb and Loretta Fowler (Santa Fe: School for Advanced Research, 2007), 142–160.

26. Thompson, "The Catch Is Limited in Indians' Fish-In," 13; Steiner, *New Indians,* 8–10.

27. Charles Wilkinson, *Messages from Frank's Landing: A Story of Salmon, Treaties, and the Indian Way* (Seattle: University of Washington Press, 2000), 30–31, 43 (Bridges quote), 32 (Frank quote); Sandra Johnson, "Guest Editorial," *Indian Voices* (February–March 1966), Folder 37, Box 3, Shirley Hill Witt Papers.

28. Wilkinson, *Messages from Frank's Landing,* 38; Janet McCloud, "The Last Indian War," pt. 2, n.d. (ca. 1965), Folder 18, Box 19, P-NIYC; Johnson, "Guest Editorial"; Dick Monaghan, "Nisqually War Quiets Down to Cease Fire," *Tacoma News Tribune,* February 14, 1962, Folder 19, Box 4, P-NIYC.

29. *Indian Survival Newsletter* (July 1966) and (March 1966), Folder 19, Box 5,

P-NIYC; "What We Request You To Do," n.d. (ca. 1966), Folder 19, Box 12, P-NIYC.

30. Don Matheson, "Summary," *Indian Survival Newsletter* (May 1966), Folder 19, Box 12, P-NIYC; Robert Casey, "Mississippi," *Survival News* (August–September 1966), Folder 19, Box 5, P-NIYC.

31. "To President Johnson, United Colonies of America," Folder 30, Box 5, P-NIYC; *Indian Survival Newsletter* (May 1966) and (March 1, 1966), Folder 19, Box 5, P-NIYC; Wilkinson, *Messages from Frank's Landing*, 46. Speaking to the commissioner of Indian affairs at a conference of tribal leaders in October 1966, Bruce Wilkie (Makah) asked the BIA simply to adhere to the position of Congress that "emphatically supports self-help, self-government, and self-determination in other parts of the world." "Statement of Makah Indian Tribe to Commissioner of Indian Affairs," October 18, 1966, Folder 30, Box 3, P-NIYC. "The Last Indian War" was reprinted in *The Catholic Worker* and other publications.

32. Bridges quoted in Wilkinson, *Messages from Frank's Landing*, 43; untitled statement, March 3, 1964, Folder 4, Box 19, P-NIYC; Janet McCloud to President Lyndon Johnson, September 12, 1965, Folder 12, Box 19, P-NIYC.

33. Darrell Houston, "Chief Steelhead's Way-Out War," *Argosy* (July 1966), Folder 5, Box 19, P-NIYC; Steiner, 62; "Columbia River Report," *Indian Survival Newsletter* (May 1966), Folder 5, Box 19, P-NIYC; Janet McCloud, "The Continuing 'Last Indian War,'" *Survival News* (1966), Folder 18, Box 19, P-NIYC; "The Draft and Your Rights," *Western Warrior* (October 1970), AIP. In 1966 SAIA changed the name of its journal from *Indian Survival Newsletter* to *Survival News*.

34. "Statement of (PFC) Sidney Mills, Yakima Indian, for Sunday, October 13, 1968," Folder: Survival of American Indians Association, Box 155, R-NCAI; Mike Layton, "Indian Says China 'Offers Better Life,'" *Seattle Post-Intelligencer*, June 7, 1972, C18.

35. Mark P. Bradley, *Imagining Vietnam and America: The Making of Postcolonial Vietnam, 1919–1950* (Chapel Hill: University of North Carolina Press, 2000), 47; Frances Fitzgerald, *Fire in the Lake: The Vietnamese and the Americans in Vietnam* (New York: Vintage, 1972), 491–492; Taylor quoted in Richard Drinnon, *Facing West: The Metaphysics of Indian-Hating and Empire-Building* (New York: New American Library, 1980), 368, 450; Jonathan Randal, "Marines Kill 61 Vietcong after a Defector's Tip, *New York Times*, January 16, 1967, 6; Ralph Blumenthal, "On a Delta River, a Test for Vietnamization," *New York Times*, February 17, 1970, 2; Meyer, *Native Americans,*, 75; Joe Starita, *The Dull Knifes of Pine Ridge: A Lakota Odyssey* (New York: Berkley Books, 1994), 279. American soldiers' practice of describing enemy racial groups as Indians began during the U.S.-Filipino War and continued into World War II, when GIs deemed fighting the Japanese "Indian fighting" and the Japanese "as good as the Indians ever were" at infiltration. See

John W. Dower, *War without Mercy: Race and Power in the Pacific War* (New York: Random House, 1986), 152. The "Buffalo Hunter" reference is found in Ronald B. Frankum Jr., *Like Rolling Thunder: The Air War in Vietnam, 1964–1975* (Lanham, Md.: Rowman and Littlefield, 2005), 96. In another example, the First U.S. Cavalry Division ran Operation Crazy Horse in 1966, suggesting an effort to track down the elusive Vietnamese-as-Sioux leader. See Gordon Rottman, *Vietnam Airborne* (Oxford: Osprey Publishing, 1990), 14.

36. "U.S. Jets Meet Heavy Fire in Attacks on Hanoi Area," *New York Times*, August 6, 1967, 1; Michael A. Elliott, *Custerology: The Enduring Legacy of the Indian Wars and George Armstrong Custer* (Chicago: University of Chicago Press, 2007), 36; John Clark Pratt, "The Lost Frontier: American Myth in the Literature of the Vietnam War," in *The Frontier Experience and the American Dream: Essays on American Literature*, ed. David Mogen et al. (College Station, Tex.: Texas A&M Press, 1989), 236; Robert Jay Lifton, "The U.S. as Blind Giant Unable to See What It Kills," *New York Times*, June 14, 1970, 14.

37. AP reporter quoted in Drinnon, *Facing West*, 459; Michael Herr, *Dispatches* (1977; rpt. Vintage Books, New York, 1991), 49, 61; Nicholas von Hoffman, "Indians Take Back an Island," *Washington Post*, December 5, 1969; Tom Hayden, *The love of possession is a disease with them* (Chicago: Holt, Rinehart and Winston, 1972), 5, 100; and see 98–118 for his extended comparison of the two contexts.

38. Takeshi Kaiko, *Into a Black Sun*, trans. Cecilia Segawa Seigle (New York: Kodanska International, 1980), 198–199; Halberstam quoted in Pratt, "The Lost Frontier," 241; John Wayne quoted in David Espey, "America and Vietnam: The Indian Subtext," *Journal of American Culture and Literature* (1994); Nelson quoted in Dotson Rader, "Who Were the Bad Guys?" *New York Times*, September 20, 1970, 119; Roxanne DeLory, "Wake Up, Whitey!" *The Red Snake* 1 (November 4, 1970), 4. Other Native Americans conflated the My Lai massacre and Native American massacres. See, for example, "Wounded Knee Is Repeated," *The Indian*, February 27, 1970, Folder: The Indian, Box 36, HPP.

39. M. Nersisyan, "Genocide Is Gravest Crime against Humanity," *Pravda*, April 24, 1965, reprinted in *Current Digest of the Soviet Press* 17 (May 19, 1965): 24–25; G. Kapralov, "Sequence after Sequence at the Festival: The Destruction of Myths," *Pravda*, July 23, 1971, reprinted in *Current Digest of the Soviet Press* 22 (August 17, 1971): 12. For coverage of the *Indianerfilme* genre, see Frank-Burkhard Habel, *Gojko Mitic, Mustangs, Marterpfahle: Die* DEFA-INDIANERFILME: Das Grosse Buch für Fans (Berlin: Schwarzkopf & Schwarzkopf, 1997); Gerd Gemunden, "Between Karl May and Karl Marx: The DEFA *Indianerfilme* (1965–1983)," *New German Critique* 82 (Winter 2001): 25–38. The *Times* of London reviewed DEFA films in a December 1975 article, "East Germany's Wounded Knee," declaring them "the best American Indian films in recent years"; Paul Moor, "East Germany's Wounded Knee," *Times* (London), December 4, 1975, 13.

40. Leroy TeCube, *Year in Nam: A Native American Soldier's Story* (Lincoln: University of Nebraska, 1999), 166–167; Tom Holm, *Strong Hearts, Wounded Souls: Native American Veterans of the Vietnam War* (Austin: University of Texas Press, 1996), 129, 9–10; Starita, *The Dull Knifes of Pine Ridge*, 279, 283; Woody Kipp, *Viet Cong at Wounded Knee: The Trail of a Blackfeet Activist* (Lincoln: University of Nebraska Press, 2004), 35–36, 43, 44, 47; Baldwin quoted in Manning Marable, *Race, Reform, and Rebellion: The Second Reconstruction in Black America, 1945–1990* (Jackson: University Press of Mississippi, 1991), 102.

41. Holm, *Strong Hearts, Wounded Souls*, 10, 118–119. Holm notes that the figure 42,000 is likely low, since army recruiters did not have a category of "American Indian." But even at that number, he argues, a much higher percentage of American Indians served than white Americans.

42. Press release, *Indian Voices* (April–May 1966), Folder 30, Box 3, P-NIYC; Mel Thom, Wisconsin Indian Leadership Conference, Folder: Great Lakes Inter-Tribal Council, Box 138, R-NCAI; Michael Connors, "My Lai and Indian Oppression," *Indian Council Talk 7* (December 1969): 1, *Indian Council Talk* folder, Box 152, R-NCAI. *Indian Council Talk* was published by the Wisconsin Indian Youth Council, a chapter of the National Indian Youth Council. The NIYC released a statement in April 1967 arguing that living as an Indian child in America was more dangerous than serving as a soldier in Vietnam; see "Life in America," April 2, 1967, Folder 31, Box 3, P-NIYC.

43. "To Editor," *Apache Drumbeat*, December 15, 1967, AIP. See also "Xmas Greetings to Servicemen," *Apache Drumbeat*, December 15, 1967, AIP.

44. Henry Hough to Robert McNamara, January 27, 1967; Johnny Belindo to Fred Harris, March 8, 1967; Henry Hough to All Who Are Interested in this Project, March 3, 1967; and Henry to John, n.d. (ca. March 1967), Folder: Indian All-Star Troupe to Entertain Troops in Vietnam, Box 149, R-NCAI.

45. Vine Deloria Jr., *Custer Died for Your Sins: An Indian Manifesto* (1969; rpt. New York: Macmillan, 1988), 28, 29, 50, 53, 77. Also see Todd Gitlin, *The Whole World Is Watching: Mass Media in the Making and Unmaking of the New Left* (Berkeley: University of California Press, 1980).

46. Vine Deloria Jr., "War between the Redskins and the Feds," *New York Times Magazine*, December 7, 1969, 49.

47. Paul Chaat Smith and Robert Allen Warrior, *Like a Hurricane: The Indian Movement from Alcatraz to Wounded Knee* (New York: New Press, 1996), 10; "Indians Again Claim Alcatraz"; Indians of All Tribes, "Proclamation: To the Great White Father and All His People," November 1969; and Patricia Silvas, "The Promise of Alcatraz," n.d., Folder: Alcatraz, Box 155, R-NCAI. A number of women participated in the occupation, including Vicky Santana (Blackfeet), Grace Thorpe (Sac and Fox), and Marilyn Miracle (Mohawk).

48. Meyer, *Native Americans*, 81; "Radio Free Alcatraz," *Indians of All Tribes*

Newsletter 1 (January 1970): 10, Folder: Alcatraz, Box 155, R-NCAI; Smith and Warrior, *Like a Hurricane*, 18; "Planning Grant Proposal to Develop an All Indian University," *Congressional Record*, March 5, 1970, 1692.

49. Quoted in Mark Hamilton Lytle, *America's Unfinished Wars: The Sixties Era from Elvis to the Fall of Richard Nixon* (Oxford: Oxford University Press, 2006), 311; "First and Last Americans," *Times* (London), March 11, 1970, 11; Henry Raynor, "Red Redskins and Pink Whites," *Times* (London), November 19, 1969, 8; Bradley H. Patterson Jr., *The Ring of Power: The White House Staff and Its Expanding Role in Government* (New York: Basic Books, 1988), 72. See also Troy Johnson, "The Occupation of Alcatraz Island: Roots of American Indian Activism," *Wicazo Sa Review* 10 (Autumn 1994): 71.

50. Smith and Warrior, *Like a Hurricane*, 24; Richard Oakes, "Alcatraz," *Indian Times* (June 1970): 2, Folder: Indian Times, Box 36, HPP; "Jane Fonda on the Warpath," *Times* (London), March 10, 1970, C10; "United Indians Invade Fort Lawton," *Indians of All Tribes Newsletter* 1 (1970): 1, Folder: Alcatraz, Box 155, R-NCAI.

51. "Indians Invade Mount Rushmore," *The Warpath* 4 (1971), AIP; "AIM Fact Sheet," n.d., 3, Folder 2, Box 1, Roger A. Finzel American Indian Movement Papers (hereafter RFAIM-P), 1965–1995, Center for Southwest Research, University Libraries, University of New Mexico; Kills Straight, "The Meaning of AIM," April 1972, Folder 2, Box 1, RFAIM-P.

52. "United Sioux Tribes Attack Crazy Horse Mt. Protectors," *The Warpath* 4 (1971); Winthrop Griffith, "The Taos Indians Have a Small Generation Gap," *New York Times*, February 21, 1971, 100; "'Let Us Develop a Model for the Former Colonial World . . .': Resolution Adopted 44 to 5 by Leaders of Thirty Tribes," in Steiner, *New Indians*, 297–298; "Marshall Plan Call by Indians," *Times* (London), August 24, 1972, 4. Henry W. Hough, NCAI Director of Research, documented the great range of Native American economic development programs facilitated by OEO monies, especially Indian Community Action Programs. See Henry W. Hough, *Development of Indian Resources* (Denver: World Press, 1967).

53. Dean J. Kotlowski, *Nixon's Civil Rights: Politics, Principle, and Policy* (Cambridge, Mass.: Harvard University Press, 2001), 193, 194, 200, 208; "President Nixon, Special Message on Indian Affairs," July 8, 1970, in *Documents of United States Indian Policy*, 3rd ed., ed. Francis Paul Prucha (Lincoln: University of Nebraska Press, 2000), 256–257. For coverage of Blue Lake, see William F. Deverell, "The Return of Blue Lake to the Taos Pueblo," *Princeton University Library Chronicle* 49 (Autumn 1987): 57–73; and R. C. Gordon-McCutchan, *The Taos Indians and the Battle for Blue Lake* (Santa Fe: Red Crane Books, 1995). On the period more broadly, see George Pierre Castile, *To Show Heart: Native American Self-Determination and Federal Indian Policy, 1960–1975* (Tucson: University of Arizona Press, 1998).

54. "Statement of Frank C. Carlucci before the Subcommittee on Indian Affairs," April 11, 1973, Folder 42, Box 29, P-NIYC; Nixon quoted in Hayden, *The love of possession*, 14. On détente as a reactive measure, see Jeremy Suri, *Power and Protest: Global Revolution and the Rise of Détente* (Cambridge, Mass.: Harvard University Press, 2003).

55. Kotlowski, *Nixon's Civil Rights*, 201, 209.

56. "The 20 Point Proposal of the Native Americans," Box 1, Folder 2, RFAIM-P; Carlucci quoted in Patterson, *Ring of Power*, 78. The Trail of Broken Treaties caravan typically is linked to AIM, which organized the protest. But it also involved the National Indian Brotherhood of Canada, the National Indian Youth Council, the newly formed Native American Rights Fund, the National American Indian Council, the National Council on Indian Work, National Indian Leadership Training, and the American Indian Committee on Alcohol and Drug Abuse. On the Trail of Broken Treaties protest and AIM's organization of it, see Deloria, *Behind the Trail of Broken Treaties*, 46–62; and Joane Nagel, *Red Power and the Resurgence of Indian Identity* (New York: Oxford University Press, 1997), 136–137, 166–171.

57. Kotlowski, *Nixon's Civil Rights*, 201; "Editorial copy," n.d., Folder 1, Box 3, P-NIYC; U.S. Congress, Senate, 94th Cong., 2nd sess., "Revolutionary Activities within the United States: The American Indian Movement," Hearing before the Subcommittee to Investigate the Administration of the Internal Security Act and Other Internal Security Laws of the Committee on the Judiciary, April 6, 1976 (Washington, D.C.: GPO, 1976), 2; Steve Hendricks, *The Unquiet Grave: The FBI and the Struggle for the Soul of Indian Country* (New York: Thunder's Mouth Press, 2006), 63–64. See also Nagel, *Red Power and the Resurgence of Indian Identity*, 177.

58. For coverage of the Wounded Knee occupation, see Smith and Warrior, *Like a Hurricane*.

59. "A Suspenseful Show of Red Power," *Time*, March 19, 1973, http://www.time.com/time/magazine/article/0,9171,906923,00.html; "Wounded Knee 1973," 13, n.d., Folder 7, Box 1, RFAIM-P.

60. Deloria, *Behind the Trail of Broken Treaties*, 80; C. V. Narasimhan, "Note for the Record," March 2, 1973 (Narasimhan summarized Bellecourt's statement); and "Representatives of American Indians Meet United Nations Correspondents," March 22, 1973, Wounded Knee, South Dakota, File 4, Series 271, Box 1, UNA; Department of State Telegram, Subj: Wounded Knee, May 1973, Box 3108, General Records of the Department of State, Subject Numeric Files 1970–1973, College Park, Md.

61. Hendricks, *The Unquiet Grave*, 69; Robert Burnette and John Koster, *The Road to Wounded Knee* (New York: Bantam Books, 1974), 235. During the 1960s Burnette, a World War II veteran, served as chairman of the Rosebud Sioux Tribal

Council and as executive director of the National Congress of American Indians; in 1972 he was national co-chairman of the Trail of Broken Treaties march on Washington.

62. Rolland Dewing, *Wounded Knee: The Meaning and Significance of the Second Incident* (New York: Irvington Publishers, 1985), 179–180; Victor Jackson, "Disorder at Wounded Knee," n.d., Folder 7, Box 1, RFAIM-P; Wilson quoted in B. D. Arcus, "Contested Boundaries: Native Sovereignty and State Power at Wounded Knee, 1973," *Political Geography* 22 (2003): 429; Martin Waldron, "U.S. Recalls Aide at Wounded Knee, *New York Times*, April 21, 1973, 11. See also John Kifner, "Indians at Wounded Knee Free 11 Held for 2 Days," *New York Times*, March 2, 1973, 1.

63. Trace A. DeMeyer, "A Series: 25 Years Later; Voices from Wounded Knee," *News from Indian Country* 12 (April 15, 1998): 8A; Starita, *The Dull Knifes of Pine Ridge*, 308; Kipp, *Viet Cong at Wounded Knee*, 48.

64. Black Elk quoted in Arcus, "Contested Boundaries," 415; Patterson, *Ring of Power*, 79.

65. Nixon aide quoted in Kotlowski, *Nixon's Civil Rights*, 216; Sneed quoted in Arcus, "Contested Boundaries," 424; Aaron Carton to Secretary Kurt Waldheim, March 5, 1973; "Mrs. Rose Daitman, March 8, 1973"; and Committee of Concern for the Traditional Indian to Secretary General, March 8, 1973, Wounded Knee, South Dakota, File 4, Series 271, Box 1, UNA. Members of the Seattle-based United Front for Defense against Political Repression protested the federal government's failure to honor treaties at Wounded Knee in their telegram to the United Nations; see Timothy Lynch to UN Genl. Assembly, March 3, 1973, Wounded Knee, South Dakota, File 4, Series 271, Box 1, UNA.

66. Burnette and Koster, *The Road to Wounded Knee*, 239; Patrick Brogan, "Wounded Knee Tense after Two Indians Die," *Times* (London), April 30, 1973, 4; Mrs. Dachine Rainer, "Siege of Wounded Knee," *Times* (London), March 15, 1973, 17.

67. Deloria, *Behind the Trail of Broken Treaties*, 81; Burnette and Koster, *The Road to Wounded Knee*, 244; Patterson, *Ring of Power*, 79.

68. Bill Zimmerman, *Airlift to Wounded Knee* (Chicago: Swallow Press, 1976), 7, 11; Marlon Brando, "That Unfinished Oscar Speech," *New York Times*, March 30, 1973, 39; "Petition by the Six Nation Iraquois [sic] Confederation Agency on Behalf of the Indians of the Oglala Nation," May 4, 1973, Wounded Knee, South Dakota, File 4, Series 271, Box 1, UNA.

69. "Representatives of American Indians Meet United Nations Correspondents," March 22, 1973, Wounded Knee, South Dakota, File 4, Series 271, Box 1, UNA; Deloria, *Trail of Broken Treaties*, 78.

70. AIM member quoted in Nagel, *Red Power and the Resurgence of Indian Iden-*

tity, 177; judge quoted in Starita, *The Dull Knifes of Pine Ridge*, 311; *Wounded Knee Legal Defense/Offense Committee Newsletter* 2 (August 6, 1974): 3, Folder 7, Box 1, RFAIM-P. For the congressional hearings on the occupation and associated documents, see "Occupation of Wounded Knee," U.S. Congress, Senate, 93rd Cong., 1st sess., *Hearings before the Subcommittee on Indian Affairs of the Committee on Interior and Insular Affairs*, June 16–17, 1973 (Washington, D.C.: GPO, 1974). On the FBI's infiltration of AIM, see Ward Churchill and Jim Vander Wall, *Agents of Repression: The FBI's Secret Wars against the Black Panther Party and the American Indian* Movement (Cambridge, Mass.; South End Press, 2002). On the trials of Wounded Knee activists, see John William Sayer, *Ghost Dancing the Law: The Wounded Knee Trials* (Cambridge, Mass.: Harvard University Press, 1997).

71. Monica Charles, "1973 Handbook on Indian Warfare: *U.S. v. Washington*," *Lummi Squol Quol* 1 (November–December 1973), Folder 35, Box 2, P-NIYC.

72. Johnson, "Guest Editorial"; Charles Wilkinson, *Blood Struggle: The Rise of Modern Indian Nations* (New York: W. W. Norton, 2005), 163, 52, 49–50.

73. "Statement of Frank C. Carlucci before the Subcommittee on Indian Affairs," April 11, 1973, Folder 42, Box 29, P-NIYC; David M. Fishlow, "ACLU's Responsibility: The Indian Dilemma," *Civil Liberties* (June 1973), Folder 35, Box 2, P-NIYC.

74. Opinion by Honorable George H. Boldt, *United States v. State of Washington*, 384 F. Supp 312 (St. Paul: West Publishing, 1975), 323, 357. In a unanimous decision the Ninth Circuit Court of Appeals upheld Boldt's decision.

75. Ibid., 315, 329.

76. Wilkinson, *Messages from Frank's Landing*, 55–56; Ralph Johnson, "Indian Treaties Cannot Be Ignored," *Seattle Post-Intelligencer*, December 13, 1976, B2; William L. Dwyer, "Remarks at the Federal Bar Association Banquet Honoring Judge George H. Boldt," in *Ipse Dixit: How the World Looks to a Federal Judge* (Seattle: University of Washington Press, 2007), 5, 8; Opinion by Honorable George H. Boldt, 329; *Lone Wolf v. Hitchcock*, 187 U.S. 553 (1903), http://caselaw.lp.find law.com/scripts/getcase.pl?court=US&vol=187&invol=553. Some legal scholars argue that the Boldt Decision is "the most significant ruling on Indian treaty law in the past century"; see Lewis Kamb, "Boldt Decision 'Very Much Alive' 30 Years Later," *Seattle Post-Intelligencer*, February 12, 2004, http://seattlepi.nwsource .com/local/160345_boldt12.html. On the Boldt Decision, see Alexandra Harmon, *Indians in the Making: Ethnic Relations and Indian Identities around Puget Sound* (Berkeley: University of California Press, 1998), 230–244.

77. "Boldt Shocked by Fishermen's Violence," *Seattle Post-Intelligencer*, 1978, NCAI Committees and Special Issues—Boldt Decision—1, Box 199, R-NCAI; Opinion by Honorable George H. Boldt, 330; *SPA v. Tuscarora Indian Nation*, 80 S. Ct. 543 (1960).

Epilogue

Nicholas Kristof, "Poems of Blood and Anger," June 9, 2004, http://www.nytimes.com/2004/06/09/opinion/poems-of-blood-and-anger.html.

1. "Indian Policy: Statement of Ronald Reagan," January 24, 1983, in *Documents of United States Indian Policy*, 3rd ed., ed. Francis Paul Prucha (Lincoln: University of Nebraska Press, 2000), 303; "Address by Robert Yellowtail in Defense of the Rights of the Crow Indians, and Indians Generally, before the Senate Subcommittee on Indian Affairs, September 9, 1919," in *Talking Back to Civilization: Indian Voices from the Progressive Era*, ed. Frederick E. Hoxie (Boston: Houghton Mifflin, 2001), 135; *United States v. Wheeler*, March 22, 1978, in Prucha, *Documents of United States Indian Policy*, 286. On self-determination, see Guy Senese, *Self-Determination and the Social Education of Native Americans* (Westport, Conn.: Praeger, 1991); and George Pierre Castile, *Taking Charge: Native American Self-Determination and Federal Indian Policy, 1975–1993* (Tucson: University of Arizona Press, 2006).

2. Patty Loew, "Hidden Transcripts in the Chippewa Treaty Rights Struggle," *American Indian Quarterly* 21 (Fall 1997): 713–728; Jim Oberly, "Spearing Fish, Playing 'Chicken' (Race and Class Warfare in Wisconsin over Fishing Rights)," *The Nation* 248 (June 19, 1989): 844–846; Eleanor Randolph, "Indian Leaders Furious at Watt Remarks," *Los Angeles Times*, January 20, 1983, B6.

3. For Neal's comment and Native Americans' response to it, see Paul De-Main, "Indian Community Demands Apology from Insulting Remarks Made about Enemy Territory by Brig. General Richard Neal," *News from Indian Country* 5 (March 15, 1991), 1, http://www.bluecorncomics.com/indctry.htm; U.S. official quoted in Rowan Scarborough, "Bin Laden's Cronies Quiet; U.S. Sees Ploy," *Washington Times*, January 24, 2002; South quoted in Tom Infield, "Alpha Company: Their War Comes Home," *Philadelphia Inquirer*, March 9, 2008, http://www.philly.com/inquirer/special/iraq/16367871.html; Riley quoted in Michael A. Elliott, *Custerology: The Enduring Legacy of the Indian Wars and George Armstrong Custer* (Chicago: University of Chicago Press, 2007), 278, 279 (Kaplan quote); Patrick J. Buchanan, "The Politics of War," WorldNetDaily, November 15, 2005, http://www.worldnetdaily.com/news/article.asp?ARTICLE_ID=47406; Biddle quoted in Brian Knowlton, "Bush Sets Out to 'Listen' to Alternatives on Iraq, *International Herald Tribune*, December 12, 2006, 6. On the NCAI protest, see Scott Starr, "Indian Country: Beyond the Green Zone in Iraq," *ZMag*, August 24, 2007, http://www.zmag.org/znet/viewArticle/14649. See also Bill Gertz, "Wartime PC Danger," *Washington Times*, May 11, 2007, A5. As in Vietnam, journalists have echoed this discourse, as a Christian Broadcasting Network reporter did in 2003 in telling Pat Robertson about "Injuns ahead of us, Injuns behind us, and

Injuns on both sides too." James William Gibson describes the reemergence of the Indian-as-enemy trope in *Warrior Dreams: Paramilitary Culture in Post-Vietnam America* (New York: Hill and Wang, 1994), 70–71.

4. "National Pundits Sadly Ignore American Indian History," *Indian Country Today*, February 8, 2006; editorial, *Native American Times*, September 12, 2001, in Paul C. Rosier, *Native American Issues* (Westport, Conn.: Greenwood Press, 2003), xi; Starr, "Indian Country"; Westerman quoted in Michael Carlson, "Actor, Activist—and the Essence of a Native American," *Sydney Morning Herald*, January 3, 2008, 16. Also see Dr. Michael Yellow Bird, Ph.D., "Why Are Indigenous (American Indian) Soldiers Serving in Iraq?" June 26, 2006, http://www.geocities.com /lakotastudentalliance/Why_Are_Indigenous_Soldiers_in_Iraqpdf.pdf.

5. Ghida Fakhry, "Native American Fights Corporations," Al Jazeera, November 23, 2006, http://english.aljazeera.net/NR/exeres/3A64E73C-25AF-468B-AD11-2EAEA4D71F78.htm.

6. Gary Rivlin, "Beyond the Reservation," *New York Times*, September 22, 2007, http://www.nytimes.com/2007/09/22/business/22tribe.html; David Peterson, "From New York to California, Indians Buying Up Land," *Minneapolis Star Tribune*, May 9, 2008, http://www.scrippsnews.com/node/33068. In 1981 the U.S. Fifth Circuit Court of Appeals ruled in *Seminole Tribe of Florida v. Butterworth* that since Florida permitted bingo games off-reservation, it had no legal authority to prohibit or establish guidelines for them on Indian reservations. As a result, the Seminole expanded their operations, earned millions of dollars in revenue, and inspired other Native American groups to do the same. In its February 1987 decision in *California v. Cabazon Band of Mission Indians*, the U.S. Supreme Court confirmed American Indians' right to establish and run gaming enterprises without state government interference.

7. George Wolfe, "California Indian Tribes Split Casino Profits to Buy Nevada and Arizona," *LaLa Times*, no. 17, http://lalatimes.com/newsfea/st_17_ tribesto.php; Nelson D. Schwartz, "Far From the Reservation, but Still Sacred?" *New York Times*, August 12, 2007.

8. *Annual Report of the Commissioner of Indian Affairs*, September 28, 1886, in Prucha, *Documents of United States Indian Policy*, 169.

Acknowledgments

This book is the product of fruitful collaboration with colleagues, librarians, archivists, friends, and family who have supported my research and writing in important and diverse ways. In particular I thank my colleagues in the History Department of Villanova University—Marc Gallicchio, Judy Giesberg, Jeffrey Johnson, Catherine Kerrison, Seth Koven, Adele Lindenmeyr, Charlene Mires, and Paul Steege. I benefited from their careful reading of all or parts of the manuscript, in informal discussions and in a faculty forum on the intersection of American Indian activism and the Vietnam War. Charlene and Judy offered especially helpful criticism during our lunchtime "chapter chat" sessions. Paul also read the entire manuscript, suggesting ways to shape the narrative during spirited conversations held over cheesesteaks or coffee. This book benefited as well from the insights of a number of scholars beyond Villanova. Thomas Borstelmann, Thompson Professor of Modern World History at the University of Nebraska, read portions of the manuscript in its early stages and helped to clarify its trajectory. Frederick Hoxie, Swanlund Professor of History at the University of Illinois, offered valuable suggestions for revising the manuscript, as did two anonymous reviewers for the Harvard University Press. I am also grateful to fellow historians who responded to sections of the manuscript at several conferences, including the annual meetings of the American Historical Association, Organization of American Historians, and American Society for Ethnohistory. In addition I thank my European colleagues who offered their perspectives as well as suggestions for European sources at the 2007 American Indian Workshop in Paris. Those conversations were, given the topic of this book (and the location of the conference), provocative and enjoyable.

I could not have conducted the research that made this book possible without the generous support of the Villanova University History Department and the Villanova University Office of Research and Supported Projects. The History Department's Summer Research Grant provided seed money for an early trip to collections of the Smithsonian Institution and to the U.S. State Department Archives in College Park, Maryland. The Office of Research and Supported Projects allowed me to explore Bureau of Indian Affairs files held in the National Archives in Washington, D.C., and to devote my summer months to writing rather than to teaching. In addition, grants and fellowships from the National Endowment for the Humanities, the D'Arcy McNickle Center at the Newberry Library, the American Philosophical Society, the Harry S. Truman Library, and the Redd Center at Brigham Young University enabled me to examine important collections such as the Library of Congress's Foreign Newspapers Archive, the Harry S. Truman Papers, the records of the National Congress of American Indians, and the papers of the National Indian Youth Council, located in the Center for Southwest Research at the University of New Mexico. In these various places I was assisted by passionate and professional archivists who made my visits both efficient and enjoyable.

The exceptional interlibrary loan staff of Falvey Memorial Library at Villanova secured dissertations, articles, and microfilm for me in a timely fashion. I am deeply grateful for their help and for their patience in piecing together my often obscure, incomplete, and international references. I thank Katya Piskacheva for translating a series of Russian-language documents and perusing multiple volumes of the *Current Digest of the Soviet Press,* and Rachel Wineman for translating several German-language documents. My thanks also to two research assistants—Karen Sause and Sydney Soderberg—for helping me locate files and citations. In the Villanova History Department, Georgi Kilroy, Chris Filiberti, and Edie Iannucci offered timely assistance in helping me prepare the manuscript.

Kathleen McDermott of the Harvard University Press offered enthusi-

asm for and support of the project from the beginning. It has been a pleasure to work with her and with members of the Harvard University Press
staff, including Sheila Barrett, Kathleen Drummy, and Susan Abel.

Portions of this book have been previously published. Parts of Chapters
4 and 5 appeared in "'They are Ancestral homelands': Race, Place, and
Politics in Cold War Native America, 1945–1961," *Journal of American
History* 92 (March 2006): 1300–26, and are used here with thanks to the
Organization of American Historians. Parts of Chapter 4 were included in
"The Association on American Indian Affairs and the Struggle for Native
American Rights, 1948–1955," *Princeton University Library Chronicle* 62
(Winter 2006): 366–391.

Finally, it gives me great pleasure to acknowledge the support that members of my family offered throughout the writing of this book. My mother,
Katherine Rosier, used her keen editorial eye to spot misplaced commas
and misused semicolons and to reflect as a non-specialist on each chapter's
readability. My two sons, Maxwell and Casey, put up with extended visits
to archives and my expeditions in search of clarity behind a closed study
door. I hope that in reading the book they come to appreciate the purpose
and the passion with which I approached the telling of this important
story of American Indian activism and patriotism and the writing of history more generally. My wife, Debra, helped me with this project in many
different ways, including reading and editing parts of the manuscript. Her
interest in the book and her constant support along the way made its writing especially rewarding.

Index